The Greek Word Study Thesaurus

The Greek Word Study Thesaurus

With Vocabulary from The Greek New Testament

Prepared by
CHRISTOPHER DALE LENZ

WIPF & STOCK · Eugene, Oregon

THE GREEK WORD STUDY THESAURUS
With Vocabulary from The Greek New Testament

Copyright © 2022 Christopher Dale Lenz. All rights reserved. Except for brief quotations in critical publications or reviews, no part of this book may be reproduced in any manner without prior written permission from the publisher. Write: Permissions, Wipf and Stock Publishers, 199 W. 8th Ave., Suite 3, Eugene, OR 97401.

Wipf & Stock
An Imprint of Wipf and Stock Publishers
199 W. 8th Ave., Suite 3
Eugene, OR 97401

www.wipfandstock.com

PAPERBACK ISBN: 978-1-6667-3791-2
HARDCOVER ISBN: 978-1-6667-9801-2
EBOOK ISBN: 978-1-6667-9802-9

VERSION NUMBER 052522

For my mother

Contents

Preface | ix

THESAURUS | 1

English Index | 201
Greek Index | 225

Preface

THE PURPOSE OF THIS thesaurus is to put many similar Greek words at the user's disposal under each entry in order to do word studies, to help find lost synonyms for a Greek word, and for reinforcing vocabulary. There are approximately 5,150 words and expressions found here. By having words with similar meanings grouped together, the user will see that learning those words is more within their grasp.

Collections of related Greek words and their definitions are organized in a way that enables more thorough word analyses. For example, searching the word "purify" will give you the most common words that mean "to cleanse, wash," such as καθαρίζω, νίπτω, and λούω, and lesser synonyms like ἁγνίζω and πλύνω, along with many of their noun and adjective forms. That's not all. You also get compounds with prepositional prefixes, such as ἐκκαθαίρω and ἀπολούομαι, other related adjectives, like ἄσπιλος, "spotless," and ἄμωμος, "without blemish," words associated more exclusively with spiritual purification: βαπτίζω (dip) and ῥαντίζω (sprinkle), words for "wipe away" (ἐξαλείφω and ἀπομάσσομαι), and more. And as you use this book, you will find that it helps to significantly develop your Greek vocabulary and improve Greek comprehension.

At the end of the thesaurus is an English word index, followed by a Greek word index, enabling the user to easily locate words in either language. So the thesaurus can also be used to simply look up a Greek word and find its English meaning or browse English words and view Greek equivalents.

Another useful feature of this thesaurus, is that in addition to lists of synonyms, there are sets of words related by category, like "animals" or "monetary terms" or "numbers." Readers will find this most helpful to compare and contrast related words. So, for example, exhaustive lists of sins and virtues are compiled under vices and virtues. A complete collection of prepositions is conveniently listed under "prepositions" with definitions grouped by case of the noun they modify, but you will also find some prepositions grouped under other headings such as "location" or "time." Where there are a lot of prepositions with the same meaning, there is a separate heading for that meaning, for example, the heading "By" has a list of six prepositions: ὑπό, παρά, διά, ἐν, ἀπό, and ἐπί. There are also full lists of conjuctions and words indicating result or purpose.

In some instances, antonyms are included under a heading. For example, under "Explain, Interpret" (ἑρμηνεύω in Greek) you also find στρεβλόω, "to misinterpret or pervert," as the last entry. But in cases where there are numerous antonyms, often a separate heading is created for them. However, in a number of entries, two opposite words are put in the heading, e.g., hot, cold, or rough, smooth, with the expectation that scholars researching that subject matter will want to learn and compare words that are opposites.

As in most greek dictionaries, the lexeme for a verb is given in its present active indicative first person singular (PAI1S) form, but the definition is stated in the infinitive form, often omitting "to," for example: ἐπιτρέπω let, permit, allow

Many Greek dictionaries provide with nouns the nominative singular ending, the genetive singular ending, and the nominative singular definite article, as: ὠτίον, ου, τό   ear. This dictionary doesn't provide that, due to the understanding that users will already be using as their primary dictionary a standard Greek to English lexicon which will be their main source for that kind of information, whereas this thesaurus is an additional, more specialized resource, even though it can also serve simply as a Greek to English dictionary.

Where the lexeme ending could be either a noun or adjective ending, adjective meanings are often included together with the corresponding noun meaning under the same entry, e.g., ἅγιος has in its definition both noun meanings: "saint, sanctuary," and adjective meanings: "holy, dedicated, set apart," based on the expectation that the user will be able to readily distinguish between them.

In some cases, idioms or colloquialisms are given as both a metaphrase equivalent and a paraphrase meaning. For example, ποιέω τὸ ἱκανόν, "to make sufficient, to satisfy or please someone." The Greek phrase literally translates as "to make sufficient," but when this expression is used in Mark

15:15, it means Pilate wishes "to satisfy" the Jewish mob by releasing to them the murderer Barabas instead of the sinless Jesus.

Where a word has a very similar-looking word that it could easily be confused with, that word often will be listed below it, so the reader may compare and differentiate them, e.g., οὗ, "where" is listed below οὔ, "no" for the purpose of comparison, not because they are related in meaning. You will find together πού, "somewhere, approximately" and ποῦ, "where? at what place?," saving the curious reader the trouble of looking it up. The word ἀργός, which means "idle," is followed by ἄργυρος, "silver," for this same reason. In another place, ἤρεμος "quiet, peaceful" is followed by ἔρημος "deserted, lonely," so the user can see the subtle difference.

In some cases, where the reader would need to look up a word elsewhere in order to know the meaning of the current entry in question, that word is provided there, e.g., εἰ τύχοι "perhaps" has below it the definition for τυγχάνω, "to happen" which makes it more clear why it means that, saving the reader from having to search it. Other examples are ψωμίον "morsel" listed below ψωμίζω "to feed," and ἠχέω "make a noise" found following κατηχέω "teach, instruct, inform, tell."

Sometimes in this dictionary there may be additional words that fill out a nexus of meaning in another place other than where the reader is looking, e.g., for words found under "more," one may find additional similar words under "extremely" or "abundance." Another example is "law" and "command," where they could have been combined under one heading, but there was enough of a distinction in meaning that it was thought reasonable to separate them into two headings and putting "see also . . ." to connect them. Many words are difficult to categorize. Words for "catch, trap" may be found under "Capture, Trap, Surround," "Hunt, Trap, Catch, Snare," "Seize, Arrest," and "Vices: Deception."

It should be pointed out that for words with multiple meanings, each of the meanings are given, not only the meaning corresponding to that heading under which it is found. So, for example, under "Location: Prepositions of," one finds that the word διά, when used with a genitive, means locationally "through." But the causative meaning, "by," which does not have to do with location, is still included in the definition. It's assumed that the user will catch on to that.

I wish the Lord's blessing on you and I pray that this thesaurus will be a help and an encouragement to you as you study Greek.

Thesaurus

A

Abandon, Forsake, Leave in a Place, see also "Go, Leave, Depart"

ἀποστρέφω—to turn away, return

ἀφίστημι—leave, desert, fall away from faith, commit apostasy, mislead, incite a revolt, abstain, shun

ἀφίημι—send away, divorce, let go, leave, desert, abandon, forgive, remit, permit, allow, not hinder

ἀνίημι—loosen, unfasten, slacken, abandon, desert, give up, cease

λείπω—to leave, leave alone, leave out, leave undone, lack, be deficient in, fall short, impersonal active 3rd person: what remains, what is wanting

καταλείπω—to leave behind, abandon, neglect, no longer relate to

ἐγκαταλείπω—to leave behind, leave out, desert, omit, forsake, abandon

ἀπολείπω—leave, leave behind, desert, forsake, abandon

περιλείπομαι—be left behind, be left remaining, remain over, survive

ὑπολείπω—leave remaining, leave behind, be left, survive

παραπίπτω—to fall to the side, fall away, forsake, to befall

μετατίθεμαι ἀπό—abandon loyalty to

στρέφω—turn, turn from one's course, change one's mind, reverse

ἔρημος—desolate, lonely, solitary, destitute, undefended, forsaken

μονόομαι—to isolate, make single or solitary, leave alone, forsake, bereave, be desolate

σαβαχθανι—forsake, Aramaic

ὀρφανός—orphan, bereft, orphaned, fatherless, friendless person

Abide, Dwell, Live

οἰκέω—dwell, live, reside, make a home

οἰκητήριον—home, dwelling place, habitation, abode

κατοικητήριον—dwelling place, abode, habitat

κατοικέω—live, settle down, dwell in, inhabit

ἐγκατοικέω—dwell among

κατοίκησις—dwelling place, habitation

κατοικία—dwelling place, habitat, settlement

κατοικίζω—cause to dwell, assign a dwelling place, cause to live in

ἐνοικέω—dwell in, live in

περιοικέω—live nearby, live in the vicinity, be a neighbor

παροικέω—live in a place without citizenship, live as a foreigner, dwell temporarily

κάθημαι—sit down, seat one's self, have a fixed abode, dwell, reside

ἐνδημέω—live in a place, stay at home, be in one's own land
μονή—room, dwelling place, mansion
ἐπισκηνόω—take up residence, reside in a tent, dwell
σκηνόω—live, dwell, camp in a tent, take up residence
σκήνωμα—tent, tabernacle, dwelling place, the human body
κατασκηνόω—to dwell, live, settle, rest, make a nest
ἔνειμι—be inside, be within
συμπάρειμι—be with, be present with someone
ἐμπεριπατέω—walk about in a place, move among the people, live among, live with
ἔμφυτος—implanted, engrafted, established in
ἀγραυλέω—live outdoors, of shepherds, dwell in the fields

Accept, Receive, Take

λαμβάνω—take, take hold of, grasp, acquire, receive, accept, collect, welcome, take on
δέχομαι—take, receive, grasp, accept, welcome
ἀποδέχομαι—to accept, receive favorably, acknowledge, welcome
ἀποδοχή—acceptance, reception
παραδέχομαι—to receive, admit, accept, welcome
προσδέχομαι—to receive favorably, accept, receive hospitably, welcome, admit into, wait for, expect
ἀνέχομαι—to put up with, be patient with, bear with, endure, accept
ἀκούω—to hear, listen, hearken, obey, give audience, receive news, be reported, understand
κομίζω—receive, receive back, be recompensed, bear, bring

Acceptable To, Pleased With

δεκτός—acceptable, pleasing, welcomed, appropriate
ἀπόδεκτος—acceptable, agreeable, pleasing
εὐπρόσδεκτος—well-received, acceptable, truly favorable, quite pleasing
εὐδοκέω—to be pleased, be favorable towards, prefer, approve, choose
εὐδοκία—delight, good pleasure, satisfaction, what pleases
χάρις—grace, goodwill, favor, mercy, kindness, a gift, thanks, exceptional favor given by God
ἀρεστός—pleasing, agreeable, proper
ἀρέσκω—to please, accommodate
ἀρεσκεία—desire to please, means of favor
εὐαρεστέω—to be well-pleasing, cause to be pleased
εὐάρεστος—well-pleasing, acceptable
εὐαρέστως—in a manner well-pleasing to one, acceptably
προσφιλής—pleasing, lovely
ἐπιστρέφω καρδίας ἐπί—to turn the heart upon, make agreeable to
ποιέω τὸ ἱκανόν—to make sufficient, to satisfy or please someone
ἀνθρωπάρεσκος—courting the favor of men, men-pleasing

Accessories, Adornments

κόσμος—world, earth, as the ordered arrangement of creation, ornament, adornment as on a woman, world system
κοσμέω—put in order, arrange, adorn, decorate, make attractive, beautify, be decked out
χρυσίον—gold, gold coin, gold ornaments
δακτύλιος—ring

χρυσοδακτύλιος—gold-ringed, adorned with gold rings

στέφανος—crown

στέμμα—wreath, garland

κράσπεδον—fringe of a garment, tassel, skirt of a hill, edge

φυλακτήριον—phylactery or amulet containing scriptures worn on the arm and forehead

διάδημα—diadem, crown, band used to bind on the turban

Accompany

συμπορεύομαι—go with, journey together, come together, assemble

συνέρχομαι—come together, assemble, go with, accompany, cohabitate

συνοδεύω—journey with, travel in company with

συνοδία—a journey in company, a company of travelers, associates on a journey, a caravan

συνέκδημος—travelling companion, fellow traveler

συνεισέρχομαι—enter with, enter together

συναναβαίνω—ascend at the same time, come/go up with

συγκαταβαίνω—come/go down with, descend from high place to a lower place together

προπέμπω—send on one's way, escort or accompany, equip for a journey

Account, Keep Records

λογίζομαι—to reckon, count, calculate, take into account, number among, consider, impute, reason, suppose, keep mental record

λόγος—word, reason, matter under discussion, account, treatise

ἐλλογέω—charge to one's account, impute, put on record

συναίρω—to take up together, check or balance accounts, take part in a thing, help in bearing, engage in a thing, undertake it, contribute, assist

οἰκονόμος τῆς πόλεως—city treasurer

ἀναπράσσω—to levy money or debts, exact the fulfillment of a promise

Accuse, Defame, see "Vices: Accuse, Defame, Talk Foolishly"

Acquire

λαμβάνω—take, take hold of, grasp, acquire, receive, accept, collect, welcome, take on

καταλαμβάνω—lay hold of, obtain, acquire, seize, attack, catch, middle: receive with the mind, comprehend

κατάσχεσις—taking possession, holding back, restraining

κατέχω—hold tightly, hold back, restrain as in prison, possess

κτάομαι—to acquire, get gain, have, possess,—procure for oneself, hold

ἐπιτυγχάνω—to obtain, attain to, reach, gain one's end, succeed in doing, succeed, acquire

τυγχάνω—to meet with, have happen, come upon, experience

περιποιέομαι—to reserve, keep safe, preserve for one's self, purchase, acquire

περιποίησις—a keeping safe, gaining possession of, preservation, obtaining, acquisition

κλείς—a key, that which serves for closing, a bar or bolt, the hook of a clasp, symbolically a means for acquiring something

εὐοδόομαι—to have a prosperous and expeditious journey, gain in business, be successful, get along well, to make a good way

πράσσω—to accomplish, achieve, bring about, do, practice, act, be busy with, cause, make, manage, transact, negotiate, to exact money

λογεία—collection for the poor

Add, Addition

ἐπιχορηγέω—furnish, supply, add

ἐπιδιατάσσομαι—to add to a will

προστίθημι—add to, increase, give, grant, do again, gather to, passive: be buried with

ἐπιτίθημι—lay upon, place upon, usually the hands, inflict, attack

ἔτι—yet, as yet, still, further, besides, moreover, hereafter, nevertheless, in addition

ἐπαθροίζομαι—gather more

Adequate, Qualified

ἱκανός—sufficient, adequate, able, enough, considerable, satisfactory

ἱκανότης—adequacy, sufficiency, fitness, capacity, capability

ἱκανόω—to make adequate, make sufficient, make capable

ἄρτιος—prepared, ready, complete, fitted to its purpose, qualified

ἀρτίζω—to get ready

ἐξαρτίζω—to thouroughly prepare, equip completely, make adequate, be complete (of time)

καταρτίζω—prepare, make adequate, mend, restore, create, perfect, make ready

κατάρτισις—adequacy, restoration, training, education, discipline

καταρτισμός—adequacy

αὐτάρκεια—self-sufficiency, not needing aid or support, adequacy

ἀρκέω—to have sufficient strength, suffice, be enough, be satisfied

Advantage

ὄφελος—furtherance, advantage, help, good, profit

ὠφέλιμος—helpful, useful, profitable, advantageous, beneficial

ὠφέλεια—usefulness, profit, source of gain, advantage, benefit, service, help, aid, assistance, utility

ἐξαγοράζομαι τὸν καιρόν—buy back the time, make good use of opportunity, work urgently

καλός—beautiful, fair, good, virtuous, advantageous, fitting

λυσιτελέω—be advantageous, be better, profit

συμφέρω—bring together, gather, collect, intransitively: be expedient, be advantageous

σύμφορος—useful, profitable, expedient, advantageous, convenient

προέχω—be first, be superior, surpass, excel, have advantage, passive: to be surpassed

ἀντιλαμβάνω—to help, support, come to the aid of, relieve

ὀνίνημι—to enjoy favor, benefit, derive enjoyment, Philemon 20

Advise

συμβουλεύω—counsel, consult, deliberate, advise, plot against

σύμβουλος—adviser, counsellor

παραινέω—to exhort, admonish, advise strongly

συμβιβάζω—join together, unite, put together in one's mind, conclude, prove, instruct, advise

Against

κατά—with genitive: against

πρός—with accusative: against

ἐπί—with accusative: against, to, up to, toward

ἀπέναντι—opposite, in front of, before, in the presence of, against, contrary

Agitate, Shake, Tremble

κινέω—set in motion, move, excite a disturbance or riot, shake

ταράσσω—agitate, trouble, disquiet, make restless, stir up, perplex

ταραχή—disturbance, commotion, tumult, sedition, movement or riot

ἔντρομος—trembling, terrified, fearful

τρέμω—tremble, quake, quiver, fear, respect

τρόμος—trembling, quaking with fear

σαλεύω—agitate, shake, be stirred up, distressed, confused

σείω—to shake, agitate, cause to quake, move, cause a disturbance

ἀποτινάσσω—shake off

ἐκτινάσσω—shake off

σεισμός—earthquake, violent shaking

ῥιπίζομαι—raise a breeze, put air in motion, e.g., for kindling a fire or cooling one's self, toss about, agitate

κλυδωνίζομαι—be tossed by waves, be agitated

ἀνεμίζομαι—agitate, drive by the wind

Agreement

συμφωνέω—be in harmony, agree with, hold the same opinions with, of clothes: match, fit together

συμφώνησις—concord, agreement

συμφωνία—music, symphony

σύμφημι—to consent, agree with

συνευδοκέω—be pleased, consent, be willing, agree to

συγκατάθεσις—joint agreement, approval

συγκατατίθεμαι—consent to, agree together, vote for

συντίθεμαι—agree

εὐνοέω—wish well, consider favorably, be well-disposed, be of a peaceable spirit, to agree with, settle a case

μεσιτεύω—to mediate, interpose between parties, act as a sponsor, pledge one's self, give surety, confirm, cause agreement

μεσίτης—mediator, one who intervenes between two, arbitrator, reconciler

ὁμοθυμαδόν—with one mind, with one accord, with one passion

ἐξομολογέω—agree, promise, consent, middle: confess, praise, thank

ἐπινεύω—assent to, consent, agree

ἐπαγγελία—promise, agreement

ἀναλογία—right relationship, compatibility, proportion, agreement between things being compared (Romans 12:6)

συγγνώμη—concession, agreement

ἀσύμφωνος—dissonant, at variance, in disagreement

ἀρνέομαι—to deny, refuse to agree

Agricultural Terms, see "Farming Terms"

All, Any, Each, Every (Totality)

ἅπας—all, the whole, altogether, everyone, everything

πᾶς—all, any, whole, total, every kind of

ἀμφότερος—each or both of two, together

ἕκαστος—each, each one, every, every one, every single one

παμπληθεί—with the whole multitude, all together

ὅλος—whole, entire, complete

ὁλόκληρος—whole, complete, intact, undamaged, entire

πλήρης—full (of), filled (with), complete, not lacking, as ripe grain πλήρωμα—a full measure, fullness, the sum total, complete amount

ἀναπληρόω—fill up, supply, refill, fulfill

πληρόω—make full, fulfill, complete, fulfill the requirements of, observe, fulfill a prophecy

ἀνταναπληρόω—to fill up, make up what is lacking, supply the balance

Allow

ἐάω—allow, permit, let, let go, leave

ἐπιτρέπω—let, permit, allow

προσεάω—allow to go farther, permit to approach, permit progress

ἀφίημι—send away, divorce, let go, leave, desert, abandon, forgive, remit, permit, allow, not hinder

συγγνώμη—concession, agreement

Alone

κατὰ μόνας—alone

μόνας—alone, left alone, forsaken, solitary, only, one and only

μονόομαι—to isolate, make single or solitary, leave alone, forsake, bereave, be desolate

ἄγαμος—unmarried, single

Although

καίπερ—even though, although, but nevertheless

καίτοι—and yet, although, even though

καίτοιγε—and yet, although indeed, as in John 4:2

κἄν—even if, and if, but if, even though

ὅμως—similarly, all the same, nevertheless, notwithstanding, still, but for all that, yet, though, likewise, in the same way, also

ὅμως μέντοι—nevertheless indeed, and yet

And, Words Marking Additive Relation Of Facts

καί—and, and then, also, yet, even

δέ—and, but, then, now

τέ—and

πάλιν—and, also, again

λοιπός—from now on, the remaining, to mark an added fact: furthermore, also, in addition, beyond that, finally

περαιτέρω—further, in addition, more than

εἶτα—then, next, afterwards, soon, furthermore, besides this

καί . . . καί, τέ . . . τέ—both . . . and

τέ . . . τέ—as . . . so, not only . . . but also

μέν . . . δέ—some . . . others, first . . . then

Angel

ἄγγελος—a messenger, envoy, one who is sent, an angel

ἰσάγγελος—like an angel

στρατιὰ οὐράνιος—heavenly hosts

ἀρχάγγελος—archangel

Anger, Indignation: see Vices: Anger, Indignation

Animals, see "Birds," "Insects," "Reptiles"

ψυχὴ ζωῆς—living creature

ζῷον—animal

θηρίον—wild animal

τετράπουν—quadruped

θρέμμα—livestock

ἀγέλη—herd

βοῦς—cattle

ταῦρος—bull

μόσχος—calf

δάμαλις—heifer

ἐρίφιον—he-goat
ἔριφος—he-goat
τράγος—he-goat
αἴγειος—of a goat
ἀμνός—lamb
ἀρήν—lamb
ἀρνίον—sheep, lamb
ποίμνη—flock
προβατικός—of sheep
πρόβατον—sheep
πάσχα—passover, passover meal, by metonymy, the lamb eaten at passover
ἵππος—horse
ὀνάριον—foal
πῶλος—foal
ὄνος—donkey
κτῆνος—beast of burden
ὑποζύγιον—pack animal
κάμηλος—camel
ὗς—sow
χοῖρος—pig
κυνάριον—small dog
κύων—dog
λέων—lion
πάρδαλις—leopard
λύκος—wolf
ἄρκος—bear
σκύμνος—cub, whelp
ἀλώπηξ—fox
ὕστριξ—porcupine

Animal Husbandry, Livestock

βόσκω—to feed, tend, or herd animals, nourish, support, maintain, graze, nurture, the stem is βοτ-
βοτήρ—herdsman, herd
σιτευτός—well-fed, fattened
σιτιστός—well-fed, fattened
ποιμαίνω—to be a shepherd, tend, guide, look after, care for
ποιμή—shepherd, herdsman
ἀρχιποίμην—chief shepherd
ἀγραυλεω—live outdoors, of shepherds, dwell in the fields
νομή—pasturage, fodder, food, a pasture
ῥάβδος—stick, rod, staff used by shepherds, scepter
βακτηρία—staff, cane used by shepherds
κέντρον—any sharp point, a horse goad, spur, prick, incentive, stinger, the center of a circle
κημόω—to muzzle an ox to keep it from eating grain while threshing
φιμόω—to muzzle, tie shut as with a muzzle, put to silence

Announce, Inform, Message

ἀγγέλλω—announce, tell, inform
ἀγγελία—message, command, order
ἄγγελος—a messenger, envoy, one who is sent, an angel
ἀναγγέλλω—inform, report, bring back tidings, announce, declare
ἀπαγγέλλω—tell, bring word, report, proclaim, inform, confess, command
καταγγελεύς—announcer, preacher
διαγγέλλω—announce throughout, publish abroad, give notice of
ἐξαγγέλλω—declare abroad, publish widely, proclaim throughout
καταγγέλλω—proclaim, make known, preach, teach
εὐαγγελίζω—to announce good news, bring glad tidings, preach the gospel
εὐαγγέλιον—good tidings, the good news of salvation through Christ, the proclamation of the grace of God given by faith in Christ

προευαγγελίζομαι—to announce or promise glad tidings beforehand, bring good news ahead of time, to have preached previously the gospel

ἀπόστολος—a messenger, delegate, apostle, one sent out with a message, ambassador, envoy

κατηχέω—teach, instruct, inform, tell

προγράφω—write previously, placard

ἐρεύγομαι—to pour forth, roar, speak out, utter, announce

σπεκουλάτωρ—soldier on special duty, executioner, courier

διασαφέω—explain, make clear or plain, unfold, narrate, tell in detail

σαφής—clear, distinct

διηγέομαι—tell fully, recount, relate in full, describe in detail

ἐκδιηγέομαι—narrate in full, relate, tell, recount, tell fully

ἐξηγέομαι—tell, relate, explain, make known, reveal

ἡγέομαι—govern, lead, think, consider

κηρύσσω—to herald with formality and authority, publish, proclaim openly, announce, preach, tell

ἐμφανίζω—to manifest, exhibit to view, disclose, make known

μηνύω—to disclose, make known, inform, report, disclose

ἦχος—a sound, blast of a trumpet, report, news

φάσις—news, report

φήμη—news, fame, report

διαφημίζω—to spread abroad one's fame or renown, spread news

ἀκοή—the sense of hearing, the ear, the thing heard, instruction, message

ἀνεκδιήγητος—unspeakable, indescribable

Answer, Reply

ἀποκρίνομαι—to answer

ἀπόκρισις—a reply, answer

ἀνταποκρίνομαι—reply, answer back, dispute

Anxiety, Distress, Worry

μέλει—it is a concern

μέριμνα—care, anxiety

μεριμνάω—be anxious about, be worried about, care for, take thought

ἀμέριμνος—free from anxiety, carefree, without worry, secure

προμεριμνάω—worry beforehand, take thought beforehand

προσδοκάω—expect, look for, wait for, anticipate, wait with anxiety

καταπονέω—to exhaust, afflict, oppress, mistreat, vex, distress

ἀνασκευάζω—unsettle, subvert, upset, disturb

μετεωρίζομαι—be unsettled, in suspense, anxious

ἐώρα—something suspended in air

σείω—to shake, agitate, cause to quake, move, cause a disturbance

θορυβάζω—be upset, stirred up

θορυβέω—cause confusion, set in a clamor, be turbulent, disturb

τυρβάζω—disturb, be troubled in mind or disquieted, be upset

ὀδύνη—consuming grief, pain, sorrow, intense anxiety

ὀδυνάομαι—be in intense pain, be in terrible anguish, be tormented

ἐξαπορέομαι—to be utterly at loss, destitute, to be in despair

περισπάομαι—be drawn away, be distracted and anxious

ἐπίστασις—an attack, disturbance, rioting, an overwhelming of responsibilities and pressures

συνοχή—constraint, straights, distress, anguish, affliction

συνέχω—surround, hem in, enclose, guard, seize, afflict, be absorbed in
σαλεύω—agitate, shake, be stirred up, distressed, confused
τάραχος—commotion, stir, tumult
ταράσσω—agitate, trouble, disquiet, make restless, stir up, perplex
ὑπωπιάζω—wear out, treat with severity, keep under control
πιάζω—to press, take or lay hold of, seize, apprehend, arrest
διαταράσσω—to agitate greatly, be deeply troubled
ἀδημονέω—to be deeply troubled, be in great distress, be upset

Approach, Come Near

ἐγγίζω—come near, approach
συντυγχάνω—to come together with, meet with, join
προσάγω—bring to, come near
προσεγγίζω—approach, come nigh
προσέρχομαι—to come to, approach, visit
προσπορεύομαι—approach, draw near
ἀπαντάω—meet
ἀπάντησις—meeting up with
ὑπαντάω—to meet, meet in battle
ὑπάντησις—drawing near to meet
συμβάλλω—meet, discuss, consult, debate, ponder, middle: help, assist
ἀπρόσιτος—unapproachable

Approximately, About, Almost, Hardly

πού—somewhere, almost, about, approximately
ποῦ—where?, at what place?
σχεδόν—close, nearby, nigh, nearly, all but, almost, just
μόλις—with difficulty, not easily, scarcely, very rarely
ὀλίγως—hardly, scarcely, just barely, only by a little
ὡς—so, thus, like, according as, with numerals: about, approximately
ὡσεί—just as if, as though, like, adverbially with numerals, about, nearly
βραχύ τι—somewhat
βραχύς—short, little, brief, for a short time, briefly, few, in a small amount

Argue, Quarrel, see also "Vices: Fighting" and "Strife, Struggle"

διαλέγομαι—discuss, argue, address
διαλογισμός—reasoning, argument, doubt, dispute
ἔρις—contention, strife, debate, rivalry, discord, quarrel, fighting
ἐρίζω—engage in strife, strive, quarrel
στάσις—a standing, insurrection, uproar, rebellion, heated quarrel
φιλονεικία—love of strife, eagerness to argue, desire to quarrel
φιλόνεικος—contentious, fond of strife, quarrelsome
παροξυσμός—sharp argument, incitement, contention, irritation
διαπαρατριβή—constant arguing
θυμομαχέω—be enraged, fight angrily
λογομαχέω—to contend about words, argue about trifling matters
λογομαχία—argument about words, petty dispute

Arrange, Organize

ἀνατάσσομαι—compile, arrange in proper order, draw up
ἐπιδιορθόω—set right, finish setting in order, make additional corrections
διόρθωσις—a making straight, restoration, reformation, reordering
τάγμα—proper order

τάξις—order, orderliness, arrangment, regularity, division of troops, rank, class of men

διατάσσω—to command, appoint, instruct, set in order

συναρμολογέομαι—to fit, join, or frame together

ἁρμόζω—fit together, join, of clothes or armor, suit, betroth, set in order, arrange harmoniously

ἁρμός—body joint, joining

συγκεράννυμι—to commingle, blend with, compose, combine, unite

Arrogance, Pride, Haughtiness, see Vices: Arrogance, Pride, Haughtiness

Ascend, Rise

ἀναβαίνω—ascend, go up, mount, board a ship, arise

ἐπιβαίνω—get upon, mount, embark, go aboard, enter

προσαναβαίνω—go up further, go up higher

ἀνέρχομαι—go up

ἀναλαμβάνω—take up, raise

ὑπολαμβάνω—suppose, take in mind, take up (Acts 1:9), receive

ἀνάλημψις—taking up, ascension, death

ἀνατέλλω—to rise, give birth to, be a descendant, bring to light, dawn

ἀνατολή—rising, the east

ἐπαίρω—lift up, raise, elevate, hoist, ascend, boast, rise up against

ἐγείρω—to arouse, cause to rise, raise to life, raise up, awaken, stand up, make war against

ἀνίστημι—raise up, rise, stand up, appear, stand forth, resurrect

ἀνάστασις—resurrection, raising to life again

ἐπιβιβάζω—cause to mount an animal, place upon, set on

ἀναβιβάζω—cause to go up or ascend, draw up, pull up

Ask For, Request, Inquire, Question, Beg

ἐπερωτάω—ask for, put a question to, interrogate, demand

ἐρωτάω—to question, ask, request, entreat, beg, beseech

ἐπερώτημα—an inquiry, question, demand, appeal, request

αἰτέω—ask for, request, beg

παραιτέομαι—ask, request, beg, give excuse, request pardon, decline, keep away from, shun, refuse to hear

αἴτημα—request

ἀπαιτέω—ask in return, demand back

ἐξαιτέομαι—ask for, demand

ἐπαιτέω—ask for more, beg, ask alms

προσαιτέω—ask for more, beg

προσαίτης—beggar

ζητέω—to seek, inquire into

ἐντυγχάνω—entreat, appeal to, plead, make intercession for, petition

δέομαι—to pray, ask for, beg, plead, beseech

δέησις—plea, prayer, request, supplication, entreaty

συνδέομαι—to join in begging, ask together

ἱκετηρία—supplication, prayer, plea

προσανατίθεμαι—lay before, submit for consideration

ἐπικαλέω—call, give a name to, middle: invoke, make an appeal to

πυνθάνομαι—to inquire, ask, learn about, demand, understand

ἐξετάζω—to search out, examine strictly, inquire, ask, try to find out

ἐτάζω—to examine, test

ἀποστοματίζω—ply with questions, interrogate, ask hostile questions

Assemble, Gather, Cause To Come Together

ἐκκλησία—church, gathering
συναγωγή—assembly, gathering
συνάγω—gather, assemble, collect
σύνειμι—be with, come together
συνέρχομαι—come with, come together, assemble, cohabitate
συμπαραγίνομαι—come together
συστρέφω—collect, come together, assemble
ἐπισυνάγω—gather, come together, convene, assemble
συμφέρω—bring together, gather, collect, intransitively: be expedient, be advantageous
προσλαμβάνω—receive, accept, take aside
ἀθροίζω—come together
συναθροίζω—gather together with others, assemble
ἐπαθροίζομαι—gather more
συνδρομή—running together of a mob, concourse, especially hostile
συντρέχω—to run with, live like, join in living
ἐπισυντρέχω—run together to a place, gather rapidly, close in

Assign, Appoint

ἀναδείκνυμι—appoint, make known publicly, commission to a position
ὁρίζω—fix, appoint, determine, decide, designate, ordain, declare
τάσσω—to appoint, assign, place, determine
ἀφορίζω—separate, set apart, exclude
μερίζω—to divide, distribute, assign, apportion
κλῆρος—a lot, a casting or drawing of lots, a piece of land, a portion, share, inheritance, fate, destiny
χειροτονέω—appoint by vote, elect, choose
καθίζω—sit, seat, set, appoint, settle, remain, tarry
καθίστημι—set one in charge of, appoint, assign one to a function
διατίθημι—make a covenant or will, testate property, dispose, arrange, settle with one
τίθημι—set, put, place, lay, appoint
δίδωμι—to give, grant, appoint
ποιέω—make, do, produce, cause to be, carry out, execute, appoint
ἀπονέμω—assign, apportion off, distribute

Association, Fellowship, Friendship

συγχράομαι—have dealings with, associate with
συναναμίγνυμι—mix together, mingle, keep company with, be intimate with one, associate
συναπάγομαι—be led away with, go with, associate with, accommodate to, condescend to
προσκαρτερέω—to persist in, be in constant readiness, continue in, spend much time in, be devoted to
κοινωνία—association, fellowship, communion, participation, sharing in
κοινωνός—partner, associate, partaker
συγκοινωνέω—to participate with others, have fellowship with, associate with
συγκοινωνός—participant with others, partner, companion, partaker
μετοχή—sharing, communion, fellowship, partnership

μέτοχος—sharing in, partaking, fellow, partner, partaker, companion

συνανάκειμαι—to recline together, feast together, associate in eating

φίλος—friend, associate, companion

χωρέω—make space for, go forward, advance, move on, have room for, accept, open one's heart to, be friendly toward

σύντροφος—nourished with, brought up with, childhood companion, foster brother

ἑταῖρος—comrade, friend, companion

συστρατιώτης—fellow soldier, associate in labors and conflicts, fellow struggler

συναγωνίζομαι—to strive together with, to help one in striving, join fervently in

συναλίζω—to eat a salt meal together, to bring together, assemble, come together, another spelling of συναυλίζω

συναυλίζω—to spend the night with, stay with, be with, live with

σύζυγος—yoked together, paired, wedded union, yoke-fellow, comrade, fellow-worker

Atonement, see "Forgiveness," "Virtues: Mercy, Forgiveness"

Attack

ἐπέρχομαι—come, arrive, come upon, overtake, attack (Luke 11:22)

ἐπιτίθημι—lay upon, place upon, usually the hands, inflict, attack

ἐφίστημι—come up to, approach, stand near, appear suddenly, be imminent, attack

κατεφίσταμαι—to rise up against, attack

καταλαμβάνω—lay hold of, obtain, acquire, seize, attack, catch, middle: receive with the mind, comprehend

ἁρπάζω—snatch greedily, carry off by force, seize, plunder, claim for one's self eagerly, overpower

συνεπιτίθημι—join in attacking

συνεφίστημι—join in attack

Authority

ἐξουσία—authority, power, license, permission, legal right

οἰκονόμος—manager, administrator

ἐπιτροπή—permission, a commission, full power, authority

ἐπιταγή—a command

κτίσις—a founding, foundation, creation, the created universe, authority (1 Peter 2:13)

δύναμις—power, might, strength, authority, force, ability

κράτος—strength, might, sovereignty, power, dominion, mastery, authority

Avoid, Abstain, Shun, Withdraw

φείδομαι—to spare in war, not destroy, use sparingly, abstain, forbear, avoid, refrain from

διατηρέω—keep, treasure up, keep free from, abstain from, avoid

ἐκτρέπομαι—to be turned aside, be dislocated, to wander, swerve, avoid

περιΐστημι—be set around, middle: avoid by going around, shun

ἀπέχω—have back, hold back, receive in full, be distanced, be sufficient (Mark 14:41), middle: hold one's self away, avoid, abstain

στέλλομαι—be on guard against, try to avoid, keep away

ὑποστέλλω—withdraw, shrink back, be timid, cower, avoid, keep silent

φεύγω—flee, seek safety from, escape, avoid, vanish

ἐκνεύω—withdraw, avoid, escape, slip out secretly

B

Bad, see also Vices: Disobedience, Sin, Guilt

κακός—bad, evil, wicked

κακία—badness, malice, ill-will, desire to injure, wickedness, evil, depravity, hatefulness

κακῶς—evil, amiss, diseased, grievously, miserably

ἥσσων—worse, less, comparative of κακός

χείρων—worse, inferior, very bad, comparative of κακός

χείριστος—worst, of lowest degree

πονηρός—bad, evil, grievous, lewd, wicked, diseased

πονηρία—wickedness, evil, malice

σαπρός—decayed, rotten, putrefied, of poor quality, bad, worthless, harmful, useless, of no value, unfit

ἀδόκιμος—failing the test, worthless, unqualified, disqualified, rejected, proven false, unfit, bad

ἄτοπος—out of place, unexpected, unusual, strange, disgusting, foul, morally wrong, evil, bad, improper

κακοποιέω—do harm, do evil

κακοποιός—evildoer, criminal, mischievous person

κακοήθεια—wickedness, malice, spitefulness

κακοῦργος—evildoer, criminal

βέβηλος—profane, worldly, ungodly, irreligious

φαῦλος—bad, evil, foul, base

ἀσθενής—without strength, weak, sick, poor, morally weak

ἁμαρτία—failure, fault, sin, guilt

διάβολος—slanderous one, Satan, the devil

σκοτία—darkness, obscurity, absence of light, ignorance, the realm of evil

σκότος—darkness, ignorance, the evil world

Baptize

βαπτίζω—baptize, ritually wash, dip

βάπτισμα—baptism

βαπτισμός—a washing, dipping in water, ablation

βαπτιστής—baptizer

λουτρόν—bath, bathing place, washing

Beautiful

καλός—beautiful, fair, good, virtuous, advantageous, fitting

ὡραῖος—timely, seasonable, in due season, ripe, in bloom, beautiful, lovely, pleasant, welcome

ἀστεῖος—well-bred, pleasing, refined, beautiful, noble, polite, town-bred

κοσμέω—put in order, arrange, adorn, decorate, make attractive, beautify, be decked out

κόσμος—world, earth, as the ordered arrangement of creation, ornament, adornment as on a woman, world system

εὐπρέπεια—beauty, fine appearance

ἀξιοπρεπής—becoming, goodly

μεγαλοπρεπής—suitable to greatness, majestic, excellent, sublime, very wonderful

εὐσχημοσύνη—presentability, good appearance, modesty, attractiveness

εὐσχήμων—decent, presentable, noble, honorable, befitting, elegant in figure and bearing, attractive, graceful, becoming, with dignity

δόξα—glory, splendor, brightness

ἔνδοξος—splendid, honored

λαμπρός—shining, bright, radiant, clear, sparkling, resplendent, elegant, luxurious

λιπαρός—luxurious, costly, rich, fat, oily, bright

ἐπιφανής—wonderful, splendid

ἀμαράντινος—unfading, undecaying, imperishable

ἀμάραντος—unfading, enduring, eternally fresh, everlasting

μαραίνω—fade, wither, dry up

Begin, Commence

ἀρχή—ruler, first in power, origin, beginning, first cause, elementary aspect, the end or corner of a thing

ἄρχω—to rule, be first, make a beginning, lead, govern

ἀρχηγός—pioneer, leader, initiator, originator, founder, prince, chief, author

ἐνάρχομαι—to begin

προενάρχομαι—to begin, begin ahead of time

εἰσέρχομαι—come into, enter into, commence

καταβολή—creation of the world, beginning, foundation

κτίζω—to create, bring into being, build

πρότερος—first, before, in front, forward, former, sooner, above, superior, foremost, beginning

ἐφίστημι—come up to, approach, stand near, appear suddenly, be imminent, attack

ἀναζωπυρέω—to rekindle, fan into flame, regain courage

ἐπεγείρω—to awaken, rouse up, stir up, incite

ἐπεισαγωγή—bringing in, letting in, introduction

Behavior, Conduct, Way Of Life, Lifestyle

ἀγωγή—way of life, conduct, behavior

ἀναστρέφω—conduct one's self, behave, live, stay, return

ἀναστροφή—mode of life, walk, conduct, conversation, behavior

διάγω—bring through, pass through (life), go through (life), (Titus 3:3)

χράομαι—make use of, employ, with adverb: act, proceed, with personal dative: deal with, treat, behave toward (Acts 27:3)

κατάστημα—condition, state, manner of life, behavior, demeanor

συνοικέω—to dwell together, live with, follow the ways of

τρόπος—way, manner, way of life, ὃν τρόπον, in which manner, as

περιπατέω—walk, conduct one's life

πορεύομαι—go, take a journey, travel, go on a business trip

στοιχέω—walk by rule or principle, live, conduct one's self

συντρέχω—to run with, live like, join in living

συναπάγομαι—be led away with, go with, associate with, accommodate to, condescend to

ὁδός—way, road, way of conduct, (Acts 24:14 "the way" referring to Christian belief in God and in the resurrection)

κατευθύνω τοὺς πόδας—make straight the feet, be obedient

τροχιὰς ὀρθὰς ποιέω τοῖς ποσίν—in straight tracks make the feet, behave properly

συσχηματίζω—form or mold after something, be formed like, be conformed to, be guided to, shape one's behavior

πολιτεύομαι—have one's citizenship or home, lead one's life as a citizen, conduct one's life

ὀρθοποδέω—walk upright, live right, act rightly

βιόω—live

βίος—life, livelihood, means of living, substance, possessions

βίωσις—manner of life, daily life

βιωτικός—of or pertaining to life, of daily life

ζάω—live, breathe, be among the living

γίνομαι—be, become, be born, come about, happen

ἐργασία—work, daily labor, business, making, building, commerce, practice, exercising, a work of art, production

ἐργάτης—worker, laborer

πραγματεία—undertakings, business, affairs, activity, occupation, the careful prosecution of an affair, dealings, the treatment of a subject, a treatise, a systematic history

πράσσω—to accomplish, achieve, bring about, do, practice, act, be busy with, cause, make, manage, transact, negotiate, to exact money

εἰσπορεύομαι καὶ ἐκπορεύομαι—coming in and going out, doing business among, dealings among

εἰσέρχομαι καὶ ἐξέρχομαι—coming in and going out, doing business among, dealings among

βάρβαρος—speaking a strange language, not Greek, barbarous, barbarian, uncivilized

ἰουδαΐζω—live by Jewish customs

Ἰουδαϊσμός—practice of Judaism, in accordance with Judaism

Χριστιανός—Christian

κοσμικός—earthly, worldly

κόσμος—world, earth, as the ordered arrangement of creation, ornament, adornment as on a woman, world system

αἰών—eternity, a very long time period, an age, world system

πνευματικός—relating to the human spirit or rational soul, as the part of man which is akin to God, spiritual, pertaining to the wind or breath, supernatural, of spiritual conduct, not physical

ψυχικός—pertaining to the natural mind, emotions, or life force, worldly, as contrasted with πνευματικός

σαρκικός—fleshly, carnal, having the nature of flesh, controlled by animal appetites, human, depraved, worldly, material, natural, physical, sensual

σάρκινος—fleshly, made of flesh, belonging to the realm of the flesh in being weak, sinful, transitory, carnal, of humanity, worldly

παλαιὸς ἄνθρωπος—the old man, meaning living according to the old sinful nature, former behavior

Being, Be, Existence, Life

εἰμί—be

γίνομαι—be, become, be born, come about, happen, take place
ὑπάρχω—to be, exist, participle: one's being, possessions, belongings, livelihood, means
προϋπάρχω—exist formerly
συμπάρειμι—be with, be present with someone
ἥκω—be present, come, arrive, as a result of reaching a place, be here, have happen, take place
ζάω—live, breathe, be among the living
βιόω—live (1 Peter 4:2)
βίος—life, livelihood, means of living, substance

Bend Over, see also "Straighten Up"

κύπτω—stoop down, bend forward, bow the head
κατακύπτω—stoop down
παρακύπτω—to stoop and look into, to look at with head lowered forward, inspect curiously
συγκύπτω—bend completely forwards, be bowed together, be doubled up

Betray, Hand Over

παραδίδωμι—give over, deliver over, betray, pass on teachings
ἀναδίδωμι—deliver, hand over, present
ἔκδοτος—given up, delivered over, surrendered, handed over, betrayed
προδότης—betrayer, traitor, one who abandons in danger

Bind, see "Fasten"

Bird

ὄρνεον—bird
ὄρνις—bird, hen
πετεινόν—bird
πτηνόν—bird
πέτομαι—fly
νοσσίον—young bird
νοσσός—young bird
νοσσιά—brood
ἀετός—eagle, vulture
κόραξ—crow, raven
περιστερά—dove, pigeon
τρυγών—dove, pigeon
ἀλέκτωρ—rooster
στρουθίον—sparrow

Birth, Procreation

γένεσις—source, origin, progeny, ancestry, lineage, birth, nativity, book of one's lineage, history
γενετή—birth
γεννητός—born, begotten
ἀρτιγέννητος—newly born
γεννάω—give birth, bear, beget, bring forth, conceive, deliver, make
γέννημα—offspring, generation, kind
καταβολὴ σπέρματος—make sperm, impregnate
συλλαμβάνω—to seize, take, catch, gather, comprehend, conceive, become pregnant
ἔγκυος—pregnant
κῦμα—billow
ἐν γαστρὶ ἔχω—to have in the womb, be pregnant
ἡ κοιλία βαστάζει—to bear in the womb, be pregnant with
κοίτην ἔχω—to have intercourse, be pregnant
τεκνογονέω—beget, bear children
τεκνογονία—childbearing
τίκτω—bring forth, bear, produce (fruit from seed), grow, give birth, be in travail
ὠδίν—birth pains, sorrow, travail
ὠδίνω—have birth pains, to travail, suffer greatly

ἔκτρωμα—an abortion, untimely birth, birth out of due time
στεῖρα—barren, hard, stiff (of men and animals)
ἀνίστημι σπέρμα—raise seed, beget
ἐξανίστημι σπέρμα—raise seed, beget
ἐξέρχομαι ἐκ τῆς ὀσφύος—come forth from the loins of, be born of
γινώσκω—know, learn, perceive, understand, acknowledge, have sexual intercourse
συνέρχομαι—come with, come together, assemble, cohabitate
κοίτη—bed, place for sleeping, the marriage bed, conception, sexual life
ἀποκυέω—give birth to
σκεῦος κτάομαι—to acquire a vessel, to take a wife, have sexual relations
παρθενία—virginity
φυσικὴν χρῆσιν—natural use, of sexual use of a woman (Romans 1:27)
συναναπαύομαι—rest with, sleep together, lie with
φύω—beget, bring forth, produce, spring up, germinate, grow

Bless
εὐλογέω—praise, bless, consecrate with solemn prayers
εὐλογία—praise, laudation, polished language, benediction, consecration, blessing, gift, of alms collected for the poor
κατευλογέω—bless

Blind, Impairment Of Sight
τυφλός—blind
μονόφθαλμος—one-eyed, missing an eye
ἀχλὺς—mist, mistiness, gloom, failure of sight, dimness

Boat, see "Sea Terms, Nautical Terms"

Bodily Excretions, Physiological Byproducts
ἱδρώς—sweat
δάκρυον—tear
πτύσμα—saliva
ἐξέραμα—vomit
ἰός—venom
χολή—gall, bile, a bitter digestive fluid from the gall bladder, the bitter liquid from the plant wormwood, something bitter
κοπρία—dung, dung heap

Body
σῶμα—body of man or animal, heavenly body, collection of people
σωματικός—bodily, corporeal
σωματικῶς—bodily (adverb)
ὁ ἔξω ἄνθρωπος—the outer man, body
σάρξ—flesh, body, natural generation, the sensual nature, human nature
σκῆνος—tent, tabernacle, the human body
σκήνωμα—tent, tabernacle, dwelling place, the human body
σκεῦος—vessel, jar, vase, utensils, furniture, military gear, equipment, luggage, one's wife (1 Thes. 4:4)
πτῶμα—corpse, dead body, carcass
κῶλον—corpse, dead body

Body Parts, Anatomy
ἀγκάλη—bent arm, arms of the sea
αἷμα—blood
ἀριστερός—left hand
ἁρμός—body joint, joining
αὐτόχειρ—one's own hands
ἁφή—ligament, bond, connection
βάσις—foot

βραχίων—arm, shoulder
γαστήρ—belly
γλῶσσα—tongue, language, people group who have the same language
γόνυ—knee
δάκτυλος—finger
δεξιός—right hand
ἔριον—wool
θηλή—nipple
θρίξ—hair
θρόμβος—clot of blood
θώραξ—chest
καρδία—heart, inner self
κέντρον—any sharp point, stinger of an insect
κέρας—horn of an animal, an extension or projection, symbol of deliverance or power, horn of salvation
κεφαλή—head, superior
κοιλία—belly, womb, seat of desires
κόλπος—lap, bay of the sea
κόμη—hair, locks
κρανίον—skull
λάρυγξ—throat
λεπίς—flake, scale
μαστός—breast
μέλος—member, part, body part
μέτωπον—forehead
μηρός—thigh
μήτρα—womb
μυελός—marrow
νῶτος—back
ὀδούς—tooth
ὄμμα—eye
ὀστέον—bone
ὀσφῦς—hip, loins, waist, belt
οὐρά—tail
οὖς—ear
ἀκοή—the sense of hearing, the ear, the thing heard, instruction, message
ὠτάριον—ear, diminutive of οὖς

ὠτίον—ear, diminutive of οὖς
ὀφθαλμός—the eye, sight
ὄψις—sight, face, countenance, outward appearance
πεζῇ—on foot
πλευρά—side of the body
πούς—foot
πρόσωπον—face, countenance, outward appearance, person
πτέρνα—heel
πτέρυξ—wing
πυγμή—fist
ῥυτίς—wrinkle
σάρξ—flesh, body, natural generation, the sensual nature, human nature
σιαγών—jaw, jaw bone, cheek
σκέλος—leg
σπλάγχνα—entrails, inner parts of the body: stomach, intestines, bowels, guts, the inner seat of emotions, where one feels compassion
στῆθος—chest
στόμα—mouth
στόμαχος—stomach
σφυδρόν—ankle
τράχηλος—neck
τρίχινος—hairy, made of hair
τύπος—mark or imprint from a blow, scar, form, pattern, example, type, figure (of something future)
χείρ—hand
χρώς—skin
ὦμος—shoulder

Booty, see "Plunder"

Break, Break Through
κλάσις—a break, a fracture
κλάω—to break e.g., bread
κατάγνυμι—to break
ἐκκλάω—break off, cut off
κατακλάω—break into pieces

συνθλάομαι—break into pieces, shatter
συντρίβω—break in pieces, tread down, crush, shatter
κλάσμα—a fragment, broken piece
διορύσσω—dig through, break through
ἐξορύσσω—dig out, pluck out

Bribery, see "Vices: Bribery"

Bring, Lead, Take, see also "Carry"
ἄγω—bring, lead, go
προάγω—precede, go before, happen previously
προσάγω—bring to, come near
περιάγω—travel about, lead around
εἰσάγω—lead into, bring in
ἐξάγω—lead out
κατάγω—lead down, bring from deep water to land, arrive at land
ἀνάγω—lead up, set sail
ἀπάγω—lead away, carry off
μετάγω—transfer, lead over, guide
χειραγωγέω—to lead by the hand
χειραγωγός—leading one by the hand
φέρω—bring, bear, carry
προσφέρω—bring before, present to, offer, make an offering to the Lord
ἐκφέρω—carry out, bring forth, produce, yield
ἀναφέρω—bring up, lead up, offer up
ἀποφέρω—carry off, bring away
ἀναλαμβάνω—take up, raise, pick up
παραλαμβάνω—receive, take with, accept, learn
συμπαραλαμβάνω—take/bring along together with, take with one as a companion
ἀπολαμβάνω—to receive from, take back, regain, recover, take aside, receive hospitably, welcome
προσλαμβάνομαι—take aside, receive, welcome
ἀπαίρω—lift off, take or carry away
ἕλκω—draw, drag off, pull
σύρω—draw, drag, before a judge, to prison, to punishment
κατασύρω—draw down, pull down, draw along, drag forcibly
προέρχομαι—go forward, go on, go prior to, precede, go in advance of another, pass on
προπορεύομαι—send before, precede, go before
ὁδηγέω—be a guide, lead on one's way, be a teacher
ὁδηγός—a leader of the way, a guide, a teacher

Building, Constructing
κατασκευάζω—to equip or furnish fully, get ready, make, build, construct, prepare, arrange
ἀνασκευάζω—to dismantle, make undone
οἰκοδομέω—to build, edify, found upon, encourage, build up, make more able, embolden
οἰκοδομή—a building, structure, construction
οἰκοδόμος—a builder, architect
ἀνοικοδομέω—to build up, wall up, build again, rebuild
ἐποικοδομέω—to build up, build upon, rebuild
συνοικοδομέω—to build together, edify together, build in with other materials
ἐπιτελέω—to complete, finish, fulfill, accomplish, discharge, pay in full
πήγνυμι—to pitch a tent, implant, fasten together, construct, build, erect, set up
ἀνορθόω—set up, make erect, build again, straighten up

δημιουργέω—to practice a trade, do work, work at, fabricate
δημιουργός—a skilled workman, builder, craftsman, architect, maker
δημιουργία—a making, creating, workmanship
ἀρχιτέκτων—chief builder, director of works, architect, engineer
τέκτων—any worker of wood, carpenter, craftsman, workman, joiner, metal-worker, sculptor, physician, master in any art, maker, builder, author
ἀποστεγάζω—uncover, remove a roof
κονιάω—to plaster over, whitewash

Building Materials
ἐνδώμησις—building material
δοκός—beam of wood
σανίς—plank
κέραμος—tile
ὕαλος—glass
ὑάλινος—of glass

Building Parts
ἀκρογωνιαῖος—cornerstone
ἀναβαθμός—stairs
ἀνάγαιον—upstairs room
ὑπερῷον—upstairs room
τρίστεγον—second or third story of a building
δῶμα—housetop
ἐνδώμησις—foundation
θεμέλιον—foundation, basis
θεμελιόω—to lay a foundation, to found, make stable, establish
ἑδραίωμα—support, foundation, mainstay
θύρα—door, entrance
θυρίς—window
κατάλυμα—room
κεφαλὴ γωνίας—cornerstone
κοιτών—bedroom
ξενία—guest room
οἴκημα—quarters
προαύλιον—forecourt
τετράγωνος—a place having four sides, laid out as a quadrangle, square
πτερύγιον—pinnacle
πύλη—gate, door, πύλαι ᾅδου (gates of hell)
πυλών—large gate of a palace, front entrance of a house through a gate or porch
στέγη—roof
στοά—porch
στῦλος—pillar
ταμεῖον—inner room, storeroom
τοῖχος—wall
ἀφεδρών—toilet

Buildings, Types Of
ἅγιος—holy place, sanctuary, saint, holy one, dedicated
ἀκροατήριον—audience hall, courtroom
ἀποθήκη—storehouse, granary, repository, barn
αὐλή—roofless enclosure, courtyard
βασίλειος—palace
γάμος—wedding hall
δεσμωτήριον—dungeon, jail, prison, place of bondage
εἰδωλεῖον—temple of an idol
ἔπαυλις—farm, dwelling, residence
θέατρον—theater
θησαυρός—treasury, store-house
ἱερόν—temple
κατάλυμα—inn, lodging place, guest chamber, dining room
κορβανᾶς—treasury
γαζοφυλάκιον—treasury
νυμφών—wedding hall
ναός—temple, shrine

οἰκία—house, dwelling, lineage, property
οἶκος—house, dwelling, lineage, property
ὀχύρωμα—castle, stronghold, fortress
πανδοχεῖον—inn, public house for reception of strangers, public lodging place
πανδοχεύς—innkeeper, host
παρεμβολή—encampment, barracks
πραιτώριον—palace, headquarters, the palace of Herod the Great where he conducted business, living quarters for the emperor's guard
πύργος—tower, watchtower
σκηνή—tent, tabernacle, dwelling place
σκηνοποιός—tentmaker
σκήνωμα—dwelling
κατασκήνωσις—nest, sheltered place to live or settle, lodging
στάδιον—arena
συναγωγή—synagogue
σχολή—unemployment, freedom from labor, leisure, school (as break from physical labor), lecture hall
ταβέρνη—inn, tavern, Three Taverns was 50 km from Rome
τήρησις—being guarded, keeping, imprisonment, custody
φυλακή—a guard, prison, watch, the shift of a sentinel's duty
μνημεῖον—monument, memorial, grave, tomb
μύλος—mill
μύλος—millstone
μυλικός—of a mill
μύλινος—of a mill
ἅλων—threshing floor
λιθόστρωτος—stone pavement (of Herod's)
φάτνη—stall
ληνός—wine press
ὑπολήνιον—wine trough, the vessel under a press to receive wine or oil, a vat

Burning, Fire, Smoke

ἅπτω—touch, hold, kindle, set on fire
ἀνάπτω—to kindle, set on fire, light
ὑφάπτω—to set on fire from underneath, to inflame unperceived
ἀνθρακιά—charcoal fire, heap of burning coals
ἄνθραξ—charcoal
ἄσβεστος—unquenchable
σβέννυμι—stop burning, extinguish fire, quench
ἐμπίμπρημι—set on fire
θεῖον—sulfur or brimstone (λίμνη τοῦ πυρὸς καὶ θείου - the lake of fire and brimstone)
θέρμη—heat, warmth
καίω—burn, ignite
κατακαίω—burn down
κάμινος—furnace
κλίβανος—oven
καπνός—smoke, visible vapors of combustion, of smoke, of things worth nothing, trifles
καῦμα—scorching heat
καυματίζω—harm by heat
καῦσις—burning
καυσόομαι—burn
καύσων—scorching heat
πῦρ—fire, flames
πυρά—bonfire
πυρόομαι—to burn with fire, set on fire, refine with fire, kindle, be sexually aroused
πύρωσις—burning, refining, trial, suffering
ἀναζωπυρέω—to rekindle, fan into flame, regain courage
σποδός—ashes

τεφρόω—reduce to ashes

τύφω—burn slowly, smoke, smolder

τυφόω—be proud or arrogant, be clouded by self-importance

φλογίζω—ignite, set on fire, kindle, inflame, arouse, excite

φλόξ—flame

φῶς—light, source of illumination, torch, bonfire

Buy, Sell, (see also under "Acquire" and "Gain")

πωλέω—to sell

ἀγοράζω—to buy, purchase, redeem, frequent the market

ἀγορά—market, place of public concourse, forum, marketplace

ἀποδίδωμι—to give back, repay, recompense, return, middle: sell

πράσσω—to accomplish, achieve, bring about, do, practice, act, be busy with, cause, make, manage, transact, negotiate, to exact money

πιπράσκω—to sell, sell into slavery

ἀνδραποδιστής—slave dealer, kidnapper

ὠνέομαι—to buy, purchase

ἐργάζομαι—to work, do business, do, perform, produce, bring about

By

ὑπό—with genitive: by, because of

παρά—with genitive: by, issuing from a person, from, on the part of

παρά—with dative: near, by, beside, alongside of

διά—with genitive: by, through, by way of

ἐν—with dative: by, near, on the grounds of, with the help of, through, because of, by reason of

ἀπό—with genitive: by, because of, as a result of, with the help of

ἐπί—with dative: by, near, on the basis of, from

C

Calm
γαλήνη—calm
σιωπάω—to be silent, become calm

Call
καλέω—to call, invite, bid, name
φωνέω—to emit a sound, speak, cry out, call, summon, send for
προσκαλέομαι—to call to oneself
προσφωνέω—to call to oneself
συγκαλέω—to call together, assemble
παρακαλέω—to urge, summon for help, encourage, comfort
μετακαλέομαι—to send for, summon, invite
κλῆσις—call, invitation, calling, social role, vocation

Capture, Trap, Surround, see also "Hunt, Trap, Catch, Snare," "Seize, Arrest"
αἰχμαλωτίζω—capture, take prisoner
ἅλωσις—a capture, conquest, catch
ζωγρέω—to take alive, capture
συλαγωγέω—take captive, prey on
περιπίπτω—fall into the hands of, encounter, run into, be seized by
θήρα—trap, net
παγίς—trap, snare, noose, pitfall, concealed danger, entanglement

κατέχω—hold tightly, hold back, restrain as in prison, possess
συνέχω—surround, hem in, enclose, guard, seize, afflict, be absorbed in
περιέχω—to encircle, surround, encompass, seize, contain
ἁρπάζω—snatch greedily, carry off by force, seize, plunder, claim for one's self eagerly, overpower
δέω—to bind, fasten, put under obligation, cause illness
συλλαμβάνω—to seize, take, catch, gather, comprehend, conceive, become pregnant
κυκλόω—go around, lead around, surround, encircle, encompass
κυκλεύω—surround
περικυκλόω—encircle, compass about, surround

Care For, Nurture
θάλπω—take care of, keep warm, cherish, comfort, foster
διακονέω—to minister, serve, take care of, wait on
ἐπισκέπτομαι—look upon, visit, care for, be concerned about, look for
σκοπέω—to watch, look out, inspect, examine, reconnoiter, premeditate, consider
ἐπισκοπέω—to look after, care for, watch over, visit, inspect, oversee

ἐπισκοπή—office of a church leader, supervisor's office, a visitation from God bringing help or salvation

ἐπίσκοπος—overseer, guardian, bishop

προνοέω—foresee, plan beforehand, be provident, provide for, take care of, take thought for

ἀγρυπνέω—to keep awake, be on the alert, attentive, circumspect, ready, keep watch over, guard, care for

ἐπιμέλεια—care, attention

ἐπιμελέομαι—to take care of, care for

παρατίθημι—put before, give, middle: entrust, commit

παραθήκη—what is entrusted to one's care

πιστεύω—to believe, think to be true, be persuaded of, place confidence in, trust, have faith, commit to, entrust to someone's care

τρέφω—nourish, support, feed, fatten, bring up, nurture, feed from the breast, take care of, rear

ἀνατρέφω—to nurse, nourish, bring up, rear

ἐκτρέφω—nourish up to maturity, nurture, bring up, rear, provide food

τεκνοτροφέω—raise children, rear

τροφός—a nurse, one who fosters or rears young

ἀναιρέω—kill, take away, abolish, middle: take up, adopt (Acts 7:21)

υἱοθεσία—adoption

Carry, Bear, see also "Bring"

φέρω—bring, bear, carry

περιφέρω—carry around

εἰσφέρω—bring into, lead into

εἰσάγω—bring into, lead into

διαφέρω—carry through, drive about, spread a message, intransitively: to differ, be worth more

προσφέρω—bring before, present to, offer, make an offering to the Lord

ἐκφέρω—carry out, bring forth, produce, yield

ἀποφέρω—carry off, bring away

ἀναφέρω—bring up, lead up, offer up

βαστάζω—bear a burden, endure

ἐκκομίζω—carry out, of a dead body

κομίζω—receive, receive back, be recompensed, bear, bring

πέμπω—send someone, send word

ἀναλαμβάνω—take up, raise

αἴρω—lift, raise up, elevate, remove, carry off, take away, kill, destroy

γόμος—freight, cargo, merchandise carried by ship

ποταμοφόρητος—carried off by flood or river, overwhelmed

φορτίζω—load, place a burden upon, cause to carry

φορτίον—burden, load, freight of a ship, obligations

ἀποφορτίζομαι—lay down a load, discharge, unload a cargo

Cause, Do

ἐπάγω—bring upon, cause something to befall one

ἐνεργέω—to work, put forth power, be active, be mighty in, bring about, cause to function, be effective

ἐργάζομαι—to work, do business, do, perform, produce, bring about

κατεργάζομαι—perform, accomplish, achieve, bring about, make ready

ποιέω—make, do, produce, cause to be, carry out, execute, appoint

τίθημι—set, put, place, lay, appoint

καθίστημι—set one in charge of, appoint, assign one to a function

ἀποκυέω—give birth to

προτίθεμαι—to place before, set forth, offer, purpose, plan beforehand τελειόω—make perfect, complete, accomplish, end, reach maturity, execute, finish, make happen

τάσσω—to appoint, assign, place, determine

διατελέω—to bring thoroughly to an end, accomplish

διεγείρω—wake up, arouse, stir up, render active

Cause, Dependency, Reason: words indicating Cause, Dependency, Reason

κρεμάννυμι—hang upon, suspend, depend upon

θεμέλιον—foundation, basis

νή—on the basis of, by

αἰτία—cause, charge for a crime, reason for an accusation, grounds for punishment

αἴτιος—cause, charge for a crime, reason for an accusation, grounds for punishment

ἀρχή—ruler, first in power, origin, beginning, first cause, elementary aspect, the corner or end of a thing

ῥίζα—root of plants, cause, source

λόγος—word, reason, matter under discussion, account, treatise

ἀφορμή—that which gives occasion and supplies matter for an undertaking, occasion, favorable circumstances, excuse

γάρ—for

ὅθεν—from where, whence, from which, from whom, wherefore, whereupon, on which occasion, upon which?

πόθεν—whence, from where, from what source, how is it that, in what way, why?

διότι—because, therefore, inasmuch as, that

χάριν—because of, on account of, for the sake of, on behalf of, for this purpose

εἰ—if, since, because

ἕνεκα—on account of, for the sake of, because of, by reason of

ἐπεί—because, since, else, otherwise, in that case, when, after

ἐπειδή—when, since, since then, because

ἐπειδήπερ—since indeed, inasmuch as, considering that, because

ὅτι—that, because

καθότι—as, according to what, in proportion to, because, in view of the fact that, to the degree that, in what manner

καθώς—just as, as, how, to the degree that, inasmuch as

ὅπου—where, to what place, in what place, whereas, insofar as, since

ὡς—so, thus, like, according as, with numerals: about, approximately

ἱνατί—why? for what reason?

λαμά, λεμά—why? transliterated from Aramaic

αὐτόματος—without any visible cause, spontaneously, on it's own

ἄλογος—unreasonable, irrational, brutish, absurd

εἰκῇ—at random, without plan or system, thoughtlessly, rashly, without reason or cause, in vain, for nothing, without purpose

Cease, Stop

παύω—to cease, bring to an end, rest, be done, stop, leave off from

ἀνάπαυσις—intermission, cessation of labor, rest, relief

καταπαύω—to make quiet, rest, be still, restrain, cause to desist, cease

ἐγκαταλείπω—to leave behind, leave in the lurch, leave out, omit, forsake, allow to end
ἐκλείπω—to fail, die out, cease
διαλείπω—stop, cease, pause
ἀποτίθημι—to put away, take off, lay aside, put aside or stop something
ἀπογίνομαι—to die, cease
ἐκκλίνω—to turn aside, deviate from, turn away from, shun, avoid, cease
κοπάζω—to abate, cease, stop, rest
ἀνίημι—loosen, unfasten, slacken, abandon, desert, give up, cease
ἀφίημι—send away, divorce, let go, leave, desert, abandon, forgive, remit, permit, allow, not hinder
ἀποστρέφω—to turn away, return
φράσσω—stop up, block, bar
ἀφαιρέω—to take away, remove, separate, passive: be deprived of
θανατόω—kill, put to death, terminate
νεκρόω—put to death
πίπτω—to fall, suffer demise, perish, befall
κλίνω—recline, incline, bend, slope, lay down, lie on a couch at meals, decline, of the day, draw to a close
σβέννυμι—to quench, put out, stop burning, extinguish fire, quell
ὑποστέλλω—withdraw, shrink back, be timid, cower, avoid, keep silent
ὑποστολή—shrinking back, evasion, ceasing, giving up
καταργέω—render ineffective, make barren, do away with, nullify, passive with ἀπό: be released from

Certain, Uncertain

βέβαιος—stable, firm, sure, steadfast, trustworthy, certain, verified
πάντως—altogether, by all means, positively, indeed, certainly
πιστός—faithful, true, to be trusted, certain, reliable, credible, believing
δῆλος—clearly visible, evident
ἀδήλως—uncertainly, aimlessly, not manifestly, dubiously
ἀδηλότης—uncertainty, obscurity, hiddenness, vagueness
μήποτε—never, on no account, lest ever, certainly not

Change, Renewal, see also "Convert, Repent"

μετάθεσις—departure, change
μεταμορφόω—to be transfigured, change appearance, transform
μετασχηματίζω—to change appearance, change the form of a person, transform, be disguised
προκοπή—progress, advancement
προκόπτω—to advance a work, go forward, progress, increase, beat forward, proceed, be spent
ἀποστρέφω—to turn away, return
στρέφω—turn, turn from one's course, change one's mind, reverse
μεθίστημι—remove, lead away, transfer
μεταστρέφω—turn around, corrupt, pervert, alter, change
μετατίθημι—transfer, change
μετατρέπω—turn into, change
περιτρέπω—turn into, change
ἀποκαθίστημι—restore to former state, establish again, restore to health
ἀποκατάστασις—restoration
ἐγείρω—raise, lift, awaken
ἰάομαι—cure, heal, make whole, restore, renew
ἀνακαινίζω—renew, renovate, restore
ἀνακαινόω—cause growth, make new, give new strength
ἀναγεννάω—be born again

παλιγγενεσία—rebirth, restoration, resurrection, regeneration, a new age
ἀλλάσσω—change, alter, transform, give in exchange, barter, repay
παραλλαγή—variation, change
μεταλλάσσω—change, alter, exchange

Child

παῖς—child, servant
παιδάριον—little boy, child, lad
παιδίον—child, infant
νήπιος—child, infant, childish
νηπιάζω—be a child, act innocently
βρέφος—unborn child, infant, babe
τέκνον—child, descendant
υἱός—son
θυγάτηρ—daughter
ταλιθα—little girl
κοράσιον—little girl, maiden

Choke, Suffocate

πνίγω—choke, strangle, of thorns crowding and hindering growth, take by the throat
πνικτός—suffocated, strangled, smothered, choked
συμπνίγω—choke utterly, press around or throng around so as to suffocate
ἀπάγχομαι—strangle, choke, middle: hang oneself

Choose, Select, Prefer

αἱρέομαι—to choose, prefer
αἱρετίζω—choose, belong to a sect
ἐξαιρέω—to pluck out, draw out, rescue, root out, choose out, select
ἐκλέγομαι—to pick out, choose, select
ἐπιλέγω—to surname, call, name, middle: choose, select
ἐκλογή—a choice, a thing or person chosen, election
ἐκλεκτός—picked out, selected

συνεκλεκτός—elected or chosen together with
χειροτονέω—to vote, appoint by vote, to elect, choose
προχειροτονέω—to choose or designate beforehand, appoint in advance
προχειρίζομαι—choose, appoint, choose in advance
ἀξιόω—to count worthy, deem deserving, regard as good
εὐδοκέω—to be pleased, be favorable towards, prefer, approve, choose
δοκιμάζω—to test, examine, prove, scrutinize, recognize as genuine after examination, approve, deem worthy, judge as good, evaluate
κρίνω—to judge, decide, evaluate, make a preference, condemn
διακρίνω—to judge between, prefer, discriminate, decide, evaluate, doubt, hesitate, take issue
προβλέπω—foresee, provide for, select in advance
προγινώσκω—to have knowledge beforehand, to foreknow, to predestinate, select in advance
ἐπισκέπτομαι—look upon, visit, care for, look for, pick out
καταφέρω ψῆφον—cast a vote
λαγχάνω—to cast lots, choose by lot, have as your portion
κληρόω—choose
κλῆρος—a lot, a casting or drawing of lots, a piece of land, a portion, share, inheritance, fate, destiny

Christian

Χριστιανός—Christian
υἱοὶ τῆς βασιλείας—sons of the king
τέκνα φωτός—children of light
πιστός—faithful, trusting, believing, confiding
οἱ ἅγιοι—the saints, holy ones

πρόβατον—sheep
ἀρνίον—lamb
ἐκκλησία—church, gathering
συναγωγή—assembly, gathering
προσήλυτος—proselyte

Citizen, Fellow Countryman
πολίτης—citizen
πολιτεία—citizenship
συμπολίτης—fellow citizen
ἀδελφός—brother, fellow countryman
συγγενής—relative, fellow countryman
συμφυλέτης—fellow tribesman
ἐντόπιος—local people, residents in a place

City
πόλις—city, town
κολωνία—colony
κωμόπολις—town
κώμη—village
ἀγρός—field, countryside, farm settlement
παρεμβολή—encampment, barracks

Class, Kind
γένος—race, stock, family, offspring, posterity, tribe, people, class, kind
τάξις—order, orderliness, arrangment, regularity, division of troops, rank, class of men
φύσις—natural state, form, character, kind, sort
ὄνομα—name, category
τύπος—mark or imprint from a blow, scar, form, pattern, example, type, figure (of something future)
γέννημα—offspring, generation, kind
ἐγκρίνω—to count in or among, admit, classify with, accept
πᾶς—all, any, whole, of every kind

πολυτρόπως—in many kinds of ways, in various manners
οἷος—what sort of, of what kind, of what manner, such as, like as
ὁποῖος—of what sort or quality, of whatsoever kind, like
ποῖος—what kind of, of what nature, what manner of
ποιός—of a certain nature, kind, or quality
ποταπός—what sort of, of what kind, how great

Cleanse, Purify, Wash
καθαίρω—purify, clean, purge, prune
καθαρίζω—purify, purge, heal
καθαρισμός—purification
καθαρότης—purification
καθαρός—clean, clear of dirt, pure, spotless, unsoiled, unblemished
ἐκκαθαίρω—clean out
διακαθαίρω—clean out
διακαθαρίζω—clean out
λούω—wash, bathe
λουτρόν—bath, bathing place, washing
ἀπολούομαι—wash away, make pure
νίπτω—wash
νιπτήρ—basin used for washing, washbasin
νίζω—wash, purge, cleanse
ἁγνίζω—to cleanse away, purify, ritually cleanse, hallow
ἁγνισμός—a ritual purification
πλύνω—wash, wash clean, bathe
ἄσπιλος—spotless, without defect, pure, clean, uncorrupted
ἄμωμος—without defect or blemish, blameless
ἁγιάζω—to hallow, dedicate, set apart for holy purposes, purify
βαπτίζω—baptize, ritually wash, dip

βαπτισμός—a washing, dipping in water, ablation
ῥαντίζω—sprinkle, purify by ritual sprinkling with blood, purge of sin
πιστικός—pure, genuine, trusted, unadulterated
ἄδολος—without guile, pure, of liquids, unadulterated, genuine
δόλος—treachery, deceit, fraud, bait
ἄκρατος—of liquids, pure, undiluted, full strength, absolute, untempered
σπογγίζω—to wipe with a sponge
ἐξαλείφω—wipe off, wipe away, obliterate, erase, blot out, eliminate
ἀπομάσσομαι—wipe off (Luke 10:11)
κονιάω—to plaster over, whitewash

Cloth, Clothing

λίνον—linen clothing, lamp wick
ὀθόνη—linen sheet
ὀθόνιον—linen strip
βύσσος—fine linen, a delicate, costly yellow Egyptian flax, byssus
βύσσινος—of fine linen
ἔριον—wool
σιρικός—made of silk, silken
ῥάκος—patch, scrap of cloth
πορφύρα—purple cloth
πορφυροῦς—purple, dyed purple, made of purple cloth
κόκκινος—scarlet, crimson, red cloth
σουδάριον—face cloth, handkerchief
λέντιον—towel, servants apron
ἔνδυμα—clothing, garment, raiment, cloak, outer garment, apparel, robe
ἐσθής—clothing, raiment, apparel, robe
ἔννυμι—clothing, dress
ἱμάτιον—clothing, garment, cloak or mantle, tunic, coat
ἱματισμός—clothing, apparel
χιτών—clothing, tunic, undergarment worn next to the skin, vestment
σινδών—linen cloth, loose undergarmen, costly linen
περιβόλαιον—clothing, mantle, veil, covering thrown around
σκέπασμα—clothing, covering
ἐπενδύτης—cloak, frock worn by fishermen, upper garment
φαιλόνης—travelling cloak for protection in stormy weather
χλαμύς—chalamys, an outer garment worn over the tunic, a short cloak worn by soldiers, magistrates
στολή—long robe worn by kings, priests
ποδήρης—long robe, reaching to the feet
ζώνη—belt
σιμικίνθιον—apron, narrow apron worn by servants, band or half-girding
κράσπεδον—fringe of a garment, skirt of a hill, tassel, edge
κόλπος—chest, breast, bosom, inlet, sea bay, fold of a garment, lap
ὑπόδημα—shoe, sandal, what is bound beneath
σανδάλιον—sandal
δέρμα—skin, hide, leather
δερμάτινος—made of leather
βυρσεύς—tanner
μηλωτή—sheepskin, outer robe or mantle
σκέπας—covering, shelter, pretense
κάλυμμα—veil, covering
καταπέτασμα—curtain, veil, drape
κειρία—band of cloth for bed-girth or for tying a linen-wrapped corpse

Cloth, Sewing

ξαίνω—to comb wool into fibers
νήθω—spin, twist fibers into thread
ὑφαίνω—weave threads into fabric
ὑφαντός—woven
πλέγμα—anything woven or braided
ἐπιράπτω—to sew on

ἐπίβλημα—patch, that which is put upon something
ἄραφος—seamless
ῥαφή—seam
ῥαφίς—needle
βελόνη—needle, any sharp point
τρῆμα—a perforation, hole, aperture, orifice, the eye of needle
τρυμαλιά—hole
τρυπάω—to pierce
γναφεύς—bleacher, fuller, one who cleans and bleaches woolen cloth, one who cards cloth or brushes it to raise the nap
κναφεύς—bleacher, fuller, one who cleans and bleaches woolen cloth, one who cards cloth or brushes it to raise the nap
ἄγναφος—unshrunk, uncarded, unbleached

Clothing, Activities Involving

ἐνδιδύσκω—to clothe, put on
ἐνδύω—to clothe, put on, wear, assume the character of
ἔνδυσις—a putting on
ἐπενδύω—to put on a garment, to put on one garment over another
ἱματίζω—to clothe
ἱμάτιον—outer garment, cloak, mantle, toga, tunic, coat, clothes
ἀμφιάζω—to clothe, adorn
ἀμφιέννυμι—to put around or on, clothe in, wear, adorn
περιβάλλω—to throw or put around, clothe, surround, encompass, enclose, embrace
ἀποβάλλω—to throw off, cast from one, reject, lose
περίκειμαι—to have placed around, wear, be surrounded
σπαργανόω—wrap in swaddling cloth, swathe (Luke 2:7)
περίθεσις—a putting on, wearing
ἐγκομβόομαι—to bind a thing to oneself, gird oneself, dress
φορέω—to carry, serve as a messenger, bear, wear, as armor or a sword, possess, be carried along
καταστολή—manner of dress, attire
ἔχω—have, hold, possess, have on, wear
ζώννυμι—gird around, put on a belt, gird up one's loins, prepare for battle
διαζώννυμι—to gird around the middle, engirdle, encompass
περιζώννυμι—be girded about, bind something about oneself
κατὰ κεφαλῆς ἔχω—have one's head covered
κατακαλύπτω—to cover, veil oneself
ὑποδέω—to put on shoes, bind or fasten under, underbind
χρυσόω—to make golden, gild, adorn with gold
ἐκδύω—to undress, strip, take off
ἀπεκδύνω—to undress, strip, take off, disarm, despoil
ἀπέκδυσις—a taking off, undressing
γυμνός—naked
γυμνότης—nakedness
γυμνιτεύω—wear rags, be poorly dressed

Colors

μέλας—black, dark, murky, obscure
λευκός—bright, radiant, brilliant, white, bleached
λευκαίνω—to make white, bleach, whiten, make bright
χρυσός—gold
ἄργυρος—silver
πορφυροῦς—purple, dyed purple, made of purple cloth
κόκκινος—scarlet, crimson, red cloth
ἐρυθρός—red

πυρρός—flame-colored, yellowish-red, orange, fiery red, blushing
πυρράζω—to be fiery red
πύρινος—of fire, fiery, hot, fiery red
χλωρός—green, grassy, fresh as new growth
ὑακίνθινος—blue, hyacinth-colored
θειώδης—sulfurous yellow

Come, Arrive
ἔρχομαι—come, go, come about
ἔλευσις—coming, advent
ἐπέρχομαι—come, arrive, come upon, overtake, attack (Luke 11:22)
ἐπιπορεύομαι—go or journey to, traverse, make a hostile inroad
ἐφικνέομαι—come to, reach
ἥκω—be present, come, arrive, as a result of reaching a place, be here, have happen, take place
καταντάω—come upon, reach, arrive at, attain to, happen to, befall
φθάνω—come before, precede, arrive at, reach, attain, come upon, happen
παραγίνομαι—come, arrive, appear
πάρειμι—be by, be at hand, to have arrived, come, be present, be ready, in store, at command
παρέρχομαι—pass by, arrive, pass away, perish, transgress
παρουσία—presence, coming, arrival, advent
ἀφικνέομαι—to reach, come to, arrive at, to reach the ears, become known

Command, see also "Law"
κελεύω—to command, order
κέλευσμα—an order, command, shouting of a command
τάσσω—to appoint, assign, place, determine
διατάσσω—to command, appoint, instruct, set in order
ἐπιτάσσω—to command, charge, enjoin
προστάσσω—to appoint, command, order
συντάσσω—to appoint, command
διαταγή—a command, ordinance
διάταγμα—a command, edict
ἐπιταγή—a command
διαστέλλομαι—to command, order, admonish, charge
ἐντέλλομαι—to command, order
ἔνταλμα—a commandment
παραγγέλλω—to command, order, announce, charge
παραγγελία—command, proclamation, announcement
ἐπιτιμάω—command, rebuke, lay a penalty on someone, admonish
ἐντολή—an order, command, charge
νόμος—law
δόγμα—command, ordinance, law

Comparison Words
οἷος—such as, like as, what sort of, of what manner, whatever kind of
ὅμοιος—similar, like, resembling, the same as, in like manner with
ὁμοίως—similarly, likewise, so, in the same way
τοιοῦτος—such as this, like that, just so, even so, so great, so small
ὁμοιότης—similarity, likeness, resemblance
ὁμοιόω—liken, compare, be similar to
ὁμοίωμα—similarity, likeness, resemblance, image, appearance
ὁμοίωσις—similarity, a becoming like, assimilation, resemblance
ὅμως—similarly, all the same, nevertheless, notwithstanding, still, but for all that, yet, though, likewise, in the same way, also
ὁμῶς—equally, likewise, alike

ἀφομοιόω—to make like, compare, be like, be similar to, portray, copy

ἔοικα—be like, resemble

συγκρίνω—to join together fitly, compound, combine, to interpret, compare, explain, measure, estimate

παρόμοιος—very similar, much like, closely resembling, nearly equal

παρομοιάζω—to be much like, be very similar to

παραπλήσιος—nearly resembling, similar, adverb: nearly, almost

παραπλησίως—similarly, likewise

συμφωνέω—be in harmony, agree with, hold the same opinions with, of clothes: match, fit together

ἀναλογία—right relationship, compatibility, proportion, agreement between things being compared (Romans 12:6)

ὡς—so, thus, like, according as, with numerals: about, approximately

οὕτως—thusly, in this way, in this manner, so, as follows

ὡσεί—just as if, as though, like

ὥσπερ—just as if, even as

ὡσπερεί—just as, like, as though, as it were

ὡσαύτως—in the same way, likewise, similarly

καθά—just as, according as, like as if, exactly as

καθό—in so far as, according as, so that, just as

καθώς—just as, as, how, to the degree that, inasmuch as

καθάπερ—just as

καθώσπερ—just as

πρός—[is] comparable to (Romans 8:18)

ἤ—than (e.g., Matthew 18:13)

ἤπερ—than (John 12:43)

Compel, Force, see also "Urge, Persuade"

ἀναγκάζω—to force, compel, constrain

ἀγγαρεύω—force to carry, compel, press into service

δέω—to bind, fasten, put under obligation, be bound to do something, be bound by illness

παραβιάζομαι—to compel by force, to constrain one by entreaties, convince by persuasion

Complain

γογγύζω—to murmur, grumble, complain, speak against in a low tone, of the cooing of doves

γογγυσμός—murmur, complaint, concealed grudging, displeasure not openly avowed

γογγυστής—murmurer, grumbler, one who discontentedly complains

διαγογγύζω—to murmur, grumble

στενάζω—to sigh, groan, moan, bewail, grumble, complain strongly

στενός—narrow, strict, exacting, close, confined

μομφή—blame, complaint, quarrel

Complete, Finish, Succeed

τελειόω—make perfect, complete, accomplish, end, reach maturity, finish, execute, make happen

τέλειος—complete, ended, perfect, full grown, adult, of full age, mature

τελειωτής—accomplisher, finisher

τελευτάω—to finish, come to an end, close, die

ἐπιτελέω—to complete, finish, fulfill, accomplish, discharge, pay in full

συντελέω—to bring to an end, complete, finish, close, be over

ἀποτελέω—to bring to an end, complete, pay a vow

ἐκτελέω—to bring to an end, accomplish, achieve

τελέω—finish, end, accomplish, fulfill, make perfect, pay taxes

τέλος—end, limit, boundary, finish, completion, last, conclusion, tax

πέρας—end, limit, boundary, finish, completion, last, conclusion, same as τέλος

περαίνω—to bring to an end, finish, accomplish, execute, be fulfilled, reach

σκοπός—goal, mark of the end of a race course

διανύω—to complete, bring to an end, accomplish, finish

ἀνύω—to accomplish, complete

πληρόω—make full, fulfill, complete, fulfill the requirements of, observe, fulfill a prophecy

ἀναπληρόω—fill up, supply, refill, fulfill

ἀπαρτισμός—completion

ἐξαρτίζω—to thouroughly prepare, equip completely, make adequate, be complete (of time)

καταρτίζω—prepare, make adequate, mend, restore, create, perfect, make ready

πληροφορέω—to fulfill, passive: have full satisfaction, be fully persuaded

ἔσχατος—the last, final, furthest, uttermost, most extreme

ὅλος—whole, entire, complete

εἰς τὸ παντελές—forever, for all time, completely

εἰς τέλος—completely

ὁλοτελής—completely

ἱκανός—sufficient, adequate, able, enough, considerable, satisfactory

παντελής—completely, fully, wholly, perfectly, absolutely

Confess, Profess Allegiance, Admit, Assert, Declare, Testify, Claim

ἐξομολογέω—agree, promise, consent, middle: confess, praise, thank

ὁμολογέω—to declare, profess, agree, middle: confess, give thanks, praise

ὁμολογουμένως—by consent of all, undeniably, beyond all question

ὁμολογία—profession, confession

φάσκω—to affirm, allege, profess, assert, claim

ἐπαγγέλλομαι—to promise, assert, profess

ἀπεῖπον—forbid, reject, renounce, denounce, disown, 2 Corinthians 4:2

ὁμολογέω—declare, profess, confess, promise, claim, give thanks, praise

ἐξηχέομαι—to proclaim, sound forth, resound

διαμαρτύρομαι—to testify, witness, insist, attest

μαρτύρομαι—to testify, witness, insist, attest

Conjunctions, Discourse Markers

γάρ—for, certainly, by all means, so

καί—and, and then, also, yet, even

ἀλλά—but, otherwise, yet, but then, however

μέν—indeed, to be sure, on the one hand

νυνὶ δέ—now, but now, and so

νυνί—now, and so

γίνομαι—there was, it happened

γέ—indeed

δή—indeed, now, then, therefore

δήπου—of course, surely, indeed

οὖν—so, therefore, then, accordingly, consequently, adversative usage: however, but, rather

εἰ μήν—surely

μενοῦν—and, surely, therefore, may be adversative: yes but, yes but even more so, as in Luke 11:28

μήτιγε—how much more

ἰδού—behold, look

πάντως—altogether, by all means, positively, indeed

ἄγε—come, look

ἴδε—look, lo, behold

ὦ—O!

ἵνα—that, in order to, as a result

ὅτι—that, because

ἄχρι—until, until the time of, before, as far as, up to, unto, as long as

κεφάλαιον—summary, main point in a letter or discourse, sum of money

λοιπός—from now on, the remaining, to mark an added fact: furthermore, also, in addition, beyond that, finally

Conquer

καταγωνίζομαι—to struggle against, prevail against, conquer

συντρίβω—break in pieces, tread down, crush, shatter

πατέω—tread, trample, crush with the feet, step on

κατακυριεύω—to gain dominion over, rule, overpower, lord it over

κατισχύω—to have power over, overpower, prevail against, defeat

νικάω—to conquer, prevail, vanquish, win victory over, be prominent

νίκη—victory, upper hand, ascendancy

νῖκος—victory, later form of νίκη

ὑπερνικάω—have complete victory, be more than conqueror

θριαμβεύω—triumph over, lead in triumph

ἡττάομαι—be defeated

ἥττημα—defeat, failure, fall

Containers

σκεῦος—vessel, jar, vase, utensils, furniture, military gear, equipment, luggage, one's wife (1 Thes. 4:4)

θήκη—receptacle, chest, sheath

ἀγγεῖον—container, vessel

ἄγγος—container, vessel

ποτήριον—cup, drink container

νιπτήρ—basin used for washing, washbasin

ἄντλημα—bucket, a container or vessel for drawing water

φιάλη—bowl, a broad, shallow bowl normally used for cooking or serving liquids

στάγμος—Jar used to contain wine or manna

ξέστης—pitcher, jar, borrowed from Latin sextarius, about a pint

ὑδρία—pitcher, water jar, a container for water

κεράμιον—jar, vessel, an earthenware container

κεραμεύς—potter, one who makes earthenware vessels

χαλκίον—kettle, metal vessel, copper, brass, or bronze container

ἀλάβαστρον—a jar made of alabaster stone, alabaster flask

ἀσκός—leather bag, wineskin

πίναξ—platter, plate, large dish

παροψίς—plate, dish, often used to serve choice foods and delicacies

τρύβλιον—bowl, dish for dipping bread

φάτνη—feed box, crib, manger, box where animals feed

λιβανωτός—bowl in which incense is burned, censer

κιβωτός—any box-like container, box, chest, coffer, ark

θησαυρός—treasure, treasury, storehouse, receptacle for valuables

γαζοφυλάκιον—offering box

γλωσσόκομον—a money box, a case for a mouthpiece

βαλλάντιον—purse, money bag, pouch

πήρα—traveler's bag, leather pouch, wallet, scrip

σαργάνη—large basket

σπυρίς—large basket

κόφινος—large basket

μόδιος—bowl, bucket, box, or basket, containing about 8 liters

Contests, Sports, Play

ἀγωνίζομαι—to contend for a prize in public games, contest, debate, contend in law, fight, struggle

ἀθλέω—compete in a contest

ἄθλησις—contest, struggle

ἀγών—an athletic contest, struggle, trial, battle, fight, race

δρόμος—a course, running, race, quick movement, flight, mission

πυκτεύω—to fight with the fists, box

γυμνασία—physical exercise, training

γυμνάζω—to train in gymnastics, exercise, practice, discipline oneself

παίζω—play, be amused, dance

Content, Satisfied

κορέννυμι—to satiate, satisfy, eat enough, be full, be content

χορτάζω—feed with herbs, grass, hay, eat one's fill, satisfy, be content

πληρόω—make full, fulfill, complete, fulfill the requirements of, observe, fulfill a prophecy

πλησμονή—satisfaction, gratification, fullness

μεστός—full, filled, very full

ἀρκέω—to have sufficient strength, suffice, be enough, be satisfied

αὐτάρκεια—self-sufficiency, not needing aid or support, adequacy

αὐτάρκης—self-sufficient, strong enough to need no aid, resourceful, contented with one's means though the slenderest

Contrast, Words Of

δέ—and, but, then, now

ἀλλά—but, otherwise, yet, but then, however, instead, on the contrary

ἀλλὰ μᾶλλον—but more, but rather

ἀλλ' ἤ—but rather, Luke 12:51

εἰ μή—except, but, however, instead, but only

μᾶλλον—more, to a greater degree, more certainly, rather, instead of, comparative of μάλα

μᾶλλον . . . ἤ—rather . . . than . . . , more . . . than . . . , as in John 3:19

μενοῦν—and, surely, therefore, may be adversative: yes but, but even more so, as in Luke 11:28

μενοῦνγε—but on the contrary, on the other hand

πάλιν—again, once more, anew, back (Mark 15:13), on the other hand, but in turn, however

μέντοι—but indeed, nevertheless, except

πλήν—but, except

τοὐναντίον—rather, on the contrary, instead

ἔτι—yet, as yet, still, further, besides, moreover, hereafter, nevertheless, in addition

μέν . . . δέ—on the one hand . . . on the other hand

μέντοι . . . δέ—on the one hand . . . on the other hand

ἐκτός—outside, without, unless, except, besides, independent of

Control, Restrain

δαμάζω—bring under control, tame, break in, bring under a yoke, make subject, subdue, overpower

ζωγρέω—to take alive, capture

βρόχος ἐπιβάλλω—put a rope upon, impose restrictions

ἐνέχω—active: to be hostile, have it in for, press upon, be urgent toward, passive, with dative: let oneself be entangled in, be under the control of

ἔνοχος—liable, deserving, guilty, answerable

εὐπερίστατος—controlling tightly, easily ensnaring

ὑπό—with accusative: under [the control of] (Galatians 3:22)

ὑποκάτω—below, under

ἐπί—with genitive or accusative: over, in charge of

συλαγωγέω—take captive, prey on

περιπίπτω—fall into the hands of, encounter, run into, be seized by

παραδίδωμι εἰς χεῖρας—deliver into the hand of, be put under control of

ἐξουσία—authority, power, license, permission, legal right

κρατέω—to take hold of, hold firmly to, grasp, seize, arrest, retain, get control of

κραταιός—powerful, strong, mighty

κατέχω—hold tightly, hold back, restrain as in prison, possess

συνέχω—surround, hem in, enclose, guard, seize, afflict, be absorbed in

ὑπερέχω—be better than, exceed, outdo, be above, govern, control

στενοχωρέομαι—be in a tight place, be crowded together, be confined

καταλαμβάνω—lay hold of, obtain, acquire, seize, attack, catch, middle: receive with the mind, comprehend

βραβεύω—to rule, be arbiter, judge, director, or umpire in public games, preside, govern, arrange, control

αὐθεντέω—to have full power over, have authority, domineer, control

βασιλεύω—to be king, reign

περικρατής—having control over, being in full command over

δοῦλος—a slave, servant

δουλόω—to put under obligation, make subservient, make a slave of

δουλεύω—to be a slave to, serve, be subject to

δουλεία—subservience, servitude, slavery, bondage

καταδουλόω—to reduce to slavery, enslave, make subservient

ἁρπάζω—snatch greedily, carry off by force, seize, plunder, claim for one's self eagerly, overpower

αἰχμαλωτίζω—capture, take prisoner

καταστέλλω—to restore order, quiet down, bring under control, repress

ὑποτάσσω—to bring under submission, subject, subordinate, passive: be submissive, obey

ἀκατάστατος—unstable, unsettled, not under control

ἀνυπότακτος—not made subject, unruly, refractory, disobedient

Converse, Discuss

ὁμιλέω—to talk with, converse with, be in company with, associate with

συνομιλέω—to talk with

συζητέω—to seek or examine together, discuss, dispute, question, inquire, reason together, talk with

συλλαλέω—to talk with, commune with, confer with

συλλογίζομαι—count together, be counted among, consider together, discuss, reason together, deliberate

διαλαλέω—to converse together, to discuss in detail, passive: be talked about, be sounded abroad

διαλογίζομαι—to reason carefully, deliberate, cast in the mind, discuss, dispute, converse about

συμβάλλω—meet, discuss, consult, debate, ponder, middle: help, assist

ἀντιβάλλω—to discuss together, exchange words, talk about

Convert, Change Behavior, Repent, see also "Change, Renewal"

μεταβάλλομαι—to turn around, transform one's self, change one's opinion, change one's mind

μεταμέλομαι—to repent, regret, feel remorse, to leave off caring about something, to change one's mind

μέλω—to be concerned, care about

μετανοέω—repent, change one's mind

μετάνοια—repentance, remorse, regret

ἐπιστρέφω—to return, turn back, change beliefs, change one's ways

ἐπιστροφή—conversion, change of one's beliefs, change of one's ways

στρέφω—turn, turn from one's course, change one's mind, reverse

γεννάω ἄνωθεν—be born again

παλιγγενεσία—rebirth, restoration, resurrection, regeneration, a new age

ἀμετανόητος—unrepentant, not to be repented of

Cooking And Kitchen Terms, See Also Under "Containers," "Food," "Measures"

σκεῦος—vessel, jar, vase, utensils, furniture, military gear, equipment, luggage, one's wife (1 Thes. 4:4)

ἀρτύω—to make ready, prepare, of foods, to season, make tasty

ὀπτός—broiled, baked, roasted, tempered, forged

ἀλήθω—to grind grain, bruise, pound

ἀλέω—to grind grain, bruise, pound

ἄλευρον—wheat flour, meal

διϋλίζω—to strain off, filter out

σινιάζω—to sift, winnow

σινίον—a sieve

σιτίον—grain, food

σαρόω—to sweep with a broom

φύραμα—lump of dough or clay

Cost, Pay, Price

μισθός—pay, wages, reward, recompense, gain, retribution

ἀνταπόδομα—repayment, retaliation

ἀποδίδωμι—to give back, repay, recompense, return, middle: sell

ἀνταποδίδωμι—to give back, repay

δίδωμι—to give

τιμή—honor, respect, worth, value of a thing, price, valuation, payment

τιμάω—to pay honor to, hold in honor, revere, reverence, value, prize, set a price on

ἀποτίνω—to repay, make atonement, make good, compensate

τίνω—pay a penalty, incur, suffer, experience retribution, undergo punishment or something bad

δαπάνη—cost, expense, outgoing

κεφάλαιον—summary, main point in a letter or discourse, sum of money, pecuniary sum total amount, principal

ὀψώνιον—allowance, pay, salary, wage, expense money, ration

ἀμοιβή—repayment, recompense

ἀρραβών—down-payment, first installment, pledge, deposit that is forfeited if the transaction fails

ἀπαρχή—first portion of a sacrifice, firstfruits, first
ἀδάπανος—free of charge, without expense, costing nothing
κομίζω—receive, receive back, be recompensed, bear, bring

Council, Assembly
γερουσία—chief counsel of a city
πρεσβυτέριον—Jewish council of elders, group of elders
συμβούλιον—council
βουλευτής—councilor, senator
δῆμος—people, family, public assembly

Country, Kingdom
ἔθνος—nation
λαός—people
πατριά—nation
φυλή—tribe
τόπος—region, place, possibility
χώρα—land, region, countryside
πολιτεία—state
βασιλεία—kingdom, dominion, reign
οἰκουμένη—inhabited world, empire
ἐπαρχεία—province, region subject to a prefect, office of a prefect
μερίς—part, district, portion, share
κολωνία—colony
πολίτευμα—place of citizenship

Courage, Boldness, see also "Strong" and "Virtues: Faith, Hope"
θαρρέω—to be of good courage, be of good cheer, be courageous, be bold
θάρσει—Imperative: Take courage! Be of good cheer!
θάρσος—courage
παρρησία—outspokenness, openness, frankness, plainness and freedom in speaking, unreservedness in speech
παρρησιάζομαι—to speak freely, speak with assurance and boldness
ἐπαίρω τὴν κεφαλήν—to lift up the head, have courage
τολμάω—to be brave, dare, bear one's self boldly, not to fear, summon up courage
τολμηρότερον—more boldly
ἀποτολμάω—be bold, be fearless
τολμητής—daring, presumptuous, arrogant
ἀνδρίζομαι—to become courageous, to be made brave, to show one's self a man, be made a man of
πείθω τὴν καρδίαν—to persuade the heart, be assured

Covered, Uncovered
καλύπτω—hide, conceal, veil, hinder from knowing, cover, keep secret
κάλυμμα—head covering, veil
περικαλύπτω—cover on the sides
ἀκατακάλυπτος—uncovered, unveiled, of the head
ἀνακαλύπτω—uncover, unveil, of the face

Criticize
ἀνακρίνω—examine, judge, inquire into, investigate, interrogate, scrutinize, criticize
διακρίνω—to judge between, prefer, discriminate, decide, evaluate, take issue, dispute, doubt, hesitate
ἀνταποκρίνομαι—reply, answer back, dispute
μωμάομαι—to blame, find fault with, mock at, criticize
ἀπελεγμός—censure, repudiation, serious criticism
ἀκατάγνωστος—not condemned or censored, above criticism

ἀνεπίλημπτος—not open to censure, irreproachable, blameless, above criticism, unrebukeable

Crooked, Straight

σκολιός—crooked, bent, dishonest, unscrupulous, unfair

ὀρθός—straight, in a straight line, right, upright, erect

εὐθύνω—to guide on course, direct, govern, steer straight, pilot a ship, straighten crooked judgements, audit accounts, call to account

εὐθύς—immediately, directly, straightway, without reserve, at once, unhindered, openly, forthrightly, Acts 8:21, 2 Peter 2:15

Crossover, Pass, Go Through, Go Around

παράγω—pass by, lead past, lead aside, mislead, depart

παραπορεύομαι—pass by

παρέρχομαι—pass by, arrive, pass away, perish, transgress

ἀντιπαρέρχομαι—pass by opposite to, pass on the other side

πάροδος—a passing by, passage

διαβαίνω—pass through, cross over

διαπεράω—pass over, cross over, sail over

διέρχομαι—travel through a region, go through, of news: spread abroad

διϊκνέομαι—go through, penetrate, pierce

περιέρχομαι—go about, wander, go around, travel around

Crowd, Group

λαός—people
ὅμιλος—crowd
ὄχλος—crowd
πλῆθος—multitude, crowd
ὀχλοποιέω—gather a crowd

νέφος—cloud (Hebrews 12:1)
κλισία—eating group
συμπόσιον—eating group
πρασιά—group of people (Mark 6:40)
σύσσωμοι—co-members, belonging to the same body
δῆμος—people, family, public assembly, crowd (Acts 15:5)

Cruelty, Mistreatment, see "Vices: Cruelty, Mistreatment"

Cry, Groan, Mourn, Weep

δακρύω—weep, shed tears
κλαίω—mourn, weep, lament, bewail
κλαυθμός—weeping, lamentation
κραυγή—crying, outcry, clamor, weeping
ἀλαλάζω—to weep loudly, wail, lament, clang
ὀλολύζω—to howl, wail, lament, cry aloud whether for joy or grief
θρηνέω—mourn, lament, sing a dirge, wail, sing funeral songs
πενθέω—to mourn, lament, be sad
πένθος—mourning, sorrow
στεναγμός—a sigh, groan
στενάζω—to sigh, groan, moan, bewail, grumble, complain strongly
στενός—narrow, strict, exacting
ἀναστενάζω—to sigh deeply, groan deeply
συστενάζω—to groan together
ταλαιπωρέω—to toil heavily, endure labors and hardships, be afflicted, be sorrowful
θορυβάζω—be upset, stirred up

Crystal

κρύσταλλος—crystal
ὕαλος—glass, something transparent like glass

Curse

κατάρα—curse, execration, imprecation

καταράομαι—to curse, doom, pronounce evil upon

ἀρά—a prayer, more commonly a prayer for evil, imprecation, curse, malediction

ἐπάρατος—accursed

ἐπικατάρατος—accursed, execrated, under God's vengeance

ἀναθεματίζω—declare one liable to the severest divine penalties, curse, bind with an oath

ἀνάθεμα—curse, oath, one cursed, a devoted thing, ordinarily in a bad sense, a person or thing cursed or damned, an execration

καταθεματίζω—to curse

κατάθεμα—a curse

Custom, Tradition

ἔθος—custom, habit

ἦθος—custom, usage, disposition, character, manners, an accustomed place, abode

ἐθίζω—to be accustomed or used to, be in the habit of

εἰωθός—custom, habit

εἰωθότως—in the customary way, as usual

συνήθεια—habitual conversation, habit, custom, the customary use

παρατηρέω—to observe carefully, watch closely, lie in wait for

νομίζω—to deem, think, suppose, passive: to be customary

Cut

κόπτω—cut, strike, smite, cut off, beat one's breast in grief, mourn

ἀποκόπτω—cut off, amputate

ἐκκόπτω—do away with, cut off, cut down, frustrate, hinder

διχοτομέω—cut in two, punish severely

πρίζω—saw in two

κατακόπτω—cut up in pieces, slay, beat, bruise, cut, gash, mangle

κατατομή—a cutting up, mutilation

τομός—sharp, cutting

τέμνω—to cut

κείρω—sheer, be shorn, cutting short the hair of the head

ξυράομαι—shear, shave, be shaved

λατομέω—to cut stones, hew out rock

λαξευτός—cut out of stones, hewn out of rock

D

Danger, Risk
κίνδυνος—danger, peril
κινδυνεύω—be in jeopardy, be in danger, put in peril, run a risk
ἐπισφαλής—prone to fall, dangerous
σφάλλω—cause to fall
παγίς—snare, trap, noose, danger
σπιλάς—a rock in the sea, a hidden danger, of those who plot, spot, stain
παραβολεύομαι—risk, expose to danger
τράχηλον ὑποτίθημι—put one's neck under, risk one's life

Darkness
σκοτία—darkness, obscurity, absence of light, ignorance, the realm of evil which opposes God
σκότος—darkness, ignorance, the evil world
σκοτεινός—dark
σκοτίζομαι—become dark
σκοτόομαι—become dark
στυγνάζω—be sad, sorrowful, become dark and gloomy, overcast
γνόφος—darkness, gloom
ζόφος—gloom
αὐχμηρός—squalid, dirty, dark and miserable
νύξ—night (darkness)

σκιά—shade, shadow, foreshadow
ἀποσκίασμα—shadow
ἐπισκιάζω—cast a shadow upon
κατασκιάζω—cast a shadow upon

Debt
ὀφείλω—to be bound, be obliged, owe, be indebted to, be due, be liable to, would that, ought
ὀφειλή—that which is owed, a debt, obligation
ὀφείλημα—that which is owed, a debt, obligation
ὀφειλέτης—a debtor
χρεοφειλέτης—debtor
προσοφείλω—to owe in return, owe besides, be still owing
καταναρκάω—to be slothful towards, press heavily upon, be a financial burden
ἐπιβαρέω—to weigh down, burden, be a financial burden
ἀβαρής—not weighing down, not financially burdensome
ἀφίημι—send away, divorce, let go, leave, desert, abandon, forgive, remit, permit, allow, not hinder
χαρίζομαι—to be agreeable, oblige, gratify, court favor, offer freely, give willingly, be pleasing, forgive, pardon, remit

Deception, Speaking Falsely, see "Vices: Deception, Speaking Falsely"

Dedicate, Consecrate

ἁγιάζω—to hallow, dedicate, set apart for holy purposes, purify

ἁγιασμός—dedication, consecration, sanctification

ἁγιωσύνη—holiness, sanctity, dedication

ἅγιος—saint, holy one, holy place, sanctuary, dedicated, set apart

ὁσιότης—dedication

ὅσιος—hallowed, sanctioned by God, dedicated, pious, devout, pure, clean

ἀνόσιος—impious, unholy, profane

ἑαυτὸν δίδωμι—to give oneself to, dedicate oneself

βαπτίζω—baptize, ritually wash, dip

περιτέμνω—to circumcise, cut around, prune, make incisions in a circle, cut off the extremity

περιτομή—circumcision

ἀκροβυστία—uncircumcision

ἐπισπάω—become uncircumcised

σπάω—to draw, pull

Defeat, see "Conquer"

Defend, Excuse

ἀπολογέομαι—to defend oneself, give a full account of, answer, excuse, speak for one's self

ἀπολογία—verbal defense, reasoned statement or argument, answer, clearing of self

ἀναπολόγητος—without defense or excuse, inexcusable

πρόφασις—pretext, alleged reason, show, pretense, what appears ostensibly, cloak, excuse, cover-up

Defiled, Unclean, Common, see "Vices: Uncleanness, Defilement"

Deny, Disregard, Neglect

ἀρνέομαι—to deny, refuse to agree

ἀπαρνέομαι—to deny, disregard, reject, deny acquaintance with

παραθεωρέω—to compare, overlook, neglect, disregard

ὑπεροράω—to overlook, take no notice of, not attend to, disregard

ἀμελέω—to be careless of, neglect, make light of, disregard

καταλείπω—to leave behind, abandon, neglect, no longer relate to

πάρεσις—passing over, letting pass, disregarding, remission

Descend, Sink, Fall

καταβαίνω—go down, come down, disembark, unboard

κατέρχομαι—go down, come down, of a ship: arrive at land

καταβιβάζω—bring down, cast down

βιβάζω—make to go up

κατάβασις—descent, slope, the act of descending

καθαιρέω—lower, take down, pull down, demolish

καθίημι—let down, send down

χαλάω—loosen, slacken, relax, let down from a higher place to a lower

δύνω—go down, sink, used of the setting sun

ἐπιδύω—go down, set (of the sun)

βυθίζω—sink, plunge into the deep

καταποντίζομαι—sink, plunge into the sea, drown

ποντος—the sea, the depths (Septuagint)

συμπίπτω—fall, completely crash down

Descendants

γένος—race, stock, family, offspring, posterity, tribe, people, class, kind
φυλή—tribe
δωδεκάφυλον—the twelve tribes
γενεά—generation, age, descendants
συγγένεια—kin, fellow countryman
συγγενής—of the same kin, related
συγγενίς—female relative
οἰκία—house, household, dwelling, property, family, lineage
οἶκος—house, household, dwelling, property, family, lineage
οἰκεῖος—member of a household, relative
οἰκιακός—member of a household, relative
πανοικεί—adverb: with one's entire household
οἱ παρ᾽ αὐτοῦ—his family, the ones near him
οἱ ἴδιοι—his own people, the ones his own
δῆμος—people, family, public assembly
ἀλλογενής—foreigner, another lineage
πάροικος—stranger, alien, foreigner

Desire: Passion, Strong Desire, see also "Vices: Greed" and "Vices: Lust"

ἐπιθυμέω—to desire greatly, long for, lust after, covet
ἐπιθυμία—deep desire, craving, lust
ἐπιθυμητής—one who greatly desires, longs for, is eager for, lusts after
θυμός—passion, intense desire, ardor, anger, fierceness, indignation, wrath
ὀρέγω—be eager for, strive for, aspire to, long for, desire
ὄρεξις—striving for, craving, lust
ἐκκαίομαι ἐν τῇ ὀρέξει—to burn with desire (Romans 1:27)
διψάω—be thirsty, desire strongly
πεινάω—be hungry, desire strongly
ἐπιποθέω—to long for, pursue with love, lust for, deeply desire, have great affection for
ἐπιπόθησις—longing, earnest desire, vehement desire, deep desire
ἐπιποθία—longing, deep desire
ζηλόω—to burn with zeal or envy, be jealous over, to desire earnestly
ζῆλος—fervor of spirit, zeal, earnest concern, jealousy, indignation
πλεονεξία—greedy desire for more, covetousness, avarice, greediness
πλεονέκτης—a greedy person, one who claims more than his due, making gain from other's losses
ἁρπαγή—the act of plundering, robbery, plunder, spoil, booty
ἅρπαξ—rapacious, ravenous, a robber, extortion, violently greedy
αἰσχροκερδής—shamefully greedy
αἰσχροκερδῶς—with shameful greed
ἡδονή—pleasure, lust, passion
κοιλία—belly, womb, seat of desires
φιλοπρωτεύω—to aspire to pre-eminence, desire to be first
σαρκὸς θέλημα—desires of the flesh, sexual desires
καταστρηνιάω—to have sexual desire, have lust, be headstrong or wanton towards
πάθημα—suffering, passion
πάθος—feeling, emotion, passion, affection, lust
πυρόομαι—to burn with fire, set on fire, refine with fire, kindle, be sexually aroused
ὁμοιοπαθής—suffering like with another, of like feelings, feeling the same kinds of desires

Desire: Want, Wish, Will
θέλησις—will, desire
θέλω—to will, desire, wish, intend, be resolved, be determined, purpose
θέλημα—a wish, will, desire
βούλομαι—to will deliberately, plan, purpose, desire, intend, wish
βούλημα—will, counsel, purpose, desire, intention
εὔχομαι—pray, wish, desire, long for
εὐδοκία—delight, good pleasure, satisfaction, what pleases
δοκέω—to be of opinion, think, suppose, to seem, be accounted
ἀξιόω—to count worthy, deem deserving, regard as good, desire
ἐπιζητέω—to inquire about, search for, seek after, seek diligently, crave, demand, desire
νοσέω—to be sick, to have morbid desire or fondness for, to dote

Destroy
ἀπόλλυμι—destroy, kill, lose, perish
συναπόλλυμαι—destroy together, perish with
ἀπώλεια—waste, ruin, loss
λύω—loose, destroy, divorce, annul
καταλύω—destroy, demolish, dismantle, tear down, abolish, annul, put an end to
λυμαίνομαι—harass, treat shamefully, ravage, ruin, injure severely
ὄλεθρος—ruin, death, destruction
ὀλοθρεύω—to ruin, destroy
ἐξολεθρεύω—utterly destroy, extirpate
ὀλοθρευτής—destroyer
πορθέω—destroy, overthrow, waste
φθορά—corruption, destruction, perishing, moral decay
φθείρω—to corrupt, destroy, deprave
διαφθείρω—to corrupt, utterly destroy, ruin
ἐρημόομαι—make desolate, lay waste, bring to desolation, strip of treasures, destroy
ἐρήμωσις—desolation
αἴρω—lift, raise up, elevate, remove, carry off, take away, kill, destroy
καθαιρέω—take down, pull down, demolish, tear down, destroy
καθαίρεσις—tearing down, destruction, demolition, incapacitating
κατεσθίω—consume, eat up, devour, exploit, prey on
ἀναλίσκω—spend, expend, consume, use up, destroy
καταναλίσκω—consume (of fire), destroy completely
καταπίνω—to devour, swallow up, destroy, passive: be overcome
ἀφανίζω—destroy, disfigure, deprive of luster, render unsightly, make ugly, passive: disappear, vanish
καταστροφή—overthrow, destruction
πτῶσις—a falling, crash, collapse, downfall, ruin, destruction
κατασκάπτω—demolish, ruin, destroy, tear down
σκάπτω—dig, till, dig a mark, delve
ἐδαφίζω—throw to the ground, raze, level to the ground, kill
ῥῆγμα—ruin, destruction, collapse, breakage, fracture
σύντριμμα—what is broken or shattered, destruction, calamity, ruin
πίπτω—to fall, suffer demise, perish, befall
καταργέω—render ineffective, make barren, do away with, nullify, passive with ἀπό: be released from
ἐκκόπτω—cut off, cut down, do away with, frustrate, hinder

ἐξαλείφω—wipe off, wipe away, obliterate, erase, blot out, eliminate

ἀποβολή—rejection, repudiation, loss, destruction, throwing away

ἀνασκευάζω—to dismantle, make undone

ἀνατρέπω—to overthrow, overturn, destroy, subvert, upset faith

Determine, Decide, Conclude, Appoint

κρίνω—to judge, decide, evaluate, make a preference, condemn

ἐπικρίνω—to give sentence, decide

πρόκριμα—an opinion formed before the facts are known, prejudgment, prejudice, preference, partiality

στηρίζω τὸ πρόσωπον—to set the face, decide firmly

ἐπιλύω—explain, expound, decide, determine, settle (a controversy)

συμβιβάζω—unite, put together in one's mind, conclude, infer, prove, decide on, instruct, advise

ὁρίζω—fix, appoint, determine, decide, designate, ordain, declare

προορίζω—to predetermine, decide beforehand, decree, foreordain, appoint beforehand, predestine

προαιρέομαι—to choose beforehand, prefer, purpose, decide in advance

τακτός—fixed, set, determined

Devil

ὁ θεὸς τοῦ αἰῶνος τούτου—the god of this age

δαιμόνιον—demon

διάβολος—devil

σατανᾶς—Satan

ὁ πονηρός—the evil one

δαιμονιώδης—demonic

δαιμονίζομαι—be demon possessed

ὁ πειράζων—the tempter

πνεῦμα πονηρόν—evil spirit

πνεῦμα ἀκάθαρτον—unclean spirit

κοσμοκράτωρ—lord of the world

Die, Death

θάνατος—death

θνῄσκω—die

θανάσιμον—deadly

θανατηφόρος—deadly, bringing death

ἀποθνῄσκω—die, be slain, be rendered ineffective

συναποθνῄσκω—die with

ἐπιθανάτιος—sentenced to die, doomed to die, appointed to die

νέκρωσις—death, deadness

νεκρός—lifeless, dead, useless, ineffective

τελευτάω—to finish, come to an end, close, die

τελευτή—the end of life, death

ἄψυχος—without a soul, lifeless

ἐκψύχω—expire, breathe out one's last breath, give up the ghost, die

ἐκπνέω—expire, breathe out one's last breath, give up the ghost, die

ἀνάλυσις—an unloosing, a dissolving, departure, death

ἀναλύω—come again, return home, depart, die

ἔξοδος—exit, departure, decease

καθεύδω—sleep, be dead

κοιμάομαι—put to sleep, make calm, quiet, still, be dead

ἐκλείπω—to fail, die out, cease

ἀπογίνομαι—to die, cease

πίπτω—to fall, suffer demise, perish, befall

ᾅδης—Hades, the Greek god of the lower regions, the netherworld, the grave, hell, the realm of the dead, death ἀφίημι τὸ πνεῦμα—release the spirit, let go the spirit, die

παραδίδωμι τὸ πνεῦμα—deliver the spirit, die

ἀπόθεσις τοῦ σκηνώματος—putting off of the earthly dwelling place, die

ἐκδημέω ἐκ τοῦ σώματος—be absent from the body, die

ἐκχύννεται τὸ αἷμα—spill or shed or pour out the blood, kill, cause death

ἀπόλλυμι τὴν ψυχήν—destroy the soul, kill, cause death

πνίγω—choke, strangle, of thorns crowding and hindering growth, take by the throat

ἀποπνίγω—choke, suffocate with water, drown

συμπνίγω—choke utterly, press around or throng around so as to suffocate

ἡμιθανής—half dead

θνητός—liable to death, mortal

φθαρτός—corruptible, perishing, mortal

ἀθανασία—deathlessness, immortality, eternity

ἄφθαρτος—uncorrupted, not liable to corruption or decay, imperishable, immortal

Different Kind

ἄλλος—another, one besides, any other, a different one, additional

ἄλλως—in another way or manner, otherwise, in some other way, differently

ἕτερος—the other, different from, other than

ἑτέρως—differently, otherwise

παρεκτός—besides, except for

διαίρεσις—a dividing, division, allotment, apportionment, variety, difference

διάφορος—different, unlike, differing or disagreeing with one another, at variance with, distinguished, remarkable, varied, the balance of an account, expenditure

διαφέρω—carry through, drive about, spread a message, intransitively: to differ, be worth more

διαστολή—difference, distinction

παραλλαγή—variation, change

ποικίλος—of various kinds, many colored, spotted, mottled, dappled, changeful, various, diversified, manifold, intricate, complex, subtle, wily, abstruse, difficult, changeable, unstable

πολυποίκιλος—manifold, much-variegated

Dig

ὀρύσσω—dig

σκάπτω—dig, till, dig a mark, delve

θάπτω—aorist ἐτάφη, to bury

ἐξορύσσω—dig out, pluck out e.g., the eyes

Direction, Spacial Orientation

ἀνατολή—rising, the east

δύσις—west, direction of the sunset

δυσμή—west, going down of the sun, usually plural

βορρᾶς—north

νότος—south, the direction of the south wind

μεσημβρία—noon, midday, south

χῶρος—northwest wind

λίψ—southwest wind, southwest

ἀριστερός—left, left hand

εὐώνυμος—of good omen, euphemism for "left" used by Greeks in place of ἀριστερός to avoid bad luck

δεξιός—right, right hand

ἀντοφθαλμέω—look into the face, face into, of a ship, head into

ἐναντίος—opposite, against, facing, opposing, meeting, contrary to

Dirty, Unclean, Impure, Rubbish

ῥύπος—dirt, filth

ῥυπαρός—dirty, filthy, foul, morally impure, degenerate

ῥυπαίνω—make dirty, soil, defile, pollute, passive: be impure

ῥυπαρία—filth, dirt, moral impurity, filthiness

ῥυπαίνομαι—be morally impure, dirty

ἀκαθαρσία—uncleanness, immorality

καθαρίζω—cleanse, purge, heal

περικάθαρμα—dirt, garbage, refuse

καθάρματα—dirt, garbage

μολύνω—make dirty, soil, smear, stain, defile, make impure

μολυσμός—defilement, spiritual pollution, filthiness, uncleanness

μῶμος—blame, disgrace, reproach, blemish, defect, flaw

μίασμα—defilement, pollution, impurity, corrupting influence

μιασμός—defilement, pollution, corruption, ungodliness

μιαίνω—defile, stain, make unclean, make unacceptable, deprave, corrupt

σπιλάς—a rock in the sea, a hidden danger, of those who plot, spot, stain

σπίλος—spot, stain, blemish, fault, shamefulness, moral wrong

σπιλόω—to stain, defile, spot, cause disgrace, make shameful

σκύβαλον—anything treated as worthless and thrown out, dung, rubbish, garbage

περίψημα—offscouring, scum, what is wiped off, dirt

Disadvantage

ἀλυσιτελής—unprofitable, detrimental

ἀνωφελής—unprofitable, useless, not advantageous

ὑστερέω—to be in need, be lacking, be wanting, fall short, arrive late

Discipline, Self-Control, see "Virtues: Self-Control, Discipline" and "Avoid, Abstain . . ."

Discouragement

ἐγκακέω—to grow weary, faint

ἐκλύομαι—to grow weary, be exhausted, faint, lose heart

κοπιάω—to grow weary, tired, to labor with exhaustion, work hard

κάμνω—grow weary, be sick, faint

ὀλιγόψυχος—fainthearted, discouraged, feebleminded

ἀθυμέω—be disheartened, dispirited, broken in spirit, dismayed

ἀποψύχω—to faint, be dismayed, lose consciousness

ῥίπτω—to throw out, let down, set down

ταπεινός—lowly, humble, of low degree, brought low with grief, depressed, downhearted, cast down

κατήφεια—shame, dejection, gloom, heaviness, depression

Discourse Types

διήγησις—narrative, account, story

ἱστορέω—to learn by inquiry, visit in order to learn from and gain information, passive participle: things learned by inquiry, historical account

μῦθος—myth, story, fable, legend

παροιμία—proverb, dark saying, metaphor illustrating truth, allegory παραβολή—a parable, a story portraying a truth, an example by which a teaching is illustrated, aphorism, proverb

ἀλληγορέω—speak allegorically or in a figure

πνευματικῶς—spiritually, figuratively, understood through the Holy Spirit

γένεσις—source, origin, progeny, ancestry, lineage, birth, nativity, book of one's lineage, history

ἀσπασμός—greeting, salutation

χαίρε—hail, rejoice, be glad, godspeed, written at the beginning or end of letters

κεφάλαιον—summary, main point in a letter or discourse, sum of money, pecuniary total, principal

ἀποτάσσομαι—to leave, say goodbye, bid farewell, part with, forsake

ἔρρωσθε—used in the closing of a letter to say, "have health" or "fare well," imperative of ῥώννυμαι

περιοχή—passage (in a book), the contents of any writing

ποίησις—a making, fabrication, creation, production, doing, a poetic composition, poem

Disobey, see "Vices: Disobedience"

Disperse, Scatter

σκορπίζω—scatter, dispense blessings, give generously

διαλύω—dissolve, scatter

διασκορπίζω—scatter abroad, disperse, winnow, throw grain into the air that it may be separated from the chaff, squander

διασπείρω—scatter abroad, disperse

διασπορά—diaspora, scattering, dispersion

ἐκχέω—pour out, give in abundance, distribute largely, flow out, stream forth, spill, squander, waste

διαμερίζω—to divide, distribute, give out parts, be divided into opposing parts, be at variance, be in discord

Dispute, Debate

συμβάλλω—meet, discuss, consult, debate, ponder, middle: help, assist

ζήτημα—question, debate, dispute

ζήτησις—inquiry, subject of questioning or debate, matter of controversy, dispute

συζητέω—to seek or examine together, to discuss, dispute, question, inquire, reason together, talk with

συζήτησις—mutual questioning, disputation, discussion, reasoning

συζητητής—disputer, debater, a learned disputant, sophist

ἐκζήτησις—speculation, idle dispute

διακατελέγχομαι—debate vigorously, strenuously refute, convince

διακρίνω—to judge between, prefer, discriminate, decide, evaluate, doubt, hesitate, take issue

διάκρισις—discernment, ability to decide

ἀντιλογία—contradiction, opposition, rebellion, strife, dispute

Division

διχοστασία—dissension, discord

σχίσμα—cleft, rent in a garment, division of opinion, schism

διαμερίζω—to divide, distribute, give out parts, be divided into opposing parts, be at variance, be in discord

διαμερισμός—division, dissension

ἀποδιορίζω—cause divisions, set up distinctions

αἱρετικός—heretical, divisive, factious

διαίρεσις—a dividing, division, allotment, apportionment, variety, difference
μεσότοιχον—dividing wall
φραγμός—fence, hedge, barrier

Divorce
ἀπολύω—set free, let go, send away, release, allow, acquit, remit, divorce
ἀφίημι—let go, send away, permit, allow, remit, divorce, leave, desert, abandon, forgive, not hinder
λύσις—a loosing, setting free, releasing, ransoming, deliverance, parting, dissolution, divorce
χωρίζω—separate, divide, part, divorce, depart
ἀποστάσιον—certificate of divorce
βιβλίον—a small scroll, record, bill of divorcement

Doubt, Unbelief, Distrust, to Turn Back or Reject because of Unbelief, to be Led Away from Faith, see also "Disobey"
ἀπιστέω—to be unfaithful, distrust
ἀπιστία—unfaithfulness, unbelief
ἄπιστος—unbelieving, unbelievable
ἀπείθεια—disobedience
ἀπειθέω—to disobey, be unbelieving
ὀλιγόπιστος—of little faith
ἐκκλίνω—to turn aside, deviate from the right course, shun, avoid, cease
ἀποστρέφω—to turn away, return
ἐπιστρέφω—to return, turn around, turn back to God, be converted, turn back (from following)
ὑποστρέφω—to turn back, return
διαστρέφω—to distort, turn away from, turn aside from the right path, pervert, corrupt, mislead
ἐκτρέπομαι—to be turned aside, be dislocated, to wander, swerve, avoid
ἀνατρέπω—to overthrow, overturn, destroy, subvert, upset faith
ἀθετέω—reject, set aside, annul
ἀνακάμπτω—turn back, return, change to former belief
ἀπωθέομαι—to thrust away, push away, repel, repudiate, reject, refuse
σαίνομαι—fawn over, flatter, passive: deluded, beguiled, moved, upset
ἀστοχέω—to deviate from, go astray, err, swerve, abandon truth
παραρρέω—to drift away, let slip, lose faith, fall away from profession
πλανάω—to lead astray, wander, cause to depart from truth, passive: be lost, be deceived, be misled
ἀποπλανάω—to lead astray, lead into error, seduce
ἐξέλκω—to lure away, be drawn away
παραφέρω—to mislead, carry away, remove, take away
συναπάγομαι—be led away with, go with, associate with, accommodate to, condescend to
σκανδαλίζω—put a stumbling block in the way, offend, cause to sin
διστάζω—to doubt, waiver
δίψυχος—double-minded, wavering, uncertain, doubting
ἀδήλως—uncertainly, aimlessly, not manifestly, dubiously
ἀστήρικτος—unstable
ἀφίστημι—leave, desert, fall away from faith, commit apostasy, mislead, incite a revolt, abstain, shun
διακρίνω—to judge between, prefer, discriminate, decide, evaluate, doubt, hesitate, take issue
διαλογισμός—reasoning, argument, doubt, dispute

Dream, Vision
ἐνύπνιον—dream

ὄναρ—dream

ἐνυπνιάζομαι—to dream, to have a divinely inspired dream

ὀπτασία—a vision, apparition seen while asleep or awake

ὅραμα—a divinely granted vision

ὅρασις—the act of seeing, the eyes, appearance, visible form, a vision, a divinely granted vision

ἔκστασις—amazement, terror, the mind being out of its normal state, an ecstatic vision

Drive Away, Drive Along

ἐλαύνω—drive, of the wind driving clouds, of sailors propelling a vessel by oars, of demons driving men

ἀπελαύνω—drive away, expel

διαφέρω—carry through, drive about, spread a message, intransitively: to differ, be worth more

ἀνεμίζομαι—agitate, drive by the wind

Drunkenness, see "Vices: Drunkenness"

Dry

ξηρός—dry, withered

ξηραίνω—to make dry, wither, waste away, become stiff, be ripe

μαραίνω—fade, wither, dry up

ἐκμάσσω—to wipe off, wipe away, wipe away one's tears

ἄνυδρος—waterless, without rain, dry

E

Eager, Earnest, Devotion

προθυμία—zeal, spirit, eagerness, inclination, readiness of mind
πρόθυμος—ready, willing, eager
προθύμως—willingly, eagerly
ἐκτένεια—intentness, earnestness
ἐκτενής—intent, earnest, assiduous, fervent, eager, without ceasing, continuous, constant, unfailing
ἐκτενῶς—earnestly, fervently, intensely, eagerly, continuously
σπεύδω—to do quickly, be eager
σπουδάζω—to hasten, do quickly, give diligence, exert one's self, endeavor, be eager, do one's best
σπουδή—haste, zeal, diligence, eagerness
σπουδαῖος—active, diligent, zealous, earnest, eager
σπουδαίως—hastily, diligently, earnestly, instantly, eagerly
εὔνοια—good will, kindness, benevolence, eagerness
ζέω τῷ πνεύματι—be fervent, show enthusiasm
ζεστός—hot, fervent, zealous
ζηλεύω—set one's heart on, be zealous, be eager
ζηλόω—to burn with zeal or envy, be jealous over, to desire earnestly
ζηλωτής—one burning with zeal, a zealot, enthusiast
φιλοτιμέομαι—to desire honor, be ambitious, aspire to
ἐπακολουθέω—to follow closely upon, imitate one's example, devote oneself to, accompany

Earth, World

γῆ—earth, ground, dirt, land, world, country, region
ἐπίγειος—human, earthly, terrestrial, existing upon the earth
κόσμος—world, earth, the ordering of creation, ornament, adornment as on a woman, world system
κοσμικός—earthly, worldly
οἰκουμένη—the inhabited world
χοϊκός—made of earth, earthy, dusty or dirty
ὑπὸ τὸν οὐρανόν—under heaven

Earth, Soil, Stone

γῆ—earth, ground, dirt, land, world, country, region
ἔδαφος—ground, basis, base, bottom
χαμαί—on the ground, on the earth, prostrate
κονιορτός—dust
χοῦς—dust
βόρβορος—mud
πηλός—clay

κεραμικός—made of clay, ceramic
ὀστράκινος—earthenware
πέτρα—bedrock
πετρῶδες—rocky ground
λίθος—stone
λίθινος—made of stone
ψῆφος—pebble
ἄμμος—sand, beach

Eat, Drink, Consume, see also "Food"

ἐσθίω—eat, devour, consume
συνεσθίω—eat together, eat with
κατεσθίω—consume, eat up, devour, exploit, prey on
βιβρώσκω—eat
βρῶσις—eating, food, meat, eating away, corrosion or rusting
βρώσιμος—edible
βόσκω—to feed, tend, or herd animals, feed, nourish, support, maintain, graze, nurture, root is βοτ-
γεύομαι—taste, try the flavor of, partake of, enjoy, experience, eat
ψωμίζω—feed with small portions, nourish, give to eat
τρώγω—gnaw, crunch, chew raw vegetables (of animals feeding), eat
τρέφω—nourish, support, feed, fatten, bring up, nurture, feed from the breast, take care of, rear
ἐκτρέφω—nourish up to maturity, nurture, bring up, rear, provide food
θηλάζω—nurse a baby, feed from the breast, give suck, suckle, to nipple
μασάομαι—bite, chew, consume, eat, devour, gnaw
μετέχω—to partake, share in, eat, drink
μεθύω—to be drunk, drink a lot

χορτάζω—feed with herbs, grass, hay, eat one's fill, satisfy, be content
συνευωχέομαι—feast together sumptuously
ἐμπίμπλημι—fill up, glut one's desire for, satisfy with food, satiate, enjoy
γαστήρ—belly, womb, stomach, glutton
φάγος—glutton, voracious man
ἀριστάω—to dine, eat a meal
ἄριστον—dinner, meal
ἄρτον—κλάω break bread, have a meal
ἀνάκειμαι—to recline at a table, dine
κατάκειμαι—lie down, lie prostrate, recline to eat
δειπνέω—to sup, eat a meal
δεῖπνον—supper, formal evening meal, feast, main meal
δοχή—feast, banquet
πεινάω—be hungry, desire strongly
πρόσπεινος—very hungry
λιμός—famine, scarcity of harvest, dearth, hunger
νηστεία—fasting, hunger
νῆστις—fasting, not eating, hunger
ἀσιτία—abstinence from food, without food
ἄσιτος—fasting, without having eaten
πόσις—a drink, drinking
ποτίζω—give to drink, furnish drink, to water, irrigate, imbue
ὑδροποτέω—to drink water
πίνω—to drink, receive refreshment, soak up
καταπίνω—to devour, swallow up, destroy, passive: be overcome
συμπίνω—drink together, drink with
διψάω—suffer thirst, be thirsty, desire strongly
δίψος—thirst

Elementary Principle

στοῖχεῖα—elementary part, the elements, basic principles, rudiments, the elements of knowledge

ἀρχή—ruler, first in power, origin, beginning, first cause, elementary aspect, the end or corner of a thing

Empty

κενός—empty, vain, devoid of truth, containing nothing, foolish, without purpose, without result, fruitless

κενόω—to empty out, drain, strip of all things, leave a place deserted, make of no account or of no effect, cause to lose power

ἐκχέω—pour out, shed forth, bestow or distribute largely, flow out, stream forth, spill, squander, waste

σχολάζω—to be at leisure, have rest from, be still, be idle, be empty, be vacant or unoccupied, be devoted to

Encouragement, Consolation

εὐθυμέω—to put in good spirits, gladden, make cheerful, be joyful, be encouraged

εὔθυμος—well disposed, kind, of good cheer, of good courage, encouraged

εὐψυχέω—to be of good courage, be of a cheerful spirit, be of good comfort, be encouraged

ἀνάψυξις—cooling, refreshing, revival, relief, encouragement

ἀναψύχω—to cool off, recover from the heat, get fresh air, revive, refresh, be encouraged, be cheered up

παρακαλέω—to urge, summon for help, encourage, comfort

παράκλησις—summoning for help, supplication, encouragement, entreaty, comfort, consolation

συμπαρακαλέομαι—to be comforted together, be encouraged together

παραμυθέομαι—to encourage, console, comfort

παραμυθία—encouragement, comfort

παραμύθιον—encouragement, comfort

μυθέομαι—to say, speak

παρηγορία—comfort, solace, relief, alleviation, consolation, assistance

End

τέλος—end, limit, boundary, finish, completion, conclusion, tax, last

τελέω—finish, end, accomplish, fulfill, make perfect, pay taxes

τελειόω—make perfect, complete, accomplish, end, reach maturity, execute, finish, make happen

συντέλεια—completion, close, end

συντελέω—to bring to an end, complete, finish, close, be over

ἔκβασις—a way out, exit, way of escape, end, result

ἐκπλήρωσις—completion

ἐκπληρόω—to bring to completion, fulfill, fill up

πλήρωμα—a full measure, fullness, the sum total, complete amount

πίμπλημι—fill, be fulfilled, accomplish, come to an end

πληρόω—make full, fulfill, complete, fulfill the requirements of, observe, fulfill a prophecy

συμπληρόω—fill up, man fully a ship, be swamped with water, of time, fulfill, approach, come to an end

ἐξαρτίζω—to thouroughly prepare, equip completely, make adequate, be complete (of time)

συντέμνω—to cut short, shorten, limit, cut off, bring to a close, end

καταργέω—render ineffective, make barren, do away with, nullify, passive with ἀπό: be released from

ἐκλείπω—to fail, die out, cease

ἄκρον—extremity, tip, farthest boundary, end

ἀποβαίνω—unboard, disembark, step off, dismount, go away, depart, resultative: to issue, result in, end in

Enjoy, Take Pleasure In, Be Fond Of Doing

φιλέω—to love, like, kiss

ἀγαπάω—to love, to be well-pleased with, to be fond of

εὐδοκέω—to be pleased, be favorable towards, prefer, approve, choose

ἀπόλαυσις—enjoyment

ἐμπίμπλημι—fill up, glut one's desire for, satisfy with food, satiate, enjoy

ἡδονή—pleasure, lust, passion

φιλήδονος—loving pleasure

φιλάγαθος—loving what is good

ἀφιλάγαθος—opposed to what is good, despising what is good

ὀνίνημι—to enjoy favor, benefit, derive enjoyment, Philemon 20

Enough, Sufficient

ἱκανός—sufficient, adequate, able, enough, considerable, satisfactory

ἀρκετός—sufficient

ἀρκέω—to have sufficient strength, suffice, be enough, be satisfied

ἀπέχω—have back, hold back, receive in full, be distanced, be sufficient (Mark 14:41), middle: hold one's self away, avoid, abstain

καθόλου—completely, entirely

ὅλος—whole, entire, complete

πᾶς—all, any, whole, total, every kind of

πληρόω—make full, fulfill, complete, fulfill the requirements of, observe, fulfill a prophecy

μεστός—full, filled, very full

πίμπλημι—fill, be fulfilled, accomplish, come to an end

εἰς τὸ παντελές—forever, for all time, completely

εἰς τέλος—completely

ὁλοτελής—completely

τελείως—fulfillment

Enter

εἴσοδος—entrance, gateway, act of entering, coming in

εἴσειμι—go into

εἰσέρχομαι—come or go into, enter

εἰσπορεύομαι—go into

ἐνδύνω—put in, envelope in, hide in, put on, sneak or creep into

ἐμβαίνω—go into, step into, embark, board (a ship)

ἐμβιβάζω—cause to embark

ἐπιβαίνω—get upon, mount, embark in, go aboard, enter

ἐπιβιβάζω—cause to mount, put in or on, lead in, cause to enter

Envy, Resentment, Bitterness, see "Vices: Envy, Resentment, Bitterness

Equipment, Supplies

σκεῦος—vessel, jar, vase, utensils, furniture, military gear, equipment, luggage, one's wife (1 Thes. 4:4)

σκευή—equipment, apparatus, furnishings, gear, tackle, rigging

ὅπλον—weapon, armament, tool, instrument

Establish

ἔμφυτος—implanted, engrafted, established in

τάσσω—to appoint, assign, place, determine

ἵστημι—stand, place, put, establish, set, continue to be, remain firmly

κτίζω—to create, bring into being, build

θεμελιόω—to lay a foundation, to found, make stable, establish

βεβαιόω—to make firm, establish, confirm, make certain, verify, cause to believe, strengthen someone

στηρίζω—to prop, set, fixate, fasten, strengthen, confirm, establish, settle, be firmly set, make steady

Eternal, see "Time: Long Duration of Time"

Ever

δήποτε—ever

ποτέ—formerly, once, at some time, ever

πώποτε—ever

Exchange

ἀλλάσσω—change, alter, transform, give in exchange, barter, repay

μεταλλάσσω—change, alter, exchange

ἀντάλλαγμα—something given in exchange

ἀντί—instead of, on behalf of, for, for this reason, in place of, in exchange for

Exorcism

ἐκβάλλω—to cast out, exorcise, throw out, banish, divorce a wife, depose a king

ἐξορκιστής—exorcist

ἐξορκίζω—to put under oath, adjure

ὁρκίζω—to put under oath, force to take an oath, adjure, charge

Experience, Undergo, Have Happen, Suffer, see also "Happen"

τυγχάνω—to meet with, have happen, come upon, experience

ἐπιτυγχάνω—to obtain, attain to, reach, gain one's end, succeed in doing, succeed, acquire

μεταλαμβάνω—to receive one's share, share in, receive, take on

φέρω—bring, carry, bear, bear up under

εἰσφέρω—bring into, lead into (Matthew 6:13)

ἐπιφέρω—cause to experience, impose on, bring on, inflict

ὑπέχω—experience, undergo, be subject to, suffer, be put under

περιέχω—to encircle, surround, encompass, come upon someone, as unexpected circumstances, seize, contain, as contained in the law

συνέχω—surround, hem in, enclose, guard, seize, afflict, be absorbed in

παρέχω—offer, present, supply, furnish, have ready, grant, bring about for someone, provide for, cause to happen

ἀναδέχομαι—to receive, accept, welcome, take upon oneself

εἰσέρχομαι—come into, enter into, commence, begin to enjoy, begin to experience, encounter

εὑρίσκω—find, come upon, discover, learn, attain, find by way of inquiry

ἔχω μέρος ἐν—have part in, experience together

γεύομαι—taste, try the flavor of, eat, partake of, enjoy, experience

θεωρέω—to look at, watch, behold, see, consider, perceive, ascertain

ὁράω—to see, behold, perceive, know, experience, take heed, beware

πίπτω—to fall, suffer demise, perish, befall

ἐμπίπτω—fall into, as into a pit, experience suddenly, be beset by, encounter unexpectedly

περιπίπτω—fall into the hands of, encounter, run into, be seized by πάσχω—to suffer, experience, feel, undergo, have a sensory experience, have passion

τίνω—pay a penalty, incur, suffer, experience retribution, undergo punishment or something bad

βαστάζω—bear a burden, endure

ἐμπλέκω—involve in, entangle

ἐπιτίθημι—lay upon, place upon, usually the hands, inflict, attack

βυθίζω—sink, plunge into the deep, thrust down, sink into ruin

Explain, Interpret

ἑρμηνεύω—to explain, expound, interpret, translate

ἑρμηνεία—interpretation

διερμηνευτής—an interpreter

διερμηνεύω—to unfold meaning, explain, expound, translate, interpret

μεθερμηνεύω—translate, interpret

δυσερμήνευτος—hard to interpret, difficult to explain

δείκνυμι—to show, expose, explain, give proof of, make known

ὑποδείκνυμι—to show by placing under the eyes, show by words or arguments, teach, explain, warn

δηλόω—to make manifest, indicate, signify, show, make clear

σημαίνω—to give a sign, signify, indicate, make known, make clear

ἀνατίθεμαι—to set forth in words, communicate, declare, explain

ἐκτίθεμαι—to expose, exhibit, set forth, declare, expound, explain, put outside, cast out

παρατίθημι—put before, offer, lay before, show to be true

διανοίγω—to open by dividing apart, to open thoroughly

διασαφέω—explain, make clear or plain, unfold, narrate, tell in detail

σαφής—clear, distinct

ἐπίλυσις—loosening, unloosing, explanation, interpretation

ἐπιλύω—explain, expound, decide, determine, settle (a controversy)

συγκρίνω—to join together, combine, compound, interpret, explain, compare, measure, estimate

φράζω—to explain, interpret, tell, expound, propound in distinct terms

στρεβλόω—to twist, turn away, torture, pervert, misinterpret

Exploit, see "Vices: Exploit"

Extremely, To A Great Extent

λίαν—very, exceedingly

ὑπερλίαν—extremely, beyond all doubt

μέγας—big, great, vast, strong

μεγάλως—greatly

μέγεθος—greatness, magnitude, size, height, stature, power

πολύς—many, often, much, mighty, great, to a great extent, with fullness

οὕτως—thusly, in this way, in this manner, so, as follows

ὡς—so, thus, like, according as, how, with numerals: about, approximately

αὐξάνω—grow, increase, augment

ὑπεραυξάνω—increase greatly

μάλιστα—especially, mostly, for the most part, most of all, about (with numbers)

ἡλίκος—how great, how extensive

ἡλικία—stature, maturity, of age

πόσος—how many, how much, how far, how long, how great

ἱκανός—sufficient, adequate, able, enough, considerable, satisfactory

πλουσίως—in abundance, extremely
ἰσχυρός—strong, mighty, powerful, vigorous, severe
εὐτόνως—vigorously
σφόδρα—exceedingly, very, most certainly
σφοδρῶς—exceedingly
ἐκ περισσοῦ—extremely, out of abundance, out of excess
καλῶς—well, in the right way, commendably, appropriately, splendidly, fitly, accurately
κατὰ βάθους—extremely

βάθος—depth, the deep, extreme, extremely
βάρος—heaviness, weight, burden, trouble, hardship, heavy, tremendous
δεινῶς—terribly, fearfully, marvelously, exceedingly
ἀνάχυσις—a pouring out, flood, effusion, excess
ἀναχέω—to pour forth
εἰς τὰ ἄμετρα—excessive, immense, without measure, boundless
ζῆλος—fervor of spirit, zeal, earnest concern, jealousy, indignation

F

Fail, see "Discouragement"

ἀδόκιμος—failing the test, worthless, unqualified, disqualified, rejected, proven false, unfit, bad

ἁμαρτία—failure, fault, sin, guilt

ἐκλείπω—to fail, die out, cease

ἐκπίπτω—to fall out of, fall off, run aground, lose, fail

Faith, Hope, Trust, Belief, Confidence, see "Virtues: Faith, Hope"

Fall

καταπίπτω—fall down

πίπτω—to fall, suffer demise, perish, befall

ἀπορίπτω—fall from, cast one's self down

ἐκπίπτω—to fall out of, fall off, run aground, lose, fail

ἐμπίπτω—fall into

ἡττάομαι—be defeated

ἥττημα—defeat, failure, fall

False, see also "Vices: Deception, Speaking Falsely"

δολόω—to falsify, beguile, ensnare, take by craft, disguise

δόλος—treachery, deceit, fraud, bait

πλαστός—formed, molded, forged, fabricated, counterfeit, based on supposition

Family, see "Kin"

Farming Terms, Agriculture, Horticulture, see also "Plant," "Animal Husbandry"

γεωργέω—to cultivate land, till, plow

γεωργός—farmer, gardener, vinedresser

ἀμπελουργός—vinedresser

ἀμπελών—vineyard

κηπουρός—keeper of a garden, gardener

κῆπος—garden, plantation, orchard

σκάπτω—dig, till, dig a mark, delve

ὀρύσσω—to dig, excavate

φραγμός—fence, hedge, barrier

ἀροτριάω—to plow, sow, beget

φυτεύω—to plant, spring forth, produce, beget, bring about, cause

σπείρω—to sow, beget, give birth, engender, scatter like seed, strew, throw about, spread abroad, broadcast, disperse

ἐπισπείρω—to sow, sow on top of

σπόριμος—grain field, what is sown

ποτίζω—give to drink, furnish drink, to water, irrigate, imbue

ἔμφυτος—implanted, engrafted, established in

ἐγκεντρίζω—to graft, join in something foreign
κεντέω—to prick, goad, spur on, sting, stab
ἐκριζόω—to uproot, root out
καθαίρω—purify, clean, purge, prune
ἀμάω—to mow, reap, gather together, collect
θερίζω—to reap, mow, do summer work
θερισμός—reaping time, harvest, the harvest crop
θεριστής—reaper, harvester
καρπός—fruit, produce, harvest
τρυγάω—to pick, gather in
ἀλοάω—to thresh out, cudgel, beat
ἀλέω—to grind, bruise, pound
λικμάω—winnow, cleanse away chaff from grain, scatter, crush, grind to powder

Farming Tools
ἄροτρον—plow
δρέπανον—sickle, scythe, curved sword
πτύον—winnowing shovel
χαλινός—bridle
ζυγός—yoke
κέντρον—any sharp point, a horse goad, spur, prick, stinger, incentive, the center of a circle
ἀξίνη—axe
ῥάβδος—stick, rod

Fasten, Stick To, Fasteners—
ἀσφαλίζω—make firm, make secure, fasten, make safe
δέω—bind, tie, fasten with chains
καταδέω—to bind on or to, to put in bonds, imprison, bind for execution
περιδέω—bind around, tie over, wrap up
δεσμεύω—put in chains, bind
δέσμη—bundle
σύνδεσμος—that which binds together, bond, of ligaments, that which is bound, a bundle
δεσμός—chain, binding, imprisonment
σειρά—chain, rope
ἅλυσις—chain
πέδη—fetter, shackle, ankle chain
σχοινίον—rope
ζευκτηρία—bands
ἱμάς—strap
ξύλον—tree, wood, firewood, club, cross, stocks
προσηλόω—nail onto
ἧλος—nail
κολλάομαι—to glue, cement, fasten together, join firmly together, cling to
κόλλα—glue
κρεμάννυμι—hang up, suspend, depend upon
κρεμάζω—hang up, suspend, depend upon
ἅπτω—touch, hold, kindle, set on fire
καθάπτω—take hold of, seize, fasten on
συνάπτω—join together, border upon, reach, extend to, touch, press closely on, join in battle, come together
ἐρείδω—fasten securely, prop
πήγνυμι—to pitch a tent, implant, fasten together, construct, build, erect, set up
στηρίζω—to prop, set, fixate, fasten, strengthen, confirm, establish, settle, be firmly set, make steady

Fasting
νηστεία—fasting, voluntary abstinence from food, hunger, the day of atonement was a public fast
νηστεύω—to fast
νῆστις—fasting, not eating, hunger
ἀσιτία—abstinence from food, without food

ἐγκρατής—disciplined, controlling one's desires, self-controlled

νηφάλιος—restrained, without wine, sober, temperate, abstinent

σωφροσύνη—sobriety, self-control, moderation, sound judgment, soundness of mind

Favorable Circumstances

ἀφορμή—occasion, opportunity, favorable circumstances for an undertaking

εὐοδόομαι—to have a prosperous and expeditious journey, gain in business, be successful, get along well, to make a good way

εἰρήνη—peace, state of tranquility, felicity, harmony, freedom from worry

ἡσυχία—quietness, silence, quiet circumstances, quiet living

εὐπρόσδεκτος—well-received, acceptable, truly favorable, pleasing

Favoritism, Prejudice, see "Vices: Favoritism, Prejudice"

Fear, Terror, Alarm

φόβος—fear, dread, terror, reverence

φοβέομαι—to be afraid, have reverence

φοβερός—inspiring fear, terrible, fearful

ἔκφοβος—stricken with fear or terror, frightened, terrified

ἐκφοβέω—to frighten away, terrify

φόβητρον—that which strikes terror, fearful thing

τρέμω—tremble, quake, quiver, fear, respect

φρίσσω—to bristle, shudder, be struck with extreme fear, be horrified

ἔντρομος—trembling, terrified, fearful

θροέομαι—to cry aloud, make a noise by outcry, be alarmed

πτύρομαι—to frighten, terrify, be afraid

πτόησις—fear, amazement, something alarming

δειλία—timidity, fearfulness, cowardice

δειλιάω—to be timid, fearful, cowardly

δειλός—timid, fearful, cowardly

ἀσθένεια—want of strength, weakness, timidity, infirmity, disease, illness, incapacity

ἀφόβως—without fear, without reverence to God, disgracefully

Festival, Observance, Celebration

εὐφραίνω—to gladden, make joyful, be merry, rejoice, celebrate

ἑορτάζω—to celebrate, keep a holiday or festival, keep a feast

ἑορτή—festival, holiday, feast, amusement in general

δοχή—feast, banquet

νεομηνία—new moon, first of the month, a special day of worship along with sabbaths (Ezekiel 46), the contracted form, νουμηνία, is in the law and historical books of the Septuagint

πάσχα—passover festival or meal, celebrated around March or April in memorial of the lamb's blood on the doorposts (Exodus 12)

πεντηκοστή—pentecost, fiftieth day after passover

σκηνοπηγία—festival of tents, feast of tabernacles, celebrated in October

ἐγκαίνια—hanukkah, feast of lights, festival of dedication of the temple

νηστεία—fasting, voluntary abstinence from food, hunger, the day of atonement was a public fast

ἡμέρα ἐξιλασμοῦ—day of atonement Leviticus 23:27

γενέσια—birthday celebration

πανήγυρις—celebration, joyful assembly, festival, holiday

κῶμος—a village festival involving drinking

Few, see "Small, Small in Number, Few, Little"

Field
ἀγρός—field, countryside, farm settlement
γεώργιον—field, cultivated land
χωρίον—field, region
χώρα—land, region, countryside
κῆπος—garden, plantation, orchard
νομή—pasturage, fodder, food, pasture

Find
ἀνευρίσκω—find, discover
εὑρίσκω—find, come upon, discover, attain, learn, find by way of inquiry
ἀκριβόω—to find out accurately, to investigate diligently, learn exactly
διερωτάω—to find out by asking, inquire, learn about
ζητέω—to seek, inquire into

Firm, Immovable
ἀσάλευτος—immovable
ἀκλινής—unswerving, steadfast, firm, unmoved, without wavering
ἀμετακίνητος—not to be moved from its place, unmoved, unmovable, firmly persistent, firm
ἀσφαλίζω—make firm, make secure, fasten, make safe
βέβαιος—stable, firm, sure, steadfast, trustworthy, certain, verified
ἐρείδω—fasten securely, prop
ῥιζόομαι—to take root, be rooted, be firmly fixed, be planted, be strengthened
στηρίζω—to prop, set, fixate, fasten, strengthen, confirm, establish, settle, be firmly set, make steady

σκληρός—hard, harsh, rough, stiff, stern, strong, violent, offensive, intolerable, demanding
θεμελιόω—to lay a foundation, to found, make stable, establish
ἑδραῖος—firm, steadfast

Fish
ἐνάλιον—sea creature
ἰχθύς—fish
ἰχθύδιον—little fish
κῆτος—big fish
ὀψάριον—fish
προσφάγιον—anything eaten in addition to bread, spoken of fish

Fishing Terms, see "Sea Terms, Nautical Terms"

Flatter
κολακεία—flattery, exaggerated praise
θαυμάζω πρόσωπον—to admire before one's face, flatter
σαίνομαι—fawn over, flatter, passive: deluded, beguiled, moved, upset

Flood
πλήμμυρα—flood
κατακλύζω—flood
κατακλυσμός—flood
ποταμοφόρητος—carried off by flood or river, overwhelmed
ἀνάχυσις—a pouring out, flood, effusion, excess

Flow, see also "Liquids, Activities Involving"
ῥέω—flow
ῥύσις—a flowing issue, flow
βρύω—cause to pour out
ἐκχέω—pour out, shed forth, bestow or distribute largely, flow out, stream forth, spill, squander, waste

ὑπερεκχύννομαι—overflow
ἅλλομαι—spring, bubble up

Foam

ἀφρός—foam
ἀφρίζω—to foam up
ἐπαφρίζω—cause to foam up

Follow

ἀκολουθέω—follow, go/come behind, join one who precedes as an attendant, be consequent upon, accompany as a disciple, be a disciple, obey
συνακολουθέω—accompany, follow together with others
κατακολουθέω—follow after
παρακολουθέω—to follow along with, accompany, attend, follow with the mind, trace or investigate a thing
ἐξακολουθέω—obey, follow, imitate
πείθω—to persuade, win over, prevail on by entreaty, induce one by words to believe, passive: trust, believe, be persuaded, obey, have confidence, be certain, be a follower
δεῦτε ὀπίσω μου—come behind me, follow me
συνέπομαι—accompany, follow with
μαθητεύω—to make a disciple of, instruct, passive: be a pupil, follow
μαθητής—learner, pupil, follower, disciple
μαθήτρια—woman disciple
συμμαθητής—fellow disciple

Food, see also "Eat, Drink, Consume"

ἄρτος—loaf of bread, food
βρῶμα—food, meat, victuals
βρῶσις—eating, food, meat, eating away, corrosion or rusting
διατροφή—food, sustenance, nourishment
τροφή—food, sustenance, nourishment
τρόφος—nurse
χόρτασμα—food, fodder
σιτίον—grain, food
σιτομέτριον—measured portion of grain, food ration, allowance
ἐπισιτισμός—foraging, providing of food; supplies, provisions, food
ψωμίον—piece of bread, fragment, bit, morsel
ψίξ—crumb
πόμα—drink, beverage
πόσις—drinking, drink
ἄλευρον—wheat flour, meal
σεμίδαλις—fine flour
ζύμη—yeast, leaven
ζυμόω—to use yeast, to leaven
ἄζυμος—unleavened
κρέας—meat, flesh of an animal
εἰδωλόθυτον—sacrificial meat
ὀψάριον—fish
προσφάγιον—anything eaten in addition to bread, spoken of fish
ᾠόν—egg
γάλα—milk
μέλι—honey
κηρίον—honeycomb
κηρήθρα—honeycomb
μάννα—manna
ῥαφανίς—radish

Foolish

μωρός—foolish, impious, godless, not making sense
μωραίνω—to be foolish, act foolishly, to make tasteless, lose flavor, of salt that has become diluted
μωρία—foolishness
ἄσοφος—unwise, foolish

ἀφροσύνη—foolishness, folly, senselessness, thoughtlessness, recklessness, folly, foolishness

ἄφρων—without reason, senseless, foolish, stupid, without reflection or intelligence, foolish, unwise

ἀσύνετος—unintelligent, without understanding, stupid, foolish, without understanding

ἀνόητος—not understood, unintelligible, unwise, without understanding, foolish

ἄνοια—lack of understanding, folly, madness, extreme fury

νωθρός—slow, sluggish, indolent, dull, languid, slothful, lazy

μυωπάζω—to see dimly, see only what is near, fail to understand

παχύνομαι—to make stupid, render dull, callous, or unable to understand

κενός—empty, vain, devoid of truth, containing nothing, foolish, without purpose, without result, fruitless

τυφλός—blind

τυφλόω—to blind

σκοτίζομαι—to darken

σκοτόομαι—to darken

ῥακά—fool (Chaldean)

Foolish Talk, see "Vices: Accuse, Defame, Talk Foolishly"

For, On Behalf Of, For The Sake Of

ἀντί—with genitive: for, on behalf of

διά—with accusative: on account of, because of, for the sake of

εἰς—with accusative: for, for the purpose of, because of, in view of, for this reason

ἐπί—with dative: on account of, for the purpose of

περί—with genitive: for, concerning, regarding, because of, on account of, on behalf of

ὑπέρ—with genitive: for, on behalf of, for the sake of, on account of, because of, concerning

ἕνεκα—on account of, for the sake of, because of, by reason of

Foreigner, Stranger

ἀλλότριος—stranger, foreigner, enemy

ἀπαλλοτριόω—alienate, estrange

ἀλλόφυλος—other tribe, foreign

ἀλλογενής—foreign, of another race

ξένος—stranger, foreigner, visitor

ξενίζω—to show hospitality to strangers, intransitive: be surprised, think strange

παρεπίδημος—stranger, sojourner, temporary resident

πάροικος—stranger, alien, foreigner

Forget

ἐπιλανθάνομαι—to forget, neglect, not care for, be overlooked

λανθάνω—to be hidden, escape the knowledge of, be in secret, be done unaware, passive: be ignorant of, forget

λήθη—forgetfulness

ἐπιλησμονή—forgetfulness

ἐκλανθάνομαι—forget entirely

Forgiveness, Reconciliation, see also "Release, Set Free" and "Virtues: Mercy"

καταλλάσσω—to reconcile, change money, exchange

καταλλαγή—reconciliation, exchange, profits of an exchange

ἀποκαταλλάσσω—to reconcile, make peace

συναλλάσσω—to reconcile, bring together again, make peace, make an alliance with, have dealings with

διαλλάσσω—to reconcile, make exchange, exchange friendship, make peace, make friends

ἀπαλλάσσω—to set free, release, let loose, settle, be reconciled

ἀλλάσσω—change, alter, transform, give in exchange, barter, repay

ἀπολύω—set free, let go, send away, release, allow, acquit, remit, divorce

ἄφεσις—a letting go, dismissal, discharge, exemption from service, divorce, liberty, pardon

ἀφίημι—send away, divorce, let go, leave, desert, abandon, forgive, remit, permit, allow, not hinder

εἰρηνεύω—keep peace, live peaceably

εἰρηνοποιέω—to make peace

εἰρηνοποιός—peacemaker

μεσίτης—mediator, one who intervenes between two, arbitrator, reconciler

χαρίζομαι—to be agreeable, oblige, gratify, court favor, offer freely, give willingly, be pleasing, forgive, pardon, remit

ἐπικαλύπτω—to hide, cover over, shroud, cover sin, forgive

ἱλάσκομαι—to forgive, show mercy, pardon, be appeased, be propitiated, expiate a wrong, make acceptable to, make reconciliation

ἱλασμός—atonement, offering for sin, means of forgiveness, sacrifice

ἱλαστήριον—atoning, propitiatory, providing for reconciliation, a sin offering, place of forgiveness, in Hebrews 9:5 called mercy-seat referring to the lid on the ark of the covenant in the holy of holies which was sprinkled with the blood of the sin offering on the day of atonement

ἐλεάω—to show mercy, pity

ἐλεήμων—merciful, compassionate

ἔλεος—mercy, compassion

ἵλεως—merciful, gracious, favorable

σπένδω—to pour libation or drink offering, pour, make a truce

ἄσπονδος—irreconcilable, neutral, heartless, not admitting truce

Form, Nature, Substance, Character, Appearance, see also "Image"

μορφή—form, shape, figure, fashion, appearance, kind, sort, nature

μόρφωσις—embodiment, form, semblance

μορφόω—to give form or shape to

σύμμορφος—conformed to, similar in form

συμμορφίζομαι—to have the same likeness, be conformed to

συμμορφόομαι—to have the same likeness, be conformed to

μεταμορφόω—to be transfigured, change appearance, transform

σχῆμα—outward form, looks, fashion, appearance, show, pretense, air of a person, form, manner, way, posture

ὑπόστασις—substance, possessions, foundation or ground of something, nature, essence, garrison of an army, subject-matter of a speech, plan of a project, confidence, hope

τύπος—mark or imprint from a blow, scar, form, pattern, example, type, figure (of something future)

εἰκών—image, representation, likeness, form, appearance, similitude, portrait

χαρακτήρ—exact representation

φύσις—how one naturally is, the natural state, one's natural bent, constitution of a person or thing, form, character, birth, kind, sort φυσικός—natural, native, in the order of nature, physical

φυσικῶς—by nature

σάρξ—flesh, body, natural generation, the sensual nature, human nature

πλάσσω—to form, fashion, make, mold

πλάσμα—what is formed or molded, an image, figure, a forgery, counterfeit, affectation of an actor

σπέρμα—descendants, seed, issue, offspring, race, origin, descent

εἶδος—appearance, form, sort, shape, figure, particular kind, nature, class

μετασχηματίζω—to change appearance, change the form of a person, transform, be disguised

Free, see also "Release, Set Free"

ἀδάπανος—free of charge, without expense, costing nothing

δωρεάν—freely, without cost, as a free gift

ἐλεύθερος—free, open to all, independent, having political and social freedom allowing for self-determination, not bound, exempt from obligation

ἀπελεύθερος—emancipated, set free

Λιβερτῖνος—free man

From

παρά—with genitive: from, issuing from a person, from the presence of

ἀπό—with genitive: from, out of, because of, as a result of, with the help of, by

ἐκ—with genitive: from, out of, away from, by, since

Fruit, see also "Plant"

καρπός—fruit, harvest

ὀπώρα—season after summer, July through early September, time of ripe fruit

σπέρμα—seed, descendants, issue

σπόρος—seed

κόκκος—seed

σῦκον—fig

ὄλυνθος—a late fig, unripe fig growing in winter not ripening but falling off in spring, untimely fig

βότρυς—cluster of grapes

ἄμπελος—grapevine

ἐλαία—olive (fruit)

στάχυς—ear of corn, head of wheat

σῖτος—wheat

σιτίον—grain, food

ἅλων—threshing area, threshed grain

κριθή—barley

κρίθινος—made of barley

κεράτιον—a little horn, carob pod (pig food)

γέννημα—that which is produced or born, a child, a product, fruit

Fulfill

ἐκπληρόω—fulfill, accomplish, make happen

πίμπλημι—fill, be fulfilled, accomplish, come to an end

πληροφορέω—to fulfill, passive: have full satisfaction, be fully persuaded

πληρόω—make full, fulfill, complete, fulfill the requirements of, observe, fulfill a prophecy

τελείωσις—fulfillment, perfection, accomplishment, completion

τελέω—finish, end, execute, fulfill, make perfect, pay taxes

ἐπιτελέω—finish, complete, fulfill, accomplish, discharge, pay in full

καταπράσσω—to accomplish, execute, achieve, gain

Full

πλήρης—full (of), filled (with), complete, not lacking

πλήρωμα—a full measure, fullness, the sum total, complete amount
πληρόω—make full, fulfill, complete
πίμπλημι—to fill full of, fill an office, satiate one's desire for, make laden a ship, fill completely, have enough of
μεστός—full, filled, very full
μεστόω—to fill full of, cause to bulge
γέμω—to be full
γεμίζω—to fill full of, load cargo or freight on a ship, charge an urn with

Funeral, Burial, Grave

κοπετός—lamentation
κομμός—a striking of the breast in lamentation, wild lament
κόπτω—cut, strike, smite, cut off, beat one's breast in grief, mourn
θρηνέω—mourn, lament, sing a dirge, wail, sing funeral songs
ὀδυρμός—complaining, lamenting
θάπτω—aorist ἐταφή, to bury, pay last dues, honor with funeral rites, inter
συνθάπτομαι—bury together with
ταφή—burial place
τάφος—tomb, grave
μνημεῖον—monument, memorial, grave, tomb
μνῆμα—memorial, monument to the dead, grave, tomb, sepulcher
συγκομίζω—to carry or bring together, collect, heap together, gather in harvest, to bury
ἐκκομίζω—to carry out in order to be buried
κομίζω—receive, receive back, be recompensed, bear, bring
ἐνταφιάζω—to prepare for burial
ἐνταφιασμός—burial, preparation for burial
προστίθημι—add to, increase, give, grant, do again, gather to, passive: be buried with

Furnishings, Household Accessories

κλίνη—bed, couch, stretcher
κλινάριον—cot
κλινίδιον—cot
κράβαττος—cot, pallet, camp bed
κοίτη—bed
δέμνιον—bed, bedding, bedstead, mattress, the marriage bed
σορός—bier, urn or receptacle for bones of the dead
προσκεφάλαιον—head cushion
καθέδρα—chair, seat, exalted seat
θρόνος—throne
τράπεζα—table
θυσιαστήριον—altar
βωμός—altar, stand, raised place, pedestal
ὑποπόδιον—footstool
κλείς—key
ἔσοπτρον—mirror

G

Gain, Earn, Do Business, see also "Advantage" and "Buy, Sell"

ὠφέλεια—profit, advantage, source of gain, usefulness, benefit, service, help, aid, assistance, utility

ὄφελος—advantage, profit, help, furtherance, good

κερδαίνω—gain, profit from, earn, win out, get

κέρδος—profit, gain

ποιέω—make, do, produce, cause to be, carry out, execute, appoint

ἐργασία—work, daily labor, business, making, building, commerce, practice, exercising, a work of art, production

ἐργάζομαι—to work, do business, do, perform, produce, bring about

προσεργάζομαι—to earn in addition, gain more in trade

πορισμός—a providing, procuring, source of gain, way to make money

ἐμπορεύομαι—to be in business, carry on business, exploit, travel for business, traffic, make a gain of, get an advantage

ἐμπορία—business, trade

ἐμπόριον—marketplace, emporium

ἔμπορος—merchant, traveler, passenger by sea

πορεία—journey, business trip, progress, way of life, conduct, going about one's business, occupation

εὐπορία—prosperity, easy passage, good business, prosperous income, abundance, wealth

πραγματεύομαι—to do business, be occupied with, be employed in a business, use capital for gain

διαπραγματεύομαι—to earn, gain, profit in business, gain in trade

καπηλεύω—to peddle for profit, deal in for profit, be a retailer

πορφυρόπωλις—dealer in purple cloth

κερματιστής—moneychanger, money exchanger

κολλυβιστής—moneychanger, money exchanger

ἀγορά—market, place of public concourse, forum, marketplace

μάκελλον—meat market, food market, slaughter house

κομίζω—receive, receive back, be recompensed, bear, bring

Gentleness, Mildness, see "Virtues: Gentleness, Mildness"

Genuine, Real, Really, see also "True"

ἀληθινός—agreeable to truth, truthful, true, real, genuine

γνήσιος—sincere, true, legitimate, noble, genuine

γνησίως—genuinely, really, truly, lawfully

δόκιμος—acceptable, approved, tried, genuine, considered good, respected

δοκίμιον—a test, trial, proving, proof, genuineness

λογικός—true to real nature

ἀνυπόκριτος—genuine, without pretense, without hypocrisy

σφραγίς—a seal, signet ring, mark of genuineness, that by which a thing is confirmed or authenticated, proof

ἀληθής—true, genuine, real, factual, reliable, trustworthy, valid

ἀληθινός—agreeable to truth, truthful, true, real, genuine

ὄντως—really, verily, truly

ἀληθῶς—really, verily, truly

ἐπ' ἀληθείας—really, verily, truly

ἐν ἀληθείᾳ—really, verily, truly

κατ' ἀλήθειαν—really, verily, truly

κυρόω—to confirm, ratify, determine, make valid, show something to be real

σωματικῶς—bodily, in reality

ἔγγυος—under good security, giving security, guarantee, guarantor

ὅλως—altogether, generally speaking, actually, as a fact, everywhere, regularly, again and again, continually, really, at all

Geography, see "Land," "Location," "Region"

Ghost

φάντασμα—ghost

πνεῦμα—wind, breath, spirit, soul, the Holy Spirit, the inner being

Give

δίδωμι—give

δόσις—a giving

δότης—giver

δόμα—gift

προδίδωμι—give beforehand

ἐπιδίδωμι—to hand over, give over, deliver, give up, surrender, yield

ἀναδίδωμι—deliver, hand over, present

παραδίδωμι—give over, deliver over, betray, pass on teachings

μεταδίδωμι—to share, impart, bestow

εὐμετάδοτος—willingly sharing, readily imparting, generous

παρατίθημι—put before, offer

τίθημι παρά—put before, turn over to

κατατίθημι—lay down, deposit, place, lay away, grant

ἐπιτίθημι—lay upon, place upon, usually the hands, inflict, attack

προστίθημι—add to, increase, give, grant, do again, gather to, passive: be buried with

παρίστημι—to stand before, present, show to be true, set before, provide, furnish, put at one's disposal

δωρέομαι—grant, give, donate

δωρεά—gift

δώρημα—gift, bounty

δῶρον—a gift, present, bribe

δωρεάν—freely, without cost, as a free gift

ἀναπληρόω—fill up, supply, refill, fulfill

προσφέρω—bring before, present to, offer, make an offering to the Lord
κλῆρος—a lot, a casting or drawing of lots, a piece of land, a portion, share, inheritance, fate, destiny
διαμερίζω—to distribute, divide, give out parts, be at variance, be in dissension
μερίζω—to divide, distribute, assign, apportion
μερισμός—distribution, parting, dividing, severance, separation
διαίρεσις—a dividing, division, allotment, apportionment, variety, difference
διαιρέω—divide into parts, cut asunder, distribute
μετρέω—measure out, mete out, estimate, give a measure
ἀντιμετρέω—repay, measure in return, give equivalent measure
διαδίδωμι—give out, offer here and there, distribute, divide, hand over
σκορπίζω—scatter, dispense blessings, give generously
ἔχω κοινός—have a share, share mutually
κοινωνέω—to share, have or do in common with, have a share of or take part in a thing with, have dealings with, do together with, form a community
κοινωνικός—willing to share, sociable, ready to communicate, beneficent
κοινωνία—association, fellowship, communion, participation, sharing in
χαρίζομαι—to show kindness, be agreeable, oblige, gratify, court favor, offer freely, give willingly, be pleasing, forgive, pardon, remit
χάρις—grace, goodwill, favor, mercy, kindness, a gift, thanks, exceptional favor given by God
χάρισμα—a gift
πλουτέω—to be rich, abound in, be generous
ἁπλότης—simplicity, sincerity, liberality, generosity
εὐλογία—praise, laudation, polished language, benediction, consecration, blessing, gift, of the alms collected for the poor
ἐλεημοσύνη—charitable giving, alms
ψωμίζω—to feed, dole out, give away
ψωμίον—bit, morsel
δεκατόω—collect tithes, passive: give a tenth
ἀποδεκατόω—give a tenth, tithe, collect a tithe

Go, Leave, Depart

ἄγω—bring, lead, go
ὑπάγω—go, depart, leave, bring under
παράγω—pass by, lead past, lead aside, mislead, depart
φεύγω—flee, seek safety from, escape, avoid, vanish
φυγή—fleeing, flight
διαφεύγω—flee, escape, get away
καταφεύγω—flee away, flee for refuge
ἐκφεύγω—flee out of, escape
ἐκβαίνω—go out of
μεταβαίνω—pass over from one place to another, remove, depart
ἀποβαίνω—unboard, disembark, step off, dismount, go away, depart, resultative: to issue, result in, end in
πορεύομαι—go, take a journey, travel, go on a business trip
ἐκπορεύομαι—go forth, go out, depart out of
χωρίζω—separate, divide, part, divorce, depart
διαχωρίζομαι—be separated, go away
ἐκχωρέω—depart from, flee from

ἀναχωρέω—go back, return, withdraw, go away, depart

ἀποχωρέω—go away, depart

ὑποχωρέω—go back, withdraw

μετατίθημι—to transfer, change

μετάθεσις—a transfer from one place to another, change, departure

ἀποδημέω—go away into foreign parts, go abroad, leave home on a journey

ἀπόδημος—away on a journey, away from home

ἔξοδος—exit, departure, decease

ἐξέρχομαι—go out

παρέρχομαι—pass by, arrive, pass away, perish, transgress

ἀπέρχομαι—go away, depart

ἄπειμι—go away, depart

ἔξειμι—go forth, go out of

ἀφίημι—send away, divorce, let go, leave, desert, abandon, forgive, remit, permit, allow, not hinder

ἀπουσία—absence, being away

ἀπολείπω—leave, leave behind, desert, forsake, abandon

καταλείπω—to leave behind, abandon, neglect, no longer relate to

ἀφίστημι—leave, desert, fall away from faith, commit apostasy, mislead, incite a revolt, abstain, shun

διΐστημι—to be later in time, to be removed in distance, come apart, separate, divide, set at variance to one another, put asunder, disjoin, stand apart, depart

ἀποτάσσομαι—to leave, say goodbye, part with, give up, forsake

ἀφανίζω—destroy, disfigure, deprive of luster, render unsightly, make ugly, passive: disappear, vanish

ἀφανισμός—disappearance, being done away with, vanishing, destruction, desolation

ἐκνεύω—withdraw, avoid, escape, slip out secretly

ἀπελαύνω—drive away, expel

ἄφιξις—departure

μεταίρω—transfer, go away, depart

God

θεός—God

θειότης—divine being, divinity

θεότης—divinity, divine nature, Godhead, deity

θεῖος—divine

ελωι—my God (Aramaic)

ηλι—my God (Hebrew)

ὕψιστος—the Most High

μεγαλωσύνη—Majesty

μεγαλοπρεπὴς δόξα—sublime glory, magnificent glory

παντοκράτωρ—almighty

κύριος—lord, master, ruler, owner

κυριακός—belonging to the Lord

κυριότης—dominion, power, lordship

ἀββά—father (Aramaic)

πατήρ—father

πνεῦμα—wind, breath, spirit, soul, the Holy Spirit, the inner being

παράκλητος—name of the Holy Spirit (John 14:26), Comforter, Counselor, called to one's aid

ἄθεος—without God

Goodness, see "Virtues: Goodness"

Gossip, see "Vices: Meddling, Busybody, Gossip"

Grace, see also "Forgiveness, Reconciliation," "Gift," "Virtues: Kindness," "Virtues:

Thankfulness," "Virtues: Mercy, Forgiveness"

χάρις—grace, goodwill, favor, mercy, kindness, a gift, thanks, exceptional favor given by God
χαρίζομαι—to be agreeable, oblige, gratify, court favor, offer freely, give willingly, be pleasing, forgive, pardon, remit
χαριτόω—show kindness, bestow favor upon, favor highly, bless
χάρισμα—a gift
εὐχαριστία—thankfulness, the giving of thanks
εὐχαριστέω—be grateful, give thanks
εὐχάριστος—thankful, grateful

Greed, see "Vices: Greed"

Grow, Growth, see also "Increase"

αὐξάνω—grow, increase, augment
αὔξησις—growth
συναυξάνομαι—grow with, grow together
ἀναβαίνω—ascend, go up, mount, board a ship, arise
μηκύνομαι—to lengthen, make long, grow
φύω—beget, bring forth, produce, spring up, germinate, grow
ἐκφύω—to generate or produce from, put forth, sprout leaves
συμφύομαι—grow with, grow together, spring up with
ἐκφέρω—carry out, bring forth, produce, yield
τίκτω—bring forth, bear, produce (fruit from seed), grow, give birth, be in travail
βλαστάνω—bud, produce, sprout leaves
ἐξανατέλλω—spring up, cause to shoot forth, sprout leaves
προβάλλω—put forward, shoot forth, sprout leaves

Guard, Watch Over, see also "Imprison"

φυλακή—a guard, prison, watch, the shift of a sentinel's duty
φυλάσσω—to keep watch, guard, guard against, keep a command, obey
φύλαξ—sentinel, guard, one who keeps watch
δεσμοφύλαξ—prison guard, jailer
φρουρέω—to keep watch, be on guard against, beware
συνέχω—surround, hem in, enclose, guard, seize, afflict, be absorbed in
τηρέω—to keep, observe, give heed to, obey, watch, protect, guard
τήρησις—being guarded, keeping, imprisonment, custody
κατακλείω—to shut up, put into prison, close
βασανιστής—questioner, torturer, prison guard
σπεκουλάτωρ—soldier on special duty, executioner

Guide, Lead, see also "Rule, Govern"

ἄγω—bring, lead, go
ἡγέομαι—govern, lead, think, consider
κατευθύνω—to make straight, set right, guide aright, lead, direct
προΐστημι—to stand before as leader, rule, manage, conduct, stand before in defense, care for, give aid
ποιμαίνω—to be a shepherd, tend, guide, look after, care for
κυβέρνησις—ability to lead
ὁδηγός—guide, leader
ἐπίτροπος—governor, manager, foreman, steward, trustee, guardian, guide, administrator

παιδαγωγός—custodian, attendant, guardian, superintendant, instructor

ἀρχηγός—pioneer, leader, initiator, originator, founder, prince, chief, author

στῦλος—pillar, support, leader

πρόδρομος—forerunner, advanced guard, a corps in the Macedonian army, a precursor

H

Hair, And Related Words
θρίξ—hair
τρίχινος—hairy, made of hair
κομάω—to wear long hair
ἐμπλοκή—braiding
πλέκω—to braid, weave, plait
πλέγμα—what is woven, entwined, braided
κείρω—sheer, be shorn, cutting short the hair of the head
ξυράομαι—shear, shave, be shaved

Happen, see also "Experience"
γίνομαι—be, become, be born, come about, be fulfilled, happen, take place, befall
ἐπιγίνομαι—happen, occur, come up
ἐνίσταμαι—happen, come about
εἰσέρχομαι—enter, arise, come into
συμβαίνω—come together, happen, turn out, come to pass
ἥκω—be present, come, arrive, be here, have happen, take place
ἐπακολουθέω—to follow closely upon, imitate one's example, devote oneself to, accompany
παρακολουθέω—to follow along with, accompany, attend, follow with the mind, trace or investigate a thing
προάγω—precede, go before, happen previously
προγίνομαι—happen previously, occur before
κατὰ συγκυρία—by coincidence, it so happened
ἔρχομαι—come, come about, happen
ποῦ φανεῖται—where will appear, what will happen 1 Peter 4:18
ἐπεισέρχομαι—happen, come into being
ἐπέρχομαι—come, arrive, come upon, overtake, attack (Luke 11:22)
ἐφίστημι—come up to, approach, stand near, appear suddenly, be imminent, attack
καταντάω—come upon, reach, arrive at, attain to, happen to, befall
συναντάω—meet, happen
ἀντάω—come opposite to, meet
ἐπιπίπτω—happen, fall upon, befall
πίπτω—to fall, suffer demise, perish, befall
φθάνω—come before, precede, arrive at, reach, attain, come upon, happen
τελειόω—make perfect, complete, accomplish, end, reach maturity, execute, finish, make happen
τελέω—finish, end, accomplish, fulfill, make perfect, pay taxes
παρέχω—offer, present, supply, furnish, have ready, grant, bring about for someone, provide for, cause to happen
παρεισάγω—cause to happen

καταφέρω—cause to happen
φέρω—bring, bear, carry, bring about
γεννάω—be born, bring about

Happy, Glad, Joyful, Cheerful, Laughter

ἱλαρότης—cheerfulness, happiness
ἱλαρός—cheerful, joyous, happy
μακαρισμός—declaration of blessedness, pronouncing of one blessed, blessedness, happiness
μακάριος—blessed, happy
μακαρίζω—to pronounce blessed, count happy, regard as happy
εὐφροσύνη—good cheer, joy, gladness, joyfulness
εὐφραίνω—to gladden, make joyful, be merry, rejoice, celebrate
χαρά—joy, gladness
χαίρω—to rejoice, be glad, at the beginning of letters: salute, greetings
συγχαίρω—to rejoice with, take part in another's joy, congratulate
συνήδομαι—to rejoice together with others, delight in
ἀσμένως—with joy, gladly
ἡδέως—with pleasure, gladly
ἥδιστα—gladly
ἀγαλλίασις—exultation, extreme joy, gladness
ἀγαλλιάω—to exult, rejoice exceedingly, be extremely joyful
σκιρτάω—to leap (for joy)
γελάω—laugh, be merry
γέλως—laughter
καταγελάω—to deride, laugh to scorn, laugh at

Hate, see "Vices: Hatred"

Health, Vigor, Strength, Healing

ὑγιαίνω—to be well, healthy, whole, sound
ὑγιής—sound, whole, well, healthy
ἰάομαι—cure, heal, make whole, restore, renew
ἴασις—healing, cure
ἴαμα—means of healing, remedy, medicine, power to heal
ἰατρός—physician
θεραπεία—nurture, care, medical service, tending to the sick, curing, healing, service to a god, worship
θεραπεύω—to care for, serve, treat, especially of a physician, heal, minister to, serve in a temple
σῴζω—to save, keep safe and sound, rescue from danger, heal
διασῴζω—save, preserve through danger, bring safely through, keep from danger, heal
καθαρίζω—cleanse, purge, heal
ἰσχύω—to be strong, to have power, be capable, be able, be healthy
ὁλοκληρία—complete health, perfect soundness, unimpaired condition of the body
ἁπλοῦς—sound, healthy, whole, without plurality, simple, singly-focused, fulfilling its purpose, generous, without guile
ῥώννυμαι—make strong, strengthen, imperative ἔρρωσθε is used in the closing of letters to say, "fare well"
κραταιόω—make strong, strengthen
καλῶς ἔχω—to be well
κομψότερον ἔχω—to get better
κομψός—well
ἀποκαθίστημι—restore to former state, establish again, restore to health

Hear

ἀκοή—the sense of hearing, the ear, the thing heard, instruction, message

ἀκούω—to hear, listen, hearken, obey, give audience, receive news, be reported, understand

εἰσακούω—give heed to, comply with an admonition, obey, listen, assent to

ἐπακούω—listen to, hear

προακούω—overhear, hear before, hear casually or carelessly or amiss, ignore, refuse to obey, pay no regard

οὖς—the ear, hearing

ἀκροατής—hearer

ἐπακροάομαι—listen to, hear

ἐνωτίζομαι—receive into the ear, give ear to, hearken, listen carefully to

κωφός—blunted, dull, deaf, lamed in tongue, dumb, speechless, mute

Heaven

οὐρανός—heaven, sky, firmament, air, any area above

ἐπουράνιος—heavenly, celestial, heavenly realms

παράδεισος—paradise, a place of blessedness, garden (of Eden)

ὕψος—height, high position, heaven

δόξα—glory, splendor, brightness, a good reputation resulting in praise and honor, pride

Heavenly Bodies, Sky

ἥλιος—the sun

στελήνη—the moon

ἀστήρ—star, planet

ἄστρον—star, constellation (Acts 7:43)

ἀστήρ πρωϊνός—morning star

φωσφόρος—morning star (actually a planet), bearer of light

φωστήρ—any bright celestial object, including sun, moon, and stars, usually stars

σώματα ἐπουράνια—heavenly bodies

νεφέλη—cloud

ὁμίχλη—fog, mist, cloud-like mass near earth's surface

ἀτμίς—steam

καπνός—smoke, vapors of combustion

ἶρις—rainbow, halo, circle of light

ἀήρ—air, sky

μεσουράνημα—midair

οὐρανός—heaven, sky, air, firmament, any area above

ἐπουράνιος—heavenly, celestial; heavenly realms

ὕψος—height, high position, heaven

ὕψωμα—height, pretension, arrogance

Hell

καταχθόνιος—underground, subterranean

χθόνιος—ground

ᾅδης—Hades, the grave, the place of the dead

γέεννα—Gehenna, hell, valley of the sons of Hinnom south of Jerusalem where unclean things were burned

ἄβυσσος—Abyss, the deep place, the place of immeasurable depth

βάθος—depth, the deep, extreme

λίμνη τοῦ πυρὸς καὶ θείου—lake of fire and brimstone (sulphur)

τὸ σκότος τὸ ἐξώτερον—the outer darkness, abode of evil spirits

σειραῖς ζόφου—chains of darkness (2 Peter 2:4)

ταρταρόω—to cast into Tartarus (2 Peter 2:4)

Help, Care For

βοήθεια—help, aid, rescue, support

βοηθέω—to help, aid, rescue, assist

βοηθός—helper

ἀντιλαμβάνω—to help, support, come to the aid of, relieve

ἀντίλημψις—help, assistance, helpful deeds, ability to help

συναντιλαμβάνομαι—to help, join in helping, come to the aid of, take part with

ἐπαρκέω—to help, aid, support

ὠφελέω—to help, aid, assist, be of use or service, benefit

ἀντέχω—to hold firmly to, cling to, be loyal to, support

ἀμύνομαι—to help, defend

συνυπουργέω—to join in helping, cooperate with

ἐπικουρέω—to act as an ally, aid, do service, make provision

ἐπικουρία—aid, help

ἑδραίωμα—support, foundation, mainstay

παρηγορία—comfort, assistance

εὐεργέτης—well-doer, benefactor

συμβάλλω—meet, discuss, consult, debate, ponder, middle: help, assist

ἐπιβλέπω—to look upon, consider, look attentively, pay respect to, take an interest, care about, help

προΐστημι—to stand before as leader, rule, manage, conduct, stand before in defense, care for, give aid

προστάτης—defender, guardian

προστάτις—helper, protector, patron

παράκλητος—comforter, helper, advocate, intercessor, assistant, called to one's aid

Hidden, Secret, Private, Unknown

κατ' ἰδίαν—privately, by one's self

ἀφανής—not manifest, hidden, secret

κρυπτός—hidden, concealed, secret

ἀπόκρυφος—hidden, secret

κρυφῇ—secretly

κρυφαῖος—hidden, concealed, in secret

κρύπτη—crypt, a covered way, vault, cellar, secret place

κρύπτω—hide, conceal, keep secret, make invisible, escape notice, keep safe, protect

ἀποκρύπτω—to hide, conceal, keep secret

περικρύβω—to conceal entirely, hide, seclude

καλύπτω—to hide, veil, keep secret, hinder from being known, cover

συγκαλύπτω—to conceal, cover up completely

παρακαλύπτομαι—to cover up, hide, conceal, make secret

ἐπικάλυμμα—covering, veil, pretext, cloak

λάθρᾳ—secretly, privately

λανθάνω—to be hidden, escape the knowledge of, be ignorant of, forget

μυστήριον—hidden thing, secret, mystery

ἄγνωστος—unknown

ἀφανίζω—destroy, disfigure, deprive of luster, render unsightly, make ugly, passive: disappear, vanish

ἄφαντος—taken out of sight, made invisible, vanished out of sight

αἴνιγμα—an obscure saying, enigma, riddle, a dim or dark image

ὑποβάλλω—to lay under, as a foundation, secretly put someone up to something, pay secretly or bribe

Hire, Rent, Lease

μισθόω—to hire, let out for hire, farm out, let, be let on contract, lease, rent

μισθός—pay, wages, reward, gain, recompense, retribution

μίσθωμα—the price agreed on in hiring, contract price, that which is let for hire, a rented real estate

ἐκδίδωμι—lease, rent, let out for hire

Hit, Strike
παίω—strike, smite, sting, hit
πληγή—blow, stripe, wound, heavy affliction, calamity, plague, distress
πλήσσω—strike, smite
τύπτω—strike, beat, smite, wound
κόπτω—cut, strike, smite, cut off
δέρω—beat, strike repeatedly, whip
πατάσσω—strike, smite with a sword, afflict, cut down, kill, slay
ῥαπίζω—smite with a rod, slap, beat
ῥάπισμα—a blow with a rod, a slap
προσκόπτω—strike against, stumble against, beat against
προσρήγνυμι—break against, break by dashing against, strike against
ῥήγνυμι—tear in pieces, rip, burst, throw into a fit, dash to the ground, break forth
κολαφίζω—strike with the fist, treat with violence, buffet, afflict
ῥαβδίζω—beat with rods or a stick
ἱμάς—thong of leather, a strap used for beating criminals or the straps which fasten sandals to the feet
μαστιγόω—scourge, whip, punish
μαστίζω—flog, scourge, whip
μάστιξ—a whip, scourge, plague, ailment, affliction
φραγελλόω—scourge, lash, whip
καταβάλλω—cast down, throw down, prostrate, knock down, hurt badly, lay (a foundation)
προσπίπτω—prostrate, fall down before, fall upon, rush upon, strike against, as wind
κρούω—to knock at a door
κεφαλιόω—bring under headings, sum up, summarize, smite or wound in the head, smite on the cheek, beat on the head

λακτίζω—to kick, strike with the foot

Hole
ὀπή—hole
τρῆμα—a perforation, hole, aperture, orifice, the eye of needle
φάραγξ—ravine
χείμαρρος—ravine
βόθυνος—pit, ditch
φρέαρ—deep pit, deep hole
χάσμα—chasm, cave
σπήλαιον—cave
φωλεός—den

Holiness, see "Virtues: Holiness, Purity"

Honesty, see "Virtues: Honesty"

Honor
τιμή—honor, respect, worth, value of a thing, price, valuation, payment
τιμάω—to honor, respect, value, set a price on, estimate the value of
τίμιος—precious, costly, prized, dear, held in honor, honored, worthy
ἔντιμος—in honor, honored, prized, valuable
δόξα—glory, splendor, brightness
δοξάζω—to praise, extol, glorify, magnify, honor, render excellent
ἔνδοξος—be given splendor, honored
ἐνδοξάζομαι—be shown as wonderful, be honored
συνδοξάζομαι—be honored with, join in receiving honor with, be glorified together with
κλέος—honor, credit, praise, good report
δόκιμος—acceptable, pleasing, tried, approved, genuine, considered good

ἐντρέπω—active: make someone ashamed, respect, mostly passive: be put to shame, be ashamed, passive with middle sense: have regard for, respect

στεφανόω—to crown, give a prize, adorn, decorate

τρέμω—tremble, quake, quiver, fear, respect

φοβέομαι—to fear, have respect

μεγαλύνω—to make great, magnify, declare great, esteem highly, extol, laud, enlarge, praise the greatness of, honor highly

ὑπερυψόω—to put one in the most high and supreme position, exalt exceedingly, give exceptional honor

ἐπιβλέπω—to look upon, consider, look attentively, pay respect to, take an interest, care about, help

πρωτοκαθεδρία—seat of honor, best seat, highest place in a meeting

πρωτοκλισία—seat of honor at a banquet, place beside the host

εὐσχήμων—decent, noble, honorable, presentable, befitting, elegant in figure and bearing, attractive, graceful, becoming, with dignity

Hope, Look Forward To

ἐλπίζω—to hope for, to hopefully trust in, to wait expectantly

ἐλπίς—hope, expectation, faith

προελπίζω—to hope beforehand, to trust in advance

ἀπελπίζω—to expect, to hope

ἀπεκδέχομαι—patiently waiting for, look forward eagerly

ἐκδέχομαι—look for, expect, wait for

ἐκδοχή—expectation, waiting

καραδοκία—eager expectation

ἀποκαραδοκία—eager desire, anxious and persistent expectation, longing

προσδοκία—expectation, looking after

προσδοκάω—expect, look for, wait for, anticipate, wait with anxiety

Hostility, see also "Vices: Hatred" and "War Terms"

ἀνθίστημι—resist, oppose, stand one's ground, be hostile toward

ἀντιδιατίθεμαι—to offer resistance, oppose, be hostile toward

ἀντίκειμαι—to be set against, lie opposite, be hostile toward

ἀντιτάσσω—to set in opposition to, meet in battle, be hostile toward

ἀντιστρατεύομαι—to make war against, actively oppose

ἐπαίρω τὴν πτέρναν—to raise the heel, oppose

ἐνέχω—active: to be hostile, have it in for, press upon, be urgent toward, passive, with dative: let oneself be entangled in, be under the control of

τάραχος—commotion, disorder, tumult

ἐξ ἐναντίας—out of opposition, contrary, hostile

ὑπεναντίος—set against, opposed, of enemies in battle, hostile, contrary to

ἐριθεία—strife, contentiousness, selfish ambition, rivalry, hostility

παροτρύνω—stir up, incite, arouse

συγκινέω—to stir up together, be set in motion, cause commotion, arouse

ἀντίδικος—opponent in a lawsuit, plaintiff, adversary, accuser

ἔχθρα—enmity, hatred, hostility

ἐχθρός—hated, hateful, hostile, at enmity with, enemy

ἀλλότριος—stranger, foreigner, enemy

ἀπέναντι—opposite, in front of, before, in the presence of, against, contrary

Hot, Cold

θέρμη—heat, warmth

θερμαίνομαι—warm oneself, dress warmly

ζεστός—boiled, hot, fervent, zealous

πυρόομαι—to burn with fire, set on fire, refine with fire, kindle, be sexually aroused

χλιαρός—lukewarm, between cold and hot, tepid, half-hearted in love or loyalty

ψῦχος—cold

ψυχρός—cold

ψύχω—make cold, cool, refrigerate

καταψύχω—make cool, refrigerate

Household Roles

οἰκονομέω—to manage a household, be a house-steward or manager

οἰκονόμος—manager, administrator

οἰκονομία—stewardship, management of a household, administration, dispensation, plan

οἰκουργός—homemaker, house-steward, house-manager

οἰκοδεσποτέω—to direct a household, rule a household, be master of a household

οἰκοδόμος—a builder, architect

οἰκέτης—house servant

θεραπεία—nurture, care, medical service, tending to the sick, curing, healing, service to a god, worship

ἀρχιτρίκλινος—head steward, president of a banquet

τρίκλινος—with three couches, a dining room with three couches, the Roman triclinium

θυρωρός—doorkeeper, porter

στρώννυμι and στρωννύω—to spread out, furnish a room, carpet a room, lay out anything to lie on or recline on, make a bed

παρασκευάζω—prepare a meal

διακονέω—to minister, serve, take care of, wait on

διακονία—service, ministry, waiting on

How, In What Way, In What Manner?

πολυμερῶς—in many portions, little by little, at many times

πολυτρόπως—in many ways, in various manners (Hebrews 1:1)

ὅν—τρόπον, in which manner, as

καθώς—just as, as, according as, to the degree that, inasmuch as, how

ὅπως—how, in what way, by what means, with subjunctive: so that, that, in order that

πόθεν—whence, from where, from what source, how is it that, in what way, why?

ὡς—so, thus, like, according as, how, with numerals: about, approximately

Humbleness, Humility, see "Virtues: Humbleness"

Hunt, Trap, Catch, Snare, see also "Capture, Trap, Surround," or "Vices: Deception"

ἀγρεύω—hunt, catch, catch in a mistake

ἄγρα—catch, that taken in hunting, booty, prey, game, a haul of fish

θήρα—trap, net

θηρεύω—hunt, catch, ensnare, catch in a mistake

παγίς—trap, snare, noose, pitfall, concealed danger, entanglement

παγιδεύω—ensnare, entrap, entangle, catch in mistake

δράσσομαι—catch, seize, trap

διώκω—to pursue, chase, hunt, persecute, strive after

καταδιώκω—to search after, track down, hunt

ἐπιλαμβάνομαι—take hold of, grasp, catch, trap, seize, arrest

σκάνδαλον—trap, offense, stumbling block

I

If, and Conditional Words
εἰ—if, since, because
εἴπερ—if indeed
ἐάν—if, if indeed, ever, when
εἴτε—if, whether
εἴτε . . . εἴτε—either . . . or, whether . . . or
πότερον . . . ἤ—whether . . . or . . . ?
ἄν—ever, would, may

Ignorant, Unlearned, Uneducated
ἀγράμματος—illiterate, unlearned, uneducated, not a scribe
ἀμαθής—unlearned, ignorant, uneducated, untaught
ἀπαίδευτος—without instruction, unschooled, ignorant, rude
ἰδιώτης—an unlearned, illiterate man, an unskilled person, layman, ignorant, rude, unlearned
ἀγνοέω—to be ignorant, to not know, to fail to understand, to be wrong
ἄγνοια—lack of knowledge, ignorance
ἀγνωσία—not knowing, ignorance, lack of knowledge, failure to understand
λανθάνω—to be hidden, escape the knowledge of, be ignorant of, forget
ἄπειρος—inexperienced, unskillful, unacquainted with

παρακούω—pay no attention to, refuse to listen to, disobey, overhear, hear what is not intended for one to hear (Mark 5:36)
ἀργός—lazy, barren, idle, slow, useless, indifferent, without thought
ἄλογος—unreasonable, irrational, brutish, absurd
καμμύω τοὺς ὀφθαλμούς—close one's eyes, refuse to learn
καμμύω—shut, close
σπερμολόγος—babbler, empty talker
πωρόω—to harden by becoming calloused, make the heart dull, lose the power of understanding, have a closed mind
πώρωσις—covering with a callous, dulled perception, stubbornness, blindness, hardness, insensibility

Image, Idol, see also "Form"
εἰκών—image, representation, likeness, form, appearance, similitude, portrait, statue
τύπος—mark or imprint from a blow, scar, form, pattern, example, type, figure (of something future)
χάραγμα—image, mark, stamp, representation
χαρακτήρ—exact representation

πλάσμα—what is formed or molded, an image, figure, a forgery, counterfeit, affectation of an actor
εἴδωλον—idol
κατείδωλος—full of idols
Χερούβ—winged creature
μοσχοποιέω—to make a calf-idol

Imitate

μιμέομαι—to mimic, imitate, represent, portray, make exactly like
μιμητής—imitator, copyist, actor,—one who represents characters, impostor
συμμιμητής—joint imitator, fellow-imitator, in following an example
ἐπακολουθέω τοῖς ἴχνεσιν—to follow in the footsteps, to imitate
περιπατέω τοῖς ἴχνεσιν—to walk in the tracks, imitate
στοιχέω τοῖς ἴχνεσιν—to be in line with the tracks, imitate
ἐξακολουθέω—obey, follow, imitate
προσποιέω—to make or act as though, pretend, simulate, feign

Important, Important in Status

μέγιστος—very important, very great, greatest
πρό—in front of, before in time, above in value
βαρύς—heavy in weight, weighty, important, burdensome, severe, stern, cruel, unsparing, grievous
ἐν βάρει—claiming importance, being weighty
πρωτοκαθεδρία—seat of honor, best seat, highest place in a meeting
βαθμός—standing, rank, status
κλῆσις—call, invitation, calling, social role, vocation
ἐξοχή—high rank, prominence, distinction
ὕψος—heaven, high position
ὑψόω—to lift high, raise up, elevate, exalt
μεγαλειότης—majesty, mighty power, prominence, importance
μεγαλωσύνη—majesty, prominence
μέγας—big, great, vast, strong, mighty, large, important
μεγιστάν—very important person
ὑπεροχή—pompous
εὐγενής—well-bred, of a noble family, important, noble-minded, open-minded, generous
κρείττων—better, greater, superior, higher in rank, more important, comparative of κρατύς used as comparative of ἀγαθός
μείζων—greater, older, more, comparative of μέγας
ἀνώτερος—higher, above, earlier, preceding
ὑπέρ—with accusative: over, above, exceeding, more than
ἐπάνω—on, above, over, more than, superior to
ὑπεράνω—above, far above
πηλίκος—how large, how important
ἐκ δεξιῶν καθίζω—seated at the right hand, be in high position
αὐξάνω—grow, increase, augment
ἐξεγείρω—to raise up, arouse, stir up, incite, raise to life, give higher status
οἱ δυνατοί—important people, the powerful ones
ἰσχυρός—strong, mighty, powerful, vigorous, severe
πρῶτος—first, earliest, before, foremost, most important, best
πρωτεύω—be first, have first place, hold highest rank
πρωτότοκος—firstborn, oldest son
πατήρ—father, forefather, progenitor, archetype, founder
ἐπιστάτης—master, lord

κεφαλή—head, superior

πρωτοστάτης—one stationed in the front ranks of an army, leader

κύριος—lord, master, ruler, owner, sir

κυρία—lady, as a title of respect for a woman

κράτιστος—superlative of κρατύς, most excellent, most noble

φαντασία—pomp, pageantry, making visible, appearance made for effect

Imprison, see also "Guard" and "Capture"

φυλακίζω—to imprison

φυλακή—a guard, prison, watch, the shift of a sentinel's duty

δεσμός—chain, binding, imprisonment

δεσμωτήριον—prison

δέσμιος—binding, bound, captive

δεσμώτης—prisoner, captive, in chains, fettered

δέω—to bind, fasten, put under obligation, cause illness

καταδέω—to bind on or to, to put in bonds, imprison, bind for execution

αἰχμάλωτος—captive, taken prisoner

συναιχμάλωτος—fellow prisoner

ἀπάγω—lead away, carry off

ἅλυσις—chain, imprisonment

Increase, see also "Grow"

αὐξάνω—grow, increase, augment

προκόπτω—to advance a work, go forward, progress, increase, beat forward, proceed, be spent

ἐπισωρεύω—to heap up, accumulate, increase greatly, collect

πλεονάζω—to be more than enough, be superfluous, go beyond bounds, take too much, have an excess of, abound in, be rich

πληθύνω—to make full, increase, multiply, grow, spread

διπλόω—to double, repay twofold

Inferiority, Of Low Position

μικρός—small, little, petty, trivial, slight, unimportant, a short time

ἀγενής—inferior, lowborn, not of noble birth, insignificant, common people, opposite: εὐγενής highborn

ἄσημος—insignificant, indistinct, of persons or cities, unnoticed, of no mark, unknown, inferior, obscure

ταπεινόω—to make low, abase, embarrass, make level, bring low, passive: be humble

ὑστερέω—to be in need, be lacking, be wanting, fall short, arrive late, be inferior

ἐλάχιστος—the smallest, least, shortest, fewest, least important

ἔσχατος—last, final, furthest, uttermost, most extreme

ἐλάσσων—smaller, less, fewer, worse than, inferior to, subservient to, younger

ἐλαττόω—make less, lower, inferior in position, be worse off, diminish in status, become less important

κενόω—to empty out, drain, strip of all things, leave a place deserted, make of no account or of no effect, cause to lose power

ἄτιμος—lacking in honor, despised, dishonored, insignificant

ὄνειδος—disgrace, reproach, censure, blame

πτῶσις—a falling, crash, collapse, downfall, ruin, destruction, worsening

πίπτω—to fall, suffer demise, perish, befall

παῖς—child, servant

παιδίσκη—slave girl, maid

δοῦλος—a slave, bondservant

δουλεύω—to be a slave to, serve, be subject to
δουλόω—to enslave, put under obligation, make subservient
σύνδουλος—fellow servant
εἰμὶ ὑπὸ ζυγόν—be under the yoke, be a slave

Infinite
ἀπέραντος—endless, boundless, infinite, countless
εἰς τὰ ἄμετρα—excessive, immense, without measure, boundless
ἀναρίθμητος—not able to be counted, countless, innumerable
μύριοι—numberless, countless, much, measureless, infinite, immense, endless, incessant, ten thousand

Insane, Out Of One's Mind
ἐξίστημι—to amaze, astonish, have wonderment, to marvel, to be out of one's mind, beside one's self, insane
μαίνομαι—to be mad, not in one's right mind, beside one's self, insane
μανία—madness, frenzy, insanity
παραφρονέω—to be beside one's self, out of one's senses, void of understanding, insane, to be a fool
παραφρονία—madness, insanity

Insects
ἀκρίς—grasshopper, locust
κώνωψ—gnat
σής—moth
μέλισσα—bee
μελίσσιος—of bees, made by bees, honeycomb, beeswax
μέλι—honey
σκώληξ—worm, grub, maggot
σκορπίος—scorpion
ἑρπετόν—reptile, creeping aninmal

Insist, Urge
διαμαρτύρομαι—to solemnly testify, strongly declare, insist, urge, earnestly ask, bear witness
μαρτύρομαι—to testify, seriously declare, insist, urge, emphatically address, call to witness
ἐμβριμάομαι—to charge with earnest admonition, sternly insist, express indignation, censure, reproach, scold, feel strongly
διϊσχυρίζομαι—to affirm stoutly, assert confidently, insist firmly
διαβεβαιόομαι—to assert confidently, state with certainty, affirm strongly

Intemperance, see "Vices: Intemperence"

Intercede
ἔντευξις—petition, supplication, intercession, prayer
ἐντυγχάνω—entreat, appeal to, plead, make intercession for, petition
ὑπερεντυγχάνω—to intercede for
μεσιτεύω—to mediate, interpose between parties, act as a sponsor, pledge one's self, give surety, confirm, cause agreement
μεσίτης—mediator, one who intervenes between two, arbitrator, reconciler

Invalidate, Deprive Of Power, Annul
ἀναιρέω—kill, take away, abolish, middle: take up, adopt (Acts 7:21)
καταλύω—destroy, demolish, dismantle, tear down, abolish, annul, put an end to, make invalid
ἀθετέω—reject, set aside, annul
ἀθέτησις—annulment, removal
ἀκυρόω—to make void, invalidate the authority of, disregard, make of no effect

περιφρονέω—despise, disregard

καταργέω—render ineffective, make barren, do away with, nullify, passive with ἀπό: be released from

κενόω—to empty out, drain, strip of all things, leave a place deserted, make of no account or of no effect, cause to lose power

Invite

καλέω—to call, invite, bid, name

παρακαλέω—to urge, summon for help, encourage, comfort

εἰσκαλέομαι—to call into one's house, call in, invite in

ἀντικαλέω—to invite back, bid again, to invite in reciprocation, invite in return

κλητός—called, invited, one who has received an invitation

φωνέω—to emit a sound, speak, cry out, call, summon, send for

J

Join, Associate

κολλάω—to glue, cement, bind, join, cling to, adhere to, attach to

προσκολλάω—to glue on or to, stick or cleave to, join to

προσκληρόομαι—to be attached to, keep company with, join lots with

προσκλίνω—to be joined to someone

ἀντέχω—to hold firmly to, cling to, be loyal to, support

Judge, Evaluate, Distinguish

κρίνω—to judge, decide, evaluate, make a preference, condemn

ἀνακρίνω—examine, judge, scrutinize, sift, question, hold an investigation, interrogate, study thoroughly

διακρίνω—to judge between, prefer, discriminate, decide, evaluate, doubt, hesitate, take issue

κρίμα—judgement, condemnation, judge's sentence, legal decision

κρίσις—judgement, legal decision, accusation, condemnation, verdict

διάκρισις—discernment, ability to decide

αὐτοκατάκριτος—condemned by one's own actions, self-condemned

δοκιμάζω—to test, examine, prove, scrutinize, recognize as genuine after examination, approve, deem worthy, try, judge as good, evaluate

δόκιμος—acceptable, pleasing, tried, approved, genuine, considered good

ἀποδοκιμάζω—to disapprove, reject, regard as unworthy

ἀποδιορίζω—cause divisions, set up distinctions

καταγινώσκω—condemn, blame, find fault with, judge to be guilty

καταβραβεύω—decide against, judge unworthy, disqualify, beguile of reward, defraud

βραβεύω—to be arbiter, judge, director, or umpire in public games, preside, govern, arrange, control

ἐξουσία—authority, power, license, permission, legal right

ῥαβδοῦχος—Roman policeman, constable, or sergeant who carried a rod or staff of office

Jump, Leap

ἅλλομαι—spring up, gush, leap, jump

ἐφάλλομαι—jump on, spring upon

ἐξάλλομαι—jump up

πηδάω—jump

ἀναπηδάω—jump up

σκιρτάω—leap, jump (for joy)

K

Kill, see also "Die, Death"

ἀποκτείνω—kill, destroy, slay, put to death, do away with

θανατόω—put to death, destroy, render extinct, kill, mortify, execute

φονεύω—to kill, slay, murder

φόνος—murder, slaughter

φονεύς—a murderer, a homicide

ἀνδροφόνος—man-killer, murderer

ἀνθρωποκτόνος—man-killer, murderer

αἷμα ἐκχέω—to spill blood, kill

διαχειρίζομαι—lay hands on in violence, seize and kill with one's hands, murder

καταστρώννυμι—slay, kill, strike down, strew over the ground, overthrow

ἐδαφίζω—throw to the ground, raze, level to the ground, kill

αἴρω—lift, raise up, elevate, remove, carry off, take away, kill, destroy

ἀναίρεσις—destroying, killing, murder, death

ἀναιρέω—kill, take away, abolish, middle: take up, adopt (Acts 7:21)

ἀπάγω—lead away, carry off, as to punishment

μάρτυς—witness, martyr

μάχαιρα—sword, death, war

σπεκουλάτωρ—soldier on special duty, executioner

θύω—to sacrifice, slay, kill, slaughter

κατασφάζω—to kill off, slaughter, slay

σφαγή—a slaughter, ἡμέρα σφαγῆς day of condemnation

σφάζω—slay, slaughter, butcher, put to death by violence, kill

πατάσσω—strike, smite with a sword, afflict, cut down, kill, slay

κοπή—act of cutting, a cut, a slaughter

θιγγάνω—to touch (with punishment of death)

κρεμάννυμι ἐπὶ ξύλου—to hang on a tree, crucify

σταυρόω—to stake, crucify

προσπήγνυμι—to fasten onto, crucify

πήγνυμι—to pitch a tent, implant, fasten together, construct, build, erect, set up

ἀνασταυρόω—crucify again

συσταυρόομαι—crucify with

καταλιθάζω—stone to death

λιθάζω—stone to death

λιθοβολέω—stone to death

ἀποκεφαλίζω—behead, cut the head off, decapitate

πελεκίζω—cut off with an axe, behead, cut off the head

ἀπάγχομαι—strangle, choke, middle: hang oneself

σταυρός—cross

ξύλον—tree, wood, firewood, club, cross, stocks

φραγέλλιον—whip
τυμπανίζω—to beat, bastinado, cudgel, torture, often to death
σικάριος—an assassin, cutthroat, terrorist
μητρολῴας—one who murders his mother
πατρολῴας—one who murders his father, a patricide

Kin, Ancestry, Genealogy, Relatives, see also "Descendants"

γονεύς—parents
πατήρ—father
μήτηρ—mother
μάμμη—grandmother
ἔκγονον—grandchild
πρόγονος—forefather
προπάτωρ—ancestor
πατρικός—of ancestors
πατρῷος—of ancestors
πατριάρχης—patriarch
σπορά—parentage
γένεσις—progeny, lineage
οἶκος—house, family, lineage
πατριά—ancestry, lineage
γενεαλογία—genealogy
γενεαλογέομαι—be descended from
ἀγενεαλόγητος—without record of ancestors
γενεά—generation, age, descendants
γένος—race, stock, family, offspring, posterity, tribe, people, class, kind
σπέρμα—descendants, seed
τέκνον—child
υἱός—son
θυγάτηρ—daughter
θυγάτριον—little daughter
παῖς—child, servant
παιδίον—child
καρπὸς τῆς ὀσφύος—offspring, fruit of the loins
καρπός τῆς κοιλίας—child, fruit of the womb
ἀνατέλλω—to rise, give birth to, be a descendant, bring to light, dawn
πρωτότοκος—firstborn, oldest son
πρωτοτόκια—birthright
ἄρσην διανοίγων μήτραν—firstborn male
ἀδελφός—brother
ἀδελφή—sister
ἀνεψιός—cousin
σύντροφος—foster brother, brought up with, nourished with, childhood companion
ἀνήρ—husband
ἄνθρωπος—man, husband
γυνή—wife
σκεῦος—vessel, jar, vase, utensils, furniture, military gear, equipment, luggage, one's wife (1 Thes. 4:4)
νυμφίος—groom
νύμφη—bride
πενθερός—father-in-law
πενθερά—mother-in-law
νύμφη—daughter-in-law
χήρα—widow
ἄτεκνος—childless
ἀπάτωρ—without father
ἀμήτωρ—without mother
ὀρφανός—orphan, bereft, orphaned, fatherless person
ἀπορφανίζω—make an orphan of, be torn away from, unwillingly separated from
νόθος—illegitimate child

Kindness, see "Virtues: Kindness"

Kiss, Embrace

καταφιλέω—to kiss in greeting or farewell, to caress

φιλέω—to love, have affection for, like, kiss

φίλημα—a greeting kiss

ἐναγκαλίζομαι—to embrace, take in one's arms

ἐπιπίπτω ἐπὶ τὸν τράχηλον—to fall upon the neck, embrace

συμπεριλαμβάνω—to embrace, throw one's arms around

Kneel

γονυπετέω—kneel down

τίθημι τὰ γόνατα—kneel down, bow in prayer

Know, Make Known, see also "True, Truth," "Think," "Virtues: Understanding," "Wisdom, Understanding"

γινώσκω—know, learn, perceive, understand, acknowledge, have sexual intercourse

γνῶσις—knowledge, understanding

γνωρίζω—to make known

γνωστός—known, well-known, notable, remarkable

γνώστης—an expert, connoisseur

καρδιογνώστης—knower of hearts

ἐπιγινώσκω—know, recognize, notice, become aware of, learn, acknowledge, know fully

ἐπίγνωσις—knowledge

οἶδα—to see, perceive, know, regard

σύνοιδα—to see together, share in knowledge, be conscious of

συνείδησις—conscience, awareness

σοφίζω—to make wise, instruct, middle: devise, reason with skill, passive: be cleverly devised

σοφία—wisdom, intelligence, specialized knowledge, insight

σοφός—wise, skilled, skillful

ἐπίσταμαι—to understand, be aware, comprehend, be acquainted with

προγινώσκω—to have knowledge beforehand, to foreknow, to predestinate, choose in advance

πρόγνωσις—foreknowledge, forethought, pre-arrangement, what is known beforehand

προοράω—to see beforehand, to keep before one's eyes, foresee, know beforehand

ἐμφανής—well-known, manifest, visible, openly known

ἐμφανίζω—to manifest, exhibit to view, disclose, make known

φαίνω—to cause to shine, bring to light, appear, make known, be seen

φανερόω—to make manifest, visible, or known, to cause to be seen

φανέρωσις—disclosure, revelation

φανερός—apparent, manifest, plainly recognized, evident, known

φανερῶς—manifestly, plainly, clearly, openly, publicly

φωτίζω—to give light, shine, illumine, bring to light, reveal

φωτισμός—brightness, revelation, enlightenment, illumination, truth

αὐγάζω—to beam upon, irradiate, be bright, shine forth, cause to be seen

ἐπίσημος—marked, stamped, of note, notable, well known

ὀνομάζω—to name, designate, call, mention a name, passive: be named, be known about, be heard of

ἀφικνέομαι—to reach, come to, arrive at, to reach the ears, become known διανέμω—distribute, allocate, deliver, dispense, give out, spread news of, circulate, cause to become known

ἐν παρρησίᾳ—in unreserved speech, openly spoken without concealment, publicly

ἀποκαλύπτω—uncover, lay open what was hidden, disclose, make known, reveal

ἀποκάλυψις—disclosure of the truth, manifestation, revelation

χρηματίζω—to give a divine message, speak, warn, to receive a title, be called

χρηματισμός—divine response, oracle, answer of God, divine revelation

ἐξηγέομαι—tell, relate, explain, make fully known, reveal

ἡγέομαι—govern, lead, think, consider

συμβιβάζω—join together, unite, put together in one's mind, conclude, prove, instruct, advise

τεκμήριον—infallible proof, convincing proof, that from which something is plainly known

δείκνυμι—to show, expose, explain, give proof of, make known

δεῖγμα—a thing shown, example

ὑποδείκνυμι—to show, warn, make known, explain

ἀποδείκνυμι—to set forth, attest, show to be true, claim, demonstrate, prove

ἀπόδειξις—proof, demonstration

ἐνδείκνυμι—to point out, show, demonstrate, prove, display

ἔνδειγμα—token, evidence, proof

ἔνδειξις—proof, sign, evidence

ἀναδείκνυμι—appoint, make known publicly, commission to a position

ἀνάδειξις—public showing forth, proclamation, announcement, inauguration, revelation

δηλόω—to make manifest, indicate, signify, show, make clear

δῆλος—clear, evident, manifest, certain

ἔκδηλος—evident, clear, manifest, conspicuous, easily known

πρόδηλος—openly evident, very obvious

δημόσιος—belonging to the people or state, public, in full view of all, openly

τραχηλίζομαι—to lay bare, uncover, expose, lay open, be easily known

τράχηλος—neck

γυμνός—naked, ill clad, unclad, stripped, exposed

L

Lamp, see also "Light"
λαμπάς—lamp, torch
φῶς—light, source of illumination, torch, bonfire
φανός—lantern
λύχνος—lamp
λυχνία—lampstand

Land
γῆ—earth, ground, dirt, land, world, country, region
χώρα—land, region, countryside
παράλιος—coastal region
χεῖλος—shore
αἰγιαλός—shore
παραθαλάσσιος—seaside
ἄμμος—beach, sand
ἀνωτερικός—inland
νῆσος—island
νησίον—small island
τόπος διθάλασσος—reef, place between seas
ἐρημία—wilderness, desert
ξηρός—dry, of land as distinct from water, withered

Language
διάλεκτος—a language or dialect, conversation, speech, discourse
φωνή—sound, tone, voice, speech, language
γλῶσσα—the tongue, the organ of speech, a language or dialect, tongue, utterance
ἑτερόγλωσσος—speaking a strange language, man of other tongue, one who speaks a foreign language

Large
μέγας—big, great, vast, strong, mighty, large
μεγαλύνω—to make great, magnify, declare great, esteem highly, extol, laud, enlarge, praise the greatness of, honor highly
πηλίκος—how large
ἡλίκος—how great, how extensive
τηλικοῦτος—so great, so large, so important, so mighty

Law, see also "Command"
νόμος—law
ἔννομος—bound to the law, lawful, legal, under law, subject to law
νομικός—pertaining to the law, one learned in the law, a lawyer
νομοθεσία—lawgiving, legislation, giving of law
νομοθετέομαι—to enact laws, to be legislated for, furnished with laws, to sanction by law, give law
νομοθέτης—lawgiver

δικαίωμα—commandment, ordinance, regulation, requirement of righteous action, a judgement, an act of righteousness

κανών—rule, measuring rod, the area over which one rules, the province assigned one, a principal or law of judging and acting

δόγμα—command, ordinance, law

Lawless, Unjust, see "Vices: Lawlessness, Injustice"

Lazy, Idle, At Leisure, Unemployed, see "Vices: Laziness"

Learn, Find Out

μαθητεύω—to make a disciple of, instruct, passive: be a pupil, follow

μαθητής—learner, pupil, disciple, follower

μανθάνω—to learn, be taught

εὑρίσκω—find, come upon, discover, attain, learn, find by way of inquiry

ἀνευρίσκω—find, discover

γινώσκω—know, learn, perceive, understand, acknowledge, have sexual intercourse

ἐπιγινώσκω—know, recognize, notice, become aware of, learn of, acknowledge, know fully

εἰς ἐπίγνωσιν ἔρχομαι—come to know, learn of, obtain knowledge of

ὁράω—to see, behold, perceive, know, learn about, experience, take heed, beware

συνοράω—learn about, understand

παραλαμβάνω—receive, take with, accept, learn

καταλαμβάνω—lay hold of, obtain, acquire, seize, attack, catch, middle: receive with the mind, comprehend

ἀκριβόω—to find out accurately, to investigate diligently, learn exactly

διερωτάω—to find out by asking, inquire, learn about

πυνθάνομαι—to inquire, ask, ascertain by inquiry, learn about

μυέω—to initiate into a religion, to instruct, to accustom one to a thing, to give one an acquaintance with

ὁδηγέω—to guide, lead on one's way, be a teacher, guide in learning

λόγιος—learned, a man of letters, skilled in literature and speech, eloquent, rational, wise

γράμμα—a letter of alphabet, any writing, document, or record, a letter or epistle, the sacred writings, scriptures, letters, learning, education, a record of debts

γραμματεύς—scribe, recorder, scholar, expert in the law

κατάσκοπος—spy, scout, one who keeps look out, a person sent to examine and report

ἐξετάζω—to search out, inquire, ask, try to find out

παρακολουθέω—to follow along with, accompany, attend, follow with the mind, trace or investigate a thing

παρακύπτω—to stoop and look into, to look at with head lowered forward, inspect curiously

ἱστορέω—to learn by inquiry, visit in order to learn from and gain information, passive participle: things learned by inquiry, historical account

Legal Terms

κριτήριον—judgement

κρίμα—judgement, verdict, sentence, legal decision, lawsuit

κρίσις—judgement, legal decision, accusation, condemnation, verdict

κρίνω—to judge, decide, evaluate, make a preference, criticize
κριτικός—able to judge, able to discern, critical
κριτής—judge, umpire, interpreter
ἀπόκριμα—verdict, judicial sentence
δικαιοκρισία—just verdict
κατάκριμα—condemnation
κατακρίνω—condemn
κατάκρισις—condemnation
ἀνακρίνω—examine, judge, investigate in court, inquire into, scrutinize, interrogate, criticize
ἀνάκρισις—investigation in court, examination, judicial hearing
ἀκατάκριτος—without trial, uncondemned
πρᾶγμα—deed, undertaking, task, act, event, occurrence, work, matter, affair, business, something important or of consequence, lawsuit, dispute
εὐνοέω—wish well, consider favorably, be well-disposed, be of a peaceable spirit, to agree with, settle a case
αἰτία—cause, reason for accusation, charge
αἰτίωμα—accusation
αἰτέω—to ask, beg, request
ἔγκλημα—accusation, complaint
λόγος—word, reason, matter under discussion, account, treatise, statement, accusation, ground, plea
ἐμφανίζω—to manifest, exhibit to view, disclose, make known
κατὰ λόγον ἀνέχομαι—to accept a complaint
ἐκζητέω—to seek out, search diligently, investigate, scrutinize, require of, bring charges against
διαγινώσκω—to ascertain exactly, determine, decide a case, inquire, examine thoroughly

διάγνωσις—deciding of a case
δικαστής—judge, avenger
ἀντίδικος—opponent in a lawsuit, plaintiff, adversary, accuser
ἄρχων—ruler, commander, chief, captain, chief magistrate, judge
ἀκούω—to hear (a case), give audience, hearken, receive news, be reported, to understand, listen, obey
διακούω—to hear through, hear to the end, hear a legal case
ἐπερωτάω—ask for, put a question to, interrogate, demand
ἀνετάζω—to examine closely, interrogate
ἐπικαλέω—call, give a name to, middle: invoke, make an appeal to
ὑπόδικος—brought to trial, liable to judgment
ἀναβάλλω—postpone, defer, adjourn a hearing
ἡμέρα σφαγῆς—day of execution
καταδικάζω—to condemn, pass judgement against, sentence someone
καταδίκη—condemnation, judgement given against one, the damages awarded
δικαιόω—to justify, make right with, deem righteous, acquit
δικαίωμα—commandment, ordinance, regulation, requirement of righteous action, a judgement, an act of righteousness
δικαίωσις—setting right, doing justice to, deeming righteous, being put right with, acquittal
ἐκδικέω—to avenge, procure justice for someone, punish a crime
ἐκδίκησις—an avenging, punishment, giving of justice
ῥήτωρ—public speaker, orator, pleader, attorney, lawyer

νομικός—pertaining to the law, one learned in the law, a lawyer

ἀπάγω—lead away, as to punishment

μαρτυρία—witness, testimony, attestation, evidence, reputation

ἀπογράφω—passive: be registered or enrolled (in a census), be entered in public records

ἀποστάσιον—divorce, notice of divorce

ἐπιδιατάσσομαι—to add to a will, add a codicil

ἀγοραῖος—court session, Acts 19:38, idle people, Acts 17:5

ἀναβολή—a putting off, delaying, postponement of a court case

Less, Lessen, Reduce

χείρων—worse, inferior, comparative of κακός

ἥσσων—worse, less

ἡσσάομαι or ἡττάομαι—be treated as inferior, be defeated

κολοβόω—to dock, curtail, shorten, reduce in number

αἴρω—lift, raise up, elevate, remove, carry off, take away, kill, destroy

Liar, Lie, Falsehood, see under "Vices: Deception, Speaking Falsely"

Lie, Recline, see also "Recline to Eat"

κεῖμαι—lie down, recline, be laid down, be situated somewhere

κατάκειμαι—lie down, lie prostrate, recline to eat

κλίνω—recline, incline, bend, slope, lay down, lie on a couch at meals, decline, of the day, draw to a close

ἀνακλίνω—cause to lie down, recline to eat, lean against, lean upon

Life, Live

ζάω—live, breathe, be among the living

ζωή—life, having vitality

ζῳογονέω—bring forth alive, give life, preserve alive, keep alive

τεκνογονέω—beget, bear children

ζῳοποιέω—make live, bear living young, germinate

συζάω—live together with, live with

συζῳοποιέω—to make one alive together with, raise to life with

ἀναζάω—live again, recover life, return to a right moral state, revive

ἀνίστημι—raise up, rise, stand up, appear, stand forth, resurrect

ἀνάστασις—resurrection, raising to life again

ἐξανάστασις—a rising up, a rising again, resurrection

ἐγείρω—to arouse, cause to rise, raise to life, raise up, awaken, stand up, make war against

ἔγερσις—a rousing, excitation, a rising up, resurrection from the dead

ἐξεγείρω—to arouse, raise up, stir up, incite, raise to life

συνεγείρω—to raise together, raise to life with

ψυχή—breath, soul, living being, person, life, inner self

σάρξ—flesh, body, natural generation, the sensual nature, human nature

ἐνδημέω ἐν τῷ σώματι—be at home in the body, be alive in this life as opposed to the next

κατασκηνόω—to dwell, live, settle, rest, make a nest

Light

φῶς—light, source of illumination, torch, bonfire

φωτίζω—to give light, shine, illumine, bring to light, reveal

φωστήρ—radiance
ἐπιφώσκω—to shine forth, dawn
φωτεινός—bright
φωτεινός—full of light
λάμπω—shine
ἐκλάμπω—shine forth
περιλάμπω—shine around
λαμπάς—lamp, torch
λαμπρός—shining, bright, radiant, clear, sparkling, resplendent, of fine things that are luxurious and elegant
λαμπρότης—brightness
φαίνω—to cause to shine, bring to light, appear, make known, be seen
ἐπιφαίνω—to show to, to bring to light, appear, give light, illuminate
φέγγος—light, radiance, glow
ἐπιφαύσκω—illuminate
ἡμέρα—day, daylight, season
αὐγή—dawn, sunlight, any bright light
αὐγάζω—to beam upon, irradiate, be bright, shine forth, cause to be seen
διαυγάζω—to shine through, dawn
διαυγής—transparent, translucent, radiant, allowing light to shine through
ἀπαύγασμα—radiance
ἀνατέλλω—to rise, give birth to, be a descendant, bring to light, dawn
ἀστραπή—bright beam
ἀστράπτω—to glisten, shine brilliantly, flash, of lightning
περιαστράπτω—shine brightly around
ἐξαστράπτω—to glisten
στίλβω—to glisten, gleam
ῥιπή—blinking, twinkling, a moment of time
δόξα—glory, splendor, brightness
λευκός—bright, radiant, brilliant, white, bleached
κατοπτρίζομαι—reflect

Liquids, Activities Involving, see also "Flow"

ἀλείφω—anoint with oil or perfume
ἐξαλείφω—wipe off, wipe away, obliterate, erase, blot out, eliminate
ἀπομάσσομαι—wipe off (Luke 10:11)
ἐκμάσσω—to wipe off, wipe away, wipe away one's tears
σπογγίζω—to wipe with a sponge
σπόγγος—sponge
ἐγχρίω—rub on, smear on, anoint as salve or oil
ἐπιχρίω—rub on, smear on, anoint as salve or oil
ἅλλομαι—spring up, bubble up
ἀντλέω—to draw water, bale a ship
βαπτίζω—baptize, ritually wash, dip
βάπτω—dip into
ἐμβάπτω—dip in
βρέχω—to make wet, rain, soak
πίνω—to drink, receive refreshment, soak up
ὑγρός—wet, moist, fluid
βρύω—cause to pour out
ἐκχέω—pour out, shed forth, bestow or distribute largely, flow out, stream forth, spill, squander, waste
ἐπιχέω—pour on, pour over
ὑπερεκχύννομαι—overflow
καταχέω—pour over, pour down upon, shower down, melt down
τήκω—melt, render liquid, dissolve into liquid
κεράννυμι—to mix, mingle, dilute, blend, pour
λούω—wash, bathe
νίζω—wash, purge, cleanse
νίπτω—wash
ἄνιπτος—unwashed
ἀπονίζω—wash off
ἀπονίπτω—wash off

πλύνω—wash, wash clean, bathe

πρόσχυσις—pouring, sprinkling, spreading

ῥαίνω—sprinkle

ῥαντίζω—sprinkle, purify by ritual sprinkling with blood, purge of sin

ῥαντισμός—sprinkling

ἐπιρραίνω—to sprinkle upon or over

περιραντίζω—sprinkle around

ῥέω—flow

ῥύσις—a flowing issue, flow, hemorrhage

ἐπιβάλλω—cast upon, put upon, splash into as waves into a ship, attend to, think on

Location, Spacial Position

ἐνθάδε—here, in this place, to this place

ὧδε—here, hither, this place, in this case, at this point, on this occasion, under these circumstances

δεῦρο—come, come here

ἐκεῖ—there, in that place, to that place

ἐκεῖσε—there, in that place, to that place

ἐπέκεινα—beyond, farther on, on yonder side

ὑπερέκεινα—beyond, on the far side

αὐτοῦ—here, in this place, there, in that place

ἀλλαχοῦ—elsewhere, somewhere else, in another direction

ὅπου—where, to what place, in what place, whereas, insofar as, since

οὗ—where, place in which, whither, to which

πού—somewhere, in a certain place, somewhere around

ποῦ—where? in what place? where is? whither?

πανταχοῦ—everywhere, in all directions, throughout

πανταχῇ—everywhere, in every place, all over

πάντη—everywhere, in every way, altogether

ἄντικρυς—opposite to, against, to indicate an offshore location near a coastal city

ἀντιπέρα—opposite, on the other side from, across from

ἔναντι—with genitive: in the presence of, against, opposite, in the eyes of, in the sight of, in front of

ἀπέναντι—opposite, in front of, before, in the presence of, against, contrary

κατέναντι—opposite, against, before, in the presence of, in the sight of, in the judgement of, in the view of

ἐναντίον—opposite, in front of, against, contrary, blowing against

ἐνώπιον—in front of, before, in the presence of, in the sight of, in the eyes of

κατενώπιον—in front of, in the presence of, before, in the sight of, in the judgement of, in the view of

κατὰ πρόσωπον—in person

πρόσωπον—face, countenance, outward appearance, person

στόμα πρὸς στόμα—face to face

ὀπίσω—behind, back, after

ἔμπροσθεν—in front of, ahead, before, in the presence of, in the sight of

ἔξωθεν—from the outside, outwardly, externally

ἔσωθεν—from within, on the inside

ὄπισθεν—from behind, behind, on the back, after

κυκλόθεν—around, on the outside, on all sides, round about

μακρόθεν—from afar, from a distance, at a distance

πόρρωθεν—from a distance, at a distance, from afar, long before, far ahead of time

πάντοθεν—from all directions, from all sides, all over, on all sides, entirely

πόθεν—whence, from some place

ὅθεν—from where, whence, from which, from whom, wherefore, because of

ἐντεῦθεν—from here, from this place, hence, thence, henceforth, thenceforth, thereupon, from this source

ἐκεῖθεν—from there, from that place, thence, thereafter, next

κἀκεῖθεν—and from there, and then, and afterward

ἄνωθεν—from above, from an earlier period, anew, again

ἀλλαχόθεν—from elsewhere, from another place, by some other way

ἔξω—outside, without

ἔσω—inside, within, into

ἐσώτερος—comparative of ἔσω, inner, interior, farther in

ἔνειμι—be inside, be within

κάτω—downward, down, below

κατώτερος—comparative of κάτω, lower

ἄνω—above, up, upward

ἐπάνω—on, above, over, more than

ὑπεράνω—above, far above

ὑποκάτω—underneath, below, beneath, under the surface of, at the foot of, down before

μακράν—far away, at a distance, far off

μακρύνω—to be put at a distance, removed far away

ἀπέχω—have back, hold back, receive in full, be distanced, be sufficient (Mark 14:41), middle: hold one's self away, avoid, abstain

πόρρω—far away, a great way off, at a distance

πορρώτερον—comparative of πόρρω, farther

πέραν—across, on the other side, beyond

πέριξ—around, all about, neighboring

πλησίον—nearby, close, neighbor

ἐγγύς—near, nigh, at hand

ἄγχι—near

ἆσσον—comparative of ἄγχι, nearer, very close, very near

κύκλῳ—in a circle, all around, around, nearby

ἐκτός—outside, without, unless, except, besides, independent of

ἐντός—within, inside, among

μεταξύ—between, in the middle of, among, meanwhile

μέσος—middle, in the middle, in the midst, between, among, between, in the center

ἀνὰ μέσον—among, in the midst, in the middle, between

ὑψηλός—high, lofty, arrogant, proud, stately, high in value, exalted

ἄχρι—until, until the time of, before, as far as, up to, unto, as long as

ἕως—while, until, as far as, to the point of, so long as, for a time, up to

μέχρι(ς)—as far as, to the degree that

Location, Prepositions Of

ἀπό—with genitive: separation from, motion away from, out of, because of, on account of, as a result of, for, with, with the help of, by

διά—with genitive: through, by way of, throughout, during, within, after, in, with, among, in spite of, in consequence of, by, on the basis of, on account of

εἰς—with accusative: into, to, toward, on, inside, among

ἐκ—with genitive: from, out of, away from

ἐν—with dative: within, in, on, at, near, among

ἐπί—with genitive: on, in, at, by, near, in the presence of, before

ἐπί—with dative: on, in, at, near, by, against, over

ἐπί—with accusative: on, across, over, as far as, to, up to, against, on top of

κατά—with genitive: down from, down into

κατά—with accusative: on, through, over, along, toward, to, down to, in, from, by, during, in agreement with, about, after, for the purpose of, because of, as a result of, in relation to

μετά—with genitive: with, among, in company with, accompanied by, on the side of, against

μετά—with accusative: after, behind, beyond

παρά—with genitive: from

παρά—with dative: near, by, beside, with, among, before

παρά—with accusative: to, toward, alongside of, by, beside, at, beyond

περί—around, about, concerning

πρό—with genitive: before, in front of, ahead of, before in time, above in value

πρός—with dative: at, by, close to, before

πρός—with accusative: to, toward, against, with, before, among

ὑπό—with genitive: under, below, underneath, under control of, by, because of

Lose, Be Lost, Suffer Loss

ἀπόλλυμι—destroy, kill, lose, perish

ζημιόω—to inflict loss, damage, or injury, fine, punish

ζημία—damage, loss, detriment

πλανάω—to lead astray, wander, cause to depart from truth, passive: be lost, be deceived, be misled

πλάνη—deception, wandering, straying, error, perversion

πλάνος—wandering, misleading, leading into error, corrupting, deceitful

ἀποτάσσομαι—to leave, say goodbye, part with possessions, forsake

ἀποβάλλω—to throw off, cast from one, reject, lose

ἀποβολή—rejection, repudiation, loss, destruction, throwing away

Love, Affection, Compassion

ἀγαπάω—to love, cherish, be well-pleased with, be fond of, desire

ἀγάπη—love, concern, affection

ἀγαπητός—beloved, dear

φιλέω—to love, like, kiss

φιλία—friendship, love

φιλαδελφία—brotherly love

φιλάδελφος—brother-loving

φιλανθρωπία—love of mankind, benevolence, affection for people

φίλανδρος—loving one's husband

φιλότεκνος—loving one's children

φίλαυτος—loving one's self, selfish

φιλόθεος—loving God

φιλόστοργος—kindly affectioned, very affectionate, loving tenderly, of the tenderness between parents and children

στέργω—to love, feel affection for

ἄστοργος—without natural affection or love, unloving

ζηλόω—to burn with zeal or envy, be jealous over, to desire earnestly

ζῆλος—fervor of spirit, zeal, earnest concern, jealousy, indignation ἐπιποθέω—to long for, pursue with love, lust for, deeply desire, have great affection for

ἐπιπόθητος—longed for

ὁμείρομαι—to desire, long for, be affectionately desirous, 1 Thes 2:8

σπλαγχνίζομαι—to be moved in one's inward parts, to be moved with compassion, have pity on

εὔσπλαγχνος—compassionate, tender hearted, showing pity

πολύσπλαγχνος—full of pity, very kind, very compassionate

συμπαθέω—to suffer with, have compassion on, have sympathy for

συμπαθής—sympathetic, compassionate

οἰκτίρω—have mercy, pity, have compassion on

οἰκτιρμός—mercy, pity, sympathy

οἰκτίρμων—merciful, compassionate

M

Magic

μαγεία—magic, sorcery, the teachings of the Magians

μαγεύω—to practice magic

μάγος—a magician, a Persian or Babylonian wise man and priest who was expert in astrology, interpreting dreams and other secret arts

βασκαίνω—to slander, malign, disparage, envy, grudge, bewitch by means of spells

φαρμακεία—remedy, cure, the use of drugs, potions, spells, poisoning, witchcraft, sorcery

φάρμακον—a drug, medicine, remedy, cure, enchanted potion, charm, spell, poison, sorcery

φαρμακός—sorcerer, magician, poisoner

Make, Create

ποιέω—make, do, produce, cause to be, carry out, execute, appoint

ποίημα—what is made, product

πλάσσω—to form, fashion, make, mold

χειροποίητος—handmade, man-made, artificial

ἀχειροποίητος—not man-made

οἰκοδομέω—to build, edify, found upon, encourage, build up, make more able, embolden

οἰκοδομή—building, structure, construction

οἰκοδόμος—a builder, architect

γεννάω—give birth, bear, beget, bring forth, conceive, deliver, make

κτίζω—to create, bring into being, build

καταρτίζω—prepare, make adequate, mend, restore, create, perfect, make ready

κτίσμα—anything created, a creature

κτίσις—creation, the created universe, world, ordinance, institution

κτίστης—creator, founder, restorer

καταβολή—creation of the world, beginning, foundation

ἐργάζομαι—to work, do business, do, perform, produce, bring about

ἔργον—work, business, deed, act, action, workmanship, occupation, matter, task

ἐργάτης—worker, laborer

συνεργός—fellow worker being of the same trade, a working together, helping in work

δημιουργός—a skilled workman, builder, craftsman, architect, maker

τέχνη—art, skill, trade, handiwork, especially of metal-work, cunning

ὁμότεχνος—of the same trade

τεχνίτης—craftsman, skilled workman, architect

τέκτων—carpenter, craftsman, builder

Man, see also "Woman"
ἀνήρ—man, husband, adult male
ἄνθρωπος—man, plural: mankind
ἄρσην—male
θῆλυς—female
εὐνοῦχος—eunuch, chamberlain, manager of a king's bedchamber, impotent male, celibate male
εὐνουχίζω—be celibate, castrate, abstain
γέρων—old man
πρεσβύτερος—elder, old man, forefather, presbyter
πρεσβύτης—old man
νεανίας—young man
νεανίσκος—young man
παρθένος—virgin, unmarried person, chaste person

Many, Much, More
πολύς—many, often, much, mighty, great, to a great extent, with fullness
ἱκανός—sufficient, adequate, able, enough, considerable, satisfactory
πόσος—how many, how much, how far, how long, how great
ποσός—of a certain quantity or magnitude
ὅσος—as many as, as great as, as long as, how great, to the degree that, so much as is enough, enough, so far as
τοσοῦτος—so many, so much, so far, so great, to the degree that
πλῆθος—crowd, multitude
πλήρης—full (of), filled (with), complete, not lacking, as ripe grain
πολλαπλασίων—many times as much, manifold
μᾶλλον—more, to a greater degree, rather, instead of, comparative of μάλα
μάλα—very much, exceedingly, quite
μάλιστα—most, superlative of μάλα
μείζων—greater, older, more, comparative of μέγας
πλείων—more, larger, further, greater
παρά—beyond (degree)
ὑπέρ—over, above, exceeding, more than, beyond, for, instead of, in behalf of, for the sake of, for the purpose of
ἐπάνω—above, atop, on the upper part, more than
ἐκπερισσῶς—more exceedingly
περισσεία—surplus, abundance, excess
περισσεύω—to be more than enough, sufficient, be abundant, abound, provide in abundance
περισσότερος—excessive
περισσοτέρως—excessive
περισσος—beyond the regular number or size, extraordinary, remarkable, more than sufficient, greater than, in surplus
πλεονάζω—to be more than enough, be superfluous, go beyond bounds, take too much, have an excess of, abound in, be rich
ὑπερβάλλω—to overshoot, outdo, surpass, prevail over, exceed, bid more
ὑπερβολή—a throwing beyond, overshooting, superiority, over-great degree, overstrained phrase, hyperbole
ὑπερβαλλόντως—extremely, exceedingly
ὑπερεκπερισσοῦ—superabundantly
ὑπερπερισσεύω—to be more abundant, be excessive, abound more and more
ὑπερπερισσῶς—extremely
προηγέομαι—to go first, take the lead, go before, precede, go first, excel, do exceedingly

τηλικοῦτος—so great, so large, so important, so mighty

τηλίκος—so great

Marriage

γαμέω—to marry, betroth, wed

γαμίζω—to give in marriage

γάμος—marriage, wedlock, a wedding, a wedding-feast

ἐπιγαμβρεύω—to marry a brother's widow, marry as next of kin

γαμίσκω—give in marriage

συζεύγνυμι—join in marriage

ἁρμόζω—fit together, join, of clothes or armor, suit, betroth, set in order, arrange harmoniously

μνηστεύω—to woo, court, seek to marry, betroth, become engaged, promise in marriage

ὕπανδρος—under a man, subject to a man, married

σύζυγος—yoked together, paired, wedded union, yoke-fellow, comrade, fellow-worker

ἑτεροζυγέω—to be mismatched, be unequally yoked

ἄγαμος—unmarried, single

παρθένος—virgin, unmarried person, chaste person

Measures, Spacial Dimensions

μέτρον—measure, size, length

μετρέω—measure out, mete out, estimate, give a measure

βῆμα—distance measured by one stride, approximately 2.5 feet, an elevated platform ascended by steps, judicial bench

κανών—rule, measuring rod, the area over which one rules, the province assigned one, a principal or law of judging and acting

κάλαμος—reed, staff, measuring reed or rod, writer's reed, pen

ὕψος—height, high position, heaven

ὑψόω—to lift high, raise up, elevate, exalt

ὑψηλός—high, lofty, arrogant, proud, stately, high in value, exalted

ταπεινόω—to make low, abase, embarrass, make level, bring low, passive: be humble

μῆκος—length, distance, height, tallness, stature

μικρός—small, little, petty, trivial, slight, a short time

μακρός—long, far, distant, remote

πλάτος—breadth, width

πλατύς—wide

εὐρύχωρος—spacious, roomy, of a road, broad, wide

στενός—narrow, strict, exacting

ἡλικία—stature, maturity, of age

βάθος—depth, the deep, extreme, extremely

βαθύς—deep

βαθύνω—make deep

πῆχυς—cubit, forearm, a measure of length equivalent to 0.46 meters

ὀργυιά—the distance measured by a man's arms outstretched, about 1.9 meters; a fathom, a nautical technical term to gauge water depth

στάδιον—arena, stadium, racecourse; stade, a measure of distance

σαββάτου ὁδός—a sabbath day's journey, about 800 meters or 2,000 paces

χοῖνιξ—choenix, a dry measure equal to around 1 liter, considered a daily grain ration sufficient for one person

σάτον—batch, measure, seah, a Hebrew measure for grain equivalent to 13.5 liters

κόρος—the largest Hebrew dry measure, holding about half a kiloliter (Luke 16:7)
βάτος—bush, thorn bush, bath (a liquid measure of about 30 liters)
μετρητής—a liquid measure of about 40 liters
ζυγός—yoke, burden (of slavery or the law), the beam of a balance
βάρος—heaviness, weight, burden, trouble, hardship, heavy, tremendous

Meddlesome, Busybody, Gossip, see "Vices: Meddlesome, Busybody, Gossip"

Medicine

κολλούριον—eye salve
ἐσμυρνισμένος οἶνος—myrrhed wine, a painkiller
σμυρνίζω—mix with myrrh
μίγμα—mixture, medicine
φάρμακον—a drug, medicine, remedy, cure, enchanted potion, charm, spell, poison, sorcery
ἴαμα—means of healing, remedy, medicine, power to heal
πήγανον—rue, shrubby plant about two feet high with medicinal value

Memory, Recall

μιμνήσκομαι—to remember, remind, recall, be mindful of
μνεία—remembrance, memory
μνήμη—remembrance, memory
μνημονεύω—to remember, be mindful of, call to mind, hold in memory, keep in mind, make mention of
ἀναμιμνήσκω—remember, remind
ὑπομιμνήσκω—remember, remind
ἐπαναμιμνήσκω—to recall to mind again, put in mind, remind
ὑπόμνησις—remembrance
ἀνάμνησις—reminder, recollection, remembrance
μνημόσυνον—memorial, remembrance
μνημεῖον—monument, memorial, grave, tomb
λογίζομαι—to reckon, count, calculate, take into account, number among, consider, impute, reason, suppose, keep mental record
συντηρέω—to protect, preserve, treasure up, remember, keep in mind
σημειόομαι—mark, note, take note of
οἶδα—to see, perceive, know, regard

Merciful, see "Virtues: Mercy, Forgiveness"

Metals

χρυσίον—gold, gold coin, gold ornaments
χρυσός—gold
χρυσοῦς—golden, made of gold
ἀργύριον—silver
ἄργυρος—silver, silver money, white metal
ἀργυροῦς—made of silver
ἀργυροκόπος—silversmith
χαλκός—bronze, copper money
χαλκοῦς—made of bronze
χαλκεύς—metalworker
χαλκολίβανον—fine bronze
σίδηρος—iron
σιδηροῦς—made of iron

Military Terms, See "War Terms"

Mix, Unite, Make Whole

συμβιβάζω—join together, unite, put together in one's mind, conclude, prove, instruct, advise

συνίστημι—to commend, recommend, approve, show, intransitive: be set together, be formed into, consist of, hold together

σύνδεσμος—that which binds together, bond, of ligaments, that which is bound, a bundle

ἀνακεφαλαιόω—to sum up, summarize an argument, bring together

ὅλος—whole, entire, complete

πᾶς—all, any, whole, total, every kind of

ἑνότης—unity

εἷς—one (number), one (indefinite referent)

κεράννυμι—to mix, mingle, dilute, blend, pour

συγκεράννυμι—to commingle, blend with, compose, combine, unite

μίγνυμι—to mix, mingle, blend, join, be united to, bring together

μίγμα—mixture, medicine

συναναμίγνυμι—mix together, mingle, keep company with, be intimate with one, associate

φύραμα—that which is mixed and kneaded, mixture of dough, lump of dough, batch, lump of clay

Mock, Ridicule, see also "Vices: Accuse, Defame, Talk Foolishly"

ἐμπαιγμονή—to mock

ἐμπαιγμός—mocking, scoffing

ἐμπαίζω—to play with, trifle with, mock, delude, deceive, trick

ἐμπαίκτης—mocker, scoffer

χλευάζω—to mock, deride, jeer, joke at

διαχλευάζω—joke at, jeer, make fun of

ἐκμυκτηρίζω—deride by turning up the nose, sneer at, scoff at, ridicule

μυκτηρίζω—to turn up the nose or sneer at, mock, deride, ridicule

καταγελάω—to deride, laugh to scorn, laugh at

Modesty, Propriety, Respect, see "Virtues: Respect, Modesty", see also "Honor"

Monetary Terms

δανείζω—active: give a loan, lend money, passive: borrow money

δάνειον—debt, loan

δανειστής—moneylender, creditor

δαπάνη—cost, expense, outgoing

τόκος—interest on a loan, usury

τοκίζω—to lend on interest

κίχρημι—lend

χρῆμα—a thing that one uses or needs, a good, property, money, gear, wealth, matter, affair, event

τράπεζα—table, moneylender's bench, hence bank

τραπεζίτης—banker, moneychanger

βάλλω—deposit, put, place, throw, cast, hurl

τίθημι—to put, place, set, deposit

παρακαθήκη—deposit, bank deposit

ἀρραβών—down-payment, first installment, pledge, deposit that is forfeited if the transaction fails

ὑποθήκη—suggestion, counsel, warning, piece of advice, pledge, mortgage

δίδωμι—to give

αἴρω—lift, raise up, elevate, remove, withdraw, take away, kill, destroy

καταλλαγή—reconciliation, exchange, profits of an exchange

καταλλάσσω—to reconcile, change money, exchange

Money

χρῆμα—a thing that one uses or needs, a good, property, money, gear, wealth, matter, affair, event

ἄργυρος—silver, silver money
χρυσός—gold money
χαλκός—bronze, copper money
νόμισμα—coin
κέρμα—coin
δηνάριον—Roman silver coin equal to a day's wage
ἀσσάριον—copper coin worth 1/16th denarius
κοδράντης—quadrans, copper coin worth ¼ assarion
λεπτόν—copper coin worth ½ quadrans
δραχμή—Greek silver coin equal to a denarius
στατήρ—stater, Greek coin worth four drachmas
μνᾶ—mina, Greek coin worth 100 denarii or 1/10 talent
τάλαντον—talent, Greek coin worth 1000 denarii

Mountain

ὄρος—mountain (different from ὅρος, boundary)
ὀρεινή—mountainous region
βουνός—hill
ὀφρῦς—cliff
κρημνός—steep slope, bank

Mouth Functions, see also "Eat, Drink, Consume"

μασάομαι—bite, chew, consume, eat, devour, gnaw
δάκνω—to bite
βρυγμός—τῶν ὀδόντων gnash the teeth
τρίζω τοὺς ὀδόντας—gnash the teeth
ἐπιλείχω—lick, lick up, lick off
λείχω—lick
ἐμπτύω—spit upon
πτύω—spit
ἐμέω—vomit, throw up, spew

Move

κινέω—set in motion, move, excite a disturbance or riot, shake
μεθίστημι—remove, lead away, transfer
χωρέω—make space for, go forward, advance, move on, have room for, accept, open one's heart to, be friendly toward
ἀποχωρίζομαι—separate, sever, part asunder, depart from, move away
μακρύνω—to be put at a distance, removed far away

Music, Song, Dance

συμφωνία—music, symphony
μουσικός—musician
κιθάρα—lyre
κιθαρίζω—play the lyre
κιθαρῳδός—harpist
αὐλός—flute
αὐλέω—play the flute
αὐλητής—flutist
σάλπιγξ—trumpet, trumpet sounds
σαλπίζω—play the trumpet
σαλπιστής—trumpeter
κύμβαλον—cymbals
χαλκὸς ἠχῶν—brass gong
ᾄδω—to sing
ᾠδή—song
ψάλλω—to sing praises, pluck strings of an instrument, sing to harp accompaniment
ψαλμός—song of praise
ὑμνέω—sing a hymn
ὕμνος—hymn
θρηνέω—to mourn, lament, sing a dirge, wail, sing funeral songs
θρῆνος—lamentation, song of grief
χορός—choral dancing, a dance, chorus, choir
ὀρχέομαι—dance

N

Name, Call

ὄνομα—name

ὀνομάζω—to name, designate, call, mention a name, passive: be named, be known about, be heard of

τοὔνομα—named, by the name of

ἐπονομάζομαι—to put a name upon, name, call, call oneself

ψευδώνυμος—falsely called, falsely so called, falsely named

καλέω—to call, invite, bid, name

ἐπικαλέω—call, give a name to, middle: invoke, make an appeal to

ἐπιλέγω—to choose, call, name

λέγω—to say, speak, to call, name

χρηματίζω—to give a divine message, speak, warn, to receive a title, be called

προσαγορεύω—to address, greet, call by a name, give a name or title to

Necessary, Inevitable, Should, Ought

δεῖ—to be bound, be necessary, it must be, ought, should

χρή—to be fated, necessary, one must, should, it behooves one, it befits one to do something

χρεία ἔχω—to have need, necessity, be in need, ought

ὀφειλή—that which is owed, a debt, obligation

ὀφείλω—to be bound, be obliged, owe, be indebted to, be due, be liable to, would that, ought

ὀφείλημα—that which is owed, a debt, obligation

ὀφειλέτης—a debtor, one who is obligated

ὄφελον—would that, O that, if only, functions as a particle introducing unattainable wishes

ἀνάγκη—force, constraint, necessity, obligation, what is inevitable, calamity, straights, distress

ἀναγκαῖος—necessary, essential, indispensable

ἀναγκαστῶς—by obligation, by constraint, inevitably, necessarily

ἐπάναγκες—necessarily, by compulsion

εὐσεβέω—to worship, reverence, live or act piously and religiously, fulfill one's duties to a deity

ἔξεστι—it is allowed, in one's power, possible, permitted, lawful, ought to

μέλλω—to be about to, intend to, be destined to, be going to περισσός—(antonym) beyond the regular number or size, abundant, profuse, more than sufficient, extraordinary, superfluous, having surplus, excessive, extravagant, unnecessary

ἀδύνατος—(antonym) incapable, unable, without strength, powerless, disabled, poor, impossible

Negation, Affirmation

ναί—yes, indeed, certainly, quite so

ἄρα—then, consequently, as a result, so, you see, to be sure, indeed

μή—not, the negative used with moods other than indicative, used in questions expecting a no answer

μήτε—nor, and not, neither

μήτι—not, interrogative particle expecting a no answer

μηδαμῶς—by no means, certainly not, no

μηδέ—and not, but not, nor, not even

μηδέπω—not yet, not as yet, nor as yet

μήπω—not yet

μηκέτι—no longer, no more, no further

μηδείς—no one, nothing

μηδέποτε—never

μήποτε—never, on no account, lest ever

οὔ—no, not, by no means

οὗ—where

οὔτε—nor

οὐχί—no, emphatic form of οὐ

οὐκ—so not, not then, surely not

οὐδαμῶς—by no means, in no way, certainly not

οὐδαμοῦ—nowhere, answering to ποῦ or οὗ or ὅπου (where?) Can be said οὐ ποῦ, no where

οὐδέ—and not, not even, neither, nor

οὐκοῦν—not therefore, so not, not then

οὔκουν—same as οὐκοῦν but losing all negative force: therefore, then, accordingly, so then, doubtless

οὐδέπω—not yet

οὔπω—not yet

οὐκέτι—no longer, no more, no further

οὐδείς—no one, nothing

οὐδέποτε—never

Neighbor

πλησίον—nearby, close, neighbor

περίοικος—neighbor, one living near

περιοικέω—to live nearby, live in the vicinity, be a neighbor

γείτων—neighbor, one of the same land and culture

συνομορέω—be next to, be next door to, border on, adjoin

ὅρος—boundary, limit

New

καινότης—newness, freshness, novelty

καινός—new, fresh, de novo, produced for the first time

νέος—young, youthful, new, fresh

ἀνακαινόω—cause growth, make new, give new strength

ἀνακαίνωσις—renewal

ἀνανεόω—to renew, make new

παλιγγενεσία—rebirth, restoration, resurrection, regeneration, a new age

πρόσφατος—fresh, recent, new

Numbers, To Number

ἀριθμός—number, amount, sum, total, quantity, a numbering, counting, numeration

ἀριθμέω—to number, count, count out, pay, count as, reckon, consider

ψηφίζω—to count up, reckon, figure out, vote for

συμψηφίζω—to reckon together, count up, add up, calculate
συγκαταψηφίζομαι—to count, be reckoned along with
ἥμισυς—one half
εἷς—one (number), one (indefinite referent)
δύο—two
τρεῖς—three
τέσσαρες—four
πέντε—five
ἕξ—six
ἑπτά—seven
ὀκτώ—eight
ἐννέα—nine
δέκα—ten
ἕνδεκα—eleven
δώδεκα—twelve
δεκατέσσαρες—fourteen
δεκαπέντε—fifteen
δέκα—eighteen
εἴκοσι(ν)—twenty
τριάκοντα—thirty
τεσσαράκοντα—forty
πεντήκοντα—fifty
ἑξήκοντα—sixty
ἑβδομήκοντα—seventy
ὀγδοήκοντα—eighty
ἐνενήκοντα—ninety
ἑκατόν—one hundred
διακόσιοι—two hundred
τριακόσιοι—three hundred
τετρακόσιοι—four hundred
πεντακόσιοι—five hundred
ἑξακόσιοι—six hundred
χίλιοι—one thousand
δισχίλιοι—two thousand
τρισχίλιοι—three thousand
τετρακισχίλιοι—four thousand
πεντακισχίλιοι—five thousand

ἑπτακισχίλιοι—seven thousand
μυριάς—ten thousand, a myriad, countless numbers
μύριοι—ten thousand, numberless, countless, measureless, immense, endless, incessant, much
δισμύριοι—twenty thousand
ἀναρίθμητος—not able to be counted, countless, innumerable
πρῶτος—first, earliest, before, foremost, most important, best
πρότερος—first, before, in front, forward, former, sooner, above, superior, foremost, beginning
δεύτερος—second, afterward
τρίτος—third
τρίτον—third part
τέταρτος—fourth, fourth part
πέμπτος—fifth
ἕκτος—sixth
ἕβδομος—seventh
ὄγδοος—eighth
ἔνατος—ninth
δέκατος—tenth, tenth part
ἑνδέκατος—eleventh
δωδέκατος—twelfth
τεσσαρεσκαιδέκατος—fourteenth
πεντεκαιδέκατος—fifteenth
ἅπαξ—once
ἐφάπαξ—at once, at one time, once for all
δίς—twice
ἅπαξ καὶ δίς—several times
τρίς—three times
τετράκις—four times
πεντάκις—five times
ἑξάκις—six times
ἑπτάκις—seven times
ἑβδομηκοντάκις—seventy times
πολλάκις—often, many times
διπλοῦς—double

τετραπλοῦς—four times, fourfold　　ζεῦγος—pair, couple
τετραπλόος—four times, fourfold　　χιλιάς—one thousand
ἑκατονταπλασίων—a hundredfold　　ἑξακισχίλιοι—six thousand

O

Oath, Vow
ὀμνύω—swear, make an oath, invoke as a witness in making an oath
ὁρκίζω—to put under oath, force to take an oath, adjure, charge
ὅρκος—an oath, that which has been pledged or promised with an oath
ὁρκωμοσία—oath, the taking of an oath, affirmation made on oath
ἐπιορκέω—to swear falsely, forswear one's self, break an oath
ἐπίορκος—perjurer, false swearer
ἐνορκίζω—put under oath
ἐξορκίζω—put under oath, adjure
εὐχή—prayer, vow

Obey, see "Virtues: Obedience"

Offend
σκάνδαλον—a trap, offense, stumbling block, temptation
σκανδαλίζω—put a stumbling block in the way, offend, cause to sin
προσκόπτω—to strike against, beat upon, stumble, take offense at
πρόσκομμα—a stumbling block, obstacle, offense
προσκοπή—a stumbling block, obstacle, offense
ἐγκόπτω—to hinder, prevent, delay, impede, thwart
ἀπρόσκοπος—not causing offense

Often
πολύς—many, often, much, mighty, great, to a great extent, with fullness
πολλάκις—often, many times
ποσάκις—how often, how many times
πυκνῶς—often, frequently
πυκνός—frequent, numerous, often
πυκνός—as often as possible
διὰ παντός—regularly, through all

Old, see also "Time: Long Duration"
παλαιότης—antiquity, obsoleteness
παλαιός—old, aged, ancient, from older time
γῆρας—old age

Open, Close
ἀνοίγω—to open, give access to
διανοίγω—to open, explain
εφφαθα—be opened, Aramaic
πλατύνω—widen, enlarge, make broad
κλείω—to close, shut, lock, bar
ἀποκλείω—to close, shut
καμμύω—to close

Opportunity, Occasion, see "Favorable Circumstances"

Oppose, Contradict

ἀντιλέγω—to speak against, oppose, contradict

ἀντιλογία—contradiction, opposition, rebellion, strife, dispute

ἀντίθεσις—opposition, contradiction

ἀναντίρρητος—indisputable, not to be contradicted, undeniable, not able to be spoken against

ἀναντιρρήτως—indisputably, without objection, without hesitation

Or

ἤ—or

ἤτοι . . . ἤ—whether. . . or, either . . . or

P

Pain, Suffering

πάθημα—suffering, passion

παθητός—subject to suffering, able to suffer, passible, destined to suffer

πάσχω—to suffer, experience, feel, undergo, have a sensory experience, have passion

προπάσχω—to suffer before

συμπάσχω—to suffer with, share the same suffering

συμπαθέω—to have compassion on, have sympathy for, join in suffering

συγκακοπαθέω—to suffer hardship with, join in suffering

κακοπάθεια—the suffering of evil, suffering distress or affliction

κακοπαθέω—to suffer or endure evils, to be afflicted, suffer distress or trouble

πόνος—hard work, toil, exhaustion, pain, anguish

αἴρω τὸν σταυρόν—to take up the cross, to suffer unto death

συγκακουχέομαι—to be ill treated along with, share persecutions, join in suffering

βασανισμός—torture, tormenting

βάσανος—torture, torment, pain

ὠδίν—birth pains, sorrow, travail

ὠδίνω—to have birth pains, travail, suffer greatly

συνωδίνω—to feel the pains of travail with, be in travail together, suffer together

ὀδυνάομαι—be in intense pain, be in terrible anguish, be tormented

ὀδύνη—pain, grief, sorrow

πύρωσις—burning, refining, trial, suffering

συγκάμπτω τὸν νῶτον—bend the back, be burdened with trouble

Part, Division, Separation

μερίς—part, district, portion, share

μέρος—part, piece, share, district, region of a country

ἀπὸ μέρους—in part

ἐκ μέρους—in part

μέλος—member, part, body part

κλῆρος—a lot, a casting or drawing of lots, a piece of land, a portion, share, inheritance, fate, destiny

πολυμερής—consisting of many parts, manifold, of diverse kinds, in many portions, fragmentary

ἀπό—with genitive: apart from

ἐκ—with genitive: one of, from

λοιπός—from now on, the remaining, to mark an added fact: furthermore, also, in addition, beyond that, finally

ἐπίλοιπος—remaining, still left

κατάλοιπος—remaining, left, the rest

λεῖμμα—remnant, what is left, remains
ὑπόλειμμα—remnant
διαμερίζω—to divide, distribute, give out parts, be divided into opposing parts, be at variance, be in discord
διαμερισμός—division, dissension
μερίζω—to divide, distribute, assign, apportion
μερισμός—distribution, parting, dividing, severance, separation
μεριστής—a divider
σχίζω—divide, rend, split into factions
αἵρεσις—sect, religious party, division, faction, heretical group, false teaching
ἀφορίζω—separate, set apart, exclude
χωρίζω—separate, divide, part, divorce, depart
ἀποχωρίζομαι—separate, sever, part asunder, depart from, move away
χωρίς—separately, apart, by oneself, besides, with no relation to

Patience, Endurance, Perseverance

μακροθυμία—patience, endurance, steadfastness, forbearance, constancy, perseverance, longsuffering
μακροθυμέω—to be patient, not lose heart, be longsuffering, be slow to avenge wrong, to endure
μακροθύμως—patiently
ἀνέχομαι—to put up with, be patient with, bear with, endure, accept
ἀνοχή—patience, toleration, forbearance
ἀνεκτός—endurable, tolerable, bearable,
ἀνεξίκακος—tolerant, forbearing, patient of ills and wrongs
τροποφορέω—to put up with, bear one's manner, endure one's character
ὑπομονή—steadfastness, constancy, endurance, patience, waiting for
ὑπομένω—to remain, abide, endure, persevere, be patient under
ὑποφέρω—to bear up, endure patiently
στέγω—endure, hold off, put up with
στέγη—roof
φέρω—bring, bear, carry
βαστάζω—carry a weight, endure
καρτερέω—to be steadfast, continue in

Pattern, Example, Type, Representation

τύπος—form, example (1 Cor.10:6), type, pattern (of something future), scar, mark (John 20:25), image (Acts 7:43)
ὑποτύπωσις—form, example, outline, pattern
τυπικῶς—as an example or warning
ἀντίτυπος—corresponding, answering to, echoing, figuring or representing something, fulfilling, substantivally: a copy, representation, antitype
ἐντυπόω—to engrave, imprint
τύπτω—strike, beat, smite, wound
ὑπογραμμός—example, pattern to be copied in writing or drawing
ὑπόδειγμα—an example to follow
σκιά—shade, shadow, foreshadow
εἰκών—image, form, representation, likeness, appearance, similitude, portrait, statue
χαρακτήρ—exact representation
παραβολή—a parable, a story portraying a truth, an example by which a teaching is illustrated, aphorism, proverb
πατήρ—father, father as a prototype or archetype of a group

συστοιχέω—to correspond to, be in the same category, of soldiers: to stand in the same line, be in the same rank, while ἀντισυστοιχέω is to be in opposite categories

στοιχεῖα—one of a series, elementary part, the elements, basic principles, rudiments, the elements of knowledge, in the order of the letters, alphabetically

Pay, see "Salary, Pay..."

Peace, Peaceful, see also "Virtues: Peace" and "Agreement"

εἰρήνη—peace, state of tranquility, felicity, harmony, freedom from worry

εἰρηνικός—peaceable, peaceful, free from worry

εἰρηνεύω—keep peace, live peaceably

ἡσυχάζω—to keep quiet, be silent, rest, cease from labor, of observing the sabbath, to lead a quiet life, hold one's peace, be still, be calm

ἡσύχιος—quiet, tranquil, peaceful, at rest, possessing an inward calm

ἡσυχία—quietness, silence, quiet circumstances, quiet living, rest

ἤρεμος—quiet, tranquil, peaceful

ἔρημος—deserted, lonely

People, Person

λαός—people

ἀνθρώπινος—human

ἄνθρωπος—man, plural: mankind

υἱοὶ τῶν ἀνθρώπων—sons of men

υἱός—son, descendant

ἀνήρ—man, husband, adult male

ἐπίγειος—earthly, terrestrial, existing upon the earth

σῶμα—body of man or animal, heavenly body, collection of people

πρόσωπον—face, countenance, outward appearance, person

σάρξ—flesh, body, natural generation, the sensual nature, human nature

σάρκινος—fleshly, made of flesh, belonging to the realm of the flesh in being weak, sinful, transitory, carnal, of humanity, worldly

σὰρξ καὶ αἷμα—human, flesh and blood

γλῶσσα—tongue, language, people group who have the same language

ψυχή—breath, soul, living being, person, life, inner self

γῆ—earth, ground, dirt, land, world, country, region

οἰκουμένη—the inhabited world

κόσμος—world, earth, as the ordered arrangement of creation, ornament, adornment as on a woman, world system

δῆμος—people, family, public assembly

Perfect

τέλειος—complete, ended, perfect, full grown, adult, of full age, mature

τελειότης—completion, perfection, wholeness, maturity

τελειόω—make perfect, complete, accomplish, end, reach maturity, execute, finish, make happen

τελείωσις—fulfillment, perfection, accomplishment, completion

ὁλοκληρία—complete health, perfect soundness, unimpaired condition of the body

Perfume, Incense

ἄρωμα—perfumed ointment, sweet scented spice

μύρον—a plant-based perfume, ointment

μυρίζω—to anoint with perfume, apply unguent to

σμύρνα—myrrh, a bitter gum and costly perfume exuding from an Arabian tree used in embalming and as antiseptic; Smyrna

ἀλόη—aloe, aloes

νάρδος—perfume of nard, East Indian fragrant additive

θυμίαμα—incense, fragrant stuffs for burning or embalming

λίβανος—frankincense the tree, perfume made from the tree

Perplexity

ἀπορία—perplexity, frustration

ἀπορέω—to be at a loss, left wanting, perplexed, in doubt, uncertain

διαπορέω—to be entirely at a loss, be perplexed, in doubt

αἴνιγμα—an obscure saying, enigma, riddle, dim image

δυσνόητος—difficult to understand

ἀνεξεραύνητος—not able to be searched out

ἀνεξιχνίαστος—untraceable, not able to be searched out

ἀγνοέω—to be ignorant, to not know, to fail to understand, to be wrong

ἀγνωσία—not knowing, ignorance, lack of knowledge, failure to understand

Perversion, Licentiousness, see "Vices: Perversion"

Physical

ψυχικός—pertaining to the natural mind, emotions, or strength, natural, worldly, opposite πνευματικός

σαρκικός—fleshly, carnal, having the nature of flesh, controlled by animal appetites, human, depraved, worldly, material, natural, physical, sensual

σάρκινος—made of flesh, natural, earthly, living in the body

σχῆμα—outward form, looks, fashion, appearance, show, pretense, air of a person, form, manner, way, posture

Pierce

ἐκκεντέω—to pierce with a sword or javelin unto death, possibly to bore the ear of slaves

νύσσω—pierce, prick, poke, jab, nudge

παίω—strike, smite, sting, hit

διϊκνέομαι—go through, penetrate, pierce

περιπείρω—pierce through, impale

τρυπάω—to pierce, bore (the ear with an awl)

τρυμαλιά—hole

Plan, Intend, Purpose

βουλεύομαι—to deliberate, consider, take counsel, resolve, purpose, think about carefully, intend

βούλομαι—to will deliberately, plan, purpose, desire, intend, wish

βουλή—will, counsel, purpose, intention, advice

βούλημα—will, counsel, purpose, intention, desire

θέλω—to will, desire, wish, intend, be resolved, be determined, purpose

θέλημα—what one wishes or has determined to do, purpose, will, command, precept, choice, desire

μελετάω—to meditate on, plot, think about, attend to, practice, rehearse

προμελετάω—to meditate beforehand, plan ahead, rehearse

προτίθεμαι—to place before, set forth, offer, purpose, plan beforehand

πρόθεσις—an offering, the offering bread in the tabernacle, a placing of something in view, a plan προνοέω—foresee, plan beforehand, be provident, provide for, take care of, take thought for

ἑκουσίως—voluntarily, willingly, of one's own free will, not forced

γνώμη—the mind, reason, judgement, opinion, intention, purpose

ἔννοια—thought, mind, intent, idea, attitude, insight, purpose

ἐπίνοια—thought, purpose, intent

οἰκονομία—stewardship, management of a household, administration, dispensation, plan

ἐφευρετής—an inventor, contriver, deviser

ἐνεδρεύω—to lie in wait for, prepare a trap for, make plans against, be in ambush

ἐπιβουλή—a plan formed against one, plot

συστροφή—coalition, conspiracy, riot, revolt, uproar

συνωμοσία—a swearing together, conspiracy, plot

συμβουλεύω—counsel, consult, deliberate, advise

συμβούλιον—counsel, consultation, deliberation, planning

σκοπέω—to watch, look out, inspect, examine, reconnoiter, premeditate, consider

ἀδήλως—(antonym) uncertainly, aimlessly, not manifestly, dubiously

δῆλος—clear, evident, manifest, certain

Plant, see also "Tree"

κῆπος—garden, plantation, orchard

φυτεία—plant

χλωρός—green, grassy, fresh as new growth

βοτάνη—herb fit for fodder, grass

χόρτος—place for grazing, grass, fodder, hay, provender, sproutings

βάτος—bush, thorn bush, bath (a liquid measure of about 30 liters)

ἄκανθα—thorn, bramble, bush, brier, thorny plant

ἀκάνθινος—thorny, woven from thorns

τρίβολος—thistle, prickly wild plant

κάλαμος—reed, staff, measuring reed or rod, writer's reed, pen

ἄψινθος—wormwood, name of star which fell into the waters and made them bitter

σίναπι—mustard

πήγανον—rue, shrubby plant about two feet high with medicinal value

ἡδύοσμον—mint

ἄνηθον—anise, dill

κύμινον—cumin

ὕσσωπος—hyssop

ἄμπελος—grapevine

ἀμπελών—vineyard

λάχανον—garden plant

ζιζάνιον—a weed, darnel, resembling wheat but grains are black

σῖτος—wheat

κρίνον—flower, lily

Plant Parts

ῥίζα—root of a plant

χόρτος—place for grazing, grass, fodder, hay, provender, the sprouting of a plant before—it develops fruit

κλάδος—branch, posterity

κλῆμα—branch

φύλλον—leaf

στιβάς—leafy branch

βάϊον—palm branch

ἄνθος—flower

ἄχυρον—chaff, straw

καλάμη—stalk, stubble

πιότης—fatness, richness, plumpness, rich sap

Plant Products, see also "Spices"

οἶνος—wine

γλεῦκος—sweet wine

σίκερα—strong drink, intoxicating beverage other than wine, liquor, intoxicant

ὄξος—sour wine, vinegar

ἔλαιον—olive oil

Plunder, Spoils, Booty, see also "Vices: Stealing"

ἁρπαγή—the act of plundering, robbery, plunder, spoil, booty

ἁρπάζω—snatch greedily, carry off by force, seize, plunder, claim for one's self eagerly, overpower

ἁρπαγμός—a plunder, booty, seizing, prize, something held by force

σκῦλα—spoils, booty, prey, plunder

λῃστής—a robber, plunderer, pirate, buccaneer, rebel

συλαγωγέω—take captive, prey on

ἄγρα—catch, that taken in hunting, booty, prey, game, a haul of fish

Point, Corner, Tip, Sharp

ἄκρον—extremity, tip, farthest boundary, end

κέρας—horn, hornlike projections on an altar, corner

κεραία—a little horn, extremity, apex, point, part of a letter, accent mark

ἀρχή—ruler, first in power, origin, beginning, first cause, elementary aspect, the end or corner of a thing

γωνία—corner

κέντρον—any sharp point, a horse goad, spur, prick, incentive, stinger, the center of a circle

βελόνη—needle, any sharp point

ὀξύς—sharp, keen, pointed, piercing, shrill, of taste, sour, pungent, of time, hasty, quick, swift

τομός—sharp, cutting

δίστομος—double-edged

αἰχμή—the point of a spear, spearmen

σκόλοψ—something pointed, stake, splinter, thorn, injurious sharp object, sharply painful affliction

ἄκανθα—thorn, bramble, bush, brier, thorny plant

τρίβολος—thistle, prickly wild plant

Poor, Needy, Poverty

πτωχεία—poverty, destitution

πτωχός—poor, destitute

πτωχεύω—be in poverty, be a beggar

ὑστέρησις—need, want, poverty

ὑστέρημα—deficiency, need, poverty, destitution, shortcoming, lack

ὑστερέω—to be in need, be lacking, be wanting, fall short, arrive late

χρεία—need, necessity

χρῄζω—need

ἐλαττονέω—have too little, diminish, have less, be inferior, lack, want

κενός—empty, vain, devoid of truth, containing nothing, foolish, without purpose, without result, fruitless

λείπω—to leave, leave alone, leave out, leave undone, lack, be deficient in, fall short, impersonal active 3rd person: what remains, what is wanting

ἐκλείπω—to fail, die out, cease

ἐνδεής—in need, needy, poor

ἐπιτήδειος—needed (James 2:16), necessary, suitable, fit

προσδέομαι—need something more, want further, need in addition

πενιχρός—poor, needy

πένης—poor man, laborer

ἀποτάσσομαι—to leave, say goodbye, part with possessions, forsake

ζημιόω—to inflict loss, damage, or injury, fine, punish

ζημία—damage, loss, detriment

Possible, Possibly, Probably, Perhaps

ἴσως—probably, perhaps

ἔξεστι—it is allowed, in one's power, possible, permitted, lawful

ἐνδέχεται—it is admitted, allowed, possible, practiced

ἀνοίγω θύραν—open the door, make possible

τόπος—region, place, possibility

ἄν—ever, would, may

ἐάν—if, if indeed, ever, when

εἰ ἄρα—whether, perhaps, possibly

ἄρα—consequently, as a result, perhaps, possibly

εἰ τύχοι—if it should happen or turn out that way, perhaps, possibly

τυγχάνω—to meet with, have happen, come upon, experience

δυνατός—strong, mighty, able, fit for service, possible (Matthew 26:39)

ἀδύνατος—(antonym) incapable, unable, without strength, powerless, disabled, impossible

ἀνένδεκτος—impossible

Power, Force

δύναμις—power, might, strength, authority, force, ability

κράτος—strength, might, sovereignty, power, dominion, mastery, authority

κραταιός—powerful, strong, mighty

κραταιόω—make strong, strengthen

ἰσχυρός—strong, mighty, powerful

ἐξουσία—authority, power, license, permission, legal right

δόξα—glory, splendor, brightness

μεγαλειότης—majesty, mighty power

μεγαλεῖος—magnificent, splendid, stately, haughty, mighty act

χείρ—hand, upholding or aid, hand of power or strength

βραχίων ὑψηλός—raised arm, great power

κέρας—horn of an animal, an extension or projection, symbol of deliverance or power, horn of salvation

σκληρός—hard, harsh, rough, stiff, stern, strong, forceful, violent, offensive, intolerable, demanding

ἐπίκειμαι—lie upon, press upon, press against a retreating enemy, be imposed, be in force, be urgent

κυρόω—to confirm, ratify, validate, conclude, decide in favor of, affirm

προκυρόω—to make valid or ratify previously, validate in advance

ἵστημι—stand, place, put, establish, set, continue to be, remain firmly

Praise, Worship, Reverence, see also "Prostrate"

αἴνεσις—praise

αἰνέω—to praise, extol

αἶνος—praise, laudatory discourse

ἐπαινέω—to praise, commend, laud

ἔπαινος—praise, commendation

ἀλληλουϊά—hallelujah, praise the Lord

δέος—reverence, awe, fear

δοξάζω—to praise, extol, glorify, magnify, honor, render excellent

ὁμολογέω—declare, profess, confess, claim, give thanks, praise

ἐξομολογέω—agree, promise, consent, middle: confess, praise, thank

εὐλογέω—praise, bless, consecrate with solemn prayers

εὐλογητός—to be praised, blessed

εὐλογία—praise, laudation, polished language, benediction, consecration, blessing, gift, of the alms collected for the poor

εὐφημία—praise, good report, the utterance of good words
εὔφημος—worthy of praise, of good report, speaking auspiciously
εὐπάρεδρος—devotion, constant waiting on the Lord, constantly attending
ἑδραῖος—firm, steadfast
θαυμάζω—to wonder, marvel, be astonished, be amazed, honor, admire, worship, respect
θαυμαστόω—to magnify
προσκυνέω—prostrate oneself before, do homage, make obeisance, worship
προσκυνητής—worshiper
κυνέω—kiss, plead
θεραπεία—nurture, care, medical service, tending to the sick, curing, healing, service to a god, worship
θεραπεύω—to care for, serve, treat, especially of a physician, heal, minister to, serve in a temple
θρησκεία—religious worship
κάμπτω τὸ γόνυ—to bow the knee, worship
λειτουργέω—to perform religious service or temple duties, minister
λειτουργία—a liturgy, temple service, the service of a minister
λειτουργός—priest, servant, minister
λειτουργικός—serving, ministering
ὀνομάζω τὸ ὄνομα κυρίου—to name the name of the Lord, say that you belong to the Lord
προσπίπτω—prostrate one's self in homage or supplication, fall down before, rush upon, beat against
σεβάζομαι—worship
σέβασμα—sanctuary, object of worship
σέβομαι—worship
εὐσεβέω—to worship, fulfill one's duties
φοβέομαι—to fear, have respect
φόβος—fear, dread, terror, reverence
μεγαλύνω—to make great, magnify, declare great, esteem highly, extol, laud, enlarge, praise the greatness of, honor highly
ὡσαννά—hosanna, save
εἰδωλολάτρης—worshiper of idols
εἰδωλολατρία—idolatry
ἀφόβως—without fear, without reverence to God, disgracefully

Pray

εὐχή—prayer, vow
εὔχομαι—to pray, wish, will, desire
προσευχή—prayer, a place set apart for the offering of prayer
προσεύχομαι—to pray
ἔντευξις—petition, prayer
ἐντυγχάνω—entreat, appeal to, plead, make intercession for, petition
ὑπερεντυγχάνω—to intercede for
αἰτέω—ask for, request, beg
αἴτημα—request
δέομαι—to pray, ask for, beg, plead, beseech
δέησις—plea, prayer, request, supplication, entreaty
ἱκετηρία—supplication, prayer, plea
ζητέω—to seek, inquire into

Preach, Proclaim

κηρύσσω—to herald with formality and authority, publish, proclaim openly, announce, preach, tell
προκηρύσσω—to announce beforehand, preach beforehand
κήρυγμα—the message proclaimed by a herald or public crier, preaching, proclamation
κῆρυξ—a herald, messenger vested with public authority, preacher of the divine word

λόγος—word, reason, matter under discussion, account, treatise, statement

θεόπνευστος—inspired by God

εὐαγγελίζω—to announce good news, bring glad tidings, preach the gospel

εὐαγγέλιον—good tidings, the good news of salvation through Christ, the proclamation of the grace of God given by faith in Christ

Precede

προάγω—precede, go before, happen previously

προπορεύομαι—send before, precede, go before

προέρχομαι—go forward, go on, go prior to, precede, go in advance of another, pass on

φθάνω—come before, precede, arrive at, reach, attain, come upon, happen

προβαίνω—go forwards, go on, move on (e.g., in age)

προτρέχω—run in front of, run before, outrun, precede

Precious Stones

λίθος τίμιος—precious stone, gem

ἴασπις—jasper

σάπφιρος—sapphire

χαλκηδών—agate

σμάραγδος—emerald

σμαράγδινος—made of emerald

σάρδιον—carnelian

χρυσόλιθος—chrysolite

χρυσόπρασος—chrysoprase

βήρυλλος—beryl

τοπάζιον—topaz

ὑάκινθος—jacinth or hyacinth

ἀμέθυστος—amethyst

μαργαρίτης—pearl

ἐλεφάντινος—made of ivory

μάρμαρος—marble

κρύσταλλος—crystal

κρυσταλλίζω—to shine like crystal

ὕαλος—glass, something transparent like glass

διοπετής—stone from heaven

Predict, Foretell

προλέγω—to say beforehand, predict, foretell, tell before, warn

προμαρτύρομαι—to testify beforehand, make known, predict

προκαταγγέλλω—to announce beforehand, promise, foretell, give notice beforehand

μαντεύομαι—to act as a seer, deliver an oracle, prophesy, soothsay, tell fortunes

Prepared, Ready

ἑτοιμασία—readiness

ἕτοιμος—ready, prepared, at hand, sure to come, certain, feasible, carried into effect, made good

ἑτοιμάζω—to make ready, prepare, provide, make arrangements

προετοιμάζω—make ready in advance

καταρτίζω—prepare, make adequate, mend, restore, create, perfect, make ready

προκαταρτίζω—make ready in advance

ἄρτιος—prepared, ready, complete, fitted to its purpose, qualified

ἀρτύω—to make ready, prepare, of foods, to season, make tasty

περιζώννυμαι τὴν ὀσφύν—gird up one's loins, get ready

σκευάζω—to prepare, make ready, dress food, provide, procure, furnish, supply, dress up, accouter, decorate

κατασκευάζω—to make ready, equip, furnish, prepare, arrange, pack up

κατασκευάζω τὴν ὁδόν—prepare the way, make ready

ἐπισκευάζομαι—get ready

παρασκευάζω—get ready
ὁπλίζω—to equip, arm, furnish with, make or get ready, prepare, harness up, train, exercise
ὅπλον—weapon, armament, tool
κατεργάζομαι—perform, accomplish, achieve, bring about, make ready
παράκειμαι—to lie beside or before, be adjacent, be at one's disposal, be close at hand, be present
στέλλω—equip, make ready, middle: avoid, guard against, shun
ἀπαρασκεύαστος—unprepared

Prepositions

ἀνά—with accusative: ἀνὰ μέσον in the midst, among, in the middle, between

ἀνά—as a prefix to verbs: up, back, again

ἀνά—as adverb, with numbers: each, apiece, by, after, in turn

ἄνευ—with genitive: without, apart from, independent of

ἀντί—with genitive: opposite, instead of, on behalf of, in place of, for, in exchange for, for this reason

ἀπό—with genitive: separation from, motion away from, out of, because of, on account of, as a result of, for, with, with the help of, by

ἄτερ—with genitive: without, apart from (Luke 22:6)

διά—with genitive: through, by way of, throughout, during, within, after, in, with, among, in spite of, in consequence of, by, on the basis of, on account of

διά—with accusative: through, on account of, because of, for the sake of

εἰς—with accusative: into, in, to, toward, on, inside, among, until, in order to, with a view to, for the purpose of, for, because of, in view of, for this reason, therefore, with reference to, against

ἐκ—with genitive: from, out of, away from, by, belonging to, of, with, for the amount of, since, after, for

ἐν—with dative: within, in, on, at, near, among, in the case of, on the grounds of, during, while, when, by, with the help of, through, because of, on account of, by reason of, with

ἐπί—with genitive: on, in, at, by, near, in the presence of, before, over, based on, in view of, in the time of, under the rule of

ἐπί—with dative: on, in, at, near, by, against, in the time of, during, because, on account of, on the basis of, from, for the purpose of, over

ἐπί—with accusative: on, across, over, as far as, to, up to, against, for, on, on top of, toward, over a period of, to the degree that, insofar as

κατά—with genitive: down from, down into, against

κατά—with accusative: according to, corresponding to, in relation to, with reference to, for the purpose of, as a result of, because of, on, through, over, along, toward, to, down to, in, from, each, by, during, in agreement with, about, after

μετά—with genitive: with, among, on the side of, by means of, through

μετά—with accusative: after, behind, beyond

παρά—with genitive: from beside, from the side of, issuing from a person, from the presence of, from, on the part of παρά—with dative: near, by, beside, alongside of, with, among, before, in the sight of

παρά—with accusative: to, toward, alongside of, by, beside, at, beyond, against

περί—with genitive: about, regarding, concerning, because of, on account of, with reference to, for

περί—with accusative: around, about, near, encircling, with, with respect to, of time: about, near

πρό—with genitive: before, in front of, ahead of, before in time, above in value

πρός—mainly with accusative: to, toward, against, with, before, at, about, among, with regard to, according to, resulting in

πρός—with genitive: necessary for, beneficial toward

πρός—with dative: at, by, close to, before

σύν—with, together with

ὑπέρ—with genitive: on behalf of, for the sake of, for, in place of, instead of, on account of, because of, in view of, with reference to, about, concerning

ὑπέρ—with accusative: exceeding, above, more than

ὑπό—with genitive: under, below, underneath, under control of, by, because of

Press, Crush

ἐπίκειμαι—lie upon, press upon, press against a retreating enemy, be imposed, be in force, be urgent

ἐπιπίπτω—happen, fall upon, befall, press upon

θλίβω—press, press hard upon, afflict, suffer hardship, throng, crowd against

ἀποθλίβω—press on all sides, squeeze, press hard, crowd against

συνθλίβω—press together, press on all sides, throng, crowd around

συντρίβω—break in pieces, tread down, crush, shatter

συνέχω—surround, hem in, enclose, guard, seize, afflict, be absorbed in

πιέζω—press, press together, press down

ψώχω—rub, rub to pieces

πατέω—tread, trample, crush with the feet, step on

καταπατέω—tread down, trample on, despise

λικμάω—winnow, cleanse away chaff from grain, scatter, crush, grind to powder

συνθλάω—crush, dash to pieces, shatter

πνίγω—choke, strangle, of thorns crowding and hindering growth, take by the throat

πνικτός—suffocated, strangled, smothered, choked

συμπνίγω—choke utterly, press around or throng around so as to suffocate

Prevent, Hinder

ἐκκλείω—shut out, not allow, prevent the approach

διακωλύω—prevent, hinder, deny

κωλύω—prevent, hinder, deny

ἐγκόπτω—prevent, hinder, impede one's course

ἐγκοπή—obstacle, a cutting off of a road, hindrance, blockage

ὄγκος—protuberance, bulk, mass, burden, weight, encumbrance, hindrance

κατέχω—hold tightly, hold back, restrain as in prison, possess

ἀθέμιτος—forbidden, unlawful, abominable

Pride, see "Vices: Arrogance, Pride, Haughtiness, Boasting"

Promise, Covenant, see also "Agreement"

ἐπαγγέλλομαι—to promise, assert, profess

ἐπαγγελία—promise, assurance

ἐπάγγελμα—promise

προεπαγγέλλομαι—to announce before, promise beforehand

ὅρκος—an oath, that which has been pledged or promised with an oath

διαθήκη—covenant, agreement, promise, of God's covenant with Abraham, of marriage, of Christ's covenant with His followers, will, testament, disposition of inheritance by a will (Hebrews 9:16)

διατίθημι—make a covenant, make a will, testate property, dispose, settle

ἀσύνθετος—bound by no covenant, faithless, disloyal, not keeping agreement, not keeping a promise

πίστις—conviction of truth, belief, faith, assurance, trust, (the) faith, as Christian belief, the promise or commitment to faith in Christ

ὁμολογέω—declare, profess, confess, promise, claim, give thanks, praise

Pronouns, Referential Words

ἐγώ—personal pronoun, I

σύ—personal pronoun, you

αὐτός—personal pronoun, he, she, it, self, same

ἐκεῖνος—demonstrative pronoun, that

οὗτος—demonstrative pronoun, this

ὅδε—demonstrative pronoun, this

οὕτως—thusly, in this way, in this manner, so, as follows

ὡς—so, thus, like, according as, how, with numerals: about, approximately

τίς, τί—interrogative pronoun, who, what, which, why?

τις, τι—indefinite pronoun, someone, a certain one, something, who?, what?

ὅς, ἥ, ὅ—relative pronoun, who, which, whom, that

ὅστις, ἥτις, ὅτι, οἵτινες, αἵτινες, ἅτινα—indefinite relative pronoun, whoever, whatever (almost always nominative)

ὅσος—as many as, as great as, as long as, how great, to the degree that, so much as is enough, enough, so far as

δεῖνα—somebody, such a one, a certain one

ἀλλήλων, ἀλλήλοις, ἀλλήλους—(no nominative), reciprocal pronouns, of one another, to one another, one another, each other

ἐμαυτοῦ, ἐμαυτῷ, ἐμαυτόν—(no nominative), reflexive pronoun, myself

σεαυτοῦ, σεαυτῷ, σεαυτόν—(no nominative), reflexive pronoun, yourself

ἑαυτοῦ, ἑαυτῷ, ἑαυτόν—(no nominative), reflexive pronoun, himself, herself, itself

ἑαυτῶν, ἑαυτοῖς, ἑαυτούς—(no nominative), reflexive pronoun, ourselves, yourselves, themselves

ἐμός—possessive pronoun, my, mine

σός—possessive pronoun, your

ἴδιος—possessive pronoun, one's own, oneself, individually, by oneself

ἡμέτερος—possessive pronoun, our

ὑμέτερος—possessive pronoun, your

ὁ—definite article, the

εἷς—one (number), one (indefinite referent)
ἐντεῦθεν—hence, thence, henceforth, thereupon, from this
ὅπου—where, to what place, in what place, in the case of
ποῦ—where
οὗ—where
ὅπως—how, in what way, by what means, with subjunctive: so that, that, in order that
πῶς—somehow, in some way, perhaps
ποῖος, α, ον—what kind? which, what?
τοιοῦτος, αὐτη, οὗτον—of such a kind, such, the sort of
ὧδε—here, hither, this place, in this case, at this point, on this occasion, under these circumstances

Proper, Improper

πρέπω—to be fitting, proper, right
ἀξιοπρεπὴς—becoming, goodly
ἄξιος—worthy, deserving, proper, befitting, sufficient for, of like value, worth as much as
ἀξίως—worthily, in a manner worthy of, suitably, properly, equivalent, comparable
ἀρεστός—pleasing, agreeable, proper
καθήκω—be fit, suitable, proper
ἐπιτήδειος—needed (James 2:16), necessary, suitable, fit
καλός—beautiful, fair, good, virtuous, advantageous, fitting
εὔθετος—well-arranged, well-fitting, easily stowed, ready for use, useful
ἀνεύθετος—unusable, inconvenient, unfavorably situated, not suitable
εὐσχήμων—elegant in figure and bearing, graceful, decent, becoming, with grace and dignity, like a gentleman, noble, honorable, befitting

δίκαιος—righteous, lawful, just, innocent, in right relation to God
δεκτός—acceptable, pleasing, welcomed, appropriate
κόσμιος—well-ordered, regular, moderate, well-behaved, discreet, quiet, decent
ἀναξίως—unworthily, in an unworthy or careless manner, in an improper manner
ἀναίδεια—shamelessness, insolence, impudence, effrontery

Property, Owner, Have, Possess

ἔχω—to have, hold, possess, wear
κατέχω—hold tightly, hold back, restrain as in prison, possess
κατάσχεσις—taking possession, holding back, restraining
ὑπάρχω—to be, exist, participle: one's being, possessions, belongings, livelihood, means
ὕπαρξις—existence, possessions, property, belongings
τὰ παρόντα—possessions, present circumstances
ἐπιβάλλω—cast upon, attend to, think on, put upon, take possession of
ἴδιος—one's own, pertaining to oneself, private, personal, not public, separate, distinct, by oneself
περιούσιος—chosen, choice, special, a distinctive possession, peculiar
κτῆμα—property
κτήτωρ—owner, possessor
κτῆσις—acquisition, possession, property
κτάομαι—to acquire, get gain, have, procure for oneself, possess, hold
κύριος—lord, master, ruler, owner
δεσπότης—lord, master, ruler, owner
οἰκοδεσπότης—master of a household

βίος—life, a course of life, manner of living, livelihood, means of living, substance, possessions

οὐσία—being, existence, one's substance, property, that which is one's own, essence, nature

σκεῦος—vessel, jar, vase, utensils, furniture, military gear, equipment, luggage, one's wife (1 Thes. 4:4)

οἰκία—house, household, dwelling, lineage, property

οἶκος—house, habitation, dwelling, lineage, property

Prophecy

προφητεία—a prophecy, inspired utterance

προφητεύω—prophesy, reveal God's will, speak inspired words, often in warnings, speak predictively, prefiguring or foreshadowing future things

προφητικός—prophetic, of prophecy, of a prophet

προφήτης—a prophet, one who declares God's word, revealer of God's counsel for the future, an inspired preacher or teacher

Prostrate

κλίνω τὸ πρόσωπον εἰς τὴν γῆν—prostrate oneself

προσκυνέω—prostrate oneself before, do homage, make obeisance, worship

κυνέω—kiss, plead

προσπίπτω—prostrate one's self in homage or supplication, fall down before, rush upon, beat against

πρηνής—headfirst, prostrate, to the ground

Protect

τηρέω—to keep, observe, give heed to, obey, watch, protect, guard

συντηρέω—to protect, preserve, treasure, remember, keep in mind

φυλάσσω—guard, keep watch, protect

διαφυλάσσω—guard carefully, keep, protect

κρύπτω—hide, conceal, keep secret, make invisible, escape notice, keep safe, protect

προστάτις—helper, protector, patron

Provide For, Supply

χορηγέω—furnish, provide, supply

ἐπιχορηγέω—provide, furnish, add

ἐπιχορηγία—provision, additional help

παρίστημι—to stand before, present, show to be true, set before, provide, furnish, put at one's disposal

πληρόω—make full, fulfill, complete

ἀναπληρόω—fill up, supply, refill, fulfill

προσαναπληρόω—provide fully, fill up or replenish in addition to, add to so as to fill up

προβλέπομαι—foresee, provide for, select in advance

προνοέω—foresee, plan beforehand, be provident, provide for, take care of, take thought for

τρέφω—nourish, support, feed, fatten, bring up, nurture, feed from the breast, take care of, rear

Psychological Faculties, Soul, Heart

καρδία—heart, inner self

ψυχή—breath, soul, living being, person, life, inner self

ἰσόψυχος—equal in soul, like-minded, similarly minded

σύμψυχος—of one mind, of one accord, like-minded, harmonious

πνεῦμα—wind, breath, spirit, soul, the Holy Spirit, the inner being

πνευματικός—spiritual, relating to the human spirit or rational soul, as the part of man which is akin to God, pertaining to the wind or breath, supernatural, of spiritual conduct, not physical

πνευματικῶς—spiritually

συνείδησις—conscience

διάνοια—mind, understanding, intention, purpose, thoughts

νόημα—mental perception, thought, mind

νοῦς—the mind, thoughts

φρήν—the mind, intellect, understanding

φρόνημα—thoughts, purposes

φρόνησις—understanding, prudence, wisdom

φρονέω—to have understanding, be wise, think, direct one's mind to a thing, hold a view, have an opinion, set the affection on

ὁ ἔσω ἄνθρωπος—the inner man, inner being

ὁ ἐν τῷ κρυπτῷ ἄνθρωπος—in the hidden man, inner being

ἔσωθεν—the inside

κοιλία—belly, womb, seat of desires

νεφρός—kidney, loins, inmost thoughts, feelings, purposes of the soul, desires

σπλάγχνα—entrails, inner parts of the body: stomach, intestines, bowels, guts, the inner seat of emotions, where one feels compassion

σπλαγχνίζομαι—to be moved in one's inward parts, to be moved with compassion, have pity on

σάρξ—flesh, body, natural generation, the sensual nature, human nature, 1 Corinthians 1:26

σαρκικός—fleshly, carnal, having the nature of flesh, controlled by animal appetites, human, depraved, worldly, material, natural, physical, sensual

Pull, Draw, Drag

ἕλκω—draw, drag off, pull

σπάομαι—draw (one's sword), pull

ἀνασπάω—draw up, pull up

ἀποσπάω—to draw off, tear away, pull out, lure away, take leave of

σύρω—draw, drag away, drag down

ἀναβιβάζω—cause to go up or ascend, draw up, pull up

Punish

κρίσις—judgement, condemnation, punishment, justice

φορέω τὴν μάχαιραν—to bear the sword, use force to punish

παιδεία—discipline, training, teaching, chastening, nurture, punishment, correction

παιδεύω—to train, teach, correct, scourge, punish, discipline

παιδευτής—teacher, instructor, preceptor, corrector, chastiser, punisher

ἐπιτιμία—punishment, penalty

ἐπιτιμάω—command, rebuke, lay a penalty on someone, admonish

τιμωρέω—punish

τιμωρία—punishment, penalty

δίκη—righteous judgement, punishment, penalty

ἐκδικέω—to avenge, procure justice for someone, punish a crime

ἐκδίκησις—an avenging, punishment

ἔκδικος—avenger, punisher

κολάζω—punish, chastise

κόλασις—punishment

ζημιόω—to inflict loss, damage, or injury, fine, punish

ζημία—damage, loss, detriment

ὀργή—anger, wrath, indignation

μαστιγόω—scourge, beat with a whip, punish

διχοτομέω—cut in two, punish severely

βασανίζω—torture, torment, cross examine by applying torture, put to the test

ἀθῷος—unpunished, guiltless

ἀθῳόω—to let go unpunished, leave unavenged, be guiltless

Purity, see "Virtues: Holiness, Purity"

Pursue, Persecute, Follow

διώκω—pursue, chase, put to flight, drive away, persecute

ἐκδιώκω—pursue and drive out, banish, persecute, oppress

διωγμός—persecution, pursuit, harassment

διώκτης—persecutor

Put, Place

τίθημι—put, place, lay, set, appoint

περιτίθημι—put around, place on, of clothing, bestow, confer upon

ἀποτίθημι—to put away, take off, lay aside, put aside or stop something

ἐκτίθεμαι—to place outside, expose, abandon, exhibit, set forth, expound, explain

ἔκθετος—placed outside, put out, abandoned, exposed

ἐπίθεσις—laying on or placing on, often the hands on someone to convey power or blessing

ἐπιτίθημι—lay upon, place upon, usually the hands, inflict, attack

ἵστημι—put, place, set, stand, establish, continue to be, remain firmly

βάλλω—throw, put, deposit

ἐμβάλλω—throw or cast into, put into

παρεμβάλλω—barricade around, erect ramparts, encamp against

βλητέος—being put, stored

ῥίπτω—to throw out, let down, set down

στηρίζω—to prop, set, fixate, fasten, strengthen, confirm, establish, settle, be firmly set, make steady

ἐγκρύπτω—hide or conceal in, put into, mix in, of yeast

ἐπιβάλλω—cast upon, attend to, think on, put upon, take possession of

R

Rain
βρέχω—to make wet, soak, rain
βροχή—rain
ὑετός—rain (event)
πρόϊμος—early rain
ὄμβρος—rainstorm, heavy rain
ὄψιμος—late rain

Rebellion, Riot
στάσις—a standing, insurrection, uproar, rebellion, heated quarrel
στασιάζω—to rebel
στασιαστής—a rebel, revolutionary
ἀποστασία—abandonment, defection, rebellion, apostasy
ἀναστατόω—to unsettle, upset, cause to revolt
ἐπίστασις—an attack, disturbance, rioting, an overwhelming of responsibilities and pressures
ἀκαταστασία—disturbance, rebellion, riot, disorder, unruliness, instability
ἐπανίστημι—rise up, rise in rebellion, rebel against
ἀφίστημι—leave, desert, fall away from faith, commit apostasy, mislead, incite a revolt, abstain, shun
ἀντιλογία—contradiction, opposition, rebellion, strife, dispute, gainsaying
λῃστής—a robber, plunderer, pirate, buccaneer, rebel
ἐπαίρω—lift up, raise, elevate, hoist, ascend, boast, rise up against
ὑπεραίρομαι—to exalt oneself, be elated, be overly proud
παραπικραίνω—to rebel, provoke, be disobedient
παραπικρασμός—rebellion, revolt
διχάζω—to divide in two, divide one against another, cause to revolt
θόρυβος—noise, uproar, clamor, excitement, applause, cheers, turmoil, tumult, confusion, riot
θορυβέω—to cause an uproar, start a riot, throw into confusion
ταραχή—trouble,—disorder, confusion, tumult, riot
ταράσσω—agitate, trouble, disquiet, make restless, stir up, perplex
ἐκταράσσω—to throw into great trouble, agitate, stir up against
σύγχυσις—confusion, tumult, uproar
συστροφή—coalition, conspiracy, riot, revolt, uproar
ἀνασείω—to shake, swing to and fro, move up and down, stir up, cause an uproar
κινέω—set in motion, move, excite a disturbance or riot, shake
σαλεύω—agitate, shake, be stirred up, distressed, confused

Rebuke, Warn

ἐπιτιμάω—command, rebuke, lay a penalty on someone, admonish

ἐλέγχω—to convict, refute, confute, expose, correct, reprehend, chasten, rebuke, reprove

ἐλεγμός—a rebuke

ἔλεγξις—refutation, rebuke

ὀνειδίζω—to reproach, upbraid, revile, disparage, reprimand, insult

ἐμβριμάομαι—to charge with earnest admonition, threaten, insist sternly, murmur against, scold

ἐπιπλήσσω—to strike upon, beat upon, rebuke

προλέγω—to say beforehand, say already, foretell, tell before, predict, warn

νουθεσία—admonition, exhortation, teaching, warning

νουθετέω—to admonish, warn, exhort, instruct

Receive

δέχομαι—take, receive, grasp, accept, welcome

διαδέχομαι—to receive in turn from a former owner, succeed

λαμβάνω—take, take hold of, grasp, acquire, receive, accept, collect, welcome, take on

λῆμψις—receiving

ἀπολαμβάνω—to take back, regain, recover, take aside, receive hospitably, welcome

μεταλαμβάνω—to receive one's share, share in, receive

μετάλημψις—receiving of a share in, sharing, taking

ὑπολαμβάνω—suppose, take in mind, take up (Acts 1:9), receive

κομίζω—bear, bring, buy, middle: obtain, be paid back, recover

λαγχάνω—to cast lots, choose by lot, have as your portion

κληρονομέω—to receive inheritance, inherit, be an heir, succeed

κλῆρος—a lot, a casting or drawing of lots, a piece of land, a portion, share, inheritance, fate, destiny

συγκληρονόμος—fellow receiver, joint heir with

κατακληρονομέω—to obtain by inheritance, make someone receive a valuable gift

μέρος—part, piece, share, district, region of a country

ἀπέχω—have back, hold back, receive in full, be distanced, be sufficient (Mark 14:41), middle: hold one's self away, avoid, abstain

Recline To Eat

ἀνάκειμαι—lie at a table, recline to eat, dine, sit down for a meal

κατάκειμαι—lie down, lie prostrate, recline to eat

ἀνακλίνω—cause to lie down, recline to eat, lean against, lean upon

κατακλίνω—recline at a table, recline to eat

ἀναπίπτω—lie back, lie down, recline to eat, sit back

Recommend, Commend,—Approve

συνίστημι—to commend, recommend, approve, show, intransitive: be set together, be formed into, consist of, hold together

συστατικός—commendatory, of recommendation

εὐδοκέω—to be pleased, be favorable towards, prefer, approve, choose

δοκιμάζω—to test, examine, prove, scrutinize, recognize as genuine after examination, approve, deem worthy, judge as good, evaluate

δόκιμος—acceptable, approved, tried, genuine, considered good, respected

ἐπαινέω—to praise, commend, laud, approve

ἐπικρίνω—to give sentence, decide

Region

γῆ—earth, ground, dirt, land, world, country, region

κλίμα—region, tract of country

μέρος—part, piece, share, district, region of a country

ὅριον—territory, region, frontier, coast

ὅρος—boundary, limit (different from ὄρος, mountain)

ὁροθεσία—placing of a boundary, definite limit, a fixed boundary

χώρα—land, region, countryside

χωρίον—field, region

περίχωρος—surrounding region

πατρίς—homeland

τόπος—region, place, possibility

κανών—rule, measuring rod, the area over which one rules, the province assigned one, a principal or law of judging and acting

Reject, Cut Off, Separate From, Exclude

ἀφορίζω—separate, set apart, exclude

ἐκκλείω—to shut out from, exclude from, be hindered from

ἐξαίρω—to remove, drive out, be quitted of, exclude

ἐκπτύω—spit out, reject

ἀποβολή—rejection, repudiation, loss, destruction, throwing away

ἀποβάλλω—to throw off, cast from one, reject, lose

ἀπόβλητος—to be rejected, thrown away as worthless

ἀδόκιμος—failing the test, worthless, unqualified, disqualified, rejected, proven false, unfit, bad

ἀποδοκιμάζω—throw out as the result of a test, reject, declare useless, think of as unworthy

φραγμός—a fence, hedge, partition, that which separates or blocks

καταλείπω—to leave behind, abandon, neglect, no longer relate to

στέλλομαι ἀπό—to avoid, shun

στέλλω—equip, make ready, middle: avoid, guard against, shun

ἀποτρέπω—to avoid, keep away from

ἀφίστημι—leave, desert, fall away from faith, commit apostasy, mislead, incite a revolt, abstain, shun

ἐκκλίνω—to turn aside, deviate from the right course, shun, avoid, turn away from, cease

ἀρνέομαι—to deny, refuse to agree

ἀπαρνέομαι—to deny, disregard, reject, deny acquaintance with

παραιτέομαι—ask, request, beg, give excuse, request pardon, decline, keep away from, shun, refuse to hear

ἀπορφανίζω—make an orphan of, be torn away from, be unwillingly separated from

ἀπεῖπον—forbid, reject, renounce, denounce, disown

ἐκβάλλω—cast out, drive out, send out, put out

ἐξωθέω—thrust out, expel, banish, drive out of the sea, run aground

ἀπωθέομαι—thrust away, push away, repel, repudiate, reject, refuse

ἀπωθέω—to push aside, reject

ἀθετέω—reject, set aside, annul

ἀποσπάω—draw off, tear away

Relations, see "Kin"

Release, Set Free

ἀπαλλάσσω—to set free, release, let loose, settle, be reconciled

ἀλλάσσω—change, alter, transform, give in exchange, barter, repay

ἀπολύω—set free, let go, send away, release, allow, acquit, remit, divorce

λύω—loose, destroy, divorce, annul

λυτρόω—to release on receipt of ransom, liberate, be ransomed

λύτρωσις—redemption, ransoming, liberation, deliverance

ἀπολύτρωσις—ransoming, redemption by payment of ransom, liberation

λυτρωτής—liberator, ransomer, redeemer

ἀντίλυτρον—ransom

λύτρον—a price paid, ransom-money, atonement, recompense

ἐξαγοράζω—to buy back, redeem

ἀγοράζω—to buy, purchase, redeem, frequent the market

ἄφεσις—a letting go, dismissal, discharge, exemption from service, divorce, liberty, pardon

ἐλευθερία—freedom, liberty, license

ἐλεύθερος—free, open to all

ἐλευθερόω—to free, set free, clear, acquit, loose, release from

δικαιόω—to justify, make right with, deem righteous, acquit

καταργέω—render ineffective, make barren, do away with, nullify, passive with ἀπό: be released from

ἄνεσις—loosening, relaxation, easement, less vigorous confinement, liberty, rest, relief

Relief, Ease From Trouble

ἀνάψυξις—refreshment, relief, revival, encouragement

ἄνεσις—loosening, relaxation, easement, less vigorous confinement, liberty, rest, relief

ἀνάπαυσις—intermission, cessation of labor, rest, relief

ἐλαφρός—light in weight, easy to bear, buoyant, not burdensome, limited in extent, insignificant in size or number

εὔκοπος—easy

εὐκοπώτερος—easier

χρηστός—good, pleasant, fit for use, useful, virtuous, easy, kind

Religion

εὐσέβεια—reverence toward God, piety, religion

εὐσεβής—devout, pious, held sacred, religious, righteous, holy, hallowed

εὐσεβῶς—religious

θεοσέβεια—religion, the service or fear of God

θεοσεβής—religious, God-fearing

θρησκεία—religion, worship

θρησκός—religious

ἐθελοθρησκία—self-imposed religion, religion from one's own initiative

δεισιδαιμονία—religion, fear of gods, superstition

δεισιδαίμων—religious, pious, fearing the gods, superstitious, bigoted

δικαιοσύνη—righteousness, justice, being in right standing with God, being acceptable to God, doing what God requires, uprightness, integrity

εὐλάβεια—discretion, caution, piety, circumspection, reverence, godly fear

εὐλαβέομαι—to be moved with fear, have reverence, act with respectful—caution εὐλαβής—undertaking prudently, cautious, circumspect, reverent, pious, religious, devout, law-abiding

ἱεροπρεπής—holy, reverent, sacred, religious

ἱερός—divine, holy, hallowed

λειτουργέω—to perform religious service or temple duties, minister

λειτουργία—a liturgy, temple service, the service of a minister

λειτουργός—priest, servant, minister

λατρεία—worship, service in a temple, service

λατρεύω—to worship, serve God, obey, serve

ἀσέβεια—godlessness, ungodliness, impiety, profaneness

ἀσεβέω—to live ungodly, be impious, act profanely, sin

ἀσεβής—godless, ungodly, impious, profane

Religious Roles

διακονέω—to minister, serve, take care of, be a deacon, wait on

διάκονος—a servant, minister, deacon

ἐπισκοπή—office of a church leader, supervisor's office, a visitation from God bringing help or salvation

ἐπισκοπέω—to watch over, visit, oversee, look after, care for, inspect

ἐπίσκοπος—overseer, guardian, bishop

ποιμή—shepherd, herdsman, shepherd of the people, pastor, minister

ἀποστολή—apostleship, the office of an apostle, a sending off, expedition, dispatching

ἀπόστολος—a messenger, delegate, apostle, one sent out with a message, ambassador, envoy

εὐαγγελιστής—evangelist, herald of good news, preacher of the gospel

πρεσβύτερος—presbyter, church leader appointed in each city, elder, old man, forefather

συμπρεσβύτερος—fellow elder

προφήτης—a prophet, one who declares God's word, revealer of God's counsel for the future, an inspired preacher or teacher

μεσσίας—the messiah, transliteration of the Hebrew word for anointed one

χριστός—anointed, the anointed one, the Christ, the messiah

ἱερατεύω—to be a priest

ἱερεύς—priest, sacrificer, minister

ἱερουργέω—to serve as a priest, perform sacred rites

ἱερωσύνη—priesthood, the office of a priest

ἱερατεία—priesthood, office of a priest

ἱεράτευμα—priesthood

ἀρχιερεύς—chief priest, high priest

ἀρχιερατικός—high priestly

ἀρχισυνάγωγος—leader of a synagogue

γραμματεύς—scribe, recorder, scholar, expert in the law

νεωκόρος—temple-keeper

ἀντίχριστος—antichrist

ψευδόχριστος—false Christ

ψευδοπροφήτης—false prophet

ψευδαπόστολος—false apostle

Remain, Continue, Stay

μένω—stay, abide, remain, wait

ἀναμένω—await, expect

διαμένω—continue, stay, remain

ἐμμένω—continue, remain

ἐπιμένω—continue, stay with

καταμένω—remain, stay

παραμένω—continue, stay, remain

περιμένω—wait for

προσμένω—keep on, remain with

ὑπομένω—to remain, abide, endure, persevere, be patient under

ἵστημι—stand, place, put, establish, set, continue to be, remain firmly

ἐφίστημι—come up to, approach, stand near, stand ready, appear suddenly, be imminent, attack

προστίθημι—add to, increase, give, grant, do again, continue, gather to, passive: be buried with

ἐκτενής—intent, earnest, assiduous, fervent, eager, without ceasing, continuous, constant, unfailing

ἐκτενῶς—earnestly, fervently, intensely, eagerly, continuously

ἀδιάλειπτος—not stopping, incessant, not leaving off from, continuous

ἀκατάπαυστος—that which cannot cease from something, never ceasing

ἀφθαρσία—unceasing, incorruptible, not undergoing decay, undying

ἐκκρέμαμαι—to hang from, depend on, listen attentively to

ἐπίκειμαι—press upon a retreating enemy, be urgent, constantly pressing, of laws: be in force

διατρίβω—to stay longer, tarry, lose time, delay

κάθημαι—sit down, seat one's self, have a fixed abode, dwell, reside

καθίζω—sit, seat, set, appoint, settle, remain, tarry

προσέχω—be attentive, watch, give heed to, beware, be devoted to

συνέχω—surround, hem in, enclose, guard, seize, afflict, be absorbed in

συνεχής—continuous, contiguous, in line with, unintermitting, constant, unceasing, persevering

ἐπέχω—to hold on to, fix attention on, watch, be alert for, take notice of, attend to, delay, stay on

εἰμὶ ἐν—continue to do, be in

μελετάω—to meditate on, plot, think about, attend to, practice, rehearse

παρατείνω—to stretch out along or beside, hold out to the last, extend, prolong, protract, lengthen

προσκαρτερέω—to persist in, be in constant readiness, continue in, spend much time in, be devoted to

διάγω—bring through, pass through (life), go through (life), (Titus 3:3)

λείπω—to leave, leave alone, leave out, leave undone, lack, be deficient in, fall short, impersonal active 3rd person: what remains, what is wanting

λοιπός—remaining, left, the rest, from now on, to mark an added fact: furthermore, also, in addition, beyond that, finally

Remove

αἴρω—remove, carry off, lift up, raise up, elevate, take from among the living, kill, destroy

ἐξαίρω—to remove, drive out, be quitted of, exclude

μεταίρω—lift up and remove to another place, transfer, go away, depart

ἀφαιρέω—to take away from, remove, separate, deprive one of

ἀφίστημι—leave, desert, fall away from faith, commit apostasy, mislead, incite a revolt, abstain, shun

μεθίστημι—remove, lead away, transfer

ἀποστεγάζω—to uncover, remove a roof

παραφέρω—to mislead, carry away, remove, take away

μεταβαίνω—pass over from one place to another, remove, depart

μετοικίζω—remove someone to another place, resettle, deport, send into exile, banish

Repent, see "Convert"

Reptile

ἑρπετόν—reptile, serpent, creeping thing

ὄφις—snake, serpent

ἀσπίς—snake, asp

ἔχιδνα—snake, viper, poisonous serpent

δράκων—dragon

βάτραχος—frog

Resistance

ἀνθίστημι—resist, oppose, stand one's ground, be hostile toward

ἀντικαθίστημι—resist, set against, oppose, withstand, reign in place of

ἀντιπίπτω—to fall against, resist

πρὸς κέντρα λακτίζω—to kick against the goads, resist

Respect, see "Virtues: Respect, Modesty," see also "Honor"

Resurrection, see "Life, Live," "Ascend, Rise," "Change, Renewal," "New"

ἀνίστημι—raise up, rise, stand up, appear, stand forth, resurrect

ἀνάστασις—resurrection, raising to life again

ἐξανάστασις—a rising up, a rising again, resurrection

ἀναζάω—live again, recover life, return to a right moral state, revive

ζῳογονέω—bring forth alive, give life, preserve alive, keep alive

ζῳοποιέω—make live, bear living young, germinate

συζάω—live together with, live with

συζωοποιέω—to make one alive together with, raise to life with

ἐγείρω—to arouse, cause to rise, raise to life, raise up, awaken, stand up, make war against

ἔγερσις—a rousing, excitation, a rising up, resurrection from the dead

ἐξεγείρω—to arouse, raise up, stir up, incite, raise to life

συνεγείρω—to raise together, raise to life with

ἀναβαίνω—ascend, go up, mount, board a ship, arise

ἀνέρχομαι—go up

ἀναλαμβάνω—take up, raise

ὑπολαμβάνω—suppose, take in mind, take up (Acts 1:9), receive

ἀνάλημψις—taking up, ascension, death

ἀνατέλλω—to rise, give birth to, be a descendant, bring to light, dawn

ἀνατολή—rising, the east

ἐπαίρω—lift up, raise, elevate, hoist, ascend, boast, rise up against

ἀναβιβάζω—cause to go up or ascend, draw up, pull up

παλιγγενεσία—rebirth, restoration, resurrection, regeneration, a new age

ἀναγεννάω—be born again

μεταμορφόω—to be transfigured, change appearance, transform

μετασχηματίζω—to change appearance, change the form of a person, transform, be disguised

μετατίθημι—transfer, change

μετατρέπω—turn into, change

ἀποκαθίστημι—restore to former state, establish again, restore to health

ἀποκατάστασις—restoration

ἰάομαι—cure, heal, make whole, restore, renew

ἀνακαινίζω—renew, renovate, restore

ἀνακαινόω—cause growth, make new, give new strength

ἀλλάσσω—change, alter, transform, give in exchange, barter, repay

μεταλλάσσω—change, alter, exchange

Rest, Pause

ἡσυχάζω—to keep quiet, be silent, rest, cease from labor, of observing the sabbath, to lead a quiet life, hold one's peace, be still, be calm

ἡσύχιος—quiet, tranquil, peaceful, at rest, possessing an inward calm

ἡσυχία—quietness, silence, quiet circumstances, quiet living

ἀναπαύω—cease from an activity to regain strength, rest, refresh, keep quiet, calm, take ease

ἀνάπαυσις—intermission, cessation of labor, rest, relief

καταπαύω—to make quiet, rest, to still, restrain, cause to desist, cease

κατάπαυσις—a putting to rest, calming, a resting place, rest

συναναπαύομαι—rest with, sleep together, lie with

ἐπαναπαύομαι—rest upon, settle upon, abide upon

τὴν κεφαλὴν κλίνω—recline the head, to lie down to rest

Result, Purpose: words indicating Result or Purpose

ἀποβαίνω εἰς—result in, issue forth, end in, turn out

ἔρχομαι εἰς—to come into, result in

ἔκβασις—a way out, exit, way of escape, an egress, end, result

τέλος—end, limit, boundary, finish, completion, last, conclusion, tax

ἄρα—consequently, as a result, perhaps, possibly

διό—therefore, for this reason, for this purpose, and so, so also, so therefore

διόπερ—emphatic therefore, for this very reason, on this very account

ἵνα—that, in order to, as a result

μενοῦν—and, surely, therefore, may be adversative: yes but, yes but even more so, Luke 11:28

οὖν—so, therefore, then, accordingly, consequently, adversative usage: however, but, rather

τοιγαροῦν—emphatic therefore indeed, for that very reason, henceforth, so then

τοίνυν—emphatic therefore indeed, so then, for that very reason, henceforth

ὡς—so, thus, like, according as, how, with numerals: about, approximately

ὥστε—therefore, for this reason, so then, so that, with the result that, as a result, so as to, for the purpose of

ἕνεκα—on account of, for the sake of, because of, by reason of

ὅπως—how, in what way, by what means, with subjunctive: so that, that, in order that

χάριν—because of, on account of, for the sake of, on behalf of, for this purpose

μή πως—so that not, how not, in order that not

μήπως—so that not, how not, in order that not

μήποτε—so that not, never, at no time, lest at any time, in order that not, whether, perhaps

κενός—(antonym) empty, vain, devoid of truth, containing nothing, foolish, without purpose, without result, fruitless

εἰκῇ—at random, without plan or system, thoughtlessly, rashly, without reason or cause, in vain, for nothing, without purpose

μάτην—in vain, senselessly, pointlessly, without result

Return, Turn

στρέφω—turn, turn from one's course, change one's mind, reverse

τροπή—turning, change, variation

ἀνατρέπω—overthrow, overturn, destroy, subvert, upset one's faith

καταστρέφω—turn over, turn under, e.g., soil with a plough, overthrow, throw down

ὑποστρέφω—return, turn back, turn around

ἐπιστρέφω—return, turn about, turn back

ἀναστρέφω—conduct one's self, behave, live, stay, return

ἀνακάμπτω—turn back, return, change to former belief

ἀναχωρέω—return, go back, withdraw, seek another place

ἐπανέρχομαι—return to, come back again

ἀπέρχομαι πρὸς ἑαυτόν—go back to one's place

ἐπανάγω—put out to sea, push off from shore, return

ἀναλύω—loose again, depart, break up, depart from life, die, return

ἀποκαθίστημι—restore to former state, establish again, restore to health

Revenge, see also "Punish"

ἐκδικέω—to avenge, procure justice for someone, punish a crime

ἐκδίκησις—an avenging, punishment

Reward, see "Salary, Pay, Recompense, Reward, Prize"

Righteous, Just, see "Virtues: Righteous, Just"

Ripen, Produce Fruit, Bear Seed

ἀκμάζω—flourish, mature, ripen, bloom

ξηραίνω—to make dry, wither, waste away, become stiff, of grain: be ripe

καρπὸν ἀποδίδωμι—bear fruit

καρπὸν φέρω—bear fruit

καρποφορέω—bear fruit

καρποφόρος—fruitful, productive

τελεσφορέω—bring to maturity, bring to perfection, bear ripe fruit

εὐφορέω—be fertile, bring forth plentifully, produce much fruit

ἄκαρπος—without fruit, barren, fruitless, unprofitable, useless

Roll

κυλίω—roll

κυλισμός—thing rolled, rolled mud, wallowing, rolling about

ἀποκυλίω—roll away

προσκυλίω—roll to or against, as moving a stone to cover an opening

Rot, Decay, Rust

φθορά—corruption, destruction, decay, rottenness, decomposition

διαφθορά—corruption, destruction, decay

φθείρω—to corrupt, destroy, deprave

σήπω—to corrupt, destroy, become rotten, decay

κατιόομαι—to rust over, cover with rust

ἰός—poison, rust

βρῶσις—eating, food, meat, eating away, corrosion or rusting

Rough, Smooth

τραχύς—rough, rugged, uneven, rocky, shaggy, sharp, harsh

τραχύνω—to make rough, rugged, uneven

τράχηλος—neck, throat

λεῖος—smooth, level, flat

πεδινός—level, flat, even, of terrain

ταπεινόω—to make low, abase, embarrass, make level, bring low, passive: be humble

ἀφελότης—smoothness, evenness, simplicity of heart, humbleness

Round, Around

περί—with accusative: around, about, concerning

τροχός—a course, as a race course or the course of the sun, anything round, a circle

κύκλος—a ring, circle, wheel, circular motion, round

κυκλόω—to encircle, surround, move in a circle, whirl around, go around

περίκειμαι—to have placed around, wear, be surrounded

Rule, Govern, see also "Guide, Lead"

ἐξουσιάζω—to exercise power over, reign, have mastery, be in authority

κατεξουσιάζω—to exercise lordship over, reign, tyrannize

κυριεύω—to be lord or master of, have legal power, rule

κατακυριεύω—to gain dominion over, rule

κύριος—lord, master, ruler, owner

κυριότης—dominion, ruling power

ῥαββι—teacher, master, lord

ἄρχω—to rule, be first, make a beginning, lead, govern

ἀρχή—ruler, first in power, origin, beginning, first cause, elementary aspect, the end or corner of a thing

ἄρχων—ruler, lord, prince, chief, chief magistrate, commander, captain, judge

τετράρχης—tetrarch, ruler over the fourth part of a region, prince with authority below a king

τετραρχέω—to be the tetrarch of

ἐθνάρχης—head of an ethnic community, governor, official

πολιτάρχης—city official

ποιμαίνω—to be a shepherd, tend, guide, look after, care for

ἡγεμονία—hegemony, government, command, leadership, going first

ἡγέομαι—govern, lead, think, consider

ἡγεμών—ruler, leader, guide, commander, chief, sovereign, provincial governor

ἡγεμονεύω—to be governor, go before, lead the way, rule, command

δυνάστης—lord, master, ruler, official

δεσπότης—lord, master, ruler, owner

βασιλεία—kingdom, dominion, reign

βασιλεύω—to be a king, rule, reign

συμβασιλεύω—reign with

βασιλεύς—king

βασίλειος—of the king, kingly, royal

βασιλικός—royal, like a king, kingly

θρόνος—throne, place of ruling, authority to rule, ruler

κοσμοκράτωρ—world ruler, lord of the world

κράτος—strength, might, sovereignty, power, dominion, mastery, authority

σεβαστός—reverenced, august, used to render the imperial name Augustus

ἀνθύπατος—proconsul, head of the government of a senatorial province εὐνοῦχος—eunuch, chamberlain, manager of a king's bedchamber,

—castrated chamberlain in charge of women, one who abstains from marriage, impotent or celebate male

ἐπίτροπος—one put in charge, guide, governor, guardian, manager, foreman, steward

πρεσβεία—embassy, ambassadors of early times were elders

πρεσβεύω—be an ambassador or envoy, be a representative

ῥαβδοῦχος—Roman policeman,— constable, or sergeant who carried a rod or staff of office

στρατηγός—commander of an army, general, governor, magistrate, praetor

στρατιώτης—army, host, soldiers

πράκτωρ—one who does or executes, an accomplisher, a tax-gatherer, a punisher, officer, constable

Run

τρέχω—to run, future and aorist have the form of δρᾰμοῦμαι

δρᾰμοῦμαι—run

δρόμος—a course, running, race, quick movement, flight, mission

τροχός—a course, as a race course or the course of the sun, anything round, a circle

περιτρέχω—run around, run about

εἰστρέχω—run into

κατατρέχω—run down to

προστρέχω—run—to

προτρέχω—run in front of, run before, outrun, precede

ἐκπηδάω—rush out

εἰσπηδάω—rush into

ὁρμάω—rush

S

Sacrifice, Offering
προσφορά—a sacrifice, offering
ἀναφέρω—bring up, lead up, offer up
ἀνάθημα—an offering, temple gift
θυσία—offering, sacrifice
θύω—to sacrifice, slay, kill, slaughter
θυσίαν ἱλάσκεσθαι τόν θεόν—an atoning sacrifice to God
θυμίαμα—incense offering, fragrant items for burning or embalming
θυμιάω—to offer incense
σφάγιον—sacrifice, offering, victim to be sacrificed
σφαγή—slaughter, ἡμέρα σφαγῆς day of condemnation
ἱερόθυτος—sacrificed to a god
κορβᾶν—Hebrew word, gift for the service of God
ἀπαρχή—first portion of a sacrifice, firstfruits, first
ὁλοκαύτωμα—whole burnt offering
ἄρτοι τῆς προθέσεως—consecrated bread, bread of offering
σπένδω—to pour libation or drink offering, pour, make a truce
ἀκροθίνιον—the choicest part, firstfruit, cream of the crop, best booty

Sacrilege
ἱεροσυλέω—to rob a temple, commit sacrilege
ἱερόσυλος—a temple-robber, sacrilegious person, desecrator
σκῦλον—spoils, booty, prey

Sadness, Sorrow, Regret
μεταμέλομαι—to repent, regret, feel remorse, to leave off caring about something, to change one's mind
λύπη—sorrow, pain, grief, annoyance, affliction, heaviness, regret, sadness
λυπέω—to make sorrowful, affect with sadness, cause grief
συλλυπέομαι—to affect with grief together, feel sorry for
περίλυπος—very sad, exceedingly sorrowful, overcome with sorrow
κατανύσσομαι τὴν καρδίαν—pricked to the heart, be greatly troubled
ἀγωνία—struggle for victory, of severe mental struggles and emotions, agony, anguish, sorrow
πικρῶς—bitterly, with agony
στυγνάζω—be sad, sorrowful, become dark and gloomy, overcast
σκυθρωπός—of a sad and gloomy countenance, sad
ἀμεταμέλητος—not regretful, not repentant
ἀλυπότερος—free from pain or grief, less sorrowful, relieved of anxiety

Safety, Freedom From Danger, Salvation, Deliverance

ἀσφάλεια—firmness, stability, certainty, undoubted truth, security from enemies, safety

ἀσφαλής—firm, reliable, certain, true, suited to confirm, safe, sure

ἀσφαλῶς—safely, assuredly, certainly

ἀσφαλίζω—make firm, make secure, make safe, fasten

κρύπτω—hide, conceal, escape notice, make invisible, keep secret, keep safe, protect

στηριγμός—steadfastness, a place of safety, firm position, stable situation

στηρίζω—to fasten, strengthen, be firmly set, establish, make steady

στερεός—strong, solid, stiff, firm, hard

φεύγω—flee away, seek safety by fleeing, escape

ἀποφεύγω—to flee from, escape

ἐκφεύγω—flee out of, flee away, seek safety in fleeing, escape

καταφεύγω—flee away, flee for refuge

ἔκβασις—a way out, exit, way of escape, an egress, end, result

φυλάσσω—guard, keep watch, protect

διαφυλάσσω—guard carefully, keep, protect

σωτήρ—rescuer, savior, deliverer

σῴζω—save, keep safe and sound, rescue from danger or destruction, deliver from penalty, heal, preserve

σωτηρία—deliverance, preservation, salvation

σωτήριον—deliverance, preservation, salvation

διασῴζω—save, preserve, bring safely through, keep from perishing, heal, rescue

ῥύομαι—rescue, deliver

εὐαγγέλιον—good tidings, the good news of salvation through Christ, the proclamation of the grace of God given through faith in Christ

ἐξαιρέω—to pluck out, draw out, rescue, root out, choose out, select

περιποιέομαι—to reserve, keep safe, preserve for one's self, purchase, acquire

φείδομαι—to spare in war, not destroy, use sparingly, abstain, forbear, avoid, refrain from

Salary, Pay, Recompense, Reward, Prize, see also "Cost, Pay, Price"—

μισθός—wages, pay, hire, fee, recompense, reward

ἀντιμισθία—recompense, requital

ἀποδίδωμι—to give back, repay, recompense, return, middle: sell

μισθαποδοσία—reward, recompense, payment of wages

μισθαποδότης—rewarder, one who pays wages

ἀνταποδίδωμι—to give back, repay

ἀνταπόδομα—repayment, requital

ἀνταπόδοσις—a reward, repayment, rendering, recompense

ὀψώνιον—allowance, pay, salary, wage, expense money, ration

βραβεῖον—prize

στέφανος—crown

στεφανόω—to crown, adorn, decorate, give a prize

Same, Equivalent Kind

ἰσότης—equality

ἴσος—equal to, the same as, like

ἰσότιμος—held in equal honor, having the same privileges, equal to

αὐτός—he, she, it, self, same

εἰκών—image, representation, likeness, form, appearance, similitude, portrait, statue

σύμμορφος—conformed to, similar in form

συμμορφίζομαι—to have the same likeness, be conformed to

συμμορφόομαι—to have the same likeness, be conformed to

ὁποῖος—of what sort or quality, of whatsoever kind, like

ὅμως—similarly, all the same, nevertheless, notwithstanding, still, but for all that, yet, though, likewise, in the same way, also

ὁμῶς—equally, like, likewise, alike, like as, equally with, together with

Sea Terms, Nautical Terms, Fishing Terms, Maritime Activities, see also "Fish"

ἁλιεύω—to fish, catch fish

ἁλιεύς—fisherman

ἅλωσις—a capture, conquest, catch

ἀμφίβληστρον—casting-net

ἀμφιβάλλω—to throw around, of clothes, to put on, throw the arms around, embrace, cast a fishnet, throw out the circular casting-net

συγκλείω—to coop up, hem in, shut, close, enclose, intercept, catch fish

δίκτυον—fishnet

σαγήνη—large net, dragnet

ναῦς—ship

ναύκληρος—ship owner, shipmaster

ναύτης—seaman, sailor, mate or companion by sea

ναυαγέω—to be shipwrecked

κιβωτός—any box-like container, box, chest, coffer, ark

σκάφη—small boat

πρῷρα—bow of a boat

πρύμνα—stern of a boat

ἄγκιστρον—fish hook

ἄγκυρα—anchor

ἀρτέμων—sail

πηδάλιον—rudder

παράσημος—emblem

πλοῖον—boat

πλοιάριον—small boat

πλέω—to sail, go by sea, float

πλόος—voyage, sailing

ἐκπλέω—sail away from

ἀποπλέω—sail from

παραπλέω—sail past

ὑποπλέω—to sail under, sail under the lee of, sail under shelter of

καταπλέω—to sail down from the high sea to shore, sail toward shore, sail downstream, sail back

διαπλέω—sail across

βραδυπλοέω—to sail slowly

εὐθυδρομέω—to sail a straight course

παραλέγομαι—to sail past, coast along

ὑποτρέχω—to run in under, sail under shelter of

παραβάλλω—sail to, come near or approach by ship

συμπληρόω—to help to fill, fill up, man fully the ships, be swamped with water in a boat, of time fulfill, approach, come

ἀνάγω—go up, set sail

ἐπανάγω—put out to sea, push off from shore, return

κατάγω—lead down, bring from deep water to land, arrive at land

κατέρχομαι—go down, come down, arrive at land

ἐξωθέω—thrust out, expel, propel, drive out of the sea, run aground

ἐπικέλλω—to bring to shore, run ashore, run aground

ἐκπίπτω—to fall out of, fall off, run aground, lose, fail

προσορμίζομαι—to moor, come to anchor near

ορμίζω—to bring into harbor, moor, anchor, put a child to sleep

εὐθύνω—to guide straight, direct, govern, steer straight, pilot a ship, audit accounts, call to account

κατέχω εἰς—to head for

βολίζω—to drop a plummet, heave the lead, take soundings

περιαιρέω—remove completely, take off from around, launch, lift anchor

ὑποζώννυμι—to undergird, brace or frap a ship

ὁ ἐπὶ τόπον πλέων—sea traveler, one sailing to a place

κυβερνήτης—captain of a ship, steersman, helmsman, pilot, guide, governor

διθάλασσος—cross-currents

ῥίπτω—to throw out, let down (as anchors), set down

κλυδωνίζομαι—be tossed by waves, be agitated

Search, Seek

ζήτησις—inquiry, subject of questioning or debate, matter of controversy, dispute

ἐκζητέω—to seek out, search diligently, investigate, scrutinize, require of, bring charges against

ἀναζητέω—to seek out, search through, make a diligent search, try to find out

ἐπιζητέω—to inquire about, search for, seek after, seek diligently, crave, demand, desire

ἐραυνάω—to search, examine, try to find out

ἐξεραυνάω—to search out carefully, search anxiously and diligently

ἀνεξεραύνητος—not able to be searched out

ἴχνος—footprint, trail, track, trace

ἀνεξιχνίαστος—untraceable, not able to be searched out

ἐξετάζω—to search out, inquire, ask, try to find out

ἀνετάζω—to examine closely, interrogate

ἐτάζω—to examine, test

καταδιώκω—to search after, track down, hunt

ἀνακρίνω—examine or judge, scrutinize, sift, question, hold an investigation, interrogate, study thoroughly

ψηλαφάω—to handle, touch, feel, feel after, grope, try to find

See, Look, View, Watch

ὁράω—to see, behold, perceive, know, experience, take heed, beware

ἀφοράω—to fix attention on, find out

καθοράω—to see clearly, perceive

προοράω—to see beforehand, foresee, know beforehand, to keep before one's eyes

ὅραμα—something seen, spectacle, a divinely revealed vision

ὅρασις—the act of seeing, the eyes, appearance, visible form, a vision, a divinely granted vision

ὁρατός—visible

ἀόρατος—invisible

εἶδος—appearance, form, sight

βλέπω—to see, discern, understand, take heed, watch out for

βλέμμα—a look, glance, seeing, what is seen

ἀναβλέπω—to look up, to recover sight, receive sight, regain sight

ἀνάβλεψις—recovery of sight, gaining sight

ἀποβλέπω—to look attentively, fix attention on

διαβλέπω—to look fixedly, stare straight before one, see clearly

ἐμβλέπω—to look at, consider, see

ἐπιβλέπω—to look upon, consider, take an interest, care about, help

περιβλέπομαι—to look around

θεωρέω—to look at, watch, behold, see, consider, perceive, ascertain

θεάομαι—to behold, view, look at, take notice, perceive

θέατρον—a theater or public show, spectacle

θεωρία—a viewing, beholding, that which is viewed, a spectacle, sight

ἀναθεωρέω—to look at attentively, to consider well, to observe accurately, behold, reflect upon

φαίνω—to cause to shine, bring to light, appear, make known, be seen

φανερόω—make manifest what was hidden, make known, reveal, appear

φανερός—apparent, manifest, evident, known, clearly seen

φανερῶς—manifestly, plainly, clearly, openly, evidently, publicly

ἐμφανίζω—to manifest, exhibit to view, disclose, make known

ἐμφανής—manifest, visible, open, well known

ἐπιφαίνω—to show to, bring to light, appear, give light, illuminate

ἐπιφάνεια—an appearing, brightness, appearance

ἀναφαίνω—bring to light, come into view, show, appear, discover

φαντάζομαι—to cause to appear, make visible, expose to view, show

πρόσωπον—face, countenance, person, appearance

ἐπέχω—to hold on to, fix attention on, watch, be alert for, take notice of, attend to, delay, stay on

ὀφθαλμός—the eye, sight

ὀπτάνομαι—appear, allow one's self to be seen, be visible to

κατοπτρίζομαι—to show in a mirror, make to reflect, to mirror, see by reflection, behold as in a glass

ἐποπτεύω—to be an overseer, to look upon, view attentively, watch

αὐτόπτης—seeing with one's own eyes, an eyewitness, autopsy, a detailed examination

ἐπόπτης—an overseer, inspector, spectator, eyewitness

παρατηρέω—to watch closely, observe carefully, attend to with the eyes

παρατήρησις—observation, close watch

παρακύπτω—to stoop and look into, to look at with head lowered forward, inspect curiously

ἀτενίζω—to give fixed attention to, to fix one's eyes on, gaze upon, fasten eyes on, stare at, look earnestly or steadfastly

τηλαυγῶς—clearly, distinctly

κατασκοπέω—to spy out, observe secretly

κατανοέω—pay attention, consider, contemplate, apprehend, discern

ἐπιδείκνυμι—show, demonstrate, cause to be seen, show to be true

σκοπέω—to watch, look out, inspect, examine, reconnoiter, premeditate, consider

Seize, Arrest, see "Capture, Trap, Surround," "Hunt, Trap"

καταλαμβάνω—lay hold of, obtain, acquire, seize, attack, catch, middle: receive with the mind, comprehend

συλλαμβάνω—to seize, take, catch, gather, comprehend, conceive, become pregnant

ἐκτείνω τὰς χεῖρας ἐπί—stretch out the hand upon, arrest

ἐπιβάλλω τὴν χεῖρα ἐπί—arrest, put hands on
ἐπιλαμβάνομαι—take hold of, grasp, catch, trap, seize, arrest
κρατέω—to be strong, be sovereign, exercise control over, get possession of, seize, hold firmly to, grasp, retain
πιάζω—take hold of, seize, grasp, arrest, take into custody, catch
συναρπάζω—seize by force, catch
περιέχω—to encircle, surround, encompass, seize, contain

Sell, see "Buy, Sell"

Send
πέμπω—send someone, send word
ἀναπέμπω—send back, send up
ἐκπέμπω—send away, send forth
μεταπέμπομαι—send for, send after, summon
προπέμπω—send on one's way, escort or accompany, equip for a journey
συμπέμπω—to send together with, dispatch at the same time
ἐξαποστέλλω—send forth, send away
ἀποστέλλω—send on a mission
συναποστέλλω—send with
ἀπολύω—set free, let go, send away, release, allow, acquit, remit, divorce
ἀφίημι—send away, divorce, let go, leave, desert, abandon, forgive, remit, permit, allow, not hinder

Sequence, words related to
καθεξῆς—in order, one after another, in sequence
ἀπὸ μιᾶς—one by one
ἀνὰ μέρος—in succession
τάξις—order, orderliness, arrangment, regularity, division of troops, rank, class of men
τροχός—a course, as a race course or the course of the sun, anything round, a circle
ἀνώτερος—higher, above, earlier, preceding
ἀπαρχή—first portion of a sacrifice, firstfruits, first
πρότερος—first, before, in front, forward, former, sooner, above, superior, foremost, beginning
ποτέ—formerly, once, at some time, ever
οὕτως—thusly, in this way, in this manner, so, as follows
διάδοχος—successor, succeeding
δευτερόπρωτος—the second after the first
ἔσχατος—last, final, furthest, uttermost, most extreme
ὕστερος—latter, last, coming after, following, behind
τέλος—end, limit, boundary, finish, completion, last, conclusion, tax
πέρας—end, limit, boundary, finish, completion, last, conclusion
περαίνω—to bring to an end, finish, accomplish, execute, be fulfilled, reach

Serve
διακονέω—to minister, serve, take care of, wait on
διακονία—service, ministry, waiting on
διάκονος—a servant, minister, deacon
θεραπεύω—to care for, serve, treat, especially of a physician, heal, minister to, serve in a temple
θεράπων—an attendant, servant
ὑπηρετέω—to serve, be helpful
ὑπηρέτης—servant, helper, assistant, minister
λειτουργέω—to perform religious service or temple duties, minister

λειτουργία—a liturgy, temple service, the service of a minister
λειτουργός—priest, servant, minister
λειτουργικός—serving, ministering
παρεδρεύω—to wait on, serve
δουλεύω—to be a slave to, serve, be subject to
δουλαγωγέω—to make a slave, bring into subjection, make ready for service
ὀφθαλμοδουλία—eye-service
προσκαρτερέω—to persist in, be in constant readiness, continue in, spend much time in, be devoted to

Sexual Misbehavior, see "Vices: Lust" or "Desire: Passion"

Shame, Disgrace, Humiliation
αἰσχύνη—shame, embarrassment, humiliation, disgrace, dishonor, indecent behavior
αἰσχύνω—to be ashamed, disgraced
ἀσχημοσύνη—shamefulness, indecent behavior, as being naked
αἰσχρότης—indecency
ἐπαισχύνομαι—to be ashamed of
καταισχύνω—to dishonor, disgrace, put to shame, make ashamed, be ashamed
ἀσχημονέω—to act disgracefully, behave indecently, be ill-mannered or rude
αἰσχρός—ugly, deformed, ill-favored, disgraceful, shameful, dishonest
ἀφόβως—disgracefully, without fear, without reverence to God
ἐντρέπω—active: make someone ashamed, respect, mostly passive: be put to shame, be ashamed, passive with middle sense: have regard for, respect
ἐντροπή—shame, respect, reverence

ταπεινόω—to make low, abase, embarrass, bring low, make level, passive: be humble
ταπείνωσις—humiliation, abasement, low status, defeat
ταπεινός—lowly, humble, of low degree, brought low with grief, depressed, downhearted, cast down
δειγματίζω—to make an example of, show as an example, disgrace publicly
παραδειγματίζω—to set forth as a public example, make an example of, expose to public disgrace, put to open shame
θεατρίζω—to bring upon the stage, set forth as a spectacle, expose to contempt, make a gazing stock, shame publicly
ἀτιμάζω—to disrespect, dishonor, treat shamefully, degrade
ἀτιμία—dishonor, disgrace, shame, disparagement
ὄνειδος—disgrace, reproach, censure, blame
ἀνεπαίσχυντος—unashamed, having no cause of shame
ἀπαλγέω—to cease to feel pain or grief, be past feeling, feel no shame, lose sensitivity, become callous

Share, see also "Give"
μετέχω—to partake, share in, eat, drink
συμμερίζω—to share, distribute in shares, take share in or with
μερίζω—to divide, distribute, assign, apportion
συμμέτοχος—sharer, partaker with another in a thing, partner
συγκοινωνός—sharer, joint partaker of a thing
κοινός—communal, shared in common, mutual, public, of meats: profane or common, defiled, ritually unclean

Shout, Cry Out

φωνέω—to emit a sound, speak, cry out, call, summon, send for

ἀναφωνέω—to cry out with a loud voice, call aloud, exclaim

ἐπιφωνέω—to call out to, shout, cry against, cry out

προσφωνέω—call to oneself, address by calling, summon, speak to

φωνή—a sound, tone, voice, speech, cry, language

ἀναβοάω—to shout, raise a cry, cry out

βοάω—to shout, raise a cry, cry for help, implore one's aid

βοή—a cry, shout

ἀνακράζω—to raise a cry, shout

κράζω—to cry out, vociferate, speak with a loud voice, shout

κραυγάζω—to cry out, cry aloud, shout

κραυγή—a crying, outcry, clamor, weeping, shout

Sickness, Disease, Weakness

ἀσθένεια—weakness, infirmity, want of strength, illness, disease

ἀσθενέω—to be weak, ill, feeble, without strength, powerless

ἀσθενής—weak, infirm, feeble, ill

κακῶς ἔχω—to have badly, to be sick

βάλλω εἰς κλίνην—put to bed due to sickness

μάστιξ—a whip, scourge, plague, ailment, affliction

μαλακία—softness, weakness, illness, sickness

νόσημα—sickness, disease

νόσος—sickness, disease, infirmity

νοσέω—to be sick, to have morbid desire for

ἄρρωστος—without strength, weak, sick, ill

κάμνω—to grow weary, be sick, faint

πονηρός—bad, evil, grievous, lewd, wicked, diseased

διαφθείρω—to corrupt, utterly destroy, ruin

δεσμός—chain, binding, imprisonment, impediment, illness

δέω—to bind, fasten, put under obligation, cause illness

λοιμός—pestilence, plague, trouble

πληγή—blow, stripe, wound, heavy affliction, calamity, plague, distress

πίμπραμαι—kindle, burn, inflame, burn with fever, swell up

πυρετός—fever, fiery heat

πυρέσσω—to have fever

δυσεντέριον—dysentery, bowel ailment, a flow of blood

λέπρα—leprosy, a cutaneous viral disease

λεπρός—leprous, a leper, scaly

ὑδρωπικός—suffering from dropsy (watery fluid collecting in tissues)

γάγγραινα—gangrene (an ulcerous, spreading inflammation)

σκωληκόβρωτος—eaten by worms

σπαράσσω—convulse, tear, rend, throw into a fit

συσπαράσσω—convulse completely, throw into a fit, tear in pieces

ῥήγνυμι—rend, rip, burst or break asunder, break up, tear in pieces, break forth, throw into a fit or into convulsions, of someone having a seizure

σεληνιάζομαι—be epileptic, be moon-struck, be a lunatic

παραλύομαι—paralyzed, disabled,— weakened, enfeebled

παραλυτικός—paralyzed, unable to walk, disabled

ξηραίνω—to make dry, wither, waste away, become stiff, be ripe ξηρός—dry, of land as distinct from water, withered

παρίημι—to let pass, to pass by, neglect, disregard, omit, loose, let go, hang down, be weakened, exhausted, relaxed

χωλός—lame, crippled, deprived of a foot, maimed

κυλλός—crooked, mutilated, crippled, maimed

ἀνάπηρος—disabled in the limbs, crippled, injured in, or bereft of, some member of the body, maimed

ἐκτρέπομαι—to be turned aside, be dislocated, to wander, swerve, avoid

ἕλκος—a wound, sore, ulcer

ἑλκόομαι—to make sore, cause to ulcerate, have sores

αἱμορροέω—to have a discharge of blood, to lose blood, to bleed

πηγὴ αἵματος—flow of blood, menstrual flow

ῥύσις αἵματος—flow of blood, menstrual flow, hemorrhage

αἱματεκχυσία—shedding of blood, cause of blood flow

ἀποψύχω—to faint, be dismayed, lose consciousness

Signal, Signify, Indicate

σύσσημον—a common sign or concerted signal, a sign given according to an agreement, token, signal

σημεῖον—sign, unusual occurance foreshadowing unexpected events soon to happen, indication, mark, token, miracle

τέρας—a miracle or wonder, prodigy, portent

παράσημος—emblem or carved figure as a distinguishing mark on ships

στίγμα—mark, scar, stamp, brand

χάραγμα—stamp, imprinted mark, graven mark, mark of the antichrist

σφραγίς—a seal, signet ring, mark of genuineness, that by which a thing is confirmed or authenticated, proof

σφραγίζω—to mark with a seal, put a seal on, seal up, confirm, prove, guarantee

κατασείω—beckon, signal with the hand, wave or motion with the hand

νεύω—to give a nod, signify by a nod, beckon, gesture

κατανεύω—gesture, nod to, make a sign, give indication by a signal, beckon

διανεύω—gesture, express one's meaning by a sign, nod to, beckon to

ἐννεύω—gesture, nod to, signify

Silent, Mute, Speechless, Quiet

ἄλαλος—speechless, mute, wanting the faculty of speech

ἄφωνος—voiceless, mute, unable to speak, inarticulate, without meaning

κωφός—blunted, dull, deaf, lamed in tongue, dumb, speechless, mute

μογιλάλος—speaking with difficulty, having a speech impediment, hardly able to speak

ἐνεός—mute, destitute of speech, unable to speak for terror, struck dumb, astounded, speechless

σιωπάω—to be silent, hold one's peace, be calm, not be able to speak

σιγή—silence, from σίζω, to hush

σιγάω—to keep silence, hold one's peace, keep secret, keep quiet about

ἡσυχάζω—to keep quiet, be silent, rest, cease from labor, of observing the sabbath, to lead a quiet life, hold one's peace, be still, be calm ἡσυχία—quietness, silence, quiet circumstances, quiet living

φιμόω—to muzzle, tie shut as with a muzzle, put to silence

ἐπιστομίζω—to bridle or stop up the mouth, put to silence

φράσσω στόμα—to stop the mouth, put to silence

φράσσω—stop up, block, bar

Sin, Guilt, see also "Bad"

ἁμαρτάνω—sin, fail of doing, do wrong, transgress

ἁμαρτία—sin, fault, failure, guilt

ἁμάρτημα—sin, fault, wrongdoing, error

ἁμαρτωλός—sinful, sinner

ἀναμάρτητος—having not sinned, guiltless, one who has done nothing wrong

προαμαρτάνω—sin previously, commit sin beforehand

πταίω—sin, stumble, err, offend

ἄπταιστος—free from sinning

παράπτωμα—sin, fall away from the right path

πτῶμα—corpse, dead body, what has fallen, a downfall, lapse into sin

ὀφείλω—to be bound, be obliged, owe, be indebted to, be due, be liable to, would that, ought

ὀφείλημα—that which is owed, a debt, obligation

ὀφειλέτης—debtor, offender

ῥᾳδιούργημα—wrongdoing, crime

ῥᾳδιουργία—wrongdoing, as taking the law lightly, lack of principle, unscrupulousness

ῥᾴδιος—light, loose

ὑπερβαίνω—sin against, go beyond (prescribed limits)

ἀγνόημα—sin through ignorance, without deliberate intent, sin committed by oversight, not consciously

δελεάζω—lure into sin, entrap, lead astray, entice, allure into wrongdoing

σκανδαλίζω—put a stumbling block in the way, offend, cause to sin

σκάνδαλον—trap, offense, stumbling block

πρόσκομμα—a stumbling block, obstacle, offense, occasion to sin

προσκοπή—a stumbling block, obstacle, offense

ἀπρόσκοπος—not causing offense, without obstacle e.g., a smooth road, without offense, blameless

ἔνοχος—liable, answerable, subject to, guilty of sin against

πονηρός—bad, evil, grievous, lewd, wicked, diseased

αἰτία—cause, reason for accusation, charge

αἴτιον—cause, reason for accusation, charge, grounds for punishment

ἀναίτιος—innocent, guiltless, not blamable

μέμφομαι—to blame, find fault, accuse

ἀνομία—lawlessness, wickedness, iniquity, sin, wrongdoing

ἀδικία—unrighteousness, injustice, wrongdoing, lawlessness, sin, evil, wickedness, violation of justice

αὐτόφωρος—caught in the act of an offense, in the very act, point blank

Sit

καθέζομαι—sit down, seat one's self

κάθημαι—sit down, seat one's self, have a fixed abode, dwell, reside

καθίζω—sit, seat, set, appoint, settle, remain, tarry

συγκάθημαι—sit together, sit down with

συγκαθίζω—cause to sit down together, place together, sit down together

παρακαθέζομαι—make to sit down beside, set beside, place near, sit down by

ἐπικαθίζω—cause to sit upon, sit upon

ἀνακαθίζω—sit up

Slander, Insult, see "Vices: Accuse, Defame, Talk Foolishly"

Sleep

καθεύδω—sleep, be dead

κοιμάομαι—put to sleep, make calm, quiet, still, be dead

κοίμησις—repose, rest, sleep

ὕπνος—sleep

ἀφυπνόω—fall asleep

νυστάζω—sleep, grow drowsy, slumber, be negligent, careless

οἱ ὀφθαλμοὶ βεβαρημένοι—the eyes being heavy, being very sleepy

οἱ ὀφθαλμοὶ καταβαρυνόμενοι—the eyes being heavy, being very sleepy

κατάνυξις—stupor, slumber, inability to think

αὐλίζομαι—to lodge, spend the night, bivouac

διανυκτερεύω—to spend the night

Slow, Delay

παρατεινω—to stretch out along or beside, hold out to the last, extend, prolong, protract, lengthen

χρονίζω—to be late, spend a long time in, tarry, linger, be slow, delay, be prolonged

βραδύς—slow, tardy, late

βραδύνω—to delay, loiter, be slow

βραδύτης—slowness

ὀκνέω—to shrink from, scruple, hesitate, delay

μακροθυμέω—to be patient, not lose heart, be longsuffering, be slow to avenge wrong, to endure

ἀναβολή—a putting off, delaying, postponement of a court case

Small, Little, Small in Number, Few, Slightly, To A Small Degree

ὀλίγος—few, little, scanty, small, slight

μικρός—small, little, petty, trivial, slight, a short time

ἐλαφρός—light in weight, easy to bear, buoyant, not burdensome, limited in extent, insignificant in size or number

ἐλάσσων—smaller, less, fewer, worse than, inferior to, subservient to, younger

ἐλασσόω—to make less or smaller, to lessen, diminish

ἐλαχύς—small, short, little

ἐλάχιστος—the smallest, least, shortest, fewest, least important

μετρίως—with measure, moderately, in due limits, temperately, a little

ἐκ μέτρου—sparingly, in a measured amount

βραχύς—short, brief, small, little, few, low, petty, trifling, insignificant

κατωτέρω—lower, below, lesser

φειδομένως—sparingly

φείδομαι—to spare in war, not destroy, use sparingly, abstain, forbear, avoid, refrain from

Smell

ὄσφρησις—sense of smell, smelling

ὀσμή—odor, fragrance, smell, aroma

ὄζω—to give off an odor, smell, stink, give off a stench

εὐωδία—fragrance, sweet odor, aroma

Sneak In, Infiltrate

παρεισέρχομαι—to slip into a group, to come or go in beside or secretly

παρείσακτος—joined falsely, introduced secretly

παρεισδύω—slip into a group stealthily, sneak in

Soft, Tender

ἁπαλός—easily yielding to pressure, of sprouting branches, soft, tender

μαλακός—soft, delicate, luxurious, effeminate, unmanly, homosexual

Sound

φθόγγος—sound, tone, voice

φθέγγομαι—to speak, give a sound, noise or cry

ἦχος—a sound, blast of a trumpet, report, news

ἠχέω—make a noise

ἀκοή—the sense of hearing, the ear, the thing heard, instruction, message

φωνέω—to emit a sound, speak, cry out, call, summon, send for

φωνή—sound, tone, voice, speech, language

μυκάομαι—roar

ὠρύομαι—roar

θόρυβος—noise, uproar, clamor, excitement, applause, cheers, turmoil, tumult, confusion, riot

ἀλαλάζω—ἀλαλάζω—to weep loudly, wail, lament, clang

συμφωνία—music, symphony

μουσικός—musician

ροιζηδόν—with a shrill noise

Sojourner, Foreigner, Pilgrim

ἐπιδημέω—live as a foreigner, dwell among other people, temporarily reside among

ἀποδημέω—go away into foreign parts, go abroad, leave home on a journey

παροικέω—live in a place without citizenship, live as a foreigner, dwell temporarily

παροικία—pilgrimage, sojourn, period spent in a foreign land, stay, time of temporary residence

ἀστατέω—be homeless, be unsettled, wander from place to place

μετοικεσία—deportation, exile, captivity, forced removal to another living place

μετοικίζω—remove someone to another place, resettle, deport, send into exile, banish

Speak, Talk, Communicate

λέγω—to say, speak, to call, name

προλέγω—to say beforehand, say already, foretell, tell before, predict, warn

φημί—declare, tell, say

λαλέω—utter a voice, speak, talk, tell, say

λαλιά—speech, dialect, mode of speech, pronunciation, accent, speech which discloses the speaker's native country, utterance

προσλαλέω—to speak to

ἐκλαλέω—to speak out, tell

ἀποφθέγγομαι—to speak out, speak forth, pronounce, say, utter

φθέγγομαι—to speak, give a sound, noise or cry

λόγια—sayings

λόγος—word, reason, matter under discussion, account, treatise, statement

πολυλογία—much speaking, long speaking

βατταλογέω—to stammer, repeat over and over, use many idle words, babble ῥῆμα—word, thing spoken, utterance, subject matter of thing spoken of, statement

παρρησιάζομαι—to speak freely, speak boldly

ῥητῶς—clearly, exactly, expressly, in express words, just as said

φωνή—sound, tone, voice, speech, language

φράζω—to explain, interpret, expound, to propound in distinct terms, to tell

παρακοινάομαι—to communicate

ὁμιλία—communication

Speech, Kinds Of

δημηγορέω—to address in a public assembly, make a speech, make an oration

διαλέγομαι—discuss, argue, address

προσφωνέω—call to oneself, address by calling, summon, speak to

ἀποκρίνομαι—to answer

χρηστολογία—attractive speech, good words

πιθανολογία—persuasive speech, convincing argumentation, enticing words

λόγιος—a man of letters, skilled in literature and speech, eloquent, rational, wise, learned

εὐτραπελία—pleasantry, humor, facetiousness, low jesting, vulgar speech

αἰσχρολογία—dirty talk, foul speaking, obscene communication

Spend, Waste

δαπανάω—to spend freely, wear out, exhaust, expend, use up, put to expense, consume, destroy

προσδαπανάω—to spend in addition to, spend besides

ἀναλίσκω—spend, expend, consume, use up, destroy

προσαναλίσκω—to spend much, to lavish or consume in addition

κατεσθίω—consume, eat up, devour, exploit, prey on

διασκορπίζω—scatter abroad, disperse, winnow, throw grain into the air that it may be separated from the chaff, squander

σκορπίζω—scatter, dispense blessings, give generously

Spices, Condiments

ἄμωμον—spice

κιννάμωμον—cinnamon

ἅλας—salt

ἅλς—salt

ἁλυκός—salty

ἄναλος—without salt

ἁλίζω—season with salt

σίναπι—mustard

πήγανον—rue, shrubby plant about two feet high with medicinal value

ἡδύοσμον—mint

ἄνηθον—anise, dill

κύμινον—cumin

Spirit, Soul

πνεῦμα—wind, breath, spirit, soul, the Holy Spirit, the inner being

πνέω—blow, breathe

πνευματικός—spiritual, relating to the human spirit or rational soul, as the part of man which is akin to God, pertaining to the wind or breath, supernatural, of spiritual conduct, not physical

πνευματικῶς—spiritually

ζῆλος—fervor of spirit, zeal, earnest concern, jealousy, indignation

ζηλόω—to burn with zeal or envy, be jealous over, to desire earnestly προθυμία—zeal, spirit, eagerness, inclination, readiness of mind

πρόθυμος—ready, willing, eager

ψυχή—breath, soul, living being, person, life, inner self

ζωή—life, having vitality

καρδία—heart, inner self

χρῖσμα—anointing oil, unguent, anointing by the Holy Spirit

χρίω—to anoint, as the anointing of Jesus Christ, the prophets, David, the apostles, and all believers, with oil of gladness or with the Holy Spirit

παράκλητος—name of the Holy Spirit (John 14:26), Comforter, Counselor, called to one's aid

Split, Tear, Rip, Break Open

σχίζω—cleave, rend, divide, split into factions

σχίσμα—a division, dissension, schism, tear

διασπάω—rend asunder, break asunder, pull in pieces, tear apart

λακάω—crack, crack open, crash, burst open

διαρρήγνυμι—rip, break asunder, burst through, rend asunder, rend clothes as show of grief

περιρήγνυμι—break off on all sides, tear off all around

ῥήγνυμι—rend, rip, burst or break asunder, break up, tear in pieces, break forth, throw into a fit or into convulsions, of someone having a seizure

σπαράσσω—convulse, tear, rend, throw into a fit

συσπαράσσω—convulse completely, throw into a fit, tear in pieces

Spoils, see "Plunder," "Vices: Stealing"

Spread, Stretch

στρώννυμι—spread, strew, furnish, spread with couches or divans, make a bed

στρώννυμι and στρωννύω—to spread out, strew, carpet a room, furnish, lay out anything to lie on or recline on, make a bed

ὑποστρωννύω—strew, spread under, spread out underneath

διανέμω—distribute, allocate, deliver, dispense, give out, spread news of, circulate, cause to become known

σπείρω—to sow, beget, give birth, engender, scatter like seed, strew, throw about, spread abroad, broadcast, disperse

ἐκπετάννυμι—spread out, stretch out

ἐκτείνω—stretch out, stretch forth, put forth

ἐπεκτείνομαι—stretch out to or towards, reach forth, try hard to

προτείνω—stretch forth, stretch out, stretch out to receive blows by tying to a beam or pillar

Stand, Set

ἵστημι—stand, place, put, establish, set, continue to be, remain firmly

στήκω—stand, persevere, persist

συνίστημι—to commend, recommend, approve, show, intransitive: be set together, be formed into, consist of, hold together

παρίστημι—to stand before, present, show to be true, set before, provide, furnish, put at one's disposal

περιΐστημι—be set around, middle: avoid by going around, shun ἐφίστημι—come up to, approach, stand near, appear suddenly, be imminent, attack

ἀνίστημι—raise up, rise, stand up, appear, stand forth, resurrect

ἐξανίστημι—make to rise up, produce, rise, stand up

ἐγείρω—arouse, cause to rise, awaken, stand up

Steal, Rob, see "Vices: Stealing"

Straighten Up

ἀνακύπτω—raise or lift one's self up, be elated, straighten up

ἀνορθόω—set up, make erect, build again, straighten up

Street

ὁδός—way, road, way of conduct

τρίβος—path

τρίβω—rub, wear away

ἄμφοδον—city street

διέξοδος—way through a city

πλατεῖα—wide street

ῥύμη—narrow street

φραγμός—fence, hedge, barrier, perhaps byway (Luke 14:23)

Strife, Struggle, see also "Vices: Fighting" and "Argue, Quarrel"

ἔρις—contention, strife, debate, rivalry, discord, quarrel, fighting

ἐρίζω—engage in strife, strive, quarrel

μάχη—severe clash, battle, fight, combat, quarrel, strife, struggle

μάχομαι—to clash severely, fight, quarrel, dispute

μάχαιρα—sword

διαμάχομαι—to protest strongly, fight, strive, struggle against, resist, contend obstinately, exert oneself greatly

θηριομαχέω—to fight with wild animals, be in serious conflict

θεομάχος—fighting against God

πολεμέω—to make war, fight, do battle, quarrel, treat as enemies, be hostile

πόλεμος—battle, fight, war

ἀγών—an athletic contest, struggle, trial, battle, fight, race

πάλη—wrestling, battle, fight

ἀγωνίζομαι—to contend for a prize in public games, contest, debate, contend in law, fight, struggle

ἐπαγωνίζομαι—to contend with, contend for

ἀνταγωνίζομαι—to struggle against, dispute with

ἄμαχος—not contentious, peaceful

Strong, Able, Capable

δύναμαι—to be able, capable, strong enough, powerful, mighty

δύναμις—power, might, strength, authority, force, ability

δυναμόω—to strengthen, enable

δυνατέω—to be powerful, mighty, able

δυνατός—strong, mighty, able, fit for service, possible

ἀδυνατέω—(antonym) to want strength, be unable to, be impossible

ἀδύνατος—(antonym) incapable, unable, without strength, powerless, disabled, poor, impossible

ἐνδυναμόω—to cause to be able, become able

ἰσχυρός—strong, mighty, powerful, vigorous, severe

ἰσχύς—strength, capability

ἰσχύω—to be strong, to have power, be capable, be able, be healthy ἐνισχύω—regain strength

ἐξισχύω—to have strength enough, be fully able, be quite able

κατισχύω—to have power over, overpower, prevail against, come to one's full strength, be fully able

στερεός—strong, solid, stiff, firm, hard

στερεόω—to make firm or solid, strengthen, (different from στερέω—to deprive, bereave, rob of)

στερέωμα—firmness, steadfastness, a solid body, foundation

στηριγμός—a propping, supporting, fixedness, steadfastness, firm position

στηρίζω—to prop, set, fixate, fasten, strengthen, confirm, establish, settle, be firmly set, make steady

ἐπιστηρίζω—to strengthen

κραταιόω—make strong, strengthen

κράτος—strength, might, sovereignty, power, dominion, mastery, authority

κραταιός—powerful, strong, mighty

οἰκοδομέω—to build, edify, found upon, encourage, build up, make more able, embolden

ἐποικοδομέω—to build up, build upon, rebuild

σθενόω—to strengthen, make strong, make more able

κατακαυχάομαι—to boast against, exult over, triumph over, have no fear of, have more power than

ἄθλησις—challenge, contest, struggle

βεβαιόω—to make firm, establish, confirm, make certain, verify, cause to believe, strengthen someone

ῥιζόομαι—to take root, be rooted, be firmly fixed, be planted, be strengthened

Stubbornness

σκληρότης—hardness, stubbornness, a resistant attitude, unreceptivity

ἀπερίτμητος καρδία καὶ τοῖς ὠσίν—obstinate, uncircumcised heart and ears

σκληροκαρδία—hard-heartedness, stubbornness, insensitivity, slowness to understand

σκληροτράχηλος—stiff-necked, stubborn, headstrong

σκληρύνω—harden, become thick, be stubborn, refuse to accept wisdom

πώρωσις—covering with a callous, dulled perception, stubbornness, blindness, hardness, insensibility

Suppose

ὑπολαμβάνω—suppose, take in mind, take up, receive

ὑπονοέω—to suppose, surmise, think, deem, suspect

ὑπόνοια—suspicion, surmising

δοκέω—to be of opinion, think, suppose, be accounted, impersonal δοκεῖ: it seems

νομίζω—to deem, think, suppose, passive: to be customary

οἴμαι—to suppose, think, expect

ἐκζήτησις—controversy, useless speculation, idle dispute

Surprise, Astonish

ἐκπλήσσομαι—to be struck with amazement, be greatly astounded

ἔκστασις—amazement, terror, the mind being out of its normal state, an ecstatic vision

ἐξίστημι—to amaze, astonish, have wonderment, to marvel, to be out of one's mind, beside one's self, insane

θαμβέομαι—to be astonished, terrified, frightened, amazed

θάμβος—astonishment, amazement, wonder

ἐκθαμβέομαι—to throw into terror or amazement, to be astounded

ἔκθαμβος—astounded, astonished, amazed, terrified, full of wonder, marveling

θαῦμα—a wonderful thing, a marvel, a miracle, admiration, amazement

θαυμάζω—to wonder at, marvel, admire, be amazed, have in admiration

θαυμάσιος—wonderful, marvelous

θαυμαστός—wonderful, marvelous, admirable, excellent, extraordinary, striking, surprising

ἐκθαυμάζω—be very amazed

ξενίζω—to show hospitality to strangers, intransitive: be surprised, think strange

ξενισμός—surprise, astonishment

συγχέω—to cause consternation, stir up tumult, confuse, passive: be confused, amazed, bewildered

Swim

κολυμβάω—dive, swim

ἐκκολυμβάω—swim out of, swim away

T

Take, Grasp, Hold, Seize, see also "Seize, Arrest"

δέχομαι—take, receive, grasp, accept, welcome

λαμβάνω—take, take hold of, grasp, acquire, receive, accept, collect, welcome, take on

ἐπιλαμβάνομαι—take hold of, grasp, catch, trap, seize, arrest

προσλαμβάνομαι—take aside, receive, welcome

ἅπτω—touch, hold, kindle, set on fire

καθάπτω—fasten to, bind on

ἔχω—have, hold, possess, have on, wear

κρατέω—to be strong, be sovereign, exercise control over, get possession of, seize, hold firmly to, grasp, retain

πιάζω—seize, lay hold of, capture (of fish), apprehend, arrest

ἁρπάζω—snatch greedily, carry off by force, seize, plunder, claim for one's self eagerly, overpower

συναρπάζω—seize by force, catch

ἄγρα—catch, that taken in hunting, booty, prey, game, a haul of fish

τίλλω—pluck, pluck off, pick

συλλέγω—gather up, collect, bring together

Taste, Words Related To, see also "Spice, Condiment"

γλυκύς—sweet

ἡδυσμός—sweet savor, sweetness

ἥδυσμα—relish, seasoning

ἡδύσματα—spices, sweet herbs

ἡδύνω—to please, gladden, make sweet, be sweet, be pleasant

ἡδύοσμον—mint

πικρία—bitterness, bitter resentment

πικρός—bitter

πικραίνω—make bitter

ἄψινθος—wormwood, a plant yielding a bitter, dark-green, alcoholic oil called gall or χολή

χολή—gall, bile, a bitter digestive fluid from the gall bladder, the bitter liquid from the plant wormwood, bitter anger

μωραίνω—to become foolish, become tasteless, lose flavor, become dull

γεύομαι—to taste, try the flavor of, partake of, enjoy, experience, eat

γεῦσις—the sense of taste

γεῦμα—a piece to taste, flavor

χυμὸς—flavor

κνίσσα—flavor

Tax, Tribute

τελέω—finish, end, accomplish, fulfill, make perfect, pay taxes τέλος—completion, result, end, finish, perfection, a toll, tax, duty

κῆνσος—census, registration for taxes, tax

ἀπογραφή—enrollment, census, listing in public records of persons often with their income and property, as the basis of a census or valuation for tax determination

ἀπογράφω—passive: be registered or enrolled (in a census), be entered in public records

δίδραχμον—two drachma, Greek coin paid annually for Jewish temple tax, about two days' wages

φόρος—tax, tribute, brought in by subjects to a ruling state or to a foreign ruler

τελώνιον—revenue office, tax collector's booth

τελώνης—tax collector

ἀρχιτελώνης—chief tax collector

Teach

διδασκαλία—teaching, instruction, doctrine

διδάσκω—to teach, instruct

διδαχή—teaching, doctrine

διδάσκαλος—teacher

διδακτός—what can be taught, teachings, precepts, instructed

διδακτικός—apt and skillful in teaching, able to teach, pertaining to teaching

θεοδίδακτος—taught by God

ἑτεροδιδασκαλέω—to teach other or different doctrine, deviating from truth

καλοδιδάσκαλος—teacher of what is good

νομοδιδάσκαλος—teacher of the Law

ψευδοδιδάσκαλος—false teacher

παιδεία—discipline, training, teaching, chastening, nurture, punishment, correction

παιδεύω—to train, teach, correct, scourge, punish, discipline

παιδευτής—instructor, teacher, trainer, punisher

σωφρονίζω—restore one to his senses, moderate, curb, control, disciple, hold one to his duty, admonish, teach to be sober, teach

ὀρθοτομέω—to hold to a straight course, teach correctly, rightly divide

νουθεσία—admonition, exhortation, teaching, warning

νουθετέω—to admonish, warn, exhort, instruct

ἐντρέφομαι—to nourish in, educate, form the mind, train

ἀνατρέφω—to nurse, nourish, bring up, rear

παραδίδωμι—give over, deliver over, betray, pass on teachings

παράδοσις—giving over, surrender, passing on of tradition through teaching, tradition

πατροπαράδοτος—handed down from forefathers or ancestors, received by tradition from fathers, teaching handed down

κατηχέω—teach, instruct, inform, tell

ἠχέω—make a noise

καθηγητής—guide, master, teacher

παραλαμβάνω—receive, take with, accept, learn

ὑποτίθημι—to place under, lay down, middle: advise, instruct

ῥαββί—teacher, master, honorable sir

ῥαββουνι—Chaldean: teacher, master, honorable sir, lord

αἵρεσις—sect, religious party, division, faction, heretical group, false teaching

Tempt, Test, Trap, Catch, see also "Take, Grasp, Hold, Seize"

πειράζω—try, attempt, endeavor, undertake, tempt, solicit to sin, test, entice, try to trap

ἐκπειράζω—to prove, put to test one's character, tempt, try to trap

πειρασμός—an experiment, attempt, trial, proving, testing, temptation

ἐτάζω—to examine, test

δοκιμάζω—to test, examine, prove, scrutinize, recognize as genuine after examination, to approve, deem worthy, try", evaluate

δοκιμασία—testing, examination

δοκιμή—proving, test, evidence of genuineness, approved character

δοκίμιον—proving, that by which something is tried or proved, a test, trial, genuineness

καταλαμβάνω—lay hold of, obtain, acquire, seize, attack, catch, middle: receive with the mind, comprehend

προλαμβάνω—to do beforehand, passive: be overtaken, be caught

ἐπιλαμβάνομαι—take hold of, grasp, catch, trap, seize, arrest

ἀγρεύω—hunt, catch, catch in a mistake

θηρεύω—hunt, catch, ensnare, catch in a mistake

παγιδεύω—ensnare, entrap, entangle, catch in mistake

δράσσομαι—catch, seize, trap

ἐνέδρα—ambush, lying in wait

ἐνεδρεύω—to lie in wait for, set an ambush

Thank, see "Virtues: Thankfulness

Think, see also "Know"

νοέω—to understand, see with insight, reflect, perceive, observe, comprehend, conceive

κατανοέω—pay attention, consider, contemplate, apprehend, discern

διάνοια—mind, understanding, intention, purpose, thoughts

διανοέωμαι—to be minded, intend, purpose, think over, suppose, be disposed

διανόημα—thought

διάνοια—mind, understanding, intention, purpose, thoughts

νόημα—mental perception, thought, the mind

ἔννοια—thought, attitude, insight, idea, purpose, intention

νοῦς—the mind, reason

εὐνοέω—wish well, consider favorably, be well-disposed, be of a peaceable spirit, to agree with, settle a case

προνοέω—foresee, plan beforehand, be provident, provide for, take care of, take thought for

πρόνοια—foresight, forethought, providential care, provision for

λογίζομαι—to reckon, count, calculate, take into account, number among, consider, impute, reason, suppose, keep mental record

λογισμός—reasoning, computation, reckoning, judgement, decision, imagination, thought

ἀναλογίζομαι—to think over, consider, ponder, consider carefully

διαλογίζομαι—to reason carefully, deliberate, cast in the mind, discuss, dispute, converse about

διαλογισμός—reasoning, argument, doubt, dispute

λόγος—word, reason, matter under discussion, account, treatise, statement

φρονέω—to have understanding, be wise, think, direct one's mind to a thing, hold a view, have an opinion, set the affection on

φροντίζω—to think, to be careful or anxious, to keep thinking about

ὁμόφρων—of one mind, concordant, like-minded

σωφρονέω—to be of sound mind, exercise self-control, be sane, be sensible, curb one's passions

ἐνθυμέομαι—to bring to mind, ponder, think deeply, deliberate, draw a conclusion about, weigh upon one's heart, form a plan

διενθυμέομαι—to think, ponder, reflect, consider carefully, think seriously about

ἐνθύμησις—thinking, consideration, thought

μελετάω—to meditate on, plot, think about, attend to, practice, rehearse

μέλει—it is a concern

ἐπιμελέομαι—to take care of, think about

ἐπιμελῶς—diligently, carefully

νήφω—be sober-minded, temperate, circumspect, restrained, watchful

ἐκνήφω—return to one's right senses, become sober, awake

ἀνανήφω—to return to soberness, recover self, return to one's right senses

βλέπω—to see, discern, understand, take heed, watch out for

ἐμβλέπω—to turn one's eyes upon, look at, to consider, behold, gaze upon, see, look straight at

ἐπιβλέπω—to look upon, consider, look attentively, pay respect to, take an interest in, care about, help

ἀποβλέπω—to look attentively, fix attention on

ὁράω—to see, behold, perceive, know, experience, take heed, beware

ἐφοράω—to look upon, regard, behold, pay attention to

ἀναθεωρέω—to look at attentively, to consider well, to observe accurately, behold, reflect upon

καταμανθάνω—to learn thoroughly, examine carefully, consider well

ἐπιβάλλω—cast upon, attend to, think on, put upon, take possession of

συμβάλλω—meet, discuss, consult, debate, ponder, middle: help, assist

ἡγέομαι—govern, lead, think, consider

ἀπερισπάστως—without distraction

βουλεύομαι—to deliberate, consider, take counsel, resolve, purpose, think about carefully, intend

ἐκκρέμαμαι—to hang from, depend on, listen attentively to

προσέχω—be attentive, watch, give heed to, beware, be devoted to

κατάνυξις—(antonym) stupor, slumber, inability to think

Threaten

ἀπειλέω—to threaten, menace

ἀπειλή—threat

προσαπειλέομαι—to add threats, threaten further

ἐπηρεάζω—mistreat, revile, slander, threaten abusively

Throw, Hurl

βάλλω—throw, cast, hurl, put, place, deposit

ἐπιβάλλω—cast upon, attend to, think on, put upon, take possession of

ἐκβάλλω—throw out

βολή—throw

ἐκβολή—a throwing out

ῥίπτω—to throw out, let down, set down
ἐπιρίπτω—throw on
κατακρημνίζω—throw down a cliff

Time

χρόνος—time, occasion, season, age
καιρός—time, occasion, season, age
διάστημα—interval
ὥρα—hour
ἡμέρα—day
μήν—month, it can also mean: indeed
ἔτος—year
αἰών—an age, eternity, a very long time, period, era
γενεά—generation, age, descendants

Time: Before In Time

πρίν—before in time, previously
πρό—in front of, before in time, above in value
πρότερος—first, before, in front, forward, former, sooner, above, superior, foremost, beginning
ἀνώτερος—higher, above, earlier, preceding
πρῶτος—first, earliest, before, foremost, most important, best
πάλαι—long ago, in olden time, in days of yore, in time gone by, formerly, for a long time
παλαιός—old, aged, ancient, from older time
ἔκπαλαι—for a long time, long ago
ἀπ' αἰῶνος—from of ages, from long ago
ἀφ' ἡμερῶν ἀρχαίων—from days of old, from long ago
πόρρωθεν—from a distance, at a distance, from afar, long before, far ahead of time
ἐχθές—yesterday, in the past
πέρυσι(ν)—last year, a year ago

προφθάνω—to outrun, anticipate, be beforehand
φθάνω—come before, precede, arrive at, reach, attain, come upon, happen
ποτέ—formerly, once, at some time, ever
τότε—then, at that time, thereupon, in those times, formerly
ἄχρι—until, until the time of, before, as far as, up to, unto, as long as
ἄχρι(ς) οὗ—until, as long as
μέχρι(ς)—until, to a given point, even so far, as far as, up to, nearly
μέχρις οὗ—until
ἤδη—already, by this time, before this, now, presently

Time: Present In Time

νῦν—now, just now
ἡ ἄρτι ὥρα—at this very moment
ἅμα—at once, at the same time, together with
ἐφάπαξ—at once, at the same time, once for all
σήμερον—today
τὸ παρόν—the present
προσφάτως—recently, newly
καινός—new, fresh, de novo, produced for the first time, latest
δεῦρο—come, come here, thus far, hitherto, of time: until now, this time, the present time
ἄρτι—now, just now, presently
εὐθύς—immediately, directly, straightway, without reserve, at once, unhindered, openly, forthrightly, Acts 8:21, 2 Peter 2:15
εὐθέως—immediately, directly, straightway, without reserve, at once

Time: Future In Time

δεύτερος—second, afterward

ὕστερος—later, afterwards, latter, last, coming after, following, behind, late, thereafter, second

ὑστερέω—to be in need, be lacking, be wanting, fall short, arrive late

ὀψέ—evening, late, after a long time

ἐγγίζω—to approach, come near

ἐγγύς—near, nigh, at hand

ἄνωθεν—again, over again, anew, from above, from on high, from the beginning

πάλιν—again, once more, anew, back (Mark 15:13), furthermore, on the other hand, in turn, however

εἰς τὸ πάλιν—again

ταχέως—very soon, quickly, at once, without delay, hastily

ἐν τάχει—very soon

ὡς τάχιστα—as soon as possible

αὔριον—tomorrow, soon

ἐπὶ θύραις—very soon, at the door

πρὸ θυρῶν—soon, before the door or antechamber

δι᾽ ἡμερῶν—a few days later

δι᾽ ἐτῶν—after years

μέλλω—to be about to, intend to, be destined to, be going to

ἐνίστημι—to be upon, threaten, be at hand, be present, be here, impend, be imminent

ἐφίστημι—come up to, approach, stand near, appear suddenly, be imminent, attack

αὔριον—tomorrow

ἐπιούσιος—daily, for today, for the coming day

τῇ ἐπιούσῃ—on the next day

τῇ ἑξῆς—on the next day

τῇ ἐπαύριον—on the next day

τῇ ἑτέρᾳ—on the next day

τῇ ἐχομένῃ—on the next day

ἐν τῷ (καθ)εξῆς—next, later, in the next day

εἶτα—then, next, afterwards, soon, furthermore

ἔπειτα—thereupon, thereafter, afterwards, hereafter, following, later, then

ἐκεῖθεν—from there, from that place, thence, thereafter, next

μετέπειτα—afterwards

μεταξύ—between, in the middle, meanwhile, among, afterward, thereupon, next, yet to come

κἀκεῖθεν—and from there, and then

Time: Other Temporal Particles, Conjunctions, Adverbs, Relative Pronouns, and Transition Words

ἀκμήν—yet, still

ἄχρι—until, within, during, to the point of, until the time of, before, as far as, up to, unto, as long as, while

ἐάν—if, if indeed, ever, when

ἐν τῷ μεταξύ—meanwhile

ἐν ᾧ—as long as

ἐπάν—when, whenever, after if, after

ἐπειδή—when, since, since then, because

ἔτι—yet, as yet, still, further, besides, moreover, hereafter, nevertheless, in addition

ἕως—while, until, as far as, to the point of, so long as, for a time, up to

ἕως οὗ—while, until

ἕως ὅτου—while, until

ὅταν—when, whenever, as often as, as long as

ὅτε—when, as long as

ὅσος—as many as, as great as, as long as, how great, to the degree that, so much as is enough, enough, so far as

ὅποτε—when
πότε—when?, how long?
ὁσάκις ἐάν—as many times as, as often as, whenever
ὡς ἄν—when, whenever, as soon as
ὡς ἐάν—when, whenever, as soon as
ἡνίκα ἄν / ἐάν—at which time, when, whenever
λοιπός—remaining, left, the rest, from now on, to mark an added fact: furthermore, also, in addition, beyond that, finally
μεσόω—to be in the middle of, be half over

Time: Prepositions Of

ἀπό—with genitive: from, from the time of, since
διά—with genitive: through, throughout, during, in, within, after
εἰς—with accusative: in, to, until
ἐκ—with genitive: since, when, from, after
ἐν—with dative: when, during, while
ἐπί—with genitive: at, when, during, in the time of
ἐπί—with dative: at, when, during, in the time of
ἐπί—with accusative: on, over a period of, at
κατά—with accusative: during, about, after, at
μετά—with accusative: after
περί—with accusative: around, about, near
πρό—with genitive: before in time
πρός—with accusative: toward, at
ὑπό—with genitive: by

Time: Times Of Day, Spans Of Time

ἀλεκτοροφωνία—before dawn, rooster's crowing, cock-crow, the third watch of the night
αὐγή—dawn, sunlight, any bright light
διαυγάζω—to shine through, dawn
ἀνατέλλω—to rise, give birth to, be a descendant, bring to light, dawn
ἐπιφώσκω—to shine forth, dawn
ὄρθρος—daybreak, dawn, cock-crow, early morning
ὀρθρινός—early in the morning
ὀρθρίζω—to get up early
πρωΐ—early morning, early in the day, early
πρωΐα—early morning
πρωϊνός—early, morning
μεσημβρία—noon, midday, south
ὀψία—late, evening, the latter part of the day
ἑσπέρα—evening, nightfall
κλίνω—recline, incline, bend, slope, lay down, lie on a couch at meals, decline, of the day: draw to a close
ὥρα πολλή—very late, a late hour
νύξ—night
ἔννυχα—at night
μεσονύκτιος—midnight
φυλακή—a guard, prison, watch, the shift of a sentinel's duty, a one-fourth period of the night
διανυκτερεύω—to spend the night
νυχθήμερον—a night and a day
δευτεραῖος—on the second day
τεταρταῖος—on the fourth day
ὀκταήμερος—on the eighth day
ἐπιούσιος—daily, for today, for the coming day
τῇ ἐπιούσῃ—on the next day
ἐφήμερος—daily, for the day
καθημερινός—daily

σάββατον—Sabbath, a week, rest
σαββατισμός—Sabbath rest, a keeping of days of rest
παρασκευή—day of preparation
προσάββατον—Friday, the fore-Sabbath, eve before the Sabbath
ἐνιαυτός—era, any long period of time, a cycle, period, one year
ἔτος—year
διετία—two-year period
διετής—two years old
τριετία—three-year period
τεσσαρακονταετής—period of forty years
ἑκατονταετής—one hundred years
τρίμηνον—three-month period
τετράμηνος—four-month period
ἡμιώριον—half an hour

Time: Seasons

ἔαρ—springtime
ἐαρίζω—to pass the spring
θέρος—summer
ὀπώρα—season after summer, July through early September, time of ripe fruit
φθινόπωρον—late autumn, fall
φθινοπωρινός—autumnal
μετόπωρον—late autumn, fall
χειμών—rainy weather, tempest, winter, the bad weather season
ψῦχος—cold, winter-time, cold weather, coolness, frost
παραχειμάζω—to spend the winter
παραχειμασία—a wintering in a place
πρόϊμος—early rain
ὄμβρος—rainstorm, heavy rain, the winter rainy season
ὄψιμος—late rain, spring rain

Time: Times Of Life

βρέφος—unborn child, infant, babe
παιδιόθεν—since childhood, from a child
νεότης—youth
νεωτερικός—youthful
ἡλικία—stature, maturity, of age
συνῆλιξ—of like or equal age
συνηλικιώτης—contemporary
ἀκμάζω—flourish, mature, ripen, bloom
ὑπέρακμος—past one's prime, past the bloom of youth
γῆρας—old age

Time: Favorable Or Unfavorable

ὡραῖος—timely, seasonable, in due season, ripe, in bloom, beautiful, lovely, pleasant, welcome
εὐκαιρέω—to have time to, have leisure to, have opportunity to, spend one's leisure time
εὐκαιρία—favorable opportunity, the right moment
εὔκαιρος—favorable time, well-timed, suitable
εὐκαίρως—favorably timed, conveniently, in season
προθεσμία—set time, fore-appointed
ἀκαιρέομαι—to lack opportunity, not have a good occasion, have no time
ἀκαίρως—unfavorable time, untimely, out of season

Time: Spend Time, Waste Time

χρονοτριβέω—to waste time, loiter, protract, spend time
διατρίβω—to stay longer, tarry, lose time, delay
τρίβω—to rub, crush, wear away, spend, waste time, use constantly
σχολάζω—to be at leisure, have rest from, be still, be idle, be empty, be vacant or unoccupied, be devoted to
ματάω—to be idle, to dally, loiter, linger, be futile

χρονίζω—to be late, spend a long time in, tarry, linger, be slow, delay, be prolonged

διαγίνομαι—pass (of time), elapse

παρέρχομαι—pass by, arrive, pass away, perish, transgress

παροίχομαι—to pass by, pass on, go on one's way, go by (of time), be bygone, be past

Time: Short Duration Of Time

βραχύς—short, small, little, low, few, brief, insignificant, trifling

διὰ βραχέων—briefly

μικρός—small, little, petty, trivial, slight, a short time

δι' ὀλίγων—in a short time, in a few

ἐν ὀλίγῳ—in a short time, in a few

πρὸς ὀλίγον—for a short time

συντόμως—briefly, shortly, immediately, concisely

σύντομος—cut short, abridged, shortened, concise, brief, curt, short

καινότης—newness, freshness, novelty

πρὸς καιρὸν (ὥρας)—for a while, not long, temporarily

πρόσκαιρος—for a while, not long, temporary

παραυτίκα—for the moment, for a little while, momentary, temporary

ταχέως—very soon, quickly, at once, without delay, hastily

ταχινός—quickly, swiftly, speedily, at a rapid rate, in a short time, soon

ταχύς—quickly, swiftly, speedily, at a rapid rate, in a short time, soon

ὀξύς—sharp, keen, pointed, piercing, shrill, pungent, hasty, quick, swift

ἄφνω—immediately, suddenly, unawares

αἰφνίδιος—unforeseen, sudden, immediate

ἐξαίφνης—immediately, suddenly, in a moment

ἐξάπινης—immediately, suddenly, in a moment

ἐξαυτῆς—immediately, at once

ἄρτι—just now, even now, presently, immediately

παραχρῆμα—immediately, forthwith, suddenly, on the spot, straightway

ἐν ῥιπῇ ὀφθαλμοῦ—in the blink of an eye, suddenly, in a moment of time

ἄτομος—an indivisible amount of time, a moment

στιγμή—a spot, point, jot, tittle, a moment, something insignificant

σπεύδω—to haste, be eager, do quickly

καινός—new, fresh, de novo, produced for the first time, latest

νέος—young, youthful, new, fresh

ἐλάσσων—smaller, less, fewer, worse than, inferior to, subservient to, younger

προκόπτω—to advance a work, go forward, progress, increase, beat forward, proceed, be spent, to be nearly over

συστέλλω—draw together, contract, shorten, abridge, limit, roll together, wrap, passive: be short, draw to a close

Time: Long Duration Of Time

ἀρχαῖος—ancient, primeval, from the beginning, early, old, old-fashioned, antiquated, primitive, former, original

παλαιότης—oldness

παλαιός—old

παλαιόω—to make old, be antiquated

ἔκπαλαι—for a long time, long ago

γηράσκω—to grow old, bring to old age

προβαίνω ἐν ἡμέραις—to be old, go before in days

μείζων—greater, older, comparative of μέγας
πρεσβύτερος—old, elder, old man, forefather, presbyter
μακροχρόνιος—a long time
ἐν μεγάλῳ—in a long time
ἐπὶ πολύ—for a long time
ἐφ᾽ ἱκανόν—for a long time, for a considerable amount of time
ἡμέρα ἐξ ἡμέρας—day after day
χρόνος ἱκανός—a considerable time
ἀεί—always, forever, eternity
ἀΐδιος—everlasting, eternal, lasting forever
αἰών—an age, forever, a long period of existence, generation, era, epoch, period
αἰώνιος—everlasting, eternal, lasting forever, unending, lasting for an age
εἰς τὸν αἰῶνα—forever
εἰς αἰῶνας αἰώνων—forever
ἀπὸ τῶν αἰώνων—from eternity
ἐκ τοῦ αἰῶνος—from eternity
χρόνοις αἰωνίοις—to times eternal
πρὸ χρόνων αἰωνίων—before times eternal
πρὸ παντὸς τοῦ αἰῶνος—before all ages
ἀπὸ τῶν αἰώνων—from ages
ἐχθὲς καὶ σήμερον καὶ εἰς τοὺς αἰῶνας—yesterday and today and forever
εἰς τὸ παντελές—forever, for all time
παντελής—completely, fully, wholly, perfectly, absolutely
διὰ παντός—always
πάντοτε—at all times, always
ἑκάστοτε—each time, on each occasion, always
εἰς τὸ διηνεκές—forever, always, to the whole length, continually, eternally, without interruption
διηνεκής—continuous, uninterrupted, always, for all time
ἐκτενής—intent, earnest, assiduous, fervent, eager, without ceasing, continuous, constant, unfailing
ἀδιάλειπτος—not stopping, incessant, not leaving off from, continuous
ἀκατάπαυστος—that which cannot cease from something, never ceasing
ἀμάραντος—unfading, enduring, eternally fresh, everlasting
μαραίνω—fade, wither, dry up
ἀπέραντος—endless, boundless, infinite, countless
ἀκατάλυτος—endless, everlasting
ἀθανασία—deathlessness, immortality, eternality
ἀφθαρσία—unceasing, incorruptible, not undergoing decay, undying
ἄφθαρτος—uncorrupted, not liable to decay, imperishable, immortal

Toil, Work, Labor, Weariness, Fatigue

κοπιάω—to grow weary, tired, to labor with exhaustion, work hard
κόπος—labor, weariness, trouble
μόχθος—toil, hard labor, hardship, distress, trouble
πόνος—hard work, toil, exhaustion, pain, anguish
συναθλέω—toil with, strive together, labor with others
ἀθλέω—compete in a contest
ἐκλύομαι—to grow weary, be exhausted, faint, lose heart

Touch, Feel

ἅπτω—touch, hold, kindle, set on fire
θιγγάνω—to touch, handle, injure, do violence to, kill
προσψαύω—to touch
ψηλαφάω—to handle, touch, feel, feel after, grope, try to find

Travel, Journey

πορεία—journey, business trip

πορεύομαι—go, travel, take a journey, go on a business trip

ὁδεύω—travel, journey

ὁδός—way, road, course of conduct

ὁδοιπορέω—travel, journey

ὁδοιπορία—journey, journeying

διοδεύω—travel through

διαπορεύομαι—pass through a place

διέρχομαι—go through

περιέρχομαι—travel about, wander

περιάγω—travel about, lead around

ἀστατέω—wander

πλανήτης—wandering, roaming, wandering star

ἀπόδημος—away on a journey, away from home

ἀποδημέω—go away into foreign parts, go abroad, leave home on a journey

Tree

δένδρον—tree, bush

ὕλη—forest, woods, felled wood, fuel

ξύλον—tree, wood, firewood, club, cross, stocks

συκῆ—fig tree

συκάμινος—mulberry tree

συκομορέα—sycamore tree

φοῖνιξ—palm tree

ἐλαία—olive (tree)

ἐλαιών—olive orchard

καλλιέλαιος—cultivated olive tree

ἀγριέλαιος—wild olive tree

Trouble, Hardship, Distress

θλῖψις—pressure, tribulation

θλίβω—press hard upon, afflict, throng, crowd against

ἀνάγκη—force, constraint, necessity, obligation, what is inevitable, calamity, straights, distress

ἀσθενής—weak, infirm, feeble, impotent, sick, without strength

βάρος—heaviness, weight, burden, trouble, hardship

βαρέω—to burden, weigh down, depress, be troubled, be sleepy

βαρύς—heavy in weight, weighty, important, burdensome, severe, stern, cruel, unsparing, grievous

καταβαρέω—press down by imposing weight, weigh down, burden, cause undue hardship

κακία—badness, malice, ill-will, desire to injure, wickedness, depravity, evil, trouble

λοιμός—pestilence, plague, trouble

κόπος—labor, weariness, trouble

οὐαί—woe

στενοχωρία—narrowness of place, limiting of one's situation, restricted by troubles

στενοχωρέομαι—be in a tight place, crowded together, confined, severely limited, under hardship

στενός—narrow, strict, exacting, close, confined

ταλαιπωρία—hardship, trouble, calamity, misery, wretchedness

ταλαίπωρος—miserable, afflicted, wretched, distressed

πληγή—blow, wound, plague, heavy affliction, calamity, distress

προσκοπή—a stumbling block, obstacle, offense

σκύλλω—to skin, flay, rend, mangle, vex, annoy, trouble

ὀχλέομαι—to disturb, trouble, vex

ἐνοχλέω—to excite, trouble, annoy, cause disturbance, afflict

παρενοχλέω—cause trouble in a matter, annoy greatly, cause extra difficulty

σκόλοψ τῇ σαρκί—thorn in the flesh, an affliction, annoyance, disability θραύω—break, shatter, smite through, bruise, oppress, enfeeble, passive: be downtrodden

καταδυναστεύω—oppress, exercise harsh control over, use one's power against

συμπνίγω—choke utterly, press around or throng around so as to suffocate

χαλεπός—hard to do, hard to bear, troublesome, dangerous, fierce, perilous

μόλις—with difficulty, not easily, scarcely, very rarely

δύσκολος—with difficulty

δυσκόλως—difficult, not easy, hard

δυσβάστακτος—hard to be borne, grievous to be borne, difficult

True, Truth, see also "Genuine" and "Know"

ἀλήθεια—truth, fact, reality, sincerity, frankness, genuineness

ἀληθής—true, genuine, real, factual, reliable, trustworthy, valid

ἀληθινός—true, real, genuine, correct

ἀληθεύω—to speak truth

φωτισμός—brightness, revelation, enlightenment, illumination, truth

γνήσιος—sincere, true, legitimate, noble, genuine

λογικός—true to real nature

ἔλεγχος—evidence, proof, a cross-examining for purpose of refutation

δοκιμή—proving, test, evidence of genuineness, approved character

ὀρθῶς—rightly, correctly, normally

ὀρθότης—correctness, soundness, rightness

ἐπανόρθωσις—correcting of faults, revisal

διόρθωμα—reform, making straight, amendment

παρατίθημι—put before, offer, lay before, show to be true

παρίστημι—to stand before, present, show to be true, set before, provide, furnish, put at one's disposal

ἀποδείκνυμι—to set forth, attest, show to be true, claim, demonstrate, prove

ἐπιδείκνυμι—show, demonstrate, cause to be seen, show to be true

ἀμήν—truly, verily, amen, let it be so

νομίμως—correctly, in conformity to custom, usage, or law

ἀκριβής—accurate, exact, precise, frugal, parsimonious

ἀκρίβεια—thoroughness, strictness, accuracy, exactness, preciseness

καλῶς—well, in the right way, commendably, appropriately, splendidly, fitly, accurately

καλός—good, beautiful, fair, fitting, virtuous, advantageous

ἀψευδής—not false, truthful

ὑγιής—sound in body, healthy, hearty, cured, in good condition, of words: wholesome, wise, accurate

ὑγιαίνω—to be well, healthy, whole, sound

βεβαίωσις—confirmation, verification

βεβαιόω—to make firm, establish, confirm, make certain, verify, cause to believe, strengthen

βέβαιος—stable, firm, sure, steadfast, trustworthy, certain, verified

συμβιβάζω—join together, unite, put together in one's mind, conclude, prove, instruct, advise

Try, Attempt, see "Tempt"

πειράζω—try, attempt, endeavor, undertake, tempt, solicit to sin, test, entice, try to trap

πειραω—try, attempt, endeavor"

ἐκπειράζω—to prove, put to test one's character, tempt, try to trap

ἐπιχειρέω—to try, undertake

δίδωμι ἐργασίαν—do one's best, give effort

Try Hard, Do Intensively, Do In Excess

σπουδάζω—to hasten, make haste, to exert one's self, endeavor, give diligence, be eager, do one's best, do quickly

σπουδή—haste, zeal, diligence, eagerness

σπουδαίως—hastily, diligently, earnestly, instantly, eagerly

σπουδὴν εἰσφέρειν—make an effort, do one's best

παρεισφέρω—apply, bring to bear

διώκω—to pursue, chase, hunt, persecute, strive after

προσκαρτερέω—to persist in, be in constant readiness, continue in, spend much time in, be devoted to

προσκαρτέρησις—persistence

προηγέομαι—to go first, take the lead, go before, precede, go first, excel, do exceedingly

ἐπισχύω—to grow strong, prevail, be urgent, persist in, insist

ἀσκέω—to practice, engage in, followed by infinitve: do one's best to, strive to

ἐξαγοράζομαι τὸν καιρόν—buy back the time, work urgently, make the best of an opportunity

ἀγωνίζομαι—to contend for a prize in public games, contest, debate, contend in law, fight, struggle

ἐκχέω—pour out, shed forth, bestow or distribute largely, flow out, give in abundance, stream forth, spill, squander, waste

σωρεύω—to heap on, pile up, be overwhelmed with

ὑπερεκτείνω—to overextend, stretch beyond measure

U

Ugly, Deformed, Unsightly, Disfigured

αἰσχρός—ugly, deformed, ill-favored, disgraceful, shameful, dishonest

αἰσχρότης—indecency, ugliness, deformity

ἀσχήμων—indecent, of the body parts that should be kept covered, unpresentable, unattractive, ugly

ἀσχημονέω—to act disgracefully, behave indecently, be ill-mannered, rude, or obscene

ἀφανίζω—destroy, disfigure, deprive of luster, render unsightly, make ugly, passive: disappear, vanish

Unable, Incapable

ἀδύνατος—incapable, unable, without strength, powerless

ἀσθένεια—want of strength, weakness, feebleness, sickliness, disease, incapacity

ἀσθενής—without strength, weak, feeble, poor, morally weak

ἀσθενέω—to be weak, feeble, sickly

καθαίρεσις—tearing down, destruction, demolition, incapacitating

ἀποθνήσκω—die, be slain, be rendered ineffective

νεκρός—lifeless, dead, useless, ineffective

Unbelievers

υἱοὶ τοῦ αἰῶνος τούτου—sons of this age

ἄπιστος—unbelieving, unbelievable

ἄδικος—unjust, evil, sinful, ungodly, unjust, dishonest, wrong

ἄνομος—destitute of law, departing from the law, lawless, wicked

ψευδάδελφος—false brother, false believer

αἵρεσις—sect, religious party, division, faction, heretical group, false teaching

οἱ ἐκ τῆς περιτομῆς—those of the circumcision, meaning Judaizers or those who wrongly required circumcision in order to be Christian

ἐθνικός—of the nations, implying pagan, heathen, unconverted

τὰ ἔθνη—the nations

Unique, Distinctive, Unusual, Extraordinary, Remarkable

ἴδιος—one's own, pertaining to oneself, private, personal, not public, separate, distinct, by oneself

περισσός—beyond the regular number or size, abundant, profuse, more than sufficient, extraordinary, superfluous, having surplus, excessive, extravagant, unnecessary περιούσιος—chosen, choice, special, a distinctive possession, peculiar

περιουσία—that which is over and above necessary expenses, surplus, plenty, abundance, wealth

τοιόσδε—of such a kind, such a one, so great, so noble, so bad, such

κατὰ μόνας—alone

μόνας—alone, left alone, forsaken, solitary, only, one and only

μονογενής—only-begotten, single, one and the same, unique

ἀγαπητός—beloved, dear, only dear

ἄτοπος—out of place, strange, extraordinary, odd, eccentric, unnatural, unusual, wrong, bad

ἀτόπως—marvelously, absurdly

γνωστός—known, notable, remarkable, extraordinary, well-known, what can be known

παράδοξος—contrary to opinion or expectation, incredible, paradoxical, unusual, unexpected, uncommon, wonderful, strange

οὐχ ὁ τυχών—unusual, extraordinary

τυγχάνω—to meet with, have happen, come upon, experience

Universe, World, Creation

καταβολή—creation of the world, beginning, foundation

κτίσις—creation, the created universe, creature, foundation, an authority created, ordinance

γῆ—earth, ground, dirt, land, world, country, region

οἰκουμένη—inhabited world, empire

κόσμος—world, earth, the ordering of creation, ornament, adornment as on a woman, world system

αἰών—eternity, a very long time period, an age, universe

Unspeakable, Inexpressible

ἄρρητος—unspeakable, unspoken, inexpressible, unutterable, not able to be described

ἀλάλητος—unutterable, inexpressible

ἀνεκλάλητος—unspeakable, cannot be expressed

Up To, As Much As, To The Degree That

ἕως—while, until, as far as, to the point of, so long as, for a time, up to

μέχρι(ς)—as far as, to the degree that

ὅσος—as many as, as great as, as long as, how great, to the degree that, so much as is enough, enough, so far as

τοσοῦτος—so many, so much, so far, so great, to the degree that

καθό—in so far as, according as, so that, just as, to the degree that

καθότι—to the degree that

καθώς—just as, as, how, to the degree that, inasmuch as

εἰς—with accusative: to the point of

ἐπί—up to

πρός—to the point of

Urge, Persuade, see also "Compel, Force"

πείθω—to persuade, win over, prevail on by entreaty, induce one by words to believe, passive: trust, believe, be persuaded, obey, have confidence, be certain, be a follower

πειθός—persuasive, enticing

πεισμονή—persuasion, treacherous or deceptive persuasion, that which persuades

ἀναπείθω—to stir up by persuasion, solicit, incite, persuade

εὐπειθής—easily persuaded, easily obeying, compliant, easy to be entreated

παρακαλέω—to urge, summon for help, encourage, comfort

παραβιάζομαι—to employ force contrary to nature, to compel by force, to constrain one by entreaties

προβιβάζω—to cause to go forward, lean forward, incite, instigate, urge, induce by persuasion

προτρέπομαι—to urge forwards, exhort, encourage, urge

Useful

χρήσιμος—useful, serviceable, good for use, good, apt, fit

χρηστός—good, pleasant, fit for use, useful, virtuous, easy, kind

εὔχρηστος—useful, serviceable, easy to make use of

εὔθετος—well-arranged, well-fitting, easily stowed, ready for use, useful

Useless, Worthless

ἀχρεῖος—useless, unprofitable, good for nothing, unserviceable, unfit for its purpose

ἄχρηστος—useless, unprofitable, unserviceable, without effect, unfit for its purpose, making no use of, unkind, cruel

ἄκαρπος—without fruit, barren, fruitless, unprofitable, useless

ἀνεύθετος—unusable, inconvenient, unfavorably situated, not suitable

ἀργός—lazy, barren, idle, slow, useless, indifferent, without thought

μάταιος—vain, empty, futile, idle, trifling, frivolous

ματαιότης—futility, emptiness, purposelessness, idleness

ματάω—to be idle, to dally, loiter, linger, be futile

νεκρός—lifeless, dead, useless, ineffective

ἀδόκιμος—failing the test, worthless, unqualified, disqualified, rejected, proven false, unfit, bad

ἀπώλεια—waste, ruin, loss

πτωχός—poor, destitute, spiritually poor, of little value

V

Value, Valuable, Treasure

τιμή—honor, respect, worth, value of a thing, price, valuation, payment

τίμιος—precious, costly, prized, dear, held in honor, honored, worthy

ἔντιμος—in honor, honored, prized, valuable, dear

βαρύτιμος—very costly, valuable

πολυτελής—expensive, of great value, very precious

πολύτιμος—expensive, very costly

ὑπερέχω—be better than, exceed, outdo, be above, govern, control

δοξάζω—to praise, extol, glorify, magnify, honor, render excellent

διαφέρω—carry through, drive about, spread a message, intransitively: to differ, be worth more

πιότης—fatness, richness, value

σιτευτός—fattened, prized

ὑψηλός—high, lofty, arrogant, proud, stately, high in value, exalted

θησαυρός—treasure, treasury, storehouse, receptacle for valuables

θησαυρίζω—to store, treasure up

ἀποθησαυρίζω—to store, hoard up, treasure up

ἀπόκειμαι—to be laid away, laid up in store, be in reserve, be awaiting, be appointed

δοκιμή—proving, test, evidence of genuineness, approved character

πιστικός—pure, genuine, trusted, unadulterated, of precious perfumes

Vehicle

ἅρμα—chariot

ῥεδή—carriage

Vices: Anger, Indignation

ὀργή—anger, wrath, indignation

ὀργίζω—be angry, furious, enraged

ὀργίλος—prone to anger, quick-tempered, wrathful, angry

παροργισμός—anger, exasperation

παροργίζω—make angry, provoke to anger, exasperate

θυμός—fury, hot temper, outburst

θυμόω—provoke to anger, passive: be extremely angry, be enraged

θυμομαχέω—be enraged, fight angrily

ἀγανάκτησις—indignation, anger, displeasure

ἀγανακτέω—be indignant, be angry, be displeased, express vexation

προκαλέω—call forth, middle: challenge, provoke, irritate

παροξύνω—prick or spur on, provoke to anger, irritate, exasperate, arouse παροξυσμός—incitement, sharp argument, provocation, sharp disagreement, irritation, exasperation

ὀξύς—sharp, quick

προσοχθίζω—be angry, be offended, be vexed

ἐμμαίνομαι—be insanely angry at

μαίνομαι—be insane

ἄνοια—folly, foolishness, irrational anger, rage, extreme fury

χολάω—be angry

διαπονέομαι—be much annoyed, be disturbed, be upset

φρυάσσω—be furious, be arrogant

βρύχω τοὺς ὀδόντας—gnashing of teeth, being furious

πρίζω—saw in two, as punishment

διαπρίω—divide with a saw, cut asunder

Vices: Arrogance, Pride, Haughtiness, Boasting

αὐθάδης—self-willed, stubborn, arrogant, dogged, contumacious, remorseless, unfeeling

ὕψωμα—height, pretension, arrogance

ὑψηλός—high, lofty, arrogant, proud, stately, high in value, exalted

ὑψηλὰ φρονέω—think highly, be haughty

ὑψηλοφρονέω—be arrogant, high-minded

ὑπερφρονέω—be arrogant, high-minded

ὑπεραίρω—middle or passive: to exalt oneself, be proud

ἐπαίρω—lift up, raise, elevate, hoist, passive: ascend, boast, be arrogant, rise up against

ὑπερηφανία—arrogance, pride

ὑπερήφανος—arrogant, proud

φυσίωσις—puffing up, inflation, pride, conceit

φυσιόω—puff up, blow up, become haughty, proud, conceited, arrogant

τυφόομαι—be puffed up with pride or self importance

τύφω—give off smoke, smolder

ἀλαζονεία—false pride, pretension, arrogance, conceit, boasting

ἀλαζών—one who arrogantly assumes too much about himself, boaster, bragger, show-off, arrogant person

κενοδοξία—vain glory, empty conceit, groundless boasting

κενόδοξος—being proud without reason, conceited, boastful

δόξα—glory, splendor, brightness, a good reputation resulting in praise and honor, pride

αὐχέω—to boast

καυχάομαι—to boast, glory

καύχημα—boasting, glorying, as the thing boasted of

καύχησις—boasting, glorying, pride, as the action

ἐγκαυχάομαι—to boast

κατακαυχάομαι—to glory against, exult over, to boast one's self, boast against, rejoice against

περπερεύομαι—to boast one's self, make self-display, speak embellishingly of one's self, brag

πέρπερος—bragger

ὑπέρογκος—immoderate, boastful, extravagant, bombastic, pompous

Vices: Bribery

ὑποβάλλω—to put someone up to something, pay secretly or bribe

ἐγκάθετος—spy, one who lies in wait, paid informant

Vices: Cruelty, Mistreatment, Violence, see also "Hit, Strike" and "Kill"

κακουχέομαι—mistreat, torment, cause to suffer

κακόω—oppress, afflict, harm, vex, maltreat, embitter, render evil to

καταπονέω—to exhaust, afflict, oppress, mistreat, vex, distress

ἀτιμάζω—to disrespect, dishonor, treat shamefully, degrade

ἀδικέω—do wrong, be in the wrong, act unjustly toward

ἐπηρεάζω—mistreat, revile, threaten abusively, slander

ὑβρίζω—to insult, scoff at, spitefully mock, revile, treat shamefully, mistreat, punish in a humiliating way, affront, outrage

ὕβρις—insult, a wrong springing from insolence, affront, injury inflicted by the violence of a tempest, damage

ὑβριστής—violent aggressor, overbearing person

λυμαίνομαι—harass, treat shamefully, ravage, ruin, injure severely

ἐξουδενέω—treat with contempt, reject

ἡττάομαι—be defeated, be overcome, be treated worse

ἥσσων—less, worse

πλήκτης—pugnacious or quarrelsome person, one who strikes others, bully

πλήσσω—strike, smite

αὐστηρός—exacting, severe, stern, austere, bitter

βαρύς—heavy in weight, weighty, important, burdensome, severe, stern, cruel, unsparing, grievous

ἀνελεήμων—unmerciful, without compassion, pitiless

ἀνέλεος—unmerciful, without compassion, pitiless

ἀνασκευάζω—unsettle, subvert, upset, disturb

ὀδυνάομαι—be in intense pain, be in terrible anguish, be tormented

θορυβέω—cause confusion, set in a clamor, cause turbulence, disturb

σείω—to shake, agitate, disturb

ταράσσω—agitate, trouble, disquiet, make restless, stir up, perplex

τυρβάζω—to disturb, trouble

ἀποτομία—abruptness, steepness in terrain, severity, sternness, harshness

ἀποτόμως—severely, sharply, harshly

σκληρός—hard, harsh, rough, stiff, stern, offensive, unmerciful

πικρός—sharp, piercing, bitter, of water, brackish, a resentful attitude, bitter, harsh, cruel

ἡττάομαι—be defeated, be treated worse

Vices: Deception, Speaking Falsely

ψεύδομαι—to lie, speak falsehoods

ψεῦδος—lie, falsehood

ψεῦσμα—lie, falsehood

ψευδής—deceitful, false, untrue

ψευδολόγος—speaking falsely, lying

ψεύστης—liar, one who breaks faith, one who is false

πλανάω—to lead astray, wander, cause to depart from truth, passive: be lost, be deceived, be misled

πλάνη—deception, wandering, straying, error, perversion

πλάνος—wandering, misleading, leading into error, corrupting, deceitful

ἀποπλανάω—to cause to go astray, lead into error, seduce

ἀπατάω—to cheat, beguile, deceive, mislead, trick, outwit

ἀπάτη—deceit, deception

ἀπάγω—lead away, carry off
ἐξαπατάω—to deceive, beguile
φρεναπατάω—to deceive
φρεναπάτης—deceiver, seducer
παραλογίζομαι—reckon falsely, miscalculate, deceive, delude by false reasoning, defraud, distort
δολιόω—deceive, deal treacherously, use fraud
δόλος—treachery, deceit, fraud, bait
δόλιος—treacherous
ὑποκρίνομαι—pretend, act a part, make believe, assume a counterfeit character, feign, impersonate
ὑπόκρισις—pretense, hypocrisy, leading people to think one thing while secretly having another motive
ὑποκριτής—actor, pretender, hypocrite, one who pretends to be other than he is
συνυποκρίνομαι—to act falsely along with others, join in their hypocrisy
πρόφασις—pretext, alleged reason, show, pretense, what appears ostensibly, cloak, excuse, cover-up
γόης—impostor, deceiver, cheat
λύκος ἐν ἐνδύμασιν προβάτων—wolf in sheep's clothing
τοῖχος κεκονιαμένος—whitewashed wall, impostor
κονιάω—to plaster over, whitewash
δίλογος—speaking one thing and meaning another, hypocritical, insincere, deceitful
εὐπροσωπέω—make a good showing or impression, put on a good front before others, appear believable
ζύμη τῶν Φαρισαίων—leaven of the Pharisees
ἐμπαίζω—to play with, trifle with, mock, delude, deceive, trick
κυβεία—craftiness, trickery, cunning
μεθοδεία—method, procedure, strategy, scheming, cunning attack, craftiness, deception, trick
βασκαίνω—bewitch, cast a spell on, cunningly deceive, malign

Vices: Defame, Accuse, Talk Foolishly

μωμάομαι—to blame, find fault with, mock at, criticize
διαβάλλω—to slander, defame, accuse, bring a complaint against
διάβολος—slanderous, falsely accusing, the devil
ἐγκαλέω—to summon, come forward as accuser against, bring charge against, call in question, accuse
ἀνακρίνω—examine, judge, criticize, investigate, inquire into, scrutinize, interrogate
κατηγορία—accusation, charge
κατήγορος—accuser
κατηγορέω—to accuse, object
ἀγορέω—speak
προαιτιάομαι—accuse previously, bring a charge against previously
μέμφομαι—to blame, find fault, accuse
μεμψίμοιρος—complaining of one's lot, discontented, blaming
συκοφαντέω—extort from, defraud, cheat, take money by false charges
καταλαλέω—to speak against, incriminate, slander
καταλαλιά—defaming, evil speaking, backbiting, slander
κατάλαλος—slanderer, backbiter, defamer, evil speaker
ὀνειδίζω—to insult, reproach, revile, upbraid, reprimand
ὀνειδισμός—insult, reproach
ἐνυβρίζω—to insult

ὑβρίζω—to insult, maltreat, be insolent, treat shamefully, to injure by speaking evil of

ὕβρις—insult, a wrong springing from insolence, affront, injury inflicted by the violence of a tempest, damage

ὑβριστής—insulter, insolent person

λοιδορέω—to slander, reproach, rail at, revile

λοιδορία—railing, reviling, slander, reproach

λοίδορος—slanderer, railer, reviler

ἀντιλοιδορέω—to insult in return, to return a reproach

δυσφημέω—defame, slander, revile

δυσφημία—defamation, ill-repute, verbal disgracement

βλασφημέω—to blaspheme, speak reproachfully, rail at, revile

βλασφημία—slander, injurious speech, reviling, blasphemy, evil speaking

βλάσφημος—slanderous, abusive, reproachful, blasphemous

χλευάζω—mock, deride, jeer, joke at

μυκτηρίζω—to turn up the nose or sneer at, mock, deride, ridicule

καταγελάω—to deride, laugh to scorn, laugh at

φλυαρέω—to talk nonsense, talk idly, prate against, bring forward idle accusations, make empty charges, accuse one falsely with malicious words

φλύαρος—foolish, trifling, silly, babbling, vain, tattling, gossipy

ἐμπαίζω—to play with, trifle with, mock, delude, deceive, trick

κενοφωνία—empty discussion, discussion of vain and useless matters, foolish talk

ματαιολογία—vain talking, empty talk, vain jangling, idle discussions

ματαιολόγος—an idle talker, one who utters empty senseless things, vain talker

λῆρος—idle talk, nonsense, idle tale

κακολογέω—to revile, speak evil of, abuse, curse

μωρολογία—foolish talk

σπερμολόγος—an empty-talker, foolish babbler

αἰσχρολογία—dirty talk, foul speaking, obscene communication

εὐτραπελία—pleasantry, humor, facetiousness, low jesting, vulgar speech

Vices: Disobedience, Sin, Guilt, see also "Doubt," see also "Sin, Guilt," see also "Bad"

παρανομέω—to transgress the law, disobey, act unlawfully

παρακοή—disobedience, unwillingness to listen

παρακούω—pay no attention to, refuse to listen to, disobey, to overhear, hear what is not intended for one to hear (Mark 5:36)

παραβαίνω—to turn aside, deviate from the way, transgress

παράβασις—transgression

παραβάτης—transgressor

παρέρχομαι—pass by, come near, disregard, transgress, pass away, perish

ἀπείθεια—disobedience

ἀπειθέω—to disobey, be unbelieving

ἀπειθής—disobedient

ἀνυπότακτος—insubordinate, unruly, disobedient

ὑποτάσσω—to bring under submission

λύω—loose, destroy, divorce, annul, to loose a law (Matthew 5:19)

ἀρνέομαι—to deny, refuse to agree

ἐκκλίνω—to turn aside, deviate from the right course, shun, avoid, cease

ἄλογος—unreasonable, irrational, brutish, absurd

πώρωσις—covering with a callous, dulled perception, stubbornness, blindness, hardness, insensibility

σκληρότης—hardness, stubbornness, a resistant attitude, unreceptivity

ἁμαρτάνω—sin, fail of doing, do wrong, transgress

παράπτωμα—sin, fall away from the right path

πταίω—sin, stumble, err, offend

ἀνομία—lawlessness, wickedness, iniquity, sin, wrongdoing

ἀδικία—unrighteousness, injustice, wrongdoing, lawlessness, sin, evil, wickedness, violation of justice

ἀγνόημα—sin through ignorance, without deliberate intent, sin committed by oversight, not consciously

ἔνοχος—liable, answerable, subject to, guilty of sin against

πονηρός—bad, evil, grievous, lewd, wicked, diseased

σκανδαλίζω—put a stumbling block in the way, offend, cause to sin

Vices: Drunkenness

μέθη—drunkenness, intoxication

μεθύω—to be drunk, drink a lot

μεθύσκομαι—get drunk, drink freely, give oneself over to excess

μέθυσος—drunkard

πότος—drinking bout, drinking party

οἰνοπότης—drunkard, one who habitually drinks in excess

οἰνοφλυγία—drunkenness, debauchery

πάροινος—drunkard, addicted to wine

κραιπάλη—drunken dissipation

κῶμος—a village festival involving drinking

Vices: Envy, Resentment, Bitterness

φθονέω—be jealous, bear ill-will or malice, bear a grudge, envy another for his good fortune

φθόνος—envy, jealousy

ζῆλος—fervor of spirit, zeal, earnest concern, jealousy, indignation

ζηλόω—to burn with zeal or envy, be jealous over, to desire earnestly

ζηλεύω—be zealous, be earnest, greatly desire

παραζηλόω—make jealous, incite to indignation

πικρός—bitter

πικρία—bitterness, bitter resentment

ἐριθεία—strife, contentiousness, selfish ambition, rivalry, hostility

ἐρεθίζω—arouse, excite, stir up, embitter, make resentful

ἐνέχω—active: to be hostile, have it in for, press upon, be urgent toward, passive, with dative: let oneself be entangled in, be under the control of

Vices: Favoritism, Prejudice

λαμβάνω πρόσωπον—receiving a person for their outward appearance, show favoritism

προσωπολημπτέω—be partial, show favoritism, treat one person better than another

προσωπολημψία—partiality, favoritism, prejudice

προσωπολήμπτης—respecter of persons, one who shows partiality, prejudiced person

ἀπροσωπολήμπτως—impartially, without respect of persons

πρόσκλισις—prejudice, bias, partiality

πρόκριμα—an opinion formed before the facts are known, prejudgment, prejudice, preference, partiality

ἀδιάκριτος—impartial, free from prejudice

Vices: Fighting, see also "Strife, Struggle" and "Argue, Quarrel"

στάσις—a standing, insurrection, uproar, rebellion, heated quarrel

ἐρίζω—engage in strife, strive, quarrel

φιλονεικία—love of strife, eagerness to contend, desire to quarrel

παροξυσμός—sharp argument, incitement, contention, irritation

διαπαρατριβή—constant arguing

θυμομαχέω—be enraged, fight angrily

λογομαχέω—to contend about words, argue about trifling matters

ἐριθεία—strife, contentiousness, selfish ambition, rivalry, hostility

Vices: Gluttony

ἐμπίμπλημι—fill up, glut one's desire for, satisfy with food, satiate, enjoy

γαστήρ—belly, womb, stomach, glutton

φάγος—glutton, voracious man

Vices: Greed, Exploitation

πλεονεξία—greedy desire for more, covetousness, avarice, greediness

πλεονεκτέω—be greedy

πλεονέκτης—a greedy person, one who claims more than his due, making gain from other's losses

φιλαργυρία—love of money, avarice

φιλάργυρος—loving money, covetous, avaricious

ἀφιλάργυρος—not loving money

αἰσχροκερδής—shamefully greedy

ἅρπαξ—rapacious, ravenous, vicious, violently greedy, extortioner, robber

ὀρέγω—be eager for, strive for, aspire to, long for, desire

κατεσθίω—consume, eat up, devour, exploit, prey on

κατασοφίζομαι—outwit, exploit with cunning, take advantage of, often with false arguments, victimize by subtlety, overtake by sophisms

ἐμπορεύομαι—be in business, carry on business, travel for business, exploit, traffic, make a gain of, get an advantage

Vices: Hatred, see also "Hostile"

μισέω—to hate, be grudging, detest, abhor

κακία—badness, malice, ill-will, desire to injure, wickedness, depravity, evil, trouble, hatred

ἐξουθενέω—despise, reject, treat of no account

καταπατέω—tread down, trample on, despise

ὀλιγωρέω—esteem little or lightly, make small account of, take no heed of, despise

πικρία—bitterness, bitter resentment

πικραίνω—be embittered

στυγητός—hated, detestable

ἀποστυγέω—abhor, hate utterly, hate violently, loathe, be disgusted, detest

θεοστυγής—hating God

καταφρονέω—despise, scorn, have contempt, look down on, disparage, disregard, slight

καταφρονητής—scoffer, despiser, scorner

περιφρονέω—despise, disregard

κατακαυχάομαι—boast against, exult over, brag, look down on, triumph over, win out over, be more powerful than

βδελύσσομαι—to detest, abhor, to render foul, render abominable βδέλυγμα—a foul thing, what is detestable, of idols and things pertaining to idolatry, abomination, a horrible thing which defiles

βδελυκτός—abominable, detestable, detested

Vices: Intemperance

ἀκρασία—lack of self-control, self-indulgent

ἀκρατής—lacking self-control, without moral restraint, intemperate

ἀσωτία—prodigality, wastefulness, recklessness, debauchery

ἀσώτως—recklessly, riotously, loosely

προπετής—reckless, rash, thoughtless

ἐλαφρία—vacillation, fickleness

ἐλαφρός—light in weight, easy to bear, insignificant

ἐντρυφάω—revel, carouse, openly indulge in, wrongfully enjoy something, delight in

τρυφάω—live in luxury, give oneself to self-indulgence

τρυφή—indulgence, luxurious living, in a good sense, enjoyment, delight

σπαταλάω—live indulgently, for sensual gratification, luxuriously

στρηνιάω—live sensually or luxuriously, indulge

στρῆνος—sensual living, luxury, sensuality

λαμπρῶς—splendidly, lavishly, luxuriously

Vices: Lawlessness, Injustice

ἀνομία—lawlessness, wickedness, iniquity, sin, wrongdoing

ἄνομος—destitute of law, departing from the law, lawless, wicked

ἀνόμως—without law, in ignorance of law

παρανομία—wrongdoing, evildoing, deliberate transgression, lawless act

παρανομέω—to transgress the law, disobey, act unlawfully

παράβασις—transgression

ἄθεσμος—lawless, unprincipled, licentious, breaking law for selfish desire, unrighteous, unjust

ἀθέμιτος—forbidden, unlawful

θέμις—law, right

ἄδικος—unjust, evil, sinful, ungodly, unjust, dishonest, wrong

ἀδίκως—unjustly, without reason, undeservedly

ἀδικία—unrighteousness, injustice, wrongdoing, lawlessness, sin, evil, wickedness, violation of justice

ἀδικέω—do wrong, be in the wrong, act unjustly toward

ἀδίκημα—unrighteous act, injustice, wrongdoing, crime

Vices: Lazy, Idle, At Leisure, Unemployed

ἀπρακτέω—to do nothing, gain nothing

ἀτακτέω—be lazy, idle, evade one's responsibilities

ἄτακτος—undisciplined, lazy, idle, disorderly, unruly

ἀτάκτως—lazily

ἀργέω—to be idle, be unemployed, do nothing, be fruitless

ἀργός—lazy, barren, idle, slow, useless, indifferent, without thought

ἄργυρος—silver, silver money, white metal

καταργέω—render ineffective, make barren, do away with, nullify, passive with ἀπό: be released from

νωθρός—lazy, sluggish, slothful, torpid, dormant

ὀκνηρός—hesitating, delaying, lazy, slow to do something because it's a bother, unready, timid, shrinking back from

ὀκνέω—to hesitate to, delay to, be slow to

χρονοτριβέω—to waste time, loiter, protract, spend time, linger

σχολάζω—to be at leisure, be still, be idle, be empty, be vacant or unoccupied, have leisure to be devoted to a thing

σχολή—spare time, leisure, rest, ease, freedom from occupation, school

ἀγοραῖος—idle people, Acts 17:5, court, Acts 19:38

Vices: Meddling, Busybody, Gossip

περίεργος—meddlesome, busy about other's affairs, superstitious, busybody

ἀλλοτριεπίσκοπος—meddler or busybody, one who minds other peoples' business, possibly a foreign supervisor

ψιθυριστής—gossiper, whisperer, secret slanderer, detractor

ψιθυρισμός—gossip, slander, whispering

Vices: Perversion, Licentiousness

πλάνη—deception, wandering, straying, error, perversion

ἀχρειόω—do wrong, become morally useless or corrupt, become perverse

διαστρέφω—to distort, turn away from, turn aside from the right path, pervert, corrupt, mislead

ἐκστρέφομαι—pervert, turn aside from correct behavior, passive: be perverted, be corrupt

φθείρω—to corrupt, destroy, deprave

φθορά—corruption, destruction, perishing, moral decay

διαφθείρω—to corrupt, utterly destroy, ruin

καταφθείρω—destroy, corrupt, deprave, ruin

σκολιός—crooked, bent, dishonest, unscrupulous, unfair

πανοῦργος—clever, in a negative sense: crafty, sly

πανουργία—treachery, trickery, deceit, craftiness, cunning

Vices: Lust, Sexual Misbehavior, Desire, see also "Desire: Passion"

πορνεύω—commit fornication, be without sexual restraint, practice prostitution

πορνεία—sexual immorality, unlawful or unnatural sexual relations, prostitution, extramarital fornication, unfaithfulness, adultery

πόρνος—sexually immoral person, fornicator

πόρνη—prostitute, harlot, whore, one who practices sexual immorality for money

ἐκπορνεύω—commit fornication, engage in illicit sex

μοιχαλίς—adulterous, lustful, unfaithful, disloyal

μοιχάω—commit adultery

μοιχεία—adultery

μοιχός—adulterer

ἐκκαίομαι ἐν τῇ ὀρέξει—to burn with lust (Romans 1:27)

ὄρεξις—striving for, craving, lust

ὀρέγω—be eager for, strive for, aspire to, long for, desire

πυρόομαι—to burn with fire, set on fire, refine with fire, kindle, be sexually aroused

ἡδονή—pleasure, lust, passion

ἀσέλγεια—licentiousness, sensuality, lustful indulgence, indecency, vice ἐπιποθέω—to long for, pursue with love, lust for, deeply desire, have great affection for

καταστρηνιάω—to have sexual desire, have lust, be headstrong or wanton towards

στρηνιάω—live sensually or luxuriously, indulge

διψάω—suffer thirst, be thirsty, desire strongly

πεινάω—be hungry, crave, desire

σαρκὸς θέλημα—desires of the flesh, sexual desires

θυμός—passion, intense desire, ardor, anger, fierceness, indignation, wrath

ἐπιθυμέω—to desire greatly, long for, lust after, covet

ζηλόω—to burn with zeal or envy, be jealous over, to desire earnestly

κοιλία—belly, womb, seat of desires

πάθος—feeling, emotion, passion, affection, lust

κοίτη—bed, place for sleeping, the marriage bed, conception, sex, sexual immorality

ἀρσενοκοίτης—a homosexual, sodomite, pederast

ἀπέρχομαι ὀπίσω σαρκὸς ἑτέρας— go behind other flesh, have homosexual intercourse

μαλακός—soft, delicate, luxurious, effeminate, unmanly, homosexual

Vices: Sorcery, Witchcraft, see also "Magic"

βασκαίνω—to slander, malign, disparage, envy, grudge, bewitch by means of spells

φαρμακεία—remedy, cure, negatively: the use of drugs, potions, spells, poisoning, witchcraft, sorcery

Vices: Stealing

κλέμμα—theft, fraud

κλέπτω—steal, acquire secretly and dishonestly

κλέπτης—thief, cheat

κλοπή—theft, secret act, fraud, stealth

ἁρπαγή—the act of plundering, robbery, plunder, spoil, booty

ἁρπαγμός—a plunder, booty, seizing, prize, something held by force

ἁρπάζω—to snatch greedily, carry off by force, seize, plunder, claim for one's self eagerly, overpower

ἁρπαγή—the act of plundering, robbery, plunder, spoil, booty

ἅρπαξ—rapacious, ravenous, a robber, extortion, violently greedy

διαρπάζω—to tear in pieces, spoil, plunder, seize

λῃστής—a robber, plunderer, pirate, rebel

συλάω—to rob

σκῦλα—spoils, booty, prey, plunder

ἱεροσυλέω—to rob a temple, commit sacrilege

ἱερόσυλος—a temple-robber, sacrilegious person, desecrator

διασείω—harass, intimidate, extort money from a person

σείω—to shake, agitate, disturb

νοσφίζομαι—keep back funds for oneself, rob, put aside secretly for oneself, misappropriate, embezzle

κατεσθίω—consume, eat up, devour, exploit, prey on

στερέω—to deprive, bereave, rob of

ἀποστερέω—to defraud, deprive of, rob someone of, passive: be bereft of

σπήλαιον—cave, den, stash place for stolen goods

Vices: Uncleanness, Defilement, see also "Dirty"

ἀκαθαρσία—filth, uncleanness, immorality

ἀκάθαρτος—unclean, defiled

ῥυπαίνομαι—be morally impure, dirty

μολύνω—make dirty, soil, smear, stain, defile, make impure

μολυσμός—defilement, uncleanness

σπίλος—spot, stain, blemish, fault, shamefulness, moral wrong

μῶμος—blame, disgrace, reproach, blemish, defect, flaw

μίασμα—defilement, pollution, impurity, corrupting influence

μιαίνω—defile, stain, make unclean, cause to be unacceptable, corrupt

ἀμίαντος—undefiled

βεβηλόω—to profane, ritually defile

ἀλίσγημα—a thing ritually defiled, a pollution

κοινόω—share in common, be a partner or partaker, of Jewish law: to make common, defile

κοινός—communal, shared in common, mutual, public, of meats: profane or common, defiled, ritually unclean

τὸ βδέλυγμα τῆς ἐρημώσεως—abomination of desolation

Vices: Wickedness, see also "Bad"

κακός—bad, evil, wicked

πονηρία—wickedness, evil, malice

φθείρω—to corrupt, destroy, deprave

Virtues: Faith, Hope, Trust, Belief, Confidence

πιστός—faithful, true, to be trusted, to be believed, trustworthy, sure, certain, credible, trusting, easily persuaded, believing, confiding

πίστις—conviction of truth, belief, faith, assurance, trust, (the) faith, as Christian belief, the promise or commitment to faith in Christ

πιστεύω—to believe, think to be true, be persuaded of, place confidence in, trust, have faith, commit to, entrust to

πείθω—to persuade, win over, prevail on by entreaty, induce one by words to believe, passive: trust, believe, be persuaded, obey, have confidence, be certain, be a follower

προσκαρτερέω—to persist in, be in constant readiness, continue in, spend much time in, be devoted to

βέβαιος—stable, firm, sure, steadfast, trustworthy, certain, verified

βεβαιόω—to make firm, establish, confirm, make certain, verify, cause to believe, strengthen someone

ἐλπίς—expectation, hope, faith, what is hoped for, the basis of hope

ἐλπίζω—to hope for, to hopefully trust in, to wait expectantly

ἀπελπίζω—to expect, hope

προελπίζω—to hope beforehand, to trust in advance

ἐκδέχομαι—look for, expect, wait for

ἀποκαραδοκία—eager desire, anxious and persistent expectation, longing

ἀληθής—true, genuine, real, factual, reliable, trustworthy, valid

παρρησιάζομαι—speak freely, speak with assurance and confidence

θαρρέω—to take courage, be of good cheer, be confident, be bold, the imperative, θάρσει, is a common greeting

Virtues: Gentleness, Mildness

πραΰτης—gentleness, humility, courtesy, considerateness, meekness

πραΰς—gentle, humble, considerate, meek, unassuming

πραϋπάθεια—gentleness

ἤπιος—gentle, mild, kind

ἐπιείκεια—gentleness, graciousness, forbearance, clemency

ἐπιεικής—gentle, kind, forbearing

εἰκών—image, likeness, form

μετριοπαθέω—deal gently with

Virtues: Goodness

ἀγαθωσύνη—goodness, generosity

ἀγαθός—good, excellent, beneficial, upright, useful, capable, worthy, noble

ἀγαθοεργέω—do good, show kindness

ἀγαθοποιέω—do good to, do what is right, live in the right way

ἀγαθοποιΐα—good deeds, doing good

ἀγαθοποιός—one doing good deeds, well-doer

καλός—good, beautiful, fair, virtuous, advantageous, fitting

καλῶς—well, in the right way, commendably, appropriately, splendidly, fitly, accurately

καλοποιέω—to do good, do what is right, do well

εὖ—good, well, well done, as an exclamation

εὖγε—good, well done, excellent, as an exclamation

εὐεργεσία—good deed, good service, well-doing

εὐεργετέω—do good, show kindness

εὐποιΐα—good deed, act of benevolence

δεκτός—acceptable, pleasing, welcomed, appropriate

ἀπόδεκτος—acceptable, agreeable, pleasing

εὐδοκία—delight, good pleasure, satisfaction, what pleases

ἀρετή—goodness, excellence, valor, nobility, virtue, merit

ἀρεστός—pleasing, agreeable

εὐάρεστος—well-pleasing, acceptable

εὐλογία—praise, laudation, polished language, benediction, consecration, blessing, gift, of the alms collected for the poor

εὐαγγελίζω—to announce good news, bring glad tidings, preach the gospel

χάρις—grace, goodwill, favor, mercy, kindness, a gift, thanks, exceptional favor given by God

ἄκακος—upright, without fault, harmless, innocent, unsuspecting, naïve

προσφιλής—pleasing, lovely

χρήσιμος—good, useful, serviceable, apt, fit

χρηστός—good, pleasant, fit for use, useful, virtuous, easy, kind

χρηστότης—goodness, benevolence, kindness, uprightness, honesty

κρείσσων—comparative of κρατύς used as comparative of ἀγαθός, better, greater, superior, higher in rank, more important

κρείττων—same as κρείσσων

βελτίων—comparative of ἀγαθός, better

βέλτιον—very well

βέλτερος—best

λυσιτελέω—to be advantageous, be better, profit

λωίων—more desirable, more agreeable, better

ὄφελος—furtherance, advantage, help, good, profit

πρῶτος—first, earliest, before, foremost, most important, best

σύμφορος—useful, profitable, expedient, advantageous, convenient

Virtues: Holiness, Purity

ἅγιος—holy, dedicated to God, sacred, consecrated, pure, saint, holy one, holy place, sanctuary

ἁγιότης—holiness, sanctity, moral purity, dedication

ἁγιωσύνη—holiness, dedication, devoted obedience to God

ἁγιάζω—make holy, consecrate, sanctify, dedicate, treat as holy, revere, set apart for holy purpose, purify, be accepted or acknowledged by God

ὅσιος—holy, sanctioned by the supreme law of God, devout, dedicated, pure, divine

ὁσίως—in a way pleasing to God, in a holy manner

ὁσιότης—holiness, dedication

ἁγνός—pure, free from sin, innocent, blameless, harmless, acceptable

ἁγνεία—purity, virginity, propriety

ἁγνότης—purity, sincerity, blamelessness, moral cleanness

ἁγνίζω—to cleanse away, purify, ritually cleanse, hallow

ἀπολούομαι—wash away, make pure

ῥαντίζω—sprinkle, purify by ritual sprinkling with blood, purge of sin

ῥαντίζομαι τὴν καρδίαν—ritually sprinkle the heart, purify the heart

ἀκέραιος—pure, unmixed, of wine, innocence from evil, sincere, harmless

ἄσπιλος—spotless, without defect, pure, clean, uncorrupted

ἄμωμος—without defect or blemish, blameless, faultless

ἀμώμητος—blameless, without reproach

ἄμεμπτος—blameless, faultless

καθαρίζω—cleanse, purge, purify, heal

βαπτίζω—baptize, ritually wash, dip

ἐξαλείφω—wipe off, wipe away, obliterate, erase, blot out, eliminate

νίπτω—wash

ἀθῷος—unpunished, guiltless, innocent

θωή—punishment

Virtues: Honesty

ἀληθής—true, genuine, real, factual, reliable, trustworthy, valid

ἀψευδής—truthful, trustworthy, without lying or deceit

εἰλικρινής—sincere, morally spotless, pure, tested by sunlight

εἰλικρίνεια—sincerity, clearness, purity of motive, integrity, judged by the light of the sun

ἀφθορία—integrity, soundness, purity, not subject to corruption

ἁπλότης—simplicity, sincerity, liberality, generosity

ἁγνῶς—sincerely, in simplicity, openly, wholeheartedly, generously, without reserve

ἄδολος—without guile, pure, of liquids, unadulterated, genuine

Virtues: Humbleness, Humility

ταπείνωσις—humiliation, abasement, low status, defeat

ταπεινός—lowly, humble, of low degree, downcast

ταπεινόω—to make low, abase, embarrass, make level, bring low, passive: be humble

ταπεινοφροσύνη—humble-mindedness, humility, unselfishness, self-abasement

ταπεινόφρων—humble, having an attitude of humility, modest

πτωχὸς τῷ πνεύματι—poor in spirit, humble

ἀφελότης—smoothness, evenness, simplicity of heart, humbleness

φελής—stone, pebble

Virtues: Kindness

δίδωμι—to give

χάρις—grace, goodwill, favor, mercy, kindness, a gift, thanks, exceptional favor given by God χαριτόω—show kindness, bestow favor upon, favor highly, bless

χαρίζομαι—to be agreeable, oblige, gratify, court favor, offer freely, give willingly, be pleasing, forgive, pardon, remit

ἐλεημοσύνη—charitable giving, alms

φιλανθρωπία—love of mankind, benevolence, affection for people, friendliness

φιλανθρώπως—friendly, kindly, in a humane manner

φιλοφρόνως—friendly, in a kind way, affectionately, hospitably, courteously

χρηστεύομαι—act kindly, be good, be kind, be gentle

χρηστότης—benevolence, goodness, kindness, uprightness, honesty

χρηστός—good, pleasant, fit for use, useful, virtuous, easy, kind

ἁπλότης—simplicity, sincerity, liberality, generosity

ἐνευλογέω—bless, act kindly toward

εὐλογέω—praise, bless, consecrate with solemn prayers, act kindly toward

εὐλογία—praise, laudation, polished language, benediction, consecration, blessing, gift, alms

Virtues: Mercy, Forgiveness, see also "Forgiveness, Reconciliation"

ἐλεάω—show mercy on, pity

ἐλεήμων—merciful, compassionate

ἐλεεινός—miserable, pitiable, wretched

ἔλεος—mercy, compassion

ἵλεως—merciful, gracious, favorable

ἱλάσκομαι—to forgive, show mercy, pardon, be appeased, be propitiated, expiate a wrong, make acceptable, make reconciliation

οἰκτιρμός—mercy, pity, sympathy

οἰκτίρω—have compassion on, pity

οἰκτίρμων—merciful, compassionate

σπλαγχνίζομαι—to be moved in one's inward parts, to be moved with compassion, have pity on

ἀπολύω—set free, let go, send away, release, allow, acquit, remit, divorce

ἀφίημι—send away, divorce, let go, leave, desert, abandon, forgive, remit, permit, allow, not hinder

ἐπικαλύπτω—to hide, cover over, shroud, cover sin, forgive

χαρίζομαι—to be agreeable, oblige, gratify, court favor, offer freely, give willingly, be pleasing, forgive, pardon, remit

ἀπαλλάσσω—to set free, release, let loose, settle, be reconciled

ἀποκαταλλάσσω—to reconcile, make peace

Virtues: Obedience

ἀκούω—to hear, listen, hearken, obey, give audience, receive news, be reported, understand

εἰσακούω—give heed to, comply with an admonition, obey, listen, assent to

ὑπακοή—obedience

ὑπακούω—to listen, obey, submit, comply, yield to, be subject to

ὑπήκοος—obedient

ὑπείκω—give way to authority, comply, concede to, obey, submit to

ἀκολουθέω—to follow, go after, be a disciple, obey

ἐξακολουθέω—obey, follow, imitate

πείθω—to persuade, win over, prevail on by entreaty, induce one by words to believe, passive: trust, believe, be persuaded, obey, have confidence, be certain, be a follower

πειθαρχέω—to obey one in authority

εὐλαβέομαι—to be moved with fear, have reverence, act with respectful—caution

ὑποταγή—subordination, subjection, submission, obedience

ὑποτάσσω—to bring under submission, subject, subordinate, passive: be submissive, obey

ὕπανδρος—under a man, subject to a man, married

τηρέω—to keep, observe, give heed to, obey, watch, protect, guard

τήρησις—a keeping, guarding, watching, obedience, vigilance

φυλάσσω—to keep watch, guard, guard against, keep a command, obey

τελέω—finish, end, execute, make happen, accomplish, fulfill, make perfect, pay taxes

ἀναπληρόω—fill up, supply, refill, fulfill, fulfill law, obey

δογματίζω—active: decree, passive: obey laws, be governed

ἐπιδέχομαι—receive as a guest, allow of, accept, admit, acknowledge one's authority

κόσμιος—modest, well-behaved

Virtues: Peace, see also "Peace, Peaceful" and "Agreement"

εἰρηνεύω—keep peace, live peaceably

ἡσύχιος—quiet, tranquil, peaceful, at rest, possessing an inward calm

σιγάω—to keep silent, hold one's peace, keep secret

ἤρεμος—quiet, tranquil, peaceful

ἄμαχος—not contentious, peaceful

σπένδω—to pour libation or drink offering, pour, make a truce

ἀποκαταλλάσσω—to reconcile, make peace

εὐνοέω—to agree with, be settled with, be at peace with

Virtues: Respect, Modesty, see also "Honor"

τιμή—honor, respect, worth, value of a thing, price, valuation, payment

εὐσχημόνως—decently, properly, with propriety, respectably

σεμνός—honorable, of good character, worthy of respect, worthy, noble

σεμνότης—propriety, serious and worthy conduct, dignity, seriousness

εὐλαβέομαι—to be moved with fear, have reverence, act with respectful—caution

αἰδώς—modesty, reverence, respect

κόσμιος—modest, well-behaved

ἐπιβλέπω—to look upon, consider, look attentively, pay respect to, take an interest, care about, help

ἐντροπή—shame, respect, reverence

ἐντρέπω—active: make someone ashamed, respect, mostly passive: be put to shame, be ashamed, passive with middle sense: have regard for, respect

θαυμάζω—to wonder, marvel, be astonished, be amazed, honor, admire, worship, respect

φοβέομαι—to fear, have respect

τρέμω—tremble, quake, quiver, fear, respect

Virtues: Righteous, Just

δίκαιος—righteous, lawful, just, innocent, in right relation to God

δικαιοσύνη—righteousness, justice, being in right standing with God, being acceptable to God, doing what God requires, uprightness, integrity

δικαίωμα—commandment, ordinance, regulation, requirement of righteous action, a judgement, an act of righteousness δικαίως—setting right, doing justice to, deeming righteous, demanding of right, a just claim, judgement of what is right, being put right with

δικαιόω—to justify, make right with, deem righteous, acquit

ἔνδικος—just, fair, deserved, based on what is right

εὐθύς—immediately, directly, straightway, without reserve, at once, unhindered, openly, forthrightly, Acts 8:21, 2 Peter 2:15

εὐθύτης—straightness, honesty, integrity, justice, Hebrews 1:8

ὀρθότης—correctness, soundness, rightness

πρέπω—to be fitting, proper, right

ἀναίτιος—innocent, guiltless, not blamable

ἀνέγκλητος—unreproachable, blameless, without accusation

ἔγκλημα—accusation, complaint

ἀνεπίλημπτος—irreproachable, blameless, above criticism, unrebukeable, without fault

Virtues: Self-Control, Discipline, see also "Avoid, Abstain . . ."

ἐγκρατεύομαι—exercise self-control, control oneself, be abstinent

ἐγκράτεια—self-control, mastery over one's behavior

ἐγκρατής—disciplined, controlling one's desires, self-controlled

νήφω—be sober-minded, temperate, circumspect, restrained, watchful

νηφάλιος—restrained, without wine, sober, temperate, abstinent

σωφροσύνη—sobriety, self-control, moderation, sound judgment, soundness of mind

σωφρονισμός—self-control, moderation, sound judgment, soundness of mind

σωφρόνως—sensibly, with self-control, temperately, moderately

σώφρων—having a sound or healthy mind, self-controlled, sensible, moderate, being able to curb desires to live an orderly life, discreet, wise, chaste, sober

χαλιναγωγέω—exercise self-control

χαλινός—bridle

παιδεύω—to train, teach, correct, scourge, punish, discipline

παιδεία—discipline, training, teaching, chastening, nurture, punishment, correction

γυμνάζω—to train in gymnastics, exercise, practice, discipline oneself

ἀφειδία—severe self-control, non-indulgence, asceticism

ὑπωπιάζω—wear out, treat with severity, keep under control

Virtues: Thankfulness

εὐχαριστία—thankfulness, the giving of thanks

εὐχαριστέω—be grateful, give thanks

εὐχάριστος—thankful, grateful

χάρις—grace, goodwill, favor, mercy, kindness, a gift, thanks, exceptional favor given by God

ἀνθομολογέομαι—to thank, praise, acknowledge

ἐξομολογέω—agree, promise, consent, middle: confess, praise, thank

ἀχάριστος—unthankful, ungrateful

Virtues: Understanding, see also "Wisdom, Understanding"

νοέω—to understand, see with insight, reflect, perceive, observe, comprehend, conceive

οἶδα—to see, perceive, know, regard

συνίημι—understand, perceive, put together in the mind, consider, be wise, be intelligent

βλέπω—to see, discern, understand, take heed, watch out for

θεωρέω—to look at, watch, behold, see, consider, perceive, ascertain

ὁράω—to see, behold, perceive, know, experience, take heed, beware

γινώσκω—know, learn, perceive, understand, acknowledge, have sexual intercourse

μανθάνω—to learn, be taught

φρόνησις—understanding, prudence, wisdom

σοφίζω—to make wise, instruct, middle: devise, reason with skill, passive: be cleverly devised

Violence, see also "Vices: Cruelty, Mistreatment, Violence"

βία—strength, force, violent action

βίαιος—violent, forcible, mighty

βιάζω—to use force, to apply force, to force, inflict violence on, suffer violence, use violence, press

βιαστής—strong, forceful, using force, violent

ὅρμημα—sudden violence, impulse, stir, longing, struggle

ὁρμή—violent movement onwards, assault, attack, onset, shock, impulse, eager initial desire for a thing

ἀνήμερος—savage, fierce, not tame

σκληρός—hard, harsh, rough, stiff, stern, strong, violent, offensive, intolerable, demanding

ἅρπαξ—rapacious, ravenous, vicious, violently greedy, extortioner, robber

ἄγριος—living or growing in the fields or woods, wild, savage, uncultivated, boorish, rude, violent in passion, vehement, furious, raging

βαρύς—heavy in weight, weighty, important, burdensome, severe, stern, cruel, unsparing, grievous

χαλεπός—hard to do, hard to bear, troublesome, dangerous, fierce, perilous

Visit

ἐπισκοπέω—to look after, care for, watch over, visit, inspect, oversee

ἐπισκέπτομαι—look upon, visit, care for, be concerned about, look for

ἐπισκοπή—office of a church leader, supervisor's office, a visitation from God bringing help or salvation

θεάομαι—to behold, look at, view, view attentively, contemplate, perceive, visit

ἱστορέω—to visit, get to know, passive participle: things learned by inquiry, historical account

παρατυγχάνω—be in a place by chance, happen to be near, chance to appear, happen to show up

W

Wage, see "Salary, Pay..."

Wall
τεῖχος—city wall
μεσότοιχον—dividing wall
χάραξ—barricade, palisade, rampart
φραγμός—fence, hedge, barrier

Wake
ἐγείρω—arouse, cause to rise, wake up
διεγείρω—wake up, arouse, stir up, render active
ἔξυπνος—roused out of sleep, awakened
ἐξυπνίζω—to awaken, cause to wake up
ἀγρυπνία—sleeplessness, the state of being awake
γρηγορέω—to watch, be cautious, be attentive, be vigilant, be alert, stay awake
διαγρηγορέω—to watch through, remain awake, become fully awake

Walk, Step
περιπατέω—walk, conduct one's life
πατέω—tread, trample, crush with the feet, step on
πεζεύω—travel on foot, go by land
ἐμβαίνω—go into, step into, embark, board (a ship)

Want, see "Desire"

War Terms, Military Terms, see "Weapons," "Guard," "Protect," "Surround"
πολεμέω—to wage war, fight, do battle, quarrel, treat as an enemy, be hostile
πόλεμος—war, fight, battle
στρατιώτης—soldier
στρατεία—warfare, an expedition, campaign, military service
στράτευμα—army, armament, expedition, campaign
στρατεύω—to engage in war, serve as a soldier, do military service, march in battle
στρατεύομαι—to make war against, be a soldier
ἀντιστρατεύομαι—to make war against, actively oppose
στρατόπεδον—camp, encampment, encamped army
στρατολογέω—to enlist soldiers, be an army officer
μάχαιρα—sword
ῥομφαία—javelin, large sword, scymitar
λεγεών—an army unit, a legion, numbering about 6,000 in the time of Augustus
λεγιών—same as λεγεών
σπεῖρα—cohort, band of soldiers

χιλίαρχος—a high-ranking Roman officer in command of a cohort
ἑκατοντάρχης—Roman officer, centurion, commander of 100 soldiers
κεντυρίων—same as ἑκατοντάρχης
κουστωδία—a guard composed of soldiers
τετράδιον—group of four soldiers
πραιτώριον—Praetorium, living quarters for the palace guard
ἱππεύς—horseman, charioteer
ἱππικόν—pertaining to horseman or chariots, cavalry
δεξιολάβος—spearman, guard, soldier
αἰχμαλωσία—captivity
αἰχμαλωτεύω—to take prisoner
αἰχμαλωτίζω—capture, take prisoner
αἰχμάλωτος—taken by the spear, taken captive, a prisoner
αἰχμή—the point of a spear or arrow, a body of spearmen
καθοπλίζω—to equip or arm fully, take arms against
ἐγείρω—to arouse, cause to rise, raise to life, to raise up, awaken, stand up, make war against
ὑπαντάω—to meet, meet in battle
ἐνεδρεύω—to lie in wait for, set an ambush
ἐνέδρα—ambush, lying in wait
ἐδαφίζω—throw to the ground, raze, level to the ground, kill
παρεμβάλλω—barricade around, erect ramparts, encamp against
χάραξ—barricade, palisade, rampart

Watchful, Alert

γρηγορέω—to watch, be vigilant, stay awake, be alert
ἀγρυπνέω—to keep awake, be on the alert, attentive, circumspect, ready, keep watch over, guard, care for
βλέπω—to see, discern, understand, take heed, watch out for
σκοπέω—to watch carefully, pay attention to, be concerned about
ἐπέχω—to hold on to, fix attention on, watch, be alert for, take notice of, attend to, delay, stay on
προσέχω—be attentive, watch, give heed to, beware, be devoted to

Water Terms, see "Weather"

ὕδωρ—water
πηγή—fountain, spring, well
ἰκμάς—moisture, as in soil
ὑετός—rain
κρύσταλλος—ice
χιών—snow
χάλαζα—hail
ἄνυδρος—waterless
ξηρός—dry, of land as distinct from water, withered

Water Body

θάλασσα—sea, lake
λίμνη—lake
λιμήν—harbor
βυθός—the deep, by implication the sea
πέλαγος—sea
κόλπος—bay, bosom, fold or lap pocket
ποταμός—river
χείμαρρος—winter torrent
πηγή—fountain, spring, well
φρέαρ—well, the pit of the abyss, deep pit
κολυμβήθρα—pool, reservoir

Wave

κῦμα—wave, billow
κλύδων—violent wave, raging water
σάλος—surging waves

Wealth, Riches, Sufficiency, Abundance, Excess

πλούσιος—rich, wealthy, opulent, abundant

πλουσίως—in abundance, extremely

πλουτέω—to be rich, abound in, be generous

πλουτίζω—to make rich, cause abundance

πλοῦτος—riches

πλεονάζω—to be more than enough, have an excess of, abound in, be rich

ὑπερπλεονάζω—to abound exceedingly, be more than

ἐκχέω—pour out, shed forth, bestow or distribute largely, give in abundance, flow out, stream forth, spill, squander, waste

περισσεύω—to be more than enough, sufficient, be abundant, abound, provide in abundance

περισσός—beyond the regular number or size, abundant, profuse, more than sufficient, extraordinary, superfluous, having surplus, excessive, extravagant, unnecessary

περισσεία—surplus, abundance, excess

περίσσευμα—abundance, that which remains over

ὑπερπερισσεύω—to be more abundant, abound more and more

περιουσία—that which is over and above necessary expenses, surplus, plenty, abundance, wealth

πλησμονή—satisfaction, gratification, fullness

κορέννυμι—to satisfy, eat enough, be full, be content

εὐπορέω—to prosper, thrive, be well off, have plenty, abound in, be rich

εὐπορία—prosperity, easy living

τὰ ἀγαθά—goods, possessions, wealth

χρῆμα—a thing that one uses or needs, a good, property, money, gear, wealth, matter, affair, event

ἁδρότης—generous gift

τιμιότης—costly merchandise, wealth

μαμωνᾶς—worldly wealth, from Μαμωνᾶ the Syrian god of riches

Weapon

ὅπλον—weapon, armament, tool, instrument

πανοπλία—weapons and armor

ξύλον—tree, wood, firewood, club, cross, stocks

ῥομφαία—large sword, scymitar

μάχαιρα—sword

λόγχη—spear

βέλος—arrow, dart

τόξον—bow

περικεφαλαία—helmet

θώραξ—breastplate

θυρεός—shield

σκεῦος—vessel, utensils, furniture, military gear, equipment, luggage

Weather, see "Wind," "Water Terms"

εὐδία—fair weather

βροντή—thunder

ἀστραπή—lightning

βρέχω—to make wet, get wet, rain, soak

βροχή—rain

ὑετός—rain

ὄμβρος—rainstorm

διεγείρω—become stormy

καύσων—scorching heat

σεισμός—storm on the sea

ὑποπνέω—blow softly, blow under, breathe gently

θύελλα—windstorm, sudden storm, tempest

τυφωνικός—of a strong wind, tempestuous
πρόϊμος—early in the season, substantivally: the early rain, the autumnal rain
χιών—snow
χειμών—bad weather, winter, tempest
χειμάζομαι—undergo bad weather
ὄψιμος—late in the season, substantivally: the late rain

Weep, see "Cry, Groan, Mourn, Weep"

Weight
βαρύς—heavy in weight, weighty, important, burdensome, severe, stern, cruel, unsparing, grievous
ἐλαφρός—light in weight, easy to bear, buoyant, not burdensome, limited in extent, insignificant in size or number
κουφίζω—to be light, be alleviated, assuaged, make light, make less heavy, lift up, relieve, lighten a ship's cargo
λίτρα—a silver coin of Sicily, as a weight, a Roman pound, about 325 grams
τάλαντον—a monetary unit equal to roughly 40 to 90 kg silver which was coined into drachmae
ταλαντιαῖος—weighing a talent, worth a talent

Welcome, Receive, Show Hospitality
δεκτός—acceptable, welcomed
δέχομαι—take, receive, grasp, accept, welcome
ἀναδέχομαι—to receive, accept, welcome, take upon oneself
ἀποδέχομαι—to accept, receive favorably, acknowledge, welcome
εἰσδέχομαι—to receive, admit, take in, welcome
ἐπιδέχομαι—receive as a guest, allow of, accept, admit, acknowledge one's authority
παραδέχομαι—accept, acknowledge, receive, receive favorably, welcome
προσδέχομαι—to receive favorably, accept, receive hospitably, welcome, admit into, wait for, expect
ὑποδέχομαι—to receive, welcome, entertain as a guest
ἀπολαμβάνω—to receive from, take back, regain, recover, take aside, receive hospitably, welcome
παραλαμβάνω—receive, take with, accept, learn
ἀσπάζομαι—to greet, bid welcome, embrace
ξενία—hospitality, entertainment of guests
ξενίζω—to show hospitality to strangers, intransitive: be surprised, think strange
ξενοδοχέω—show hospitality
ξένος—stranger, foreigner
φιλόξενος—loving strangers, hospitable
φιλοξενία—hospitality

Wilderness, Rural Place, Country
ἐρημία—wilderness, desert
ἔρημος—τόπος—deserted place, lonely place
ἄνυδρος τόπος—waterless, dry place
ἀγρός—field, countryside, farm settlement
χώρα—land, region, countryside, mostly rural and sparsely populated in contrast with a metropolis (Luke 21:21)

Willing
ἑκούσιος—voluntary, willing

ἑκουσίως—voluntarily, willingly, of one's own accord, purposely

αὐθαίρετος—voluntary, of free choice, of one's own choosing

ἑκών—unforced, voluntary, willing, of one's own will, of one's own accord

ἄκων—not of one's own will, unwillingly, against the will, not willing

Wind

ἄνεμος—wind

πνεῦμα—wind, breath, spirit, soul, the Holy Spirit, the inner being

πνέω—blow, breathe

πνοή—breath, wind

ὑποπνέω—blow softly, blow under, breathe gently

θύελλα—windstorm, sudden storm, tempest

λαῖλαψ—windstorm, squall, violent forceful wind

τυφωνικός—of a strong wind, tempestuous

νότος—south wind

εὐρακύλων—violent agitation raising mighty waves, northeaster

Wisdom, Understanding, see also "Know, Make Known," "True, Truth," "Think," "Virtues: Understanding"—

φρόνησις—understanding, prudence, wisdom

φρόνιμος—intelligent, wise, prudent

φρονίμως—wisely, prudently

σωφρονέω—to be of sound mind, exercise self-control, be sane, be sensible, curb one's passions

σωφρονισμός—self-control, moderation, sound judgment, soundness of mind

σωφροσύνη—self-control, moderation, sound judgment, sobriety, soundness of mind

σοφία—wisdom, intelligence, specialized knowledge, insight

σοφός—wise, skilled, skillful

σοφίζω—to make wise, instruct, middle: devise, reason with skill, passive: be cleverly devised

φιλοσοφία—love of wisdom, human wisdom, philosophy

φιλόσοφος—philosopher, one given to the pursuit of wisdom or learning

νουνεχῶς—wisely, discreetly, sensibly

ἀκούω—to hear, listen, hearken, obey, give audience, receive news, understand, be reported

νοέω—to understand, see with insight, reflect, perceive, observe, comprehend, conceive

κατανοέω—pay attention, consider, contemplate, apprehend, discern

ἐπίσταμαι—to understand, be aware, comprehend, be acquainted with

ἐπιστήμων—intelligent, experienced, having expertise

συνίημι—understand, perceive, put together in the mind, consider, be wise, be intelligent

σύνεσις—knowledge, understanding, what is understood, intelligence

συνετός—intelligent, having understanding, wise, learned, prudent

οἶδα—to see, perceive, know, regard

βλέπω—to see, discern, understand, take heed, watch out for

θεωρέω—to look at, watch, behold, see, consider, perceive, ascertain

ὁράω—to see, behold, perceive, know, experience, take heed, beware

συνοράω—learn about, understand

μανθάνω—to learn, be taught

ψηφίζω—to count up, reckon, figure out, vote for

γινώσκω—know, learn, perceive, understand, acknowledge, have sexual intercourse

γνῶσις—knowledge, understanding

ἐπιγινώσκω—to recognize, to know, to become thoroughly acquainted with, to know accurately, learn about, acknowledge

ἐπίγνωσις—knowledge

καταλαμβάνω—lay hold of, obtain, acquire, seize, attack, catch, middle: receive with the mind, comprehend

εὔσημος—intelligible, well-marked, clear and definite, distinct, easy to understand

κατάδηλος—easily understood, thoroughly clear, plain, evident

αἰσθάνομαι—to perceive, grasp, understand

αἴσθησις—perception, cognition, capacity to understand, discernment, judgement

αἰσθητήριον—faculty of the mind for understanding, capacity to understand

μάγος—a wise man and priest, a magician

Wish, see "Desire"

With

σύν—with, accompanied by, together with

ἅμα—at once, at the same time, together with

ἀμφότερος—each or both of two, together

μεταξύ—between, in the middle, among

ὁμοῦ—together

σύμφυτος—planted together, grown together, united with, closely identified with, one with

κοινός—communal, shared in common, mutual, public, of meats: profane or common, defiled, ritually unclean

Without, or Words Indicating Dissociation

ἄνευ—without, independent of, apart from

ἄτερ—without, apart from

χωρίς—without, separated from, apart from, outside of, independent of, without any relation to

ἐκτός—outside, the outer part of something, besides, independent of, followed by εἰ μή: unless, except

Witness, Testify

ἐπιμαρτυρέω—to testify, witness

μαρτυρέω—to witness, testify, give a good report, speak well of

μαρτυρία—witness, testimony, attestation, evidence, reputation

μαρτύριον—testimony, witness

συμμαρτυρέω—bear witness with, bear joint witness, testify in support

ἀμάρτυρος—without witness, unattested, without testimony

συνεπιμαρτυρέω—to attest together with, join in bearing witness, unite in adding testimony

καταμαρτυρέω—to bear witness against, testify against

μάρτυς—a witness, spectator, martyr, record

ψευδομαρτυρέω—to give false witness

ψευδομαρτυρία—false testimony

ψευδόμαρτυς—a false witness

Woman

γυνή—woman, wife

γυναικεῖος—female

πρεσβῦτις—old woman

γυναικάριον—idle, frivolous, silly woman
γραώδης—characteristic of old women, silly
παρθένος—virgin, maiden, girl, unmarried person, chaste person
κοράσιον—girl, damsel, maiden
θῆλυς—female, feminine

Womb, see "Body Parts"

Wood

ξύλον—tree, wood, firewood, club, cross, stocks
ξύλινος—wooden
ὕλη—forest, felled wood, fuel
φρύγανον—firewood
ἄνθραξ—charcoal
δοκός—beam of wood, shaft of timber
κάρφος—splinter, speck
θύϊνος—citron wood, ornamental wood from citron tree

Word

ῥῆμα—word, thing spoken, utterance, statement, plural: message, speech
γραφή—writing, thing written, the Scripture, a portion of the Scripture
λόγος—word, reason, matter under discussion, account, treatise, statement
ἔπος—word

Work, Function, Do, Operate

ἔργον—work, business, deed, act, action, workmanship, occupation, matter, task
ἐνέργεια—action, function, energy
ἐνεργέω—to work, put forth power, be active, be mighty in, bring about, cause to function, be effective
ἐργάζομαι—to work, do business, do, perform, produce, bring about
ἐνέργημα—activity, experience
ἐργασία—work, daily labor, business, making, building, commerce, practice, exercising, a work of art, production
ἐργάτης—worker, laborer
συνεργέω—work together with, help in work, cooperate with, assist
κατεργάζομαι—perform, accomplish, achieve, bring about, make ready
πραγματεία—undertakings, business, affairs, activity, occupation, the careful prosecution of an affair, dealings, the treatment of a subject, a treatise, a systematic history
πρᾶξις—a doing, deed, transaction, business, affair, the result or issue of business, a practical result, an acting, practice, action, exercise, function, practical ability, dexterity
πράσσω—to accomplish, achieve, bring about, do, practice, act, be busy with, cause, make, manage, transact, negotiate, to exact money
πρᾶγμα—deed, undertaking, task, act, event, occurrence, work, matter, affair, business, something necessary or expedient or important or of consequence, lawsuit, dispute
ποιέω—make, do, produce, cause to be, carry out, execute, appoint
ποίησις—a making, fabrication, creation, production, doing, a poem
ποιητής—maker, producer, author, poet, performer
ἕξις—a practice, habit, exercise, skill
κοινωνέω—to share, have or do in common with, have a share of or take part in a thing with, have dealings with, do together with, form a community
προκόπτω—to advance a work, progress, go forward, proceed, of time: be spent

χράομαι—make use of, employ, with adverb: act, proceed, with personal dative: deal with, behave toward (Acts 27:3)
ἀπόχρησις—consumption, using up
οἰκονομία—stewardship, management of a household, administration, dispensation, plan
δρόμος—a course, running, race, quick movement, flight, mission
ἐκδαπανάομαι—spend oneself fully, give oneself completely, do something to the limit of one's capacity
δαπανάω—to spend freely, exhaust, use up

Worship, see "Praise"

Worthy

ἄξιος—worthy, deserving, proper, befitting, sufficient for, of like value, worth as much as
ἀξίως—worthily, in a manner worthy of, suitably, properly
ἀξιόω—to count worthy, deem deserving, regard as good
καταξιόω—to consider worthy, hold in high esteem, regard as worthy
ἀνάξιος—unworthy, not held as worthy of, undeserving
ἀναξίως—unworthily, in an unworthy or careless manner, in an improper manner
ἱκανός—sufficient, adequate, able to, enough, considerable, satisfactory, many

Wound, Harm

κακοποιέω—do harm, do evil, do wrong, do injury to
κακόω—oppress, afflict, harm, maltreat, embitter, render evil to, vex
κακός—of a bad nature, evil, wicked
κακῶς ἔχειν—to have badly, be sick
κάκωσις—ill treatment, ill usage, affliction, injury
βλαβερός—hurtful, injurious, harmful
βλάπτω—hurt, harm, injure
τραυματίζω—to wound, hurt
τραῦμα—a wound
μώλωψ—a bruise, wound
ὕβρις—insult, a wrong springing from insolence, affront, injury inflicted by the violence of a tempest, damage
φθείρω—to corrupt, destroy, deprave
λυμαίνομαι—harass, treat shamefully, ravage, ruin, injure severely
ἀδικέω—do wrong, be in the wrong, act unjustly toward
δάκνω—to bite, figuratively: cause harm to
κολαφίζω—strike with the fist, treat with violence, buffet, afflict
τύπτω—strike, beat, smite, wound
πατέω—tread, trample, crush with the feet, step on
πληγή—blow, stripe, wound, heavy affliction, calamity, plague, distress
δέρω—flay, skin, beat, thrash, strike repeatedly, whip
σαπρός—rotten, putrefied, corrupted by one and no longer fit for use, of poor quality, bad, worthless, harmful
καταστροφή—overthrow, destruction

Wrap, Roll, Fold

ἐντυλίσσω—wrap, roll up, fold up, of burial preparation
ἑλίσσω—roll up something, as a scroll
ἕλιγμα—package, roll
ἐνειλέω—wrap in, passive: be engaged in or with
εἴλω—roll up
συστέλλω—place together, draw together, shorten, abridge, limit, roll together, wrap

πτύσσω—fold up, roll up
ἀναπτύσσω—unroll

Writing, Words Pertaining To

ἀναγινώσκω—to read, usually aloud
ἀνάγνωσις—a reading, public reading
γράμμα—a letter of the alphabet, any record, document, letter, epistle, the sacred writings, scriptures, learning, education
γραπτός—written
γραφή—writing, thing written, the Scripture, a portion of the Scripture
γράφω—to write, record, compose
καταγράφω—write down
ἐγγράφω—engrave, inscribe, write on, record
ἐπιγράφω—to write on, inscribe
ἐπιγραφή—an inscription, title, legend
προγράφω—to write previously
χειρόγραφον—handwritten account, record of charges
ἐλλογέω—charge to one's account, keep record
ἐντυπόω—to engrave, imprint
βιβλαρίδιον—little scroll
βιβλίον—document
βίβλος—a written book, scroll, record
κάλαμος—pen
μέλας—ink
κεφαλίς—wooden head of a scroll, by metonymy: scroll
μεμβράνα—parchment sheet
χάρτης—sheet of paper
πινακίδιον—tablet
πλάξ—tablet
σφραγίς—a seal, signet ring, mark of genuineness, that by which a thing is confirmed or authenticated, proof
σφραγίζω—to mark with a seal, put a seal on, seal up, confirm, prove, guarantee
κατασφραγίζω—secure with a seal
ἐπιστέλλω—to send one a message, write instructions, instruct by letter
ἐπιστολή—letter, epistle
ἰῶτα—the eighth and smallest Hebrew letter called a "jot"
κεραία—a little horn, extremity, apex, point, part of a letter, accent mark
λόγος—word, reason, account, matter under discussion, treatise
καταλέγω—to enlist, enroll, put on a list
νόμος—law
τίτλος—a title, inscription

Y

Yield

εἴκω—to concede, withdraw, yield, give way, draw back, retire, shrink from, grant, allow, submit

ὑπείκω—give way to authority, comply, concede to, obey, submit to

ἐπιδίδωμι—to give besides, give in dowry, give freely, contribute as benevolence, hand over, give over, give up, surrender, yield

English Index

abandon, 2
abasement, 185
abate, 27
abhor, 179
abide, 2
ability, 119, 154
able, 154
abolish, 45, 85
abomination, 180
abortion, 18
about, 10
above, 98
abroad, 167
abstain, 13
abstinence, 60, 188
absurd, 26, 178
abundance, 102, 192
abuse, 175
abyss, 76, 191
accent mark, 118
accept, 3, 130, 193
acceptable, 3, 125
access, 111
accessories, 3
accompany, 4, 12, 145, 195
accomplish, 25, 33, 66
account, 4
accounting, 4
accurate, 168
accursed, 41
accuse, 94, 149, 176
achieve, 25, 66, 196
acquire, 4, 23, 130

acquit, 65, 94, 132, 186, 188
activity, 196
addition, 5
adequate, 5, 36, 55
adhere, 87
adjure, 56, 111
administration, 197
admit, 34, 193
admonish, 5, 32, 130, 158
adorn, 31
adornments, 3
adultery, 181
advance, 121
advantage, 5
advent, 32
advice, 5, 116, 158
affection, 90, 99
affirmation, 85, 108
affliction, 113, 167, 175, 197
after, 97, 99, 122
afterwards, 162
against, 5, 112
age, 111, 161, 165
agitate, 6
agreeable, 3, 125, 184
agreement, 6, 124, 187
agriculture, 59
aid, 5, 76
ailment, 147
alabaster flask, 35
alarm, 61
alert, 191
alien, 64

alike, 142
alive, 95
all, 6
alleviate, 54
allotment, 70
allow, 7
allowance, 141
almighty, 71
almost, 10
aloe, 116
alone, 7
alphabet, 198
already, 161
altar, 67
alter, 27
although, 7
always, 166
amazement, 61, 155
ambush, 191
amen, 168
amount, 108
amputate, 41
anatomy, 18
ancestor, 17, 89
anchor, 142
ancient, 111, 161
and, 7, 34
angel, 7
anger, 173
anguish, 113, 140
animal, 7, 8
animal husbandry, 8
anise, 117, 152
ankle, 19
announce, 8, 120

English Index

annul, 45, 85
anoint, 96, 115
another, 47
answer, 9, 43, 152
antichrist, 133
anticipation, 79
antitype, 114
anxiety, 9
any, 6
apart from, 195
apostasy, 129
apostle, 9, 133
appeal, 11, 120
appearance, 15, 65, 82, 143
appoint, 12, 46
apportion, 12, 70, 146
apprehend, 157, 159
approach, 10
approve, 69, 130
approximately, 10
apron, 30
arbitrator, 6, 85
archery, 192
architect, 20
arena, 22
argument, 10, 43, 152, 179
arise, 74, 135
ark, 142
arm, 18
armament, 190
armor, 192
army, 190
aroma, 150
around, 98, 99, 138
arouse, 11, 190
arrangement, 10, 145
arrest, 144
arrive, 32
arrogance, 174
arrow, 192
as, 32
as much as, 171
ascend, 11, 135
ascertain, 144
asceticism, 188
ashes, 22

ask, 11, 120
assault, 189
assembly, 12, 39, 40
assert, 34
assign, 12
assist, 76, 196
associate, 12, 87
assurance, 39, 183
astonish, 155
astray, 50, 99, 175
asunder, 114, 174
at leisure, 180
athletic, 36
atonement, 61, 65, 140
attach, 87
attack, 13, 189
attain, 4
attempt, 168
attention, 25, 143
attentive, 190, 191
attest, 195
attire, 31
attitude, 159
attractive, 14
authentic, 69
author, 15
authority, 13, 138
autumn, 164
avarice, 179
avenge, 127
avoid, 13, 131
await, 79
awaken, 11, 135, 190
aware, 90
awe, 119
axe, 60

babble, 151, 177
babe, 28
back, 19
backbiting, 176
bad, 14, 183
bake, 38
bands, 60
banish, 56, 131
banker, 105
banquet, 61
baptize, 14, 43

barley, 66
barn, 21
barracks, 22
barren, 18
barricade, 190
barrier, 190
based on, 26
basin, 35
basket, 36
bath, 104
bathe, 29
battle, 79, 154, 190
bay, 191
be, 16
beach, 92
beam, 196
bear, 8, 20, 25, 57
beat, 78
beautiful, 14
because, 26, 35, 64, 66, 122
beckon, 148
becoming, 15
bed, 67
bee, 85
befall, 59, 74
before, 161
beg, 11, 120
beget, 17
beggar, 118
beginning, 15, 145, 161
begotten, 17
beguile, 50, 59, 175
behavior, 15, 187
behead, 88
behind, 97
behold, 143
being, 16
belief, 183
belly, 19
belongings, 125
below, 98
belt, 30
bend over, 17
benediction, 18
benefactor, 77
beneficial, 184
benefit, 5

benevolence, 186
bent, 40
beseech, 11, 120
beside, 23
betray, 17, 69
beverage, 63
beware, 143, 191
bewildered, 156
bewitch, 182
beyond, 97
biased, 178
big, 92
bile, 18
billow, 191
bind, 60
bird, 17
birth, 17
birthday, 61
bishop, 133
bite, 53, 106, 197
bitterness, 140, 157, 178
blame, 149, 176
blameless, 40, 188
blaspheme, 177
bleach, 31
bleeding, 148
blemish, 48
blend, 105
bless, 18, 119, 186
blind, 18
blockage, 123
blood, 18
bloom, 137
blow, 194
blue, 32
board, 11, 55
boasting, 174
boat, 142
bodily excretions, 18
body, 18
body parts, 18
boldness, 39
bonds, 84
bone, 19
bonfire, 92
booty, 118
born, 17
born again, 27, 38, 135

borrow, 105
bound, 33
boundary, 131
boundless, 85
bow, 90, 142
bowl, 35
box, 36
boxing, 36
boy, 28
brag, 174
braid, 74
branch, 117
brave, 39
bread, 63
breadth, 103
break, 19
break open, 153
break through, 19
breast, 19
breastplate, 192
breath, 194
bribery, 69, 174
bridle, 60
briefly, 165
brier, 117
bright, 96
brimstone, 22
bring, 20, 56
broadcast, 153
broil, 38
broken, 20
bronze, 104
brood, 17
brother, 89
bruise, 197
brutish, 178
bucket, 35
buffet, 197
building, 20, 21
building materials, 21
building parts, 21
buildings, types of, 21
bull, 7
bully, 175
bundle, 60
buoyant, 193
burden, 25, 167, 193
burial, 67

burning, 22
bury, 47, 67
bush, 117, 167
business, 23, 25, 68, 196
busybody, 181
but, 34, 36
buy, 23
by, 23, 99, 122
bygone, 165
byway, 154

calamity, 45
calculate, 4, 109, 159
calf, 7
call, 11, 24, 86, 107, 147
callous, 155
calm, 24, 115, 187
cavalry, 191
camel, 8
capable, 5, 154
captivity, 24, 72, 84, 191
capture, 24
carcass, 18
care, 9, 145
care for, 24, 76
caress, 90
cargo, 25
carnal, 116
carpenter, 21
carriage, 173
carry, 25
cast, 160
catch, 24, 80, 142, 144, 159
category, 29
cattle, 7
cause, 56
cause, words indicating, 26
cave, 78
cease, 26
celebration, 61
celestial, 76
cement, 60
censer, 35
censure, 39
census, 158
centurion, 191

English Index

ceramic, 53
certain, 27, 62, 168
certainly, 108
chaff, 60, 117
chain, 60
chair, 67
change, 27, 135
change behavior, 38
character, 65
charcoal, 22, 196
charge, 32, 94, 149
chariot, 173, 191
charitable, 186
chase, 128
chasten, 127
cheat, 176
cheek, 19
cheer, 39, 54
cheerful, 75
cherish, 99
chest, 19
chew, 53
chief, 138
child, 28, 89
childbearing, 17
choke, 28
choose, 12, 28
chorus, 106
Christ, 133
Christian, 28
church, 12, 29, 133
cinnamon, 152
circular, 138
circumcise, 43
circumspect, 188
citizenship, 29, 39
citron, 196
city, 29
claim, 34
clamor, 151
clang, 151
clash, 154
class, 29
clay, 53
cleanse, 29
clearly, 143
cliff, 106
cling, 60, 87

cloak, 30
closed, 111
cloth, 30
cloth, sewing, 30
clothe, 31
clothing, 30
cloud, 76
club, 167, 192
coast, 92, 131, 142
coffer, 36
cohabitate, 18
cohort, 190
coin, 106
cold, 79
collapse, 45
collect, 4, 130
colony, 29, 39
colors, 31
combat, 154
combustion, 22
come, 10, 32
comfort, 24, 54
comforter, 153
command, 32
commander, 138
commandment, 93, 94
commence, 15
commend, 130
commission, 12
commitment, 124, 183
communal, 146
communicate, 151
communion, 12
companion, 12
company, 12
comparable, 33
comparison words, 32
compassion, 99, 186
compel, 33, 171
compensate, 38
compile, 10
complaint, 33, 176
complete, 6, 33, 54, 66, 115
comply, 186
compose, 198
comprehend, 159, 194
compulsion, 107

conceal, 39, 77
concede, 199
conceited, 174
conceive, 17, 159
concern, 9, 24
conclude, 46, 54
concord, 6
condemnation, 87, 127
condiment, 152
conduct, 15
confer, 37
confess, 34
confidence, 183
confined, 167
confirm, 56
conflict, 154
conform, 65, 142
conjunctions, 34
conquer, 35
conscience, 90, 127
consecrate, 18, 43, 184
consent, 6
consequently, 136
consider, 4, 159
considerable, 55, 102
consolation, 54
conspiracy, 129
constant, 134
constellation, 76
constraint, 33, 107, 167
constructing, 20
consult, 38
consume, 45, 53
container, 35
contemplate, 159, 194
contempt, 179
contend, 154, 169
content, 36
contention, 10, 154, 179
contests, 36
continue, 133
continuous, 166
contradict, 112
contrary, 6, 36
contrast, words of, 36
control, 37
controversy, 49
contumacious, 174

English Index

convene, 12
conversation, 15, 37
convert, 38
convict, 130
convulsions, 147
cooking and kitchen
    terms, 38
cool, 80
copper, 104
corn, 66
corner, 118
cornerstone, 21
corporeal, 18
corpse, 18
correct, 168
correction, 127, 158, 188
correspond, 115
corrosion, 53
corruptible, 47
corruption, 48, 137, 181
cost, 38, 105, 141
costly, 173
cot, 67
couch, 67
council, 39
counsel, 5, 116
count, 4
countenance, 115, 144
counterfeit, 59, 176
counting, 108
country, 39, 92, 131
countryman, 29
courage, 39
course, 145
courtesy, 183
courtroom, 21
courtyard, 21
covenant, 124
covered, 31, 39
covet, 44, 179
cowardice, 61
crack, 153
craftiness, 176
craftsman, 21, 101
craving, 44, 181
crazy, 85
create, 15, 101
creation, 52, 171

credit, 78
crime, 149
crimson, 31
crippled, 148
criticize, 39
crooked, 40, 181
cross, 113, 167, 196
crossover, 40
crow, 17
crowd, 40
crown, 141
crucify, 88
cruelty, 175
crumb, 63
crunch, 53
crush, 20, 123
cry, 40
cry out, 147
crystal, 40, 121
cub, 8
cubit, 103
cultivate, 59
cumin, 117, 152
cunning, 176
cup, 35
cure, 75, 104
curse, 41, 177
curtain, 30
cushion, 67
custody, 145
custom, 41
customary, 155
cut, 41
cut off, 131
cymbals, 106

daily, 163
damned, 41
damsel, 196
dance, 106
dangerous, 42, 168
daring, 39
darkness, 42
dart, 192
daughter, 28
dawn, 96, 163
day, 161, 163
deacon, 133

dealings, 23, 196
death, 46, 88
debate, 36, 38, 49, 154
debauchery, 178, 180
debt, 42, 105
decay, 137
deception, 59, 175
decide, 39, 46, 87
declare, 8, 34, 85, 151
decorate, 3
dedicate, 43, 184
deed, 196
defame, 176
defeat, 35, 59
defect, 183
defense, 43, 77
defilement, 48, 182
deformed, 170
defraud, 176
degenerate, 48
degree, 171
deity, 71
delay, 150, 164
deliberate, 37, 159
delight, 184
deliverance, 17, 69, 132, 141
delude, 50, 176
demise, 59
demolish, 45
demon, 46
den, 78
denarius, 106
deny, 43
depart, 70, 137
dependency
    words indicating, 26
deportation, 134, 151
deposit, 38, 69, 105
depravity, 14, 181
depressed, 48
deprive, 182
deprive of power, 85
depth, 103
deride, 177
descend, 43
descendants, 44
describe, 9

English Index

desecrate, 140, 182
desert, 2, 92, 193
deserted, 54
deserving, 197
designate, 12, 28, 107
desire, 44, 55, 99, 179, 182
despise, 179
destined, 107
destroy, 45
determine, 12, 46
detest, 179
deviate, 178
devil, 14, 46
devised, 194
devotion, 52, 134, 169
devour, 45, 53
devout, 43, 133, 185
dialect, 92
diaspora, 49
die, 46
different kind, 47
difficult, 116, 168
dig, 20, 47, 59
dignity, 187
diligence, 52, 169
dill, 117, 152
dilute, 105
diminished, 150
dimness, 18
dine, 53, 130
diqualified, 59
direct, 72
direction, 47, 97
dirt, 52
dirty, 48, 183
disabled, 147
disadvantage, 48
discern, 159, 189, 194
disciple, 63, 93
discipline, 127, 158, 188
disclose, 9, 90, 144
discontent, 33, 176
discord, 10, 49, 154
discouragement, 48
discourse markers,
  conjunctions, 34
discourse types
  allegory, 48

historical, 48
lineage, 49
metaphor, 48
myth, 48
narrative, 48
nativity, 49
parable, 49
poem, 49
proverb, 48
treatise, 151
discover, 62, 93
discriminate, 39
discuss, 37
disease, 147
disfigured, 45, 170
disgrace, 48, 146
disguise, 59
disgusting, 14
dish, 35
disheartened, 48
dishonor, 146
dislocated, 148
dismayed, 48
disobedience, 14, 177
disown, 131
disparage, 130, 179
dispatch, 145
dispensation, 80, 197
disperse, 49
dispute, 10, 37, 49, 112
disregard, 43, 86
dissension, 49, 153
dissipation, 178
dissociation, words
  marking, 195
distance, 97, 103
distinction, 47
distinctive, 170
distinguish, 87
distort, 176
distress, 9, 167
distribute, 12, 70, 146
district, 131
distrust, 50
disturbance, 6
dive, 156
diverse, 113
divide, 146, 153, 190

divine, 71, 133, 185
division, 49, 113, 145
divorce, 50, 114
do, 25, 196
do intensively, 169
doctrine, 158
document, 198
dog, 8
dominion, 35, 119, 138
donkey, 8
doomed, 46
door, 21
doorkeeper, 80
double, 109
double-edged, 118
doubt, 50, 87
dough, 38
dove, 17
down payment, 105
downhearted, 48
downtrodden, 168
dowry, 199
drachma, 106
drag, 20, 127
dragnet, 142
dragon, 135
drain, 54
draw, 20, 127
dread, 61
dream, 50
drink, 53, 63
drive along, 51
drive away, 51
dropsy, 147
drowsy, 150
drunkenness, 178
dry, 51
dull, 64
dumb, 148
dung, 18, 48
dungeon, 21
during, 162
dust, 52
duty, 107
dwell, 2
dwelling, 22
dysentary, 147

English Index

each, 6
eagerness, 52, 153, 169
eagle, 17
ear, 19
earlier, 161
earn, 68
earnest, 52, 99, 169
earth, 52
earthly, 116
earthquake, 6
ease, 132
east, 47
eat, 53, 130
edict, 32
edify, 20
education, 93, 158
effective, 196
effeminate, 182
effort, 169
egg, 63
either, 82, 112
elapse, 165
elder, 133, 139
elect, 28
elegant, 15, 125
elementary principle, 54
elevate, 11
eliminate, 46
eloquent, 152
elsewhere, 97
embalm, 116
embark, 55
embarrassment, 146
embezzle, 182
embitter, 178
emblem, 142, 148
embrace, 90, 193
emerald, 121
emotional, 140
empire, 39
employ, 197
empty, 54, 172
empty-talker, 177
encampment, 190
encircle, 138
encounter, 56
encouragement, 54, 172
encumbrance, 123

end, 26, 33, 54
endeavor, 168
endless, 166
endurance, 57, 114
enemy, 79, 154, 190
energy, 196
engage in, 169
engaged to, 103
engineer, 21
engrafted, 59
engrave, 198
enigma, 77
enjoy, 55
enlist, 190
enmity, 79
enough, 55
enraged, 173
enroll, 198
ensnare, 159
entangle, 24, 159
enter, 55
entertain, 193
enthusiasm, 52
entice, 159
entire, 6
entrance, 21
entreat, 11, 120, 171
entrust, 25
envy, 178
epileptic, 147
epistle, 198
epistolary discourse types
    closing, 49
    farewell, 49
    greeting, 49
    rejoicing, 49
    summary, 49
equal, 141
equip, 20, 121
equipment, 55, 192
equivalent, 141
era, 161, 166
erect, 20, 40
error, 149, 175
escape, 13, 141
escort, 4
essence, 65
establish, 55, 153

eternal, 166
eternity, 161
eunuch, 102, 139
evaluate, 87
evangelist, 133
even, 7
evening, 163
ever, 56, 82, 162
everlasting, 166
every, 6
everywhere, 97
evident, 27
evil, 14, 42, 149, 178, 183
example, 114
exasperate, 173
exceedingly, 57
excellent, 184
except, 36
excess, 178, 192
excessive, 102
exchange, 56, 68, 105
exclude, 131
excretions, 18
excuse, 43
execute, 12, 25, 88
exempt, 66
exercise, 36, 188
exert, 169
exhausted, 48, 166
exhibit, 144
exhort, 5, 158
exile, 134, 151
existence, 16
exorcism, 56
expect, 155
expectation, 79
expel, 51, 131
expend, 152
expense, 38, 141
expensive, 173
experience, 56
experienced, 194
expertise, 194
expiate, 65, 186
expire, 46
explain, 9, 57, 91
exploitation, 68, 179
expose, 57

English Index

expound, 57
extinct, 88
extinguish, 22
extol, 78, 119
extortion, 176
extramarital, 181
extraordinary, 170
extravagant, 170, 192
extremely, 57
exultation, 75
eye of a needle, 31
eyes, 19, 143
eyewitness, 144

fabricate, 21
face, 19
facing, 48
faction, 114, 170
factual, 168
fail, 59
faint, 48, 147
fair, 14
faith, 183
faithful, 27
fall, 43, 59, 149, 164
false, 59, 170
falsehood, 95, 175
fame, 9
family, 89
famine, 53
far, 98
farm, 21, 62
farming terms, 59
farming tools, 60
fasten, 60
fasting, 60
father, 89
fathom, 103
fatigue, 166
fatten, 53
fattened, 8
fault, 14, 149
favor, 28, 55, 72, 185
favorable, 3
favorable circumstances, 61
favoritism, 178
fear, 61, 119, 132

fearless, 39
feast, 53, 61
fee, 141
feeble, 147
feed, 53
feel, 57, 166
fellowship, 12
female, 195
feminine, 196
fence, 190
fervent, 52
fervor, 44
festival, 61
fever, 147
few, 150
fiber, 30
field, 62
fierce, 189
fig, 66
fig tree, 167
fight, 36, 169, 190
fighting, 10, 154, 179
figure, 65
filth, 48, 182
finally, 35
find, 62, 143
find out, 93
fine appearance, 15
finger, 19
finish, 33, 54, 66
fire, 22
firewood, 196
firm, 27, 62
firmament, 76
first, 15, 109
firstfruits, 140
fish, 62
fish hook, 142
fisherman, 142
fishing terms, 62
fishnet, 142
fist, 19
fitting, 125
fixate, 60
fixed, 62
flames, 22
flash, 96
flat, 138

flatter, 62
flavor, 157
flee, 13, 70, 141
flesh, 19, 115
fleshly, 116
float, 142
flock, 8
flog, 78
flood, 62
flour, 38, 63
flourish, 137
flow, 62, 97
flower, 117
flute, 106
foal, 8
foam, 63
fold, 197
follow, 63, 128
following (in time), 162
folly, 64
fondness, 55
food, 63
foolish, 63
foolish talk, 176
foot, 18
footstool, 67
for, 34, 64
forbearance, 13, 114
force, 33, 119, 189
forehead, 19
foreigner, 64, 151
foreknowledge, 90
foresee, 143
foreshadow, 114, 148
forest, 167
foretell, 121
forethought, 159
forever, 166
forget, 64
forgiveness, 64, 72, 186
form, 65
former, 161
fornication, 181
forsake, 2
fortress, 22
foul, 14
foundation, 21
founder, 15

English Index

fountain, 191
fox, 8
fracture, 19
fragment, 20
fragrance, 116, 150
frankencense, 116
fraud, 59, 176, 182
free, 65, 132
free choice, 194
freight, 25
frequent, 111
fresh, 108
friendship, 12, 99, 186
frivolous, 172
frog, 135
from, 23, 66, 98, 122
front, 97
fruit, 60, 66
fruitful, 137
frustration, 116
fulfill, 34, 66
fulfilled, 55
full, 6, 66
function, 196
funeral, 67
furious, 173, 189
furnace, 22
furnish, 20, 69, 121, 126
furnishings, 55, 67
furthermore, 7
futile, 172

gain, 4, 23, 68
gall, 18
games, 36
gangrene, 147
garbage, 48
garden, 59, 117
garment, 30
gash, 41
gate, 21
gathering, 12
gaze, 144
gear, 55, 192
gehenna, 76
gem, 121
genealogy, 89

generation, 17, 44, 115, 161
generosity, 186
generous, 69, 192
gentleness, 183
genuine, 69, 168
germinate, 18, 72
gesture, 148
ghost, 69
gift, 69
gild, 31
gird, 31
girl, 28
give, 69
give over, 17
glad, 75
gladden, 54
glance, 143
glass, 21, 40, 121
glisten, 96
gloomy, 42, 140
glorify, 78, 119
glory, 119
glow, 96
glue, 60
gluttony, 53, 179
gnashing, 106, 174
gnat, 85
gnaw, 53
go, 70
go around, 40
go through, 40
goad, 8, 60
goat, 8
God, 71
godly, 132
gold, 31, 104
gong, 106
goodness, 184
goods, 192
goodwill, 185
gospel, 8, 121
gossip, 181
gossipy, 177
govern, 72, 138
grace, 71, 184, 188
graceful, 15, 125
grain, 38, 63, 66

grant, 12, 69, 199
grapes, 66
grapevine, 117
grasp, 3, 130, 145, 157
grass, 117
grasshopper, 85
grateful, 72, 188
grave, 67, 76
great, 92
greatly, 57
greed, 44, 179
green, 32
greeting, 90, 193
grief, 14, 40, 140, 168
grind, 38
groan, 40
grope, 166
ground, 52
group, 40
grow, 72, 84
grudge, 178
grumble, 33
guard, 72, 126, 141, 191
guardian, 77
guest, 193
guide, 20, 72
guilt, 87, 149, 177
guiltless, 188
gymnastics, 36

habitual, 41
Hades, 76
hail, 49, 191
hair, 19, 74
hall, 21
hallelujah, 119
hallowed, 43, 132
hand, 18
hand over, 17
handle, 166
handmade, 101
handwritten, 198
hang, 60, 88
happen, 32, 56, 74
happiness, 75
harbor, 143, 191
hardly, 10
hardship, 113, 167

English Index

harlot, 181
harm, 197
harmony, 6
harp, 106
harsh, 175, 189
harvest, 60, 66
hasten, 169
hatred, 179
haughtiness, 174
have, 125
hay, 117
head, 19
headquarters, 22
headstrong, 155
healing, 75, 104
hear, 76
heart, 19, 126, 153
heat, 22
heathen, 170
heaven, 76
heavenly bodies, 76
heaviness, 140, 167
heavy, 193
heed, 76, 186
heel, 19
heifer, 7
height, 103
heir, 130
hell, 46, 76
helmet, 192
helmsman, 143
help, 5, 25, 76
hemorrhage, 148
herald, 9, 120
herbs, 117, 157
herd, 7
here, 97
hereafter, 162
heretical, 170
hewn, 41
hidden, 64, 77
hill, 106
hinder, 123
hip, 19
hire, 77
history, 49
hit, 78
hog, 8

hold, 145, 157, 166
hole, 78
holiday, 61
holiness, 43, 132, 184
home, 2
homeless, 151
homosexual, 182
honesty, 185
honey, 63
honor, 78, 119, 173, 187
hope, 79, 183
horn, 19, 118
horrified, 61
horse, 8
horseman, 191
horticulture, 59
hospitality, 186, 193
hostility, 79, 135, 154, 179
hot, 79
hour, 161
house, 22
household accessories, 67
household roles, 80
housetop, 21
how, 80, 125
however, 35, 36
human, 18, 115
humane, 186
humbleness, 48, 185
humiliation, 146, 175
humor, 152
hundred, 109
hunger, 53, 60
hunt, 80
hurl, 160
hurt, 197
husband, 89
hymn, 106
hypocrite, 176
hyssop, 117

ice, 191
idea, 117, 159
idle, 164, 180
idol, 82
if, 82
ignite, 22
ignorance, 42, 178

ignorant, 82
illicit, 181
illiterate, 82
illness, 147
illumination, 90, 95
image, 65, 82
imitate, 63, 83
immediately, 161
immense, 85
imminent, 162
immorality, 182
immovable, 62
impale, 116
impede, 123
important, 83
imposter, 176
impregnate, 17
imprint, 198
imprison, 72, 84
improper, 125
impure, 48, 183
impute, 4
in, 99
in season, 164
inasmuch, 171
incapable, 170
incense, 115, 140
incessant, 134
incite, 172
income, 68
increase, 5, 72, 84
incriminate, 176
indebted, 42
indecency, 146, 181
indeed, 34, 108
independence, 66
independent of, 195
indicate, 148
indignation, 173
induce, 171
indulgence, 179, 180
ineffective, 170
inevitable, 107
inexpressible, 171
infant, 28
inferiority, 84, 95
infiltrate, 151
infinite, 85

210

infirmity, 147
inflammation, 147
inflict, 13, 56
inform, 8, 158
inhabit, 2
inherit, 130
iniquity, 149
injury, 148, 175, 197
injustice, 149, 178, 180
ink, 198
inland, 92
inn, 21
innkeeper, 22
innocent, 187
innovation, 27
innumerable, 85
inquire, 11, 62, 143
insane, 85
inscription, 198
insects, 85
insensitivity, 155
inside, 97
insight, 194
insignificant, 84, 150
insist, 85
insolence, 177
inspired, 121
instead, 36
instruct, 158
insubordination, 177
insult, 175, 176
insurrection, 10, 129, 179
integrity, 185
intelligence, 90, 194
intemperance, 180
intend, 45, 116, 159
intercession, 11, 85, 120
intercourse, 17
interpret, 57
interrogate, 11, 94
interval, 161
intestines, 19
into, 98
intoxication, 178
invalidate, 85
investigate, 62, 143
invisible, 77
invite, 24, 86

invoke, 11, 107
iron, 104
irrational, 26, 82, 174
irrigate, 59
irritate, 173
island, 92
isolate, 7
issue, 62, 66, 136
ivory, 121

jab, 116
jail, 21
jailer, 72
jangling, 177
jar, 35, 38
jaw, 19
jealousy, 178
jeapardy, 42
jeer, 177
join, 10, 60, 87
joint, 18
jot, 198
journey, 70, 167
joyful, 75
judaizers, 170
judge, 39, 87
judgement, 93, 127
jump, 87
just, 187
justice, 94, 127
justify, 188

keep, 126, 187
kettle, 35
key, 67
kick, 78
kill, 45, 47, 88
kin, 44, 89
kind, 29
kindle, 22
kindness, 185
kinds of, 152
king, 138
kingdom, 39
kiss, 90
knee, 19
kneel, 90
knock, 78

know, 90, 194
knowledge, 93
labor, 166, 196
lacking, 48, 118
lake, 191
lamb, 8
lame, 148
lamentation, 40, 67, 151
lamp, 92
lampstand, 92
land, 39, 62, 92
language, 92, 152
lantern, 92
lap, 19
lapse, 149
large, 92
last, 145
late, 162
latter, 145, 162
laugh at, 177
laughter, 75
launch, 143
lavish, 180
law, 32, 92
lawful, 187
lawlessness, 149, 170, 178, 180
lawyer, 94
lay, 128
lazy, 172, 180
lead, 20, 72
leader, 138
leaf, 117
leap, 87
learn, 90, 93, 189
learned, 194
learner, 63
lease, 77
least, 84
leather, 30
leave, 2, 70
leaven, 63, 176
lecture hall, 22
left, 47
leg, 19
legal terms, 93
legion, 190
legislation, 92

English Index

legitimate, 69, 168
leisure, 164
length, 103
leopard, 8
leprosy, 147
less, 95
let, 7
letters, 93, 198
level, 138
lewd, 14, 178
liable, 42, 149
liar, 175
libation, 140
liberality, 186
liberate, 132
license, 13
licentious, 180
lick, 106
lie, 95
life, 16, 95
lifeless, 46
lifestyle, 15
ligament, 18
light, 95
lighten, 193
lightning, 192
like, 32, 55, 141
likeness, 65, 82, 142
lily, 117
lineage, 17, 44
linen, 30
linger, 164
lion, 8
liquids, 96
list, 198
listen, 76
little, 150
liturgy, 133
live, 2, 95
livelihood, 17
livestock, 8
load, 25
loan, 105
loathe, 179
location, 97, 98
lock, 111
lodge, 21, 150
lofty, 174

loins, 18
loiter, 164
lonely, 193
longing, 44, 100
longsuffering, 114
look, 143
loose, 132
lord, 71, 138
lose, 59, 99
lost, 99
loud, 147
love, 55, 99
lovely, 14
low position, 84
lower, 43
lowly, 185
lump, 105
lust, 44, 181
luxurious, 180
lyre, 106

maggot, 85
magic, 101
magistrate, 138
magnify, 78, 119
maiden, 28, 196
maimed, 148
majesty, 71
make, 101
male, 102
malice, 14, 179
malign, 176
man, 102
manage, 72, 139
manger, 35
manifest, 90, 144
manifold, 47
mankind, 115
manna, 63
manner, 80
many, 102
marble, 121
maritime activities, 142
mark, 148
marketplace, 23, 68
marriage, 18, 103
marrow, 19
martyr, 195

marvel, 155
master, 138
material, 116
matter, 151, 196
maturity, 115, 164
may, 82
meal, 38, 53
meaning, 26, 57, 121, 151, 160, 196
meanwhile, 162
measureless, 85
measures, 103
measuring rod, 103
meat, 63
meddling, 181
mediate, 6, 65, 85
medicine, 104
meditate, 160
meekness, 183
meet, 10
melt, 96
member, 113
memorial, 22, 67
memory, 104
menace, 160
menstrual, 148
merchandise, 192
merchant, 68
mercy, 65, 72, 186
mercy-seat, 65
merit, 184
merry, 75
message, 8, 120
messenger, 7, 8
messiah, 133
metals, 104
midday, 163
middle, 98
midnight, 163
mighty, 92
mildness, 183
military terms, 190
milk, 63
millstone, 22
mimic, 83
mina, 106
mind, 127, 159, 194
mingle, 12, 105

English Index

minister, 24, 133, 145
mint, 117, 152
miracle, 148
mirror, 67
misappropriate, 182
misery, 167
misleading, 50, 99, 175
mission, 145, 197
mistreatment, 175
mix, 104
mock, 105, 176
moderation, 61
modesty, 185, 187
moisture, 191
moment, 161
momentary, 165
monetary terms, 105
money, 23, 105
moneychanger, 68
month, 161
monument, 67
moon, 76
moor, 143
more, 102
morning, 163
morsel, 63
mortal, 47
moth, 85
mother, 89
motion, 106
mount, 11
mountain, 106
mourn, 40, 67
mouth, 19
mouth functions, 106
move, 106
much, 102
mud, 52
mulberry tree, 167
multiply, 84
multitude, 40
murder, 88
murmer, 33
music, 106
mustard, 117, 152
mute, 148
mutilate, 41
mutual, 146, 195

muzzle, 8, 149
myrrh, 116
mystery, 77

nail, 60
naked, 31
name, 24, 107
nard, 116
narrate, 9
narrow, 103
nation, 39
natural, 116
nature, 18, 65
nautical terms, 142
near, 23, 98
nearly, 10
necessary, 107
neck, 19
needle, 31, 118
needy, 118
negation, 108
neglect, 2, 43, 64, 131
negotiate, 23
neighbor, 108
nest, 22
net, 24, 142
never, 108
nevertheless, 7, 36
new, 108
news, 9
night, 42, 163
nipple, 19
no, 108
noble, 187
nod, 148
noise, 151
nonsense, 177
north, 47
northeaster, 194
nothing, 54
notice, 90, 144, 191
nourishment, 25, 53, 63
novelty, 108
now, 34, 161
nullify, 45, 86
numbers, 108
numerous, 111
nurse, 25, 53

nurture, 24

oath, 41, 111, 124
obedience, 63, 76, 186, 199
objection, 112
obligation, 33, 42, 107
obliterate, 46
obscurity, 27, 42, 116
observance, 61, 144
obstacle, 111, 123
obstinate, 155
obtain, 4, 130
occasion, 61, 112, 161
occupation, 16, 196
occur, 74
odd, 171
odor, 150
offend, 111, 149, 189
offer, 69
offering, 65, 140
officer, 190
official, 138
offspring, 17, 44
often, 111
ointment, 115
old, 111, 161, 165
olive, 66
olive oil, 118
olive tree, 167
on, 99
only-begotten, 171
open, 111
operate, 196
opinion, 155
opportunity, 61, 164
opposite, 6, 48, 97
opposition, 49, 79, 112, 135
oppress, 168, 175
opulent, 192
or, 82, 112
orange, 32
oration, 152
orchard, 117
ordain, 12
order, 32, 145
ordered, 10

English Index

orderly, 188
ordinance, 32, 93
organize, 10
origin, 17
ornament, 3
otherwise, 47
ought, 107
out of, 98
outcry, 147
outrun, 121, 139
outside, 97
oven, 22
overextend, 169
overflow, 63
overlook, 64
overpower, 13, 35, 37
overtake, 13
overthrow, 45
overturn, 137
overwhelmed, 62
owe, 42
owner, 125

pagan, 170
pain, 113
palace, 21
palm tree, 167
paper, 198
paradise, 76
paradoxical, 171
paralyzed, 147
parchment, 198
pardon, 65, 72, 132, 186
parents, 89
part, 113
partake, 12, 53, 146
partiality, 46, 178
participate, 12
partner, 12, 146
pass, 40
passage, 49
passible, 113
passion, 44, 113, 181
Passover, 61
past, 161
pastor, 133
pasture, 8, 62
patch, 30, 31

path, 154
patience, 114
pattern, 65, 114
pause, 27, 136
pavement, 22
pay, 38, 141
peace, 115, 187
pearl, 121
pebble, 53
peculiar, 171
pederast, 182
pen, 198
penalty, 38, 127
pentecost, 61
people, 39, 115
perceive, 90, 127, 143, 159
perfect, 33, 66, 115
perform, 25, 196
perfume, 115
perhaps, 119
peril, 42, 168
period, 161
perish, 45, 99
permission, 7, 13
perplexity, 10, 116
persecute, 128
perseverance, 114
persistence, 62, 169
person, 115
persuade, 171
perversion, 181
petition, 11, 85, 120
philosophy, 194
physical, 116
physiological byproducts, 18
pierce, 31, 116
piety, 132
pig, 8
pigeon, 17
pilgrim, 151
pillar, 21
pinnacle, 21
pioneer, 15
pious, 43
pirate, 118
pit, 78
pitcher, 35

pity, 186
place, 97, 128, 153
plague, 167, 197
plan, 116, 159
plank, 21
plant, 117
plant parts, 117
plant products, 118
plaster, 21
plate, 35
platter, 35
play, 36
plead, 11, 85, 120
pleasing, 3, 14, 184
pleasure, 55
pledge, 38, 124
plenty, 192
plot, 117
plow, 59, 60
pluck, 141
plummet, 143
plunder, 13, 118, 182
point, 118
policeman, 139
pollution, 48, 183
pompous, 83, 174
ponder, 159
pool, 191
poor, 118
porch, 21
porcupine, 8
portion, 113
possess, 4, 125
possessions, 157, 192
possible, 119
posterity, 44
potter, 35
pouch, 36
pour, 62, 96
poverty, 118
power, 13, 119, 138
powerless, 170
practice, 16
praetorium, 191
praise, 78, 119
prate, 177
prayer, 11, 85, 120
preach, 8, 120, 133

precede, 20, 63, 121, 145
precepts, 158
precious, 78, 173
precious stones, 121
predestinate, 90
predestine, 46
predict, 121
preference, 28, 46
pregnant, 17
prejudice, 178
premeditate, 117
prepared, 5, 121
prepositions, 98, 122
prepositions of time, 163
presence, 32
present, 69
presentable, 15
presently, 161, 165
preservation, 126, 141
press, 123
pressure, 167
pretension, 174, 176
prevail, 35
prevent, 123
previously, 161
prey, 24, 118
price, 38, 173
pride, 174
priest, 133
prince, 73, 138
principal, 93, 103
principle, 15, 54
prison, 21, 22, 72, 84
prisoner, 191
private, 77
prize, 78, 141, 173
probably, 119
proclaim, 8, 120
proconsul, 138
procreation, 17
prodigal, 180
produce, 72, 101
produce fruit, 137
product, 66
production, 196
profane, 14, 183
profess allegiance, 34
profit, 68

progress, 27, 84, 196
prolong, 134, 150
prominence, 83
promise, 34, 124
pronounce, 151
pronouns, 124
proof, 91
proper, 125
property, 125, 192
prophecy, 121, 126, 133
propiety, 187
propitiation, 65, 186
prosperous, 61, 192
prostitution, 181
prostrate, 126
protect, 126, 141
prove, 159
provide, 25, 69, 126
province, 39
proving, 69
provision, 77
provoke, 173
prudent, 194
prune, 29, 60
psychological faculties, 126
publicly, 144, 146
publish, 8, 120
puffed up, 174
pugnacious, 175
pull, 127
punishment, 127, 188
pupil, 93
purchase, 23
pure, 43
purge, 29
purify, 29, 184
purple, 31
purpose, 45, 116, 159
purpose, words indicating, 136
purse, 36
pursue, 128, 169
put, 128

qualified, 5
quantity, 108
quarrel, 10, 154, 179

quench, 22
questioning, 11, 49
quickly, 162
quiet, 115, 148

race, 29, 36
radiance, 15, 96
radish, 63
rain, 129, 191, 192
rainbow, 76
rainstorm, 192
raise, 11, 154
rampart, 191
rank, 83
ransom, 132
rapacious, 179
rather, 36
ration, 141
raven, 17
ravenous, 44, 179, 189
raze, 45, 191
reach, 32
readiness, 134
reading, 198
ready, 121, 191
real, 69
reality, 168
really, 69
reap, 60
rear, 25
reason, 136, 159
reason
    words indicating, 26
rebellion, 10, 129, 179
rebirth, 28, 38, 135
rebuke, 32, 127, 130
recall, 104
receive, 3, 130, 193
recently, 161
receptacle, 35
recklessness, 180
reckon, 4, 159
recline, 95, 130
recline to eat, 130
recognize, 90
recommend, 130
recompense, 23, 141

English Index

reconcile, 6, 64, 85, 186, 187
record, 198
recordkeeping, 4
recover, 130
red, 31
redeemer, 132
redemption, 23, 132
reduce, 95
reed, 117
reef, 92
referential words, pronouns, 124
refining, 22
reflection, 144, 159, 188
refrain, 13
refreshment, 54, 132
refute, 49
regard, 188
regeneration, 38, 135
region, 39, 92, 131
regret, 38, 140
regulation, 93, 94
reign, 39, 138
reject, 59, 85, 131
relations, 89
relatives, 44, 89
relaxation, 132
release, 65, 66, 132, 186
reliable, 27
relief, 54, 132
religion, 132
religious roles, 133
relish, 157
remain, 133
remarkable, 170
remedy, 75, 104
remember, 104
remind, 104
remit, 65
remnant, 114
remorse, 38, 140
remove, 134
rend, 153
rendering, 141
renewal, 27, 108, 135
renovate, 27
rent, 77

repay, 23, 38, 141
repent, 38, 140
reply, 9
report, 9
repose, 150
representation, 65, 82, 114
reprimand, 130, 176
reproach, 40, 146, 176, 188
reptile, 85, 135
reputation, 195
request, 11, 120
rescue, 76, 141
resentment, 178
reservoir, 191
resettle, 134, 151
reside, 2
residence, 21
resistance, 79, 135, 154
respect, 78, 132, 187
resplendent, 15
rest, 26, 115, 132, 136, 150
restoration, 27, 135
restrain, 37, 123, 188
restriction, 167
result, words indicating, 136
resurrection, 11, 95, 135
retain, 157
return, 137
reveal, 90
revenge, 137
reverence, 61, 119, 132, 187
revile, 176
revive, 95, 135
revolt, 129
revolutionary, 129
reward, 141
riches, 192
richness, 173
riddle, 116
ridicule, 105, 177
right, 47, 125
righteousness, 132, 187
ring, 138
riot, 129
rip, 153

ripen, 137
rise, 11
rising, 135
risk, 42
rivalry, 10, 79, 154, 179
river, 191
road, 154
roaming, 167
roar, 151
roast, 38
robbery, 118, 182
robe, 30
rocky, 138
rod, 60
roll, 137, 197
room, 21
rooster, 17
root, 117
rooted, 62
rope, 60
rot, 137
rough, 138
round, 138
rubbish, 48
rudder, 142
rude, 146
rue, 104, 117, 152
rugged, 138
ruin, 45
rule, 72, 93, 138
ruler, 103
run, 139
rush, 139
rust, 137

sabbath, 61, 136, 164
sacred, 132
sacrifice, 65, 140
sacrilege, 140, 182
sadness, 40, 140
safety, 141
sail, 142
sailor, 142
saint, 28, 43
salary, 38, 141
saliva, 18
salt, 152
salvation, 141

English Index

salve, 104
same, 141
sanctification, 43
sanctity, 184
sanctuary, 21, 43, 120
sand, 53
sandal, 30
sap, 117
sapphire, 121
Satan, 46
satiate, 179
satisfactory, 5, 197
satisfied, 36
savage, 189
save, 141
savior, 141
savor, 157
sayings, 151
scale, 19
scar, 19
scarcely, 10
scarlet, 31
scatter, 49, 153
schism, 49, 153
scholar, 93
scold, 130
scorching, 22, 192
scorn, 105, 179
scorpion, 85
scourge, 127, 158, 188
scribe, 133
scripture, 198
scroll, 198
scrutinize, 39, 87, 176
sculptor, 21
scum, 48
sea, 191
sea terms, 142
seah, 103
seal, 148, 198
seam, 31
seaman, 142
search, 11, 93, 143
seaside, 92
season, 161
seasoning, 38, 152, 157
seat, 149
secret, 77

secretly, 151
sect, 170
secure, 62
seduce, 175
see, 143
seed, 59
seek, 11, 62, 143
seems, 155
seize, 13, 144
seizure, 147
select, 28
self-control, 188
self-indulgence, 180
sell, 23, 38
senator, 39
send, 145
senseless, 64
sensible, 160, 188
sensual, 18, 116
sensuality, 180
sentence, 46
separate, 50
separate from, 131
separation, 113
sepulcher, 67
sequence, 145
serpent, 135
servant, 28
serve, 145
set, 55, 128, 153
set apart, 43, 185
set time, 164
settle, 3, 56
seventy, 109
severe, 167, 175
sewing, 30
sexual, 18, 182
sexual misbehavior, 181
shadow, 42
shaft, 196
shake, 6
shame, 146, 183
shape, 65
share, 69, 146
sharing in, 12
sharp, 118
shatter, 20
shave, 41, 74

shear, 41
sheep, 8
sheepskin, 30
shepherd, 8, 72, 138
shield, 192
shine, 95
ship, 142
shipwreck, 142
shoes, 31
shore, 92, 142
should, 107
shoulder, 19
shout, 147
shovel, 60
show, 57, 144
shower, 96
show-off, 174
shun, 13, 131
shut, 111
sickle, 60
sickness, 147
sift, 38
sigh, 40
sign, 148
signal, 148
signet, 198
signify, 148
silent, 148
silk, 30
silly, 177
silver, 31, 104
silversmith, 104
similar, 32, 142
similitude, 114
sin, 14, 149, 177
since, 82
sincere, 69, 168, 185
single, 7
sink, 43
sister, 89
sit, 149
skill, 196
skin, 19
skull, 19
sky, 76
slain, 46
slander, 176
slaughter, 88, 140

217

English Index

slay, 88
sleep, 150
sleeplessness, 190
slight, 150, 179
slope, 106
slothful, 180
slow, 150
sluggish, 64
slumber, 150
sly, 181
small, 84, 150
smear, 96
smell, 150
smite, 41, 78, 197
smoke, 22
smolder, 23
smooth, 138
smother, 28
snake, 135
snare, 24, 80
snatch, 13, 118, 157
sneak in, 151
sneer, 177
snow, 191, 193
so, 34, 136
soak, 96
sober, 61
sobriety, 188
sodomite, 182
soft, 151
soil, 52
sojourner, 64, 151
solace, 54
soldier, 190
solitary, 7
somewhere, 97
son, 28
song, 106
soon, 162
sophisms, 179
sorcery, 182
sore, 148
sorrow, 40, 113, 140
soul, 126, 152
sound, 92, 151
soundings, 143
soundness, 168
source, 17

south, 47
sovereign, 138
sovereignty, 13, 119
sow, 8, 59, 153
spacial orientation, 47
spare, 141
sparrow, 17
speak, 151
spear, 118, 191, 192
spearman, 191
speck, 196
spectacle, 146
spectator, 144
speculate, 155
speech, 92, 152
speechless, 148
spend, 152
sperm, 17
spice, 115, 152
spicy, 157
spill, 62, 96
spirit, 152
spiritual, 127
spit, 106
splinter, 118, 196
split, 153
spoils, 118
sponge, 96
sports, 36
spotless, 29
spread, 153
spring, 63, 164, 191
spring up, 96
sprinkle, 97
sprout, 72, 117
squall, 194
squander, 49, 54, 152
squeeze, 123
stable, 62
staff, 8, 117
stairs, 21
stalk, 117
stall, 22
stand, 153
star, 76
stare, 144
state, 39
status, 83

stay, 3, 133
steadfast, 27, 62
stealing, 182
stealthily, 151
stench, 150
step, 190
stern, 142, 175
steward, 80
stick to, 60
stiff-necked, 155
still, 162
sting, 116
stinger, 19
stink, 150
stomach, 19
stone, 52
stoop, 17
stop, 26
storehouse, 21
stormy, 192
straight, 40
straighten up, 154
straights, 167
strange, 171
stranger, 64
strangle, 28, 88
strap, 60
stream, 62
street, 154
strength, 75, 119, 154
stretch, 153
stretcher, 67
strew, 153
strife, 10, 49, 79, 154, 179
strike, 78
strive, 169
strong, 154
stronghold, 22
structure, 20
struggle, 36, 154, 169
stubbornness, 155, 178
stumbling, 50, 111, 149
stupid, 64
stupor, 150
subdue, 37
subject, 152
submission, 37
submit, 186, 199

English Index

subordination, 187
subservient, 37
substance, 65
subterranean, 76
subtlety, 179
succeed, 33, 61, 145
succession, 145
suckle, 53
suddenly, 165
suffering, 56, 113
sufficient, 5, 34, 36, 55, 192, 197
suffocate, 28
suitable, 125
sulfur, 22
summarize, 105
summer, 164
summon, 24, 86, 145
sun, 76
sup, 53
superfluous, 170, 192
superior, 83
superstitious, 132
supplication, 11, 85, 120
supplies, 55
supply, 69, 121, 126
support, 76
suppose, 155, 159
sure, 27
surging, 191
surpass, 102
surplus, 192
surprise, 155
surrender, 17, 69, 199
surround, 24, 138
suspense, 9
sustenance, 63
swaddling cloth, 31
swear, 111
sweat, 18
sweep, 38
sweet, 157
swim, 156
sword, 154, 190, 192
sycamore tree, 167
sympathy, 100, 186
synagogue, 12, 22

tabernacles, 61
table, 67
tablet, 198
tail, 19
take, 3, 20, 130, 157
talent, 106
talk, 37, 151
tame, 37
tanner, 30
tarry, 134, 150, 164
tartarus, 76
task, 196
taste, 53, 157
tasteless, 157
tattling, 177
tavern, 22
tax, 157
tax collector, 158
tax collector's booth, 158
teach, 158
teacher, 133
tear, 153
tears, 18, 40
tell, 8, 120, 151
tempest, 192
temple, 21, 133
temporary, 165
temptation, 111, 159
tender, 151
tent, 22
tentmaker, 22
terminate, 27
terrestrial, 52
territory, 131
terror, 61
test, 159
testament, 124
testate, 12
testify, 34, 85, 195
tetrarch, 138
than, 33
thankfulness, 188
thanks, 72
that, 124
theater, 21
theft, 182
then, 34, 161
thence, 98

there, 97
therefore, 34, 136
thigh, 19
think, 155, 159
thirsty, 53
this, 124
thistle, 117
thorn, 117, 118, 167
though, 7
thoughts, 127
thousand, 109
thread, 30
threaten, 160
thresh, 60
threshing floor, 22
throat, 19
throne, 67
through, 23, 98
throw, 160
thunder, 192
thusly, 124
tidings, 8
tie, 60
tile, 21
till, 47
time, 161
timely, 164
timidity, 61
tip, 118
tithe, 70
title, 107
to, 122
today, 161
toga, 31
together, 6, 195
toil, 166
toilet, 21
toll, 158
tomb, 67
tomorrow, 162
tone, 151
tongue, 19, 92
tooth, 19
torch, 92
torment, 113, 175
totality, 6
touch, 166
toward, 99

English Index

towel, 30
tower, 22
town, 29
trace, 143
trade, 68
tradition, 41, 158
trafficking, 179
training, 36, 158, 188
traitor, 17
trample, 123, 190
tranquility, 115, 187
transact, 23
transfigure, 65
transform, 27, 135
transgress, 149, 177
translate, 57
transparent, 40, 96
trap, 24, 80, 159
travail, 17, 113
travel, 167
treachery, 176
tread, 123, 190
treasure, 21, 36, 173
treasurer, 4
treatise, 151
tree, 167
tremble, 6, 61
trial, 94, 113
tribe, 29, 39, 44
tribulation, 167
tribute, 157
trick, 175
trifling, 150, 177
trip, 167
triumph, 35
trouble, 9, 140, 167
true, 69, 168
trumpet, 106
trust, 183
trustworthy, 27, 62, 185
truth, 158, 168
truthful, 185
try, 168
tunic, 30
turn, 38, 137
twinkling, 96
type, 65, 114

ugly, 170
ulcer, 148
umpire, 37
unable, 170
unattractive, 170
unaware, 64
unbelief, 50, 170, 177
unceasing, 134, 166
uncertain, 27, 50
uncleanness, 48, 182
unconscious, 148
uncover, 39
uncultivated, 189
under, 99
undergo, 56
understanding, 90, 127, 159, 188, 194
undertake, 168
undress, 31
uneducated, 82
unemployed, 180
uneven, 138
unfair, 181
unfaithful, 50
unfit, 59, 172
ungodly, 14, 170
unguent, 115
unique, 170
unite, 104
universe, 171
unknown, 77
unlearned, 82
unleavened, 63
unmerciful, 175
unnecessary, 108
unoccupied, 54
unprofitable, 48, 172
unqualified, 59
unreasonable, 26
unrighteousness, 149, 178
unroll, 198
unroof, 21
unruly, 177
unsearchable, 116
unsightly, 170
unspeakable, 171
unstable, 50
until, 161, 162, 171

untimely, 164
untraceable, 116
unusual, 170
unutterable, 171
unveil, 39
unwise, 63
up to, 171
upbraid, 130, 176
upper room, 21
upright, 132
uproar, 10, 129
upset, 9, 40, 129, 174, 175
urge, 85, 171
urgent, 169
urn, 67
useful, 172, 184
useless, 172
usury, 105
utensils, 38
utterance, 152
vacant, 54
vagueness, 27
vain, 54, 174
valid, 69, 168
valuable, 78, 173
value, 38, 78, 173
vanquish, 35
variation, 28
variety, 47, 50
vase, 35, 38
vat, 22
vehicle, 173
veil, 30, 31, 39
venom, 18
verdict, 93
verification, 27, 168
vessel, 18, 35, 38
vexation, 9, 173
vices, 173
victimize, 179
victory, 35
view, 143
vigilant, 191
vigor, 75
village, 29
vinegar, 118
vineyard, 59, 117
violation, 149, 178

violence, 175, 189
viper, 135
virgin, 103, 196
virginity, 18
virtue, 183
virtuous, 184
vision, 50, 143
visit, 10, 189
visitor, 64
vocation, 83
voice, 147, 151
void, 85
voluntary, 193
vomit, 18, 106
voracious, 53, 179
vote, 28
vow, 111
voyage, 142
vulture, 17

wages, 38, 106, 141
wail, 40, 151
waist, 19
wait, 133
waiting, 79
wake, 190
walk, 15, 190
wall, 21, 190
wallet, 36
wander, 50, 99, 151, 167
want, 45
wanting, 118
wanton, 182
war, 79, 154, 190
war terms, 190
warm, 79
warn, 121, 130
wash, 29, 96
waste, 54, 152, 192
waste time, 164
watch, 141, 143
watch over, 72
watchful, 191
water body, 191
water terms, 191
wavering, 50
waves, 143, 191
way, 154

way of life, 15
way, manner, 80
weakness, 147, 170
wealth, 68, 105, 192
weapon, 55, 192
wear, 31
weariness, 48, 147, 166
weather, 192
weave, 30
wed, 103
wedding hall, 21
weed, 117
weep, 40
weight, 104, 193
weighty, 83, 167, 193
welcome, 3, 130, 193
well-timed, 164
west, 47
what manner?, 80
wheat, 63, 66, 117
when, 162
whenever, 163
where, 97, 125
whether, 82, 112
while, 162
whip, 78
white, 31
whitewashed, 21, 176
whither, 97
wholeness, 6, 115
whore, 181
wickedness, 14, 149, 183
widen, 111
width, 103
wife, 89, 195
wilderness, 92, 193
will, 45, 116, 124
willing, 52, 193
willingly, 194
wind, 194
window, 21
windstorm, 192
wine, 118, 178
wine press, 22
wineskin, 35
wing, 19
winnow, 38, 60
winter, 164

wipe, 30, 51, 96
wisdom, 127, 194
wise, 160
wish, 45
witchcraft, 182
with, 99, 122, 195
withdraw, 13, 199
wither, 51
withered, 148
without, 195
withstand, 135
witness, 195
woe, 167
wolf, 8
woman, 195
womb, 17, 19
wonder, 155
wood, 21, 196
woods, 167
wool, 30
word, 151, 196
work, 166, 196
workmanship, 21, 101, 196
world, 52, 171
worldly, 116
worm, 85
wormwood, 117
worry, 9
worse, 95
worship, 119, 132
worth, 173
worthless, 172
worthy, 78, 173, 197
would, 82
wound, 148, 197
woven, 30
wrap, 197
wrath, 173
wrestling, 154
wrinkle, 19
writing, 198
wrong, 14, 149
wrongdoing, 178

year, 161
yeast, 63
yellow, 32

English Index

yes, 108
yesterday, 161
yet, 7, 162

yield, 199
yoke, 60
yoked, 13, 103

zeal, 44, 52, 53, 152

Greek Index

ἀβαρής, 42
ἀββά, 71
ἄβυσσος, 76
ἀγαθοεργέω, 184
ἀγαθοποιέω, 184
ἀγαθοποιΐα, 184
ἀγαθοποιός, 184
ἀγαθός, 184
ἀγαθωσύνη, 184
ἀγαλλίασις, 75
ἀγαλλιάω, 75
ἄγαμος, 7, 103
ἀγανακτέω, 173
ἀγανάκτησις, 173
ἀγαπάω, 55, 99
ἀγάπη, 99
ἀγαπητός, 99, 171
ἀγγαρεύω, 33
ἀγγεῖον, 35
ἀγγελία, 8
ἀγγέλλω, 8
ἄγγελος, 7, 8
ἄγγος, 35
ἄγε, 35
ἀγέλη, 7
ἀγενεαλόγητος, 89
ἀγενής, 84
ἁγιάζω, 29, 43, 185
ἁγιασμός, 43
ἅγιοι, 28
ἅγιος, 21, 43, 184
ἁγιότης, 184
ἁγιωσύνη, 43, 185
ἀγκάλη, 18
ἄγκιστρον, 142

ἄγκυρα, 142
ἄγναφος, 31
ἁγνεία, 185
ἁγνίζω, 29, 185
ἁγνισμός, 29
ἀγνοέω, 82, 116
ἀγνόημα, 149, 178
ἄγνοια, 82
ἁγνός, 185
ἁγνότης, 185
ἁγνῶς, 185
ἀγνωσία, 82, 116
ἄγνωστος, 77
ἀγορά, 23, 68
ἀγοράζω, 23, 132
ἀγοραῖος, 95, 181
ἀγορέω, 176
ἄγρα, 80, 118, 157
ἀγράμματος, 82
ἀγραυλέω, 3, 8
ἀγρεύω, 80, 159
ἀγριέλαιος, 167
ἄγριος, 189
ἀγρός, 29, 62, 193
ἀγρυπνέω, 25, 191
ἀγρυπνία, 190
ἄγχι, 98
ἄγω, 20, 70, 72
ἀγωγή, 15
ἀγών, 36, 154
ἀγωνία, 140
ἀγωνίζομαι, 36, 154, 169
ἀδάπανος, 39, 66
ἀδελφή, 89
ἀδελφός, 29, 89

ἀδηλότης, 27
ἀδήλως, 27, 50, 117
ἀδημονέω, 10
ᾅδης, 46, 76
ἀδιάκριτος, 179
ἀδιάλειπτος, 134, 166
ἀδικέω, 175, 180, 197
ἀδίκημα, 180
ἀδικία, 149, 178, 180
ἄδικος, 170, 180
ἀδίκως, 180
ἀδόκιμος, 14, 59, 131, 172
ἄδολος, 30, 185
ἁδρότης, 192
ἀδυνατέω, 154
ἀδύνατος, 108, 119, 154, 170
ᾄδω, 106
ἀεί, 166
ἀετός, 17
ἄζυμος, 63
ἀήρ, 76
ἀθανασία, 47, 166
ἀθέμιτος, 123, 180
ἄθεος, 71
ἄθεσμος, 180
ἀθετέω, 50, 85, 131
ἀθέτησις, 85
ἀθλέω, 36, 166
ἄθλησις, 36, 155
ἀθροίζω, 12
ἀθυμέω, 48
ἀθῷος, 128, 185
ἀθῳόω, 128
αἴγειος, 8

Greek Index

αἰγιαλός, 92
ἀΐδιος, 166
αἰδώς, 187
αἷμα, 18, 47, 88, 115
αἷμα ἐκχέω, 88
αἱματεκχυσία, 148
αἱμορροέω, 148
αἴνεσις, 119
αἰνέω, 119
αἴνιγμα, 77, 116
αἶνος, 119
αἱρέομαι, 28
αἵρεσις, 114, 158, 170
αἱρετίζω, 28
αἱρετικός, 49
αἴρω, 25, 45, 88, 95, 105, 113, 134
αἴρω τὸν σταυρόν, 113
αἰσθάνομαι, 195
αἴσθησις, 195
αἰσθητήριον, 195
αἰσχροκερδής, 44, 179
αἰσχροκερδῶς, 44
αἰσχρολογία, 152, 177
αἰσχρός, 146, 170
αἰσχρότης, 146, 170
αἰσχύνη, 146
αἰσχύνω, 146
αἰτέω, 11, 94, 120
αἴτημα, 11, 120
αἰτία, 26, 94, 149
αἴτιον, 149
αἴτιος, 26
αἰτίωμα, 94
αἰφνίδιος, 165
αἰχμαλωσία, 191
αἰχμαλωτεύω, 191
αἰχμαλωτίζω, 24, 37, 191
αἰχμάλωτος, 84, 191
αἰχμή, 118, 191
αἰών, 16, 161, 166
αἰώνιος, 166
ἀκαθαρσία, 48, 182
ἀκάθαρτος, 183
ἀκαιρέομαι, 164
ἀκαίρως, 164
ἄκακος, 184
ἄκανθα, 117, 118

ἀκάνθινος, 117
ἄκαρπος, 137, 172
ἀκατάγνωστος, 39
ἀκατακάλυπτος, 39
ἀκατάκριτος, 94
ἀκατάλυτος, 166
ἀκατάπαυστος, 134, 166
ἀκαταστασία, 129
ἀκατάστατος, 37
ἀκέραιος, 185
ἀκλινής, 62
ἀκμάζω, 137, 164
ἀκμήν, 162
ἀκοή, 9, 19, 76, 151
ἀκολουθέω, 63, 186
ἀκούω, 3, 76, 94, 186, 194
ἀκρασία, 180
ἀκρατής, 180
ἄκρατος, 30
ἀκρίβεια, 168
ἀκριβής, 168
ἀκριβόω, 62, 93
ἀκρίς, 85
ἀκροατήριον, 21
ἀκροατής, 76
ἀκροβυστία, 43
ἀκρογωνιαῖος, 21
ἀκροθίνιον, 140
ἄκρον, 55, 118
ἀκυρόω, 85
ἄκων, 194
ἀλάβαστρον, 35
ἀλαζονεία, 174
ἀλαζών, 174
ἀλαλάζω, 40, 151
ἀλάλητος, 171
ἄλαλος, 148
ἅλας, 152
ἀλείφω, 96
ἀλεκτοροφωνία, 163
ἀλέκτωρ, 17
ἄλευρον, 38, 63
ἀλέω, 38, 60
ἀλήθεια, 168
ἀληθεύω, 168
ἀληθής, 69, 168, 183, 185
ἀληθινός, 69, 168
ἀλήθω, 38

ἀληθῶς, 69
ἁλιεύς, 142
ἁλιεύω, 142
ἁλίζω, 152
ἀλίσγημα, 183
ἀλλ᾽ ἤ, 36
ἀλλά, 34, 36
ἀλλὰ μᾶλλον, 36
ἀλλάσσω, 28, 56, 65, 132, 136
ἀλλαχόθεν, 98
ἀλλαχοῦ, 97
ἀλληγορέω, 49
ἀλληλουϊά, 119
ἀλλήλων, ἀλλήλοις, ἀλλήλους, 124
ἀλλογενής, 44, 64
ἅλλομαι, 63, 87, 96
ἄλλος, 47
ἀλλοτριεπίσκοπος, 181
ἀλλότριος, 64, 79
ἀλλόφυλος, 64
ἄλλως, 47
ἀλοάω, 60
ἄλογος, 26, 82, 178
ἀλόη, 116
ἅλς, 152
ἁλυκός, 152
ἀλυπότερος, 140
ἅλυσις, 60, 84
ἀλυσιτελής, 48
ἅλων, 22, 66
ἀλώπηξ, 8
ἅλωσις, 24, 142
ἅμα, 161, 195
ἀμαθής, 82
ἀμαράντινος, 15
ἀμάραντος, 15, 166
ἁμαρτάνω, 149, 178
ἁμάρτημα, 149
ἁμαρτία, 14, 59, 149
ἀμάρτυρος, 195
ἁμαρτωλός, 149
ἄμαχος, 154, 187
ἀμάω, 60
ἀμέθυστος, 121
ἀμελέω, 43
ἄμεμπτος, 185

Greek Index

ἀμέριμνος, 9
ἀμετακίνητος, 62
ἀμεταμέλητος, 140
ἀμετανόητος, 38
ἀμήν, 168
ἀμήτωρ, 89
ἀμίαντος, 183
ἄμμος, 53, 92
ἀμνός, 8
ἀμοιβή, 38
ἄμπελος, 66, 117
ἀμπελουργός, 59
ἀμπελών, 59, 117
ἀμύνομαι, 77
ἀμφιάζω, 31
ἀμφιβάλλω, 142
ἀμφίβληστρον, 142
ἀμφιέννυμι, 31
ἄμφοδον, 154
ἀμφότερος, 6, 195
ἀμώμητος, 185
ἄμωμον, 152
ἄμωμος, 29, 185
ἄν, 82, 119
ἀνά, 122
ἀνὰ μέρος, 145
ἀνὰ μέσον, 98, 122
ἀναβαθμός, 21
ἀναβαίνω, 11, 72, 135
ἀναβάλλω, 94
ἀναβιβάζω, 11, 127, 135
ἀναβλέπω, 143
ἀνάβλεψις, 143
ἀναβοάω, 147
ἀναβολή, 95, 150
ἀνάγαιον, 21
ἀναγγέλλω, 8
ἀναγεννάω, 27, 135
ἀναγινώσκω, 198
ἀναγκάζω, 33
ἀναγκαῖος, 107
ἀναγκαστῶς, 107
ἀνάγκη, 107, 167
ἀνάγνωσις, 198
ἀνάγω, 20, 142
ἀναδείκνυμι, 12, 91
ἀνάδειξις, 91
ἀναδέχομαι, 56, 193

ἀναδίδωμι, 17, 69
ἀναζάω, 95, 135
ἀναζητέω, 143
ἀναζωπυρέω, 15, 22
ἀνάθεμα, 41
ἀναθεματίζω, 41
ἀναθεωρέω, 144, 160
ἀνάθημα, 140
ἀναίδεια, 125
ἀναίρεσις, 88
ἀναιρέω, 25, 85, 88
ἀναίτιος, 149, 188
ἀνακαθίζω, 150
ἀνακαινίζω, 27, 135
ἀνακαινόω, 27, 108, 135
ἀνακαίνωσις, 108
ἀνακαλύπτω, 39
ἀνακάμπτω, 50, 137
ἀνάκειμαι, 53, 130
ἀνακεφαλαιόω, 105
ἀνακλίνω, 95, 130
ἀνακράζω, 147
ἀνακρίνω, 39, 87, 94, 143, 176
ἀνάκρισις, 94
ἀνακύπτω, 154
ἀναλαμβάνω, 11, 20, 25, 135
ἀνάλημψις, 11, 135
ἀναλίσκω, 45, 152
ἀναλογία, 6, 33
ἀναλογίζομαι, 159
ἄναλος, 152
ἀνάλυσις, 46
ἀναλύω, 46, 137
ἀναμάρτητος, 149
ἀναμένω, 133
ἀναμιμνήσκω, 104
ἀνάμνησις, 104
ἀνανεόω, 108
ἀνανήφω, 160
ἀναντίρρητος, 112
ἀναντιρρήτως, 112
ἀνάξιος, 197
ἀναξίως, 125, 197
ἀνάπαυσις, 26, 132, 136
ἀναπαύω, 136
ἀναπείθω, 171

ἀναπέμπω, 145
ἀναπηδάω, 87
ἀνάπηρος, 148
ἀναπίπτω, 130
ἀναπληρόω, 7, 34, 69, 126, 187
ἀναπολόγητος, 43
ἀναπράσσω, 4
ἀναπτύσσω, 198
ἀνάπτω, 22
ἀναρίθμητος, 85, 109
ἀνασείω, 129
ἀνασκευάζω, 9, 20, 46, 175
ἀνασπάω, 127
ἀνάστασις, 11, 95, 135
ἀναστατόω, 129
ἀνασταυρόω, 88
ἀναστενάζω, 40
ἀναστρέφω, 15, 137
ἀναστροφή, 15
ἀνατάσσομαι, 10
ἀνατέλλω, 11, 89, 96, 135, 163
ἀνατίθεμαι, 57
ἀνατολή, 11, 47, 135
ἀνατρέπω, 46, 50, 137
ἀνατρέφω, 25, 158
ἀναφαίνω, 144
ἀναφέρω, 20, 25, 140
ἀναφωνέω, 147
ἀναχέω, 58
ἀνάχυσις, 58, 62
ἀναχωρέω, 71, 137
ἀνάψυξις, 54, 132
ἀναψύχω, 54
ἀνδραποδιστής, 23
ἀνδρίζομαι, 39
ἀνδροφόνος, 88
ἀνέγκλητος, 188
ἀνεκδιήγητος, 9
ἀνεκλάλητος, 171
ἀνεκτός, 114
ἀνελεήμων, 175
ἀνέλεος, 175
ἀνεμίζομαι, 6, 51
ἄνεμος, 194
ἀνένδεκτος, 119

225

Greek Index

ἀνεξεραύνητος, 116, 143
ἀνεξίκακος, 114
ἀνεξιχνίαστος, 116, 143
ἀνεπαίσχυντος, 146
ἀνεπίλημπτος, 40, 188
ἀνέρχομαι, 11, 135
ἄνεσις, 132
ἀνετάζω, 94, 143
ἄνευ, 122, 195
ἀνεύθετος, 125, 172
ἀνευρίσκω, 62, 93
ἀνέχομαι, 3, 114
ἀνεψιός, 89
ἄνηθον, 117, 152
ἀνήμερος, 189
ἀνήρ, 89, 102, 115
ἀνθίστημι, 79, 135
ἀνθομολογέομαι, 188
ἄνθος, 117
ἀνθρακιά, 22
ἄνθραξ, 22, 196
ἀνθρωπάρεσκος, 3
ἀνθρώπινος, 115
ἀνθρωποκτόνος, 88
ἄνθρωπος, 16, 18, 89, 102, 115, 127
ἀνθύπατος, 138
ἀνίημι, 2, 27
ἄνιπτος, 96
ἀνίστημι, 11, 95, 135, 154
ἀνίστημι σπέρμα, 18
ἀνόητος, 64
ἄνοια, 64, 174
ἀνοίγω, 111
ἀνοίγω θύραν, 119
ἀνοικοδομέω, 20
ἀνομία, 149, 178, 180
ἄνομος, 170, 180
ἀνόμως, 180
ἀνορθόω, 20, 154
ἀνόσιος, 43
ἀνοχή, 114
ἀνταγωνίζομαι, 154
ἀντάλλαγμα, 56
ἀνταναπληρόω, 7
ἀνταποδίδωμι, 38, 141
ἀνταπόδομα, 38, 141
ἀνταπόδοσις, 141

ἀνταποκρίνομαι, 9, 39
ἀντάω, 74
ἀντέχω, 77, 87
ἀντί, 56, 64, 122
ἀντιβάλλω, 38
ἀντιδιατίθεμαι, 79
ἀντίδικος, 79, 94
ἀντίθεσις, 112
ἀντικαθίστημι, 135
ἀντικαλέω, 86
ἀντίκειμαι, 79
ἄντικρυς, 97
ἀντιλαμβάνω, 5, 76
ἀντιλέγω, 112
ἀντίλημψις, 77
ἀντιλογία, 49, 112, 129
ἀντιλοιδορέω, 177
ἀντίλυτρον, 132
ἀντιμετρέω, 70
ἀντιμισθία, 141
ἀντιπαρέρχομαι, 40
ἀντιπέρα, 97
ἀντιπίπτω, 135
ἀντιστρατεύομαι, 79, 190
ἀντιτάσσω, 79
ἀντίτυπος, 114
ἀντίχριστος, 133
ἀντλέω, 96
ἄντλημα, 35
ἀντοφθαλμέω, 48
ἄνυδρος, 51, 191
ἄνυδρος τόπος, 193
ἀνυπόκριτος, 69
ἀνυπότακτος, 37, 177
ἄνω, 98
ἄνωθεν, 38, 98, 162
ἀνωτερικός, 92
ἀνώτερος, 83, 145, 161
ἀνωφελής, 48
ἀξίνη, 60
ἀξιοπρεπὴς, 15, 125
ἄξιος, 125, 197
ἀξιόω, 28, 45, 197
ἀξίως, 125, 197
ἀόρατος, 143
ἀπ' αἰῶνος, 161
ἀπαγγέλλω, 8
ἀπάγχομαι, 28, 88

ἀπάγω, 20, 84, 88, 95, 176
ἀπαίδευτος, 82
ἀπαίρω, 20
ἀπαιτέω, 11
ἀπαλγέω, 146
ἀπαλλάσσω, 65, 132, 186
ἀπαλλοτριόω, 64
ἀπαλός, 151
ἀπαντάω, 10
ἀπάντησις, 10
ἅπαξ, 109
ἅπαξ καὶ δίς, 109
ἀπαρασκεύαστος, 122
ἀπαρνέομαι, 43, 131
ἀπαρτισμός, 34
ἀπαρχή, 39, 140, 145
ἅπας, 6
ἀπατάω, 175
ἀπάτη, 175
ἀπάτωρ, 89
ἀπαύγασμα, 96
ἀπείθεια, 50, 177
ἀπειθέω, 50, 177
ἀπειθής, 177
ἀπειλέω, 160
ἀπειλή, 160
ἄπειμι, 71
ἀπεῖπον, 34, 131
ἄπειρος, 82
ἀπεκδέχομαι, 79
ἀπεκδύνω, 31
ἀπέκδυσις, 31
ἀπελαύνω, 51, 71
ἀπελεγμός, 39
ἀπελεύθερος, 66
ἀπελπίζω, 79, 183
ἀπέναντι, 6, 79, 97
ἀπέραντος, 85, 166
ἀπερισπάστως, 160
ἀπερίτμητος καρδία καὶ τοῖς ὠσίν, 155
ἀπέρχομαι, 71
ἀπέρχομαι ὀπίσω σαρκὸς ἑτέρας, 182
ἀπέρχομαι πρὸς ἑαυτόν, 137
ἀπέχω, 13, 55, 98, 130
ἀπιστέω, 50

ἀπιστία, 50
ἄπιστος, 50, 170
ἁπλότης, 70, 185, 186
ἁπλοῦς, 75
ἀπό, 23, 66, 98, 113, 122, 163
ἀπὸ μέρους, 113
ἀπὸ μιᾶς, 145
ἀπὸ τῶν αἰώνων, 166
ἀποβαίνω, 55, 70
ἀποβαίνω εἰς, 136
ἀποβάλλω, 31, 99, 131
ἀποβλέπω, 143, 160
ἀπόβλητος, 131
ἀποβολή, 46, 99, 131
ἀπογίνομαι, 27, 46
ἀπογραφή, 158
ἀπογράφω, 95, 158
ἀποδείκνυμι, 91, 168
ἀπόδειξις, 91
ἀποδεκατόω, 70
ἀπόδεκτος, 3
ἀποδέχομαι, 3, 193
ἀποδημέω, 71, 151, 167
ἀπόδημος, 71, 167
ἀποδίδωμι, 23, 38, 141
ἀποδιορίζω, 49, 87
ἀποδοκιμάζω, 87
ἀποδοχή, 3
ἀπόθεσις τοῦ σκηνώματος, 47
ἀποθήκη, 21
ἀποθησαυρίζω, 173
ἀποθλίβω, 123
ἀποθνήσκω, 46, 170
ἀποκαθίστημι, 27, 75, 135, 137
ἀποκαλύπτω, 91
ἀποκάλυψις, 91
ἀποκαραδοκία, 79, 183
ἀποκαταλλάσσω, 64, 186, 187
ἀποκατάστασις, 27, 135
ἀπόκειμαι, 173
ἀποκεφαλίζω, 88
ἀποκλείω, 111
ἀποκόπτω, 41
ἀπόκριμα, 94

ἀποκρίνομαι, 9, 152
ἀπόκρισις, 9
ἀποκρύπτω, 77
ἀπόκρυφος, 77
ἀποκτείνω, 88
ἀποκυέω, 18, 25
ἀποκυλίω, 137
ἀπολαμβάνω, 20, 130, 193
ἀπόλαυσις, 55
ἀπολείπω, 2, 71
ἀπόλλυμι, 45, 99
ἀπόλλυμι τὴν ψυχήν, 47
ἀπολογέομαι, 43
ἀπολογία, 43
ἀπολούομαι, 29, 185
ἀπολύτρωσις, 132
ἀπολύω, 50, 65, 132, 145, 186
ἀπομάσσομαι, 30, 96
ἀπονέμω, 12
ἀπονίζω, 96
ἀπονίπτω, 96
ἀποπλανάω, 50, 175
ἀποπλέω, 142
ἀποπνίγω, 47
ἀπορέω, 116
ἀπορία, 116
ἀπορίπτω, 59
ἀπορφανίζω, 89, 131
ἀποσκίασμα, 42
ἀποσπάω, 127, 131
ἀποστασία, 129
ἀποστάσιον, 50, 95
ἀποστεγάζω, 21, 134
ἀποστέλλω, 145
ἀποστερέω, 155, 182
ἀποστολή, 133
ἀπόστολος, 9, 133
ἀποστοματίζω, 12
ἀποστρέφω, 2, 27, 50
ἀποστυγέω, 179
ἀποτάσσομαι, 49, 71, 99, 118
ἀποτελέω, 33
ἀποτίθημι, 27, 128
ἀποτινάσσω, 6
ἀποτίνω, 38
ἀποτολμάω, 39

ἀποτομία, 175
ἀποτόμως, 175
ἀποτρέπω, 131
ἀπουσία, 71
ἀποφέρω, 20, 25
ἀποφεύγω, 141
ἀποφθέγγομαι, 151
ἀποφορτίζομαι, 25
ἀπόχρησις, 197
ἀποχωρέω, 71
ἀποχωρίζομαι, 106, 114
ἀποψύχω, 48, 148
ἀπρακτέω, 180
ἀπρόσιτος, 10
ἀπρόσκοπος, 111, 149
ἀπροσωπολήμπτως, 178
ἄπταιστος, 149
ἅπτω, 22, 60, 157, 166
ἀπωθέομαι, 50, 131
ἀπωθέω, 131
ἀπώλεια, 45, 172
ἀρά, 41
ἄρα, 119, 136
ἆρα, 108
ἄραφος, 31
ἀργέω, 180
ἀργός, 82, 172, 180
ἀργύριον, 104
ἀργυροκόπος, 104
ἄργυρος, 31, 104, 106, 180
ἀργυροῦς, 104
ἀρεσκεία, 3
ἀρέσκω, 3
ἀρεστός, 3, 125
ἀρετή, 184
ἀρήν, 8
ἀριθμέω, 108
ἀριθμός, 108
ἀριστάω, 53
ἀριστερός, 18, 47
ἄριστον, 53
ἀρκετός, 55
ἀρκέω, 5, 36, 55
ἄρκος, 8
ἅρμα, 173
ἁρμόζω, 11, 103
ἁρμός, 11, 18

Greek Index

ἀρνέομαι, 6, 43, 131, 177
ἀρνίον, 8, 29
ἀροτριάω, 59
ἄροτρον, 60
ἁρπαγή, 44, 118, 182
ἁρπαγμός, 118, 182
ἁρπάζω, 13, 24, 37, 118, 157, 182
ἅρπαξ, 44, 179, 182, 189
ἀρραβών, 38, 105
ἄρρητος, 171
ἄρρωστος, 147
ἀρσενοκοίτης, 182
ἄρσην, 89, 102
ἄρσην διανοίγων μήτραν, 89
ἀρτέμων, 142
ἄρτι, 161, 165
ἀρτιγέννητος, 17
ἄρτιος, 5, 121
ἄρτοι τῆς προθέσεως, 140
ἄρτον κλάω, 53
ἄρτος, 63
ἀρτύω, 38, 121
ἀρχάγγελος, 7
ἀρχαῖος, 165
ἀρχή, 15, 26, 54, 118, 138
ἀρχηγός, 15, 73
ἀρχιερατικός, 133
ἀρχιερεύς, 133
ἀρχιποίμην, 8
ἀρχισυνάγωγος, 133
ἀρχιτέκτων, 21
ἀρχιτελώνης, 158
ἀρχιτρίκλινος, 80
ἄρχω, 15, 138
ἄρχων, 94, 138
ἄρωμα, 115
ἀσάλευτος, 62
ἄσβεστος, 22
ἀσέβεια, 133
ἀσεβέω, 133
ἀσεβής, 133
ἀσέλγεια, 181
ἄσημος, 84
ἀσθένεια, 61, 147, 170
ἀσθενέω, 147, 170
ἀσθενής, 14, 147, 167, 170

ἀσιτία, 53, 60
ἄσιτος, 53
ἀσκέω, 169
ἀσκός, 35
ἀσμένως, 75
ἄσοφος, 63
ἀσπάζομαι, 193
ἀσπασμός, 49
ἄσπιλος, 29, 185
ἀσπίς, 135
ἄσπονδος, 65
ἀσσάριον, 106
ἆσσον, 98
ἀστατέω, 151, 167
ἀστεῖος, 14
ἀστὴρ πρωϊνός, 76
ἀστήρικτος, 50
ἄστοργος, 99
ἀστοχέω, 50
ἀστραπή, 96, 192
ἀστράπτω, 96
ἀσύμφωνος, 6
ἀσύνετος, 64
ἀσύνθετος, 124
ἀσφάλεια, 141
ἀσφαλής, 141
ἀσφαλίζω, 60, 62, 141
ἀσφαλῶς, 141
ἀσχημονέω, 146, 170
ἀσχημοσύνη, 146
ἀσχήμων, 170
ἀσωτία, 180
ἀσώτως, 180
ἀτακτέω, 180
ἄτακτος, 180
ἀτάκτως, 180
ἄτεκνος, 89
ἀτενίζω, 144
ἄτερ, 122, 195
ἀτιμάζω, 146, 175
ἀτιμία, 146
ἄτιμος, 84
ἄτομος, 165
ἄτοπος, 14, 171
ἀτόπως, 171
αὐγάζω, 90, 96
αὐγή, 96, 163
αὐθάδης, 174

αὐθαίρετος, 194
αὐθεντέω, 37
αὐλέω, 106
αὐλή, 21
αὐλητής, 106
αὐλίζομαι, 150
αὐλός, 106
αὐξάνω, 57, 72, 83, 84
αὔξησις, 72
αὔριον, 162
αὐστηρός, 175
αὐτάρκεια, 5, 36
αὐτάρκης, 36
αὐτοκατάκριτος, 87
αὐτόματος, 26
αὐτόπτης, 144
αὐτός, 124, 141
αὐτοῦ, 97
αὐτόφωρος, 149
αὐτόχειρ, 18
αὐχέω, 174
αὐχμηρός, 42
ἀφ' ἡμερῶν ἀρχαίων, 161
ἀφαιρέω, 27, 134
ἀφανής, 77
ἀφανίζω, 45, 71, 77, 170
ἀφανισμός, 71
ἄφαντος, 77
ἀφεδρών, 21
ἀφειδία, 188
ἀφελότης, 138, 185
ἄφεσις, 65, 132
ἀφή, 18
ἀφθαρσία, 134, 166
ἄφθαρτος, 47, 166
ἀφθορία, 185
ἀφίημι, 2, 7, 27, 42, 50, 65, 71, 145, 186
ἀφίημι τὸ πνεῦμα, 47
ἀφικνέομαι, 32, 90
ἀφιλάγαθος, 55
ἀφιλάργυρος, 179
ἄφιξις, 71
ἀφίστημι, 2, 50, 71, 129, 131, 134
ἄφνω, 165
ἀφόβως, 61, 120, 146
ἀφομοιόω, 33

Greek Index

ἀφοράω, 143
ἀφορίζω, 12, 114, 131
ἀφορμή, 26, 61
ἀφρίζω, 63
ἀφρός, 63
ἀφροσύνη, 64
ἄφρων, 64
ἀφυπνόω, 150
ἄφωνος, 148
ἀχάριστος, 188
ἀχειροποίητος, 101
ἀχλὺς, 18
ἀχρεῖος, 172
ἀχρειόω, 181
ἄχρηστος, 172
ἄχρι, 35, 98, 161, 162
ἄχρι(ς) οὗ, 161
ἄχυρον, 117
ἀψευδεῖν, 168
ἀψευδής, 185
ἄψινθος, 117, 157
ἄψυχος, 46

βαθμός, 83
βάθος, 58, 103
βαθύνω, 103
βαθύς, 103
βάϊον, 117
βακτηρία, 8
βαλλάντιον, 36
βάλλω, 105, 128, 160
βάλλω εἰς κλίνην, 147
βαπτίζω, 14, 29, 43, 96, 185
βάπτισμα, 14
βαπτισμός, 14, 30
βαπτιστής, 14
βάπτω, 96
βάρβαρος, 16
βαρέω, 167
βάρος, 58, 104, 167
βαρύς, 83, 167, 175, 189, 193
βαρύτιμος, 173
βασανίζω, 128
βασανισμός, 113
βασανιστής, 72
βάσανος, 113

βασιλεία, 39, 138
βασίλειος, 21, 138
βασιλεύς, 138
βασιλεύω, 37, 138
βασιλικός, 138
βάσις, 18
βασκαίνω, 101, 176, 182
βαστάζω, 25, 57, 114
βάτος, 104, 117
βάτραχος, 135
βατταλογέω, 151
βδέλυγμα, 180
βδελυκτός, 180
βδελύσσομαι, 179
βέβαιος, 27, 62, 168, 183
βεβαιόω, 56, 155, 168, 183
βεβαίωσις, 168
βέβηλος, 14
βεβηλόω, 183
βελόνη, 31, 118
βέλος, 192
βέλτερος, 184
βέλτιον, 184
βελτίων, 184
βῆμα, 103
βήρυλλος, 121
βία, 189
βιάζω, 189
βίαιος, 189
βιαστής, 189
βιβάζω, 43
βιβλαρίδιον, 198
βιβλίον, 50, 198
βίβλος, 198
βιβρώσκω, 53
βίος, 16, 17, 126
βιόω, 16, 17
βίωσις, 16
βιωτικός, 16
βλαβερός, 197
βλάπτω, 197
βλαστάνω, 72
βλασφημέω, 177
βλασφημία, 177
βλάσφημος, 177
βλέμμα, 143
βλέπω, 143, 160, 189, 191, 194

βλητέος, 128
βοάω, 147
βοή, 147
βοήθεια, 76
βοηθέω, 76
βοηθός, 76
βόθυνος, 78
βολή, 160
βολίζω, 143
βόρβορος, 52
βορρᾶς, 47
βόσκω, 8, 53
βοτάνη, 117
βοτήρ, 8
βότρυς, 66
βουλεύομαι, 116, 160
βουλευτής, 39
βουλή, 116
βούλημα, 45, 116
βούλομαι, 45, 116
βουνός, 106
βοῦς, 7
βραβεῖον, 141
βραβεύω, 37, 87
βραδύνω, 150
βραδυπλοέω, 142
βραδύς, 150
βραδύτης, 150
βραχίων, 19
βραχίων ὑψηλός, 119
βραχύ τι, 10
βραχύς, 10
βρέφος, 28, 164
βρέχω, 96, 129, 192
βροντή, 192
βροχή, 129, 192
βρόχος ἐπιβάλλω, 37
βρυγμὸς τῶν ὀδόντων, 106
βρύχω τοὺς ὀδόντας, 174
βρύω, 62, 96
βρῶμα, 63
βρώσιμος, 53
βρῶσις, 53, 63, 137
βυθίζω, 43, 57
βυθός, 191
βυρσεύς, 30
βύσσινος, 30

Greek Index

βύσσος, 30
βωμός, 67

γάγγραινα, 147
γαζοφυλάκιον, 21, 36
γάλα, 63
γαλήνη, 24
γαμέω, 103
γαμίζω, 103
γαμίσκω, 103
γάμος, 21, 103
γάρ, 26, 34
γαστήρ, 19, 53, 179
γέ, 34
γέεννα, 76
γείτων, 108
γελάω, 75
γέλως, 75
γεμίζω, 67
γέμω, 67
γενεά, 44, 89, 161
γενεαλογέομαι, 89
γενεαλογία, 89
γενέσια, 61
γένεσις, 17, 49, 89
γενετή, 17
γεννάω, 17, 75, 101
γεννάω ἄνωθεν, 38
γέννημα, 17, 29
γεννητός, 17
γένος, 29, 44, 89
γερουσία, 39
γέρων, 102
γεῦμα, 157
γεύομαι, 53, 56
γεῦσις, 157
γεωργέω, 59
γεώργιον, 62
γεωργός, 59
γῆ, 52, 92, 115, 131, 171
γῆρας, 111, 164
γηράσκω, 165
γίνομαι, 16, 17, 34, 74
γινώσκω, 18, 90, 93, 189, 195
γλεῦκος, 118
γλυκύς, 157
γλῶσσα, 19, 92, 115

γλωσσόκομον, 36
γναφεύς, 31
γνήσιος, 69, 168
γνησίως, 69
γνόφος, 42
γνώμη, 117
γνωρίζω, 90
γνῶσις, 90, 195
γνώστης, 90
γνωστός, 90, 171
γογγύζω, 33
γογγυσμός, 33
γογγυστής, 33
γόης, 176
γόμος, 25
γονεύς, 89
γόνυ, 19
γονυπετέω, 90
γράμμα, 93, 198
γραμματεύς, 93, 133
γραπτός, 198
γραφή, 158, 196, 198
γράφω, 198
γραώδης, 196
γρηγορέω, 190, 191
γυμνάζω, 36, 188
γυμνασία, 36
γυμνιτεύω, 31
γυμνός, 31, 91
γυμνότης, 31
γυναικάριον, 196
γυναικεῖος, 195
γυνή, 89, 195
γωνία, 118

δαιμονίζομαι, 46
δαιμόνιον, 46
δαιμονιώδης, 46
δάκνω, 106, 197
δάκρυον, 18
δακρύω, 40
δακτύλιος, 3
δάκτυλος, 19
δαμάζω, 37
δάμαλις, 7
δανείζω, 105
δάνειον, 105
δανειστής, 105

δαπανάω, 152, 197
δαπάνη, 38, 105
δέ, 7, 36
δέησις, 11, 120
δεῖ, 107
δεῖγμα, 91
δειγματίζω, 146
δείκνυμι, 57, 91
δειλία, 61
δειλιάω, 61
δειλός, 61
δεῖνα, 124
δεινῶς, 58
δειπνέω, 53
δεῖπνον, 53
δεισιδαιμονία, 132
δεισιδαίμων, 132
δέκα, 109
δεκαπέντε, 109
δεκατέσσαρες, 109
δέκατος, 109
δεκατόω, 70
δεκτός, 3, 125, 193
δελεάζω, 149
δέμνιον, 67
δένδρον, 167
δεξιολάβος, 191
δεξιός, 19, 47
δέομαι, 11, 120
δέος, 119
δέρμα, 30
δερμάτινος, 30
δέρω, 78
δεσμεύω, 60
δέσμη, 60
δέσμιος, 84
δεσμός, 60, 84, 147
δεσμοφύλαξ, 72
δεσμωτήριον, 21, 84
δεσμώτης, 84
δεσπότης, 125, 138
δεῦρο, 97, 161
δεῦτε ὀπίσω μου, 63
δευτεραῖος, 163
δευτερόπρωτος, 145
δεύτερος, 109, 161
δέχομαι, 3, 130, 157, 193
δέω, 24, 33, 60, 84, 147

Greek Index

δή, 34
δῆλος, 91, 117
δηλόω, 57, 91
δημηγορέω, 152
δημιουργέω, 21
δημιουργία, 21
δημιουργός, 21, 101
δῆμος, 39, 40, 44, 115
δημόσιος, 91
δηνάριον, 106
δήποτε, 56
δήπου, 34
δἰ ἐτῶν, 162
δἰ ἡμερῶν, 162
δι᾽ ὀλίγων, 165
διά, 23, 64, 98, 122, 163
διὰ βραχέων, 165
διὰ παντός, 111, 166
διαβαίνω, 40
διαβάλλω, 176
διαβεβαιόομαι, 85
διαβλέπω, 144
διάβολος, 14, 46
διαγγέλλω, 8
διαγίνομαι, 165
διαγινώσκω, 94
διάγνωσις, 94
διαγογγύζω, 33
διαγρηγορέω, 190
διάγω, 15, 134
διαδέχομαι, 130
διάδημα, 4
διαδίδωμι, 70
διάδοχος, 145
διαζώννυμι, 31
διαθήκη, 124
διαίρεσις, 47, 50, 70
διαιρέω, 70
διακαθαίρω, 29
διακαθαρίζω, 29
διακατελέγχομαι, 49
διακονέω, 24, 80, 133, 145
διακονία, 80, 145
διάκονος, 133, 145
διακόσιοι, 109
διακούω, 94
διακρίνω, 28, 39, 49, 50, 87

διάκρισις, 49, 87
διακωλύω, 123
διαλαλέω, 38
διαλέγομαι, 10, 152
διαλείπω, 27
διάλεκτος, 92
διαλλάσσω, 65
διαλογίζομαι, 38, 159
διαλογισμός, 10, 50, 159
διαλύω, 49
διαμαρτύρομαι, 34, 85
διαμάχομαι, 154
διαμένω, 133
διαμερίζω, 49, 70, 114
διαμερισμός, 49, 114
διανέμω, 91, 153
διανεύω, 148
διανοέομαι, 159
διανόημα, 159
διάνοια, 127, 159
διανοίγω, 57, 111
διανυκτερεύω, 150, 163
διανύω, 34
διαπαρατριβή, 10, 179
διαπεράω, 40
διαπλέω, 142
διαπονέομαι, 174
διαπορεύομαι, 167
διαπορέω, 116
διαπραγματεύομαι, 68
διαπρίω, 174
διαρπάζω, 182
διαρρήγνυμι, 153
διασαφέω, 9, 57
διασείω, 182
διασκορπίζω, 49, 152
διασπάω, 153
διασπείρω, 49
διασπορά, 49
διαστέλλομαι, 32
διάστημα, 161
διαστολή, 47
διαστρέφω, 50, 181
διασῴζω, 75, 141
διαταγή, 32
διάταγμα, 32
διαταράσσω, 10
διατάσσω, 11, 32

διατελέω, 26
διατηρέω, 13
διατίθημι, 12, 124
διατρίβω, 134, 164
διατροφή, 63
διαυγάζω, 96, 163
διαυγής, 96
διαφέρω, 25, 47, 51, 173
διαφεύγω, 70
διαφημίζω, 9
διαφθείρω, 45, 147, 181
διαφθορά, 137
διάφορος, 47
διαφυλάσσω, 126, 141
διαχειρίζομαι, 88
διαχλευάζω, 105
διαχωρίζομαι, 70
διδακτικός, 158
διδακτός, 158
διδασκαλία, 158
διδάσκαλος, 158
διδάσκω, 158
διδαχή, 158
δίδραχμον, 158
δίδωμι, 12, 38, 69, 105, 185
δίδωμι ἐργασίαν, 169
διεγείρω, 26, 190, 192
διενθυμέομαι, 160
διέξοδος, 154
διερμηνευτής, 57
διερμηνεύω, 57
διέρχομαι, 40, 167
διερωτάω, 62, 93
διετής, 164
διετία, 164
διηγέομαι, 9
διήγησις, 48
διηνεκής, 166
διθάλασσος, 143
διϊκνέομαι, 40, 116
διΐστημι, 71
διϊσχυρίζομαι, 85
δικαιοκρισία, 94
δίκαιος, 125, 187
δικαιοσύνη, 132, 187
δικαιόω, 94, 132, 188
δικαίωμα, 93, 94, 187

Greek Index

δικαίως, 188
δικαίωσις, 94
δικαστής, 94
δίκη, 127
δίκτυον, 142
δίλογος, 176
διό, 136
διοδεύω, 167
διόπερ, 136
διοπετής, 121
διόρθωμα, 168
διόρθωσις, 10
διορύσσω, 20
διότι, 26
διπλοῦς, 109
διπλόω, 84
δίς, 109
δισμύριοι, 109
διστάζω, 50
δίστομος, 118
δισχίλιοι, 109
διϋλίζω, 38
διχάζω, 129
διχοστασία, 49
διχοτομέω, 41, 128
διψάω, 44, 53, 182
δίψος, 53
δίψυχος, 50
διωγμός, 128
διώκτης, 128
διώκω, 80, 128, 169
δόγμα, 32, 93
δογματίζω, 187
δοκέω, 45, 155
δοκιμάζω, 28, 87, 131, 159
δοκιμασία, 159
δοκιμή, 159, 168, 173
δοκίμιον, 69, 159
δόκιμος, 69, 78, 87, 131
δοκός, 21
δόλιος, 176
δολιόω, 176
δόλος, 30
δολόω, 59
δόμα, 69
δόξα, 15, 78, 96, 119, 174
δοξάζω, 78, 119, 173
δόσις, 69

δότης, 69
δουλαγωγέω, 146
δουλεία, 37
δουλεύω, 37, 85, 146
δοῦλος, 37, 84
δουλόω, 37, 85
δοχή, 53, 61
δράκων, 135
δραμοῦμαι, 139
δράσσομαι, 80, 159
δραχμή, 106
δρέπανον, 60
δρόμος, 36, 139, 197
δύναμαι, 154
δύναμις, 13, 119, 154
δυναμόω, 154
δυνάστης, 138
δυνατέω, 154
δυνατοί, 83
δυνατός, 119, 154
δύνω, 43
δύο, 109
δυσβάστακτος, 168
δυσεντέριον, 147
δυσερμήνευτος, 57
δύσις, 47
δύσκολος, 168
δυσκόλως, 168
δυσμή, 47
δυσνόητος, 116
δυσφημέω, 177
δυσφημία, 177
δώδεκα, 109
δωδέκατος, 109
δωδεκάφυλον, 44
δῶμα, 21
δωρεά, 69
δωρεάν, 66, 69
δωρέομαι, 69
δώρημα, 69
δῶρον, 69

ἐάν, 82, 119, 162
ἔαρ, 164
ἐαρίζω, 164
ἑαυτὸν δίδωμι, 43
ἑαυτοῦ, ἑαυτῷ, ἑαυτόν, 124

ἑαυτῶν, ἑαυτοῖς, ἑαυτούς, 124
ἐάω, 7
ἑβδομήκοντα, 109
ἑβδομηκοντάκις, 109
ἕβδομος, 109
ἐγγίζω, 10, 162
ἐγγράφω, 198
ἔγγυος, 69
ἐγγύς, 98, 162
ἐγείρω, 11, 27, 95, 135, 154, 190, 191
ἔγερσις, 95, 135
ἐγκάθετος, 174
ἐγκαίνια, 61
ἐγκακέω, 48
ἐγκαλέω, 176
ἐγκαταλείπω, 2, 27
ἐγκατοικέω, 2
ἐγκαυχάομαι, 174
ἐγκεντρίζω, 60
ἔγκλημα, 94, 188
ἐγκομβόομαι, 31
ἐγκοπή, 123
ἐγκόπτω, 111, 123
ἐγκράτεια, 188
ἐγκρατεύομαι, 188
ἐγκρατής, 61, 188
ἐγκρίνω, 29
ἐγκρύπτω, 128
ἔγκυος, 17
ἐγχρίω, 96
ἐγώ, 124
ἐδαφίζω, 45, 88, 191
ἔδαφος, 52
ἑδραῖος, 62, 120
ἑδραίωμα, 21, 77
ἐθελοθρησκία, 132
ἐθίζω, 41
ἐθνάρχης, 138
ἐθνικός, 170
ἔθνος, 39
ἔθος, 41
εἰ, 26
εἰ ἄρα, 119
εἰ μή, 35, 36
εἰ μήν, 35
εἰ τύχοι, 119

Greek Index

εἶδος, 66, 143
εἰδωλεῖον, 21
εἰδωλόθυτον, 63
εἰδωλολάτρης, 120
εἰδωλολατρία, 120
εἴδωλον, 83
εἰκῇ, 26, 136
εἴκοσι(ν), 109
εἴκω, 199
εἰκών, 65, 82, 114, 142
εἰλικρίνεια, 185
εἰλικρινής, 185
εἴλω, 197
εἰμί, 16
εἰμὶ ἐν, 134
εἰμὶ ὑπὸ ζυγόν, 85
εἴπερ, 82
εἰρηνεύω, 65, 115, 187
εἰρήνη, 61, 115
εἰρηνικός, 115
εἰρηνοποιέω, 65
εἰρηνοποιός, 65
εἰς, 64, 98, 122, 136, 163, 171
εἷς, 105, 109, 125
εἰς αἰῶνας αἰώνων, 166
εἰς ἐπίγνωσιν ἔρχομαι, 93
εἰς τὰ ἄμετρα, 58, 85
εἰς τέλος, 34, 55
εἰς τὸ διηνεκές, 166
εἰς τὸ πάλιν, 162
εἰς τὸ παντελές, 34, 55, 166
εἰς τὸν αἰῶνα, 166
εἰσάγω, 20, 25
εἰσακούω, 76, 186
εἰσδέχομαι, 193
εἴσειμι, 55
εἰσέρχομαι, 15, 55, 56, 74
εἰσέρχομαι καὶ ἐξέρχομαι, 16
εἰσκαλέομαι, 86
εἴσοδος, 55
εἰσπηδάω, 139
εἰσπορεύομαι, 55
εἰσπορεύομαι καὶ ἐκπορεύομαι, 16
εἰστρέχω, 139

εἰσφέρω, 25, 56
εἶτα, 7, 162
εἴτε...εἴτε, 82
εἰωθός, 41
εἰωθότως, 41
ἐκ, 18, 47, 66, 99, 113, 122, 163
ἐκ δεξιῶν καθίζω, 83
ἐκ μέρους, 113
ἐκ μέτρου, 150
ἐκ περισσοῦ, 58
ἐκ τοῦ αἰῶνος, 166
ἕκαστος, 6
ἑκάστοτε, 166
ἑκατόν, 109
ἑκατονταετής, 164
ἑκατονταπλασίων, 110
ἑκατοντάρχης, 191
ἐκβαίνω, 70
ἐκβάλλω, 56, 131, 160
ἔκβασις, 54, 136, 141
ἐκβολή, 160
ἔκγονον, 89
ἐκδαπανάομαι, 197
ἐκδέχομαι, 79, 183
ἔκδηλος, 91
ἐκδημέω ἐκ τοῦ σώματος, 47
ἐκδίδωμι, 78
ἐκδιηγέομαι, 9
ἐκδικέω, 94, 127, 137
ἐκδίκησις, 94, 127, 137
ἔκδικος, 127
ἐκδιώκω, 128
ἔκδοτος, 17
ἐκδοχή, 79
ἐκδύω, 31
ἐκεῖ, 97
ἐκεῖθεν, 98, 162
ἐκεῖνος, 124
ἐκεῖσε, 97
ἐκζητέω, 94, 143
ἐκζήτησις, 49, 155
ἐκθαμβέομαι, 156
ἔκθαμβος, 156
ἐκθαυμάζω, 156
ἔκθετος, 128
ἐκκαθαίρω, 29

ἐκκαίομαι ἐν τῇ ὀρέξει, 44, 181
ἐκκεντέω, 116
ἐκκλάω, 19
ἐκκλείω, 123, 131
ἐκκλησία, 12, 29
ἐκκλίνω, 27, 50, 131, 178
ἐκκολυμβάω, 156
ἐκκομίζω, 25
ἐκκόπτω, 41, 45
ἐκκρέμαμαι, 134, 160
ἐκλαλέω, 151
ἐκλάμπω, 96
ἐκλανθάνομαι, 64
ἐκλέγομαι, 28
ἐκλείπω, 27, 46, 54, 59, 118
ἐκλεκτός, 28
ἐκλογή, 28
ἐκλύομαι, 48, 166
ἐκμάσσω, 51
ἐκμυκτηρίζω, 105
ἐκνεύω, 13, 71
ἐκνήφω, 160
ἑκούσιος, 193
ἑκουσίως, 117, 194
ἔκπαλαι, 161, 165
ἐκπειράζω, 159, 169
ἐκπέμπω, 145
ἐκπερισσῶς, 102
ἐκπετάννυμι, 153
ἐκπηδάω, 139
ἐκπίπτω, 59, 142
ἐκπλέω, 142
ἐκπληρόω, 54, 66
ἐκπλήρωσις, 54
ἐκπλήσσομαι, 155
ἐκπνέω, 46
ἐκπορεύομαι, 70
ἐκπορνεύω, 181
ἐκπτύω, 131
ἐκριζόω, 60
ἔκστασις, 51, 155
ἐκστρέφομαι, 181
ἐκταράσσω, 129
ἐκτείνω, 144, 153
ἐκτείνω τὰς χεῖρας ἐπί, 144

Greek Index

ἐκτελέω, 34
ἐκτένεια, 52
ἐκτενής, 52, 134, 166
ἐκτενῶς, 52, 134
ἐκτίθεμαι, 57, 128
ἐκτινάσσω, 6
ἐκτός, 36, 98, 195
ἕκτος, 109
ἐκτρέπομαι, 13, 50, 148
ἐκτρέφω, 25, 53
ἔκτρωμα, 18
ἐκφέρω, 20, 25, 72
ἐκφεύγω, 70, 141
ἐκφοβέω, 61
ἔκφοβος, 61
ἐκφύω, 72
ἐκχέω, 49, 54, 62, 96, 169, 192
ἐκχύννεται τὸ αἷμα, 47
ἐκχωρέω, 70
ἐκψύχω, 46
ἑκών, 194
ἐλαία, 66, 167
ἔλαιον, 118
ἐλαιών, 167
ἐλασσόω, 150
ἐλάσσων, 84, 150, 165
ἐλαττονέω, 118
ἐλαττόω, 84
ἐλαύνω, 51
ἐλαφρία, 180
ἐλαφρός, 180
ἐλάχιστος, 84, 150
ἐλαχύς, 150
ἐλεάω, 65, 186
ἐλεγμός, 130
ἔλεγξις, 130
ἔλεγχος, 168
ἐλέγχω, 130
ἐλεεινός, 186
ἐλεημοσύνη, 70, 186
ἐλεήμων, 65, 186
ἐλευθερία, 132
ἐλεύθερος, 66, 132
ἐλευθερόω, 132
ἔλευσις, 32
ἐλεφάντινος, 121
ἕλιγμα, 197

ἑλίσσω, 197
ἑλκόομαι, 148
ἕλκος, 148
ἕλκω, 20, 127
ἐλλογέω, 4, 198
ἐλπίζω, 79, 183
ἐλπίς, 79, 183
ελωι, 71
ἐμαυτοῦ, ἐμαυτῷ, ἐμαυτόν, 124
ἐμβαίνω, 55, 190
ἐμβάλλω, 128
ἐμβάπτω, 96
ἐμβιβάζω, 55
ἐμβλέπω, 144, 160
ἐμβριμάομαι, 85, 130
ἐμέω, 106
ἐμμαίνομαι, 174
ἐμμένω, 133
ἐμός, 124
ἐμπαιγμονή, 105
ἐμπαιγμός, 105
ἐμπαίζω, 105, 176, 177
ἐμπαίκτης, 105
ἐμπεριπατέω, 3
ἐμπίμπλημι, 53, 55, 179
ἐμπίμπρημι, 22
ἐμπίπτω, 56, 59
ἐμπλέκω, 57
ἐμπλοκή, 74
ἐμπορεύομαι, 68, 179
ἐμπορία, 68
ἐμπόριον, 68
ἔμπορος, 68
ἔμπροσθεν, 97
ἐμπτύω, 106
ἐμφανής, 90, 144
ἐμφανίζω, 9, 90, 94, 144
ἔμφυτος, 3, 55, 59
ἐν, 23, 44, 56, 95, 99, 122, 134, 163, 181
ἐν ἀληθείᾳ, 69
ἐν βάρει, 83
ἐν γαστρὶ ἔχω, 17
ἐν μεγάλῳ, 166
ἐν ὀλίγῳ, 165
ἐν παρρησίᾳ, 91
ἐν ῥιπῇ ὀφθαλμοῦ, 165

ἐν τάχει, 162
ἐν τῷ (καθ) ἑξῆς, 162
ἐν τῷ μεταξύ, 162
ἐν ᾧ, 162
ἐναγκαλίζομαι, 90
ἐνάλιον, 62
ἔναντι, 97
ἐναντίον, 97
ἐναντίος, 48
ἐνάρχομαι, 15
ἔνατος, 109
ἐνδεής, 118
ἔνδειγμα, 91
ἐνδείκνυμι, 91
ἔνδειξις, 91
ἕνδεκα, 109
ἑνδέκατος, 109
ἐνδέχεται, 119
ἐνδημέω, 3, 95
ἐνδημέω ἐν τῷ σώματι, 95
ἐνδιδύσκω, 31
ἔνδικος, 188
ἐνδοξάζομαι, 78
ἔνδοξος, 15, 78
ἔνδυμα, 30
ἐνδυναμόω, 154
ἐνδύνω, 55
ἔνδυσις, 31
ἐνδύω, 31
ἐνδώμησις, 21
ἐνέδρα, 159, 191
ἐνεδρεύω, 117, 159, 191
ἐνειλέω, 197
ἔνειμι, 3, 98
ἕνεκα, 26, 64, 136
ἐνενήκοντα, 109
ἐνεός, 148
ἐνέργεια, 196
ἐνεργέω, 25, 196
ἐνέργημα, 196
ἐνευλογέω, 186
ἐνέχω, 37, 79, 178
ἐνθάδε, 97
ἐνθυμέομαι, 160
ἐνθύμησις, 160
ἐνιαυτός, 164
ἐνίσταμαι, 74
ἐνίστημι, 162

Greek Index

ἐνισχύω, 155
ἐννέα, 109
ἐννεύω, 148
ἔννοια, 117, 159
ἔννομος, 92
ἔννυμι, 30
ἔννυχα, 163
ἐνοικέω, 2
ἐνορκίζω, 111
ἑνότης, 105
ἐνοχλέω, 167
ἔνοχος, 37, 149, 178
ἔνταλμα, 32
ἐνταφιάζω, 67
ἐνταφιασμός, 67
ἐντέλλομαι, 32
ἐντεῦθεν, 98, 125
ἔντευξις, 85, 120
ἔντιμος, 78, 173
ἐντολή, 32
ἐντόπιος, 29
ἐντός, 98
ἐντρέπω, 79, 146, 187
ἐντρέφομαι, 158
ἔντρομος, 6, 61
ἐντροπή, 146, 187
ἐντρυφάω, 180
ἐντυγχάνω, 11, 85, 120
ἐντυλίσσω, 197
ἐντυπόω, 114, 198
ἐνυβρίζω, 176
ἐνυπνιάζομαι, 51
ἐνύπνιον, 50
ἐνώπιον, 97
ἐνωτίζομαι, 76
ἕξ, 109
ἐξ ἐναντίας, 79
ἐξαγγέλλω, 8
ἐξαγοράζομαι τὸν καιρόν, 5, 169
ἐξαγοράζω, 132
ἐξάγω, 20
ἐξαιρέω, 28, 141
ἐξαίρω, 131, 134
ἐξαιτέομαι, 11
ἐξαίφνης, 165
ἑξάκις, 109
ἑξακισχίλιοι, 110

ἐξακολουθέω, 63, 83, 186
ἑξακόσιοι, 109
ἐξαλείφω, 30, 46, 96, 185
ἐξάλλομαι, 87
ἐξανάστασις, 95, 135
ἐξανατέλλω, 72
ἐξανίστημι, 154
ἐξανίστημι σπέρμα, 18
ἐξαπατάω, 176
ἐξάπινης, 165
ἐξαπορέομαι, 9
ἐξαποστέλλω, 145
ἐξαρτίζω, 5, 34, 54
ἐξαστράπτω, 96
ἐξαυτῆς, 165
ἐξεγείρω, 83, 95, 135
ἔξειμι, 71
ἐξέλκω, 50
ἐξέραμα, 18
ἐξεραυνάω, 143
ἐξέρχομαι, 71
ἐξέρχομαι ἐκ τῆς ὀσφύος, 18
ἔξεστι, 107, 119
ἐξετάζω, 11, 93, 143
ἐξηγέομαι, 9, 91
ἑξήκοντα, 109
ἑξῆς, 162
ἐξηχέομαι, 34
ἕξις, 196
ἐξίστημι, 85, 155
ἐξισχύω, 155
ἔξοδος, 46, 71
ἐξολεθρεύω, 45
ἐξομολογέω, 6, 34, 119, 188
ἐξορκίζω, 56, 111
ἐξορκιστής, 56
ἐξορύσσω, 20, 47
ἐξουδενέω, 175
ἐξουθενέω, 179
ἐξουσία, 13, 37, 87, 119
ἐξουσιάζω, 138
ἐξοχή, 83
ἐξυπνίζω, 190
ἔξυπνος, 190
ἔξω, 98
ἔξωθεν, 97

ἐξωθέω, 131, 142
ἔοικα, 33
ἑορτάζω, 61
ἑορτή, 61
ἐπ' ἀληθείας, 69
ἐπαγγελία, 6, 124
ἐπαγγέλλομαι, 34, 124
ἐπάγγελμα, 124
ἐπάγω, 25
ἐπαγωνίζομαι, 154
ἐπαθροίζομαι, 5, 12
ἐπαινέω, 119, 131
ἔπαινος, 119
ἐπαίρω, 11, 39, 129, 135, 174
ἐπαίρω τὴν κεφαλήν, 39
ἐπαίρω τὴν πτέρναν, 79
ἐπαισχύνομαι, 146
ἐπαιτέω, 11
ἐπακολουθέω, 52, 74
ἐπακολουθέω τοῖς ἴχνεσιν, 83
ἐπακούω, 76
ἐπακροάομαι, 76
ἐπάν, 162
ἐπάναγκες, 107
ἐπανάγω, 137, 142
ἐπαναμιμνήσκω, 104
ἐπαναπαύομαι, 136
ἐπανέρχομαι, 137
ἐπανίστημι, 129
ἐπανόρθωσις, 168
ἐπάνω, 83, 98, 102
ἐπάρατος, 41
ἐπαρκέω, 77
ἐπαρχεία, 39
ἔπαυλις, 21
ἐπαύριον, 162
ἐπαφρίζω, 63
ἐπεγείρω, 15
ἐπεί, 26
ἐπειδή, 26, 162
ἐπειδήπερ, 26
ἐπεισαγωγή, 15
ἐπεισέρχομαι, 74
ἔπειτα, 162
ἐπέκεινα, 97
ἐπεκτείνομαι, 153

ἐπενδύτης, 30
ἐπενδύω, 31
ἐπέρχομαι, 13, 32, 74
ἐπερωτάω, 11, 94
ἐπερώτημα, 11
ἐπέχω, 134, 144, 191
ἐπηρεάζω, 160, 175
ἐπί, 6, 23, 37, 64, 99, 122, 163, 171
ἐπὶ θύραις, 162
ἐπὶ πολύ, 166
ἐπιβαίνω, 11, 55
ἐπιβάλλω, 97, 125, 128, 160
ἐπιβάλλω τὴν χεῖρα ἐπί, 145
ἐπιβαρέω, 42
ἐπιβιβάζω, 11, 55
ἐπιβλέπω, 77, 79, 144, 160, 187
ἐπίβλημα, 31
ἐπιβουλή, 117
ἐπιγαμβρεύω, 103
ἐπίγειος, 52, 115
ἐπιγίνομαι, 74
ἐπιγινώσκω, 90, 93, 195
ἐπίγνωσις, 90, 195
ἐπιγραφή, 198
ἐπιγράφω, 198
ἐπιδείκνυμι, 144, 168
ἐπιδέχομαι, 187, 193
ἐπιδημέω, 151
ἐπιδιατάσσομαι, 5, 95
ἐπιδίδωμι, 69, 199
ἐπιδιορθόω, 10
ἐπιδύω, 43
ἐπιείκεια, 184
ἐπιεικής, 184
ἐπιζητέω, 45, 143
ἐπιθανάτιος, 46
ἐπίθεσις, 128
ἐπιθυμέω, 44, 182
ἐπιθυμητής, 44
ἐπιθυμία, 44
ἐπικαθίζω, 150
ἐπικαλέω, 11, 94, 107
ἐπικάλυμμα, 77
ἐπικαλύπτω, 65, 186

ἐπικατάρατος, 41
ἐπίκειμαι, 119, 123, 134
ἐπικέλλω, 142
ἐπικουρέω, 77
ἐπικουρία, 77
ἐπικρίνω, 46, 131
ἐπιλαμβάνομαι, 80, 145, 157, 159
ἐπιλανθάνομαι, 64
ἐπιλέγω, 28, 107
ἐπιλείχω, 106
ἐπιλησμονή, 64
ἐπίλοιπος, 113
ἐπίλυσις, 57
ἐπιλύω, 46, 57
ἐπιμαρτυρέω, 195
ἐπιμέλεια, 25
ἐπιμελέομαι, 25, 160
ἐπιμελῶς, 160
ἐπιμένω, 133
ἐπινεύω, 6
ἐπίνοια, 117
ἐπιορκέω, 111
ἐπίορκος, 111
ἐπιούσιος, 162, 163
ἐπιπίπτω, 74, 123
ἐπιπίπτω ἐπὶ τὸν τράχηλον, 90
ἐπιπλήσσω, 130
ἐπιποθέω, 44, 100, 182
ἐπιπόθησις, 44
ἐπιπόθητος, 100
ἐπιποθία, 44
ἐπιπορεύομαι, 32
ἐπιράπτω, 30
ἐπιρίπτω, 161
ἐπιρραίνω, 97
ἐπίσημος, 90
ἐπισιτισμός, 63
ἐπισκέπτομαι, 24, 28, 189
ἐπισκευάζομαι, 121
ἐπισκηνόω, 3
ἐπισκιάζω, 42
ἐπισκοπέω, 24, 133, 189
ἐπισκοπή, 25, 133, 189
ἐπίσκοπος, 25, 133
ἐπισπάω, 43
ἐπισπείρω, 59

ἐπίσταμαι, 90, 194
ἐπίστασις, 9, 129
ἐπιστάτης, 83
ἐπιστέλλω, 198
ἐπιστήμων, 194
ἐπιστηρίζω, 155
ἐπιστολή, 198
ἐπιστομίζω, 149
ἐπιστρέφω, 38, 50, 137
ἐπιστρέφω καρδίας ἐπί, 3
ἐπιστροφή, 38
ἐπισυνάγω, 12
ἐπισυντρέχω, 12
ἐπισφαλής, 42
ἐπισχύω, 169
ἐπισωρεύω, 84
ἐπιταγή, 13, 32
ἐπιτάσσω, 32
ἐπιτελέω, 20, 33, 66
ἐπιτήδειος, 118, 125
ἐπιτίθημι, 5, 13, 57, 69, 128
ἐπιτιμάω, 32, 127, 130
ἐπιτιμία, 127
ἐπιτρέπω, 7
ἐπιτροπή, 13
ἐπίτροπος, 72, 139
ἐπιτυγχάνω, 4, 56
ἐπιφαίνω, 96, 144
ἐπιφάνεια, 144
ἐπιφανής, 15
ἐπιφαύσκω, 96
ἐπιφέρω, 56
ἐπιφωνέω, 147
ἐπιφώσκω, 96, 163
ἐπιχειρέω, 169
ἐπιχέω, 96
ἐπιχορηγέω, 5, 126
ἐπιχορηγία, 126
ἐπιχρίω, 96
ἐποικοδομέω, 20, 155
ἐπονομάζομαι, 107
ἐποπτεύω, 144
ἐπόπτης, 144
ἔπος, 196
ἐπουράνιος, 76
ἑπτά, 109
ἑπτάκις, 109

ἑπτακισχίλιοι, 109
ἐραυνάω, 143
ἐργάζομαι, 23, 25, 68, 101, 196
ἐργασία, 16, 68, 196
ἐργάτης, 16, 101, 196
ἔργον, 101, 196
ἐρεθίζω, 178
ἐρείδω, 60, 62
ἐρεύγομαι, 9
ἐρημία, 92, 193
ἐρημόομαι, 45
ἔρημος, 2
ἔρημος τόπος, 115, 193
ἐρήμωσις, 45
ἐρίζω, 10, 154, 179
ἐριθεία, 79, 178, 179
ἔριον, 19, 30
ἔρις, 10, 154
ἐρίφιον, 8
ἔριφος, 8
ἑρμηνεία, 57
ἑρμηνεύω, 57
ἑρπετόν, 85
ἐρυθρός, 31
ἔρχομαι, 32, 74
ἔρχομαι εἰς, 136
ἐρωτάω, 11
ἐσθής, 30
ἐσθίω, 53
ἐσμυρνισμένος οἶνος, 104
ἔσοπτρον, 67
ἑσπέρα, 163
ἔσχατος, 34, 84, 145
ἔσω, 98
ἔσωθεν, 97, 127
ἐσώτερος, 98
ἐτάζω, 11, 143, 159
ἑταῖρος, 13
ἑτέρᾳ, 162
ἑτερόγλωσσος, 92
ἑτεροδιδασκαλέω, 158
ἑτεροζυγέω, 103
ἕτερος, 47
ἑτέρως, 47
ἔτι, 5, 36, 162
ἑτοιμάζω, 121
ἑτοιμασία, 121
ἕτοιμος, 121
ἔτος, 161, 164
εὖ, 184
εὐαγγελίζω, 8, 121
εὐαγγέλιον, 8, 121, 141
εὐαγγελιστής, 133
εὐαρεστέω, 3
εὐαρέστως, 3
εὖγε, 184
εὐγενής, 83, 84
εὐδία, 192
εὐδοκέω, 3, 28, 55, 130
εὐδοκία, 3, 45, 184
εὐεργεσία, 184
εὐεργετέω, 184
εὐεργέτης, 77
εὔθετος, 125, 172
εὐθέως, 161
εὐθυδρομέω, 142
εὐθυμέω, 54
εὔθυμος, 54
εὐθύνω, 40, 143
εὐθύς, 40, 161, 188
εὐθύτης, 188
εὐκαιρέω, 164
εὐκαιρία, 164
εὔκαιρος, 164
εὐκαίρως, 164
εὐκοπώτερος, 132
εὐλάβεια, 132
εὐλαβέομαι, 132, 187
εὐλαβής, 133
εὐλογέω, 18, 119, 186
εὐλογητός, 119
εὐλογία, 18, 70, 119, 186
εὐμετάδοτος, 69
εὐνοέω, 6, 94, 159, 187
εὔνοια, 52
εὐνουχίζω, 102
εὐνοῦχος, 102, 139
εὐοδόομαι, 5, 61
εὐπάρεδρος, 120
εὐπειθής, 172
εὐπερίστατος, 37
εὐποιΐα, 184
εὐπορέω, 192
εὐπορία, 68, 192
εὐπρέπεια, 15
εὐπρόσδεκτος, 3, 61
εὐπροσωπέω, 176
εὐρακύλων, 194
εὑρίσκω, 56, 62, 93
εὐρύχωρος, 103
εὐσέβεια, 132
εὐσεβέω, 107, 120
εὐσεβής, 132
εὐσεβῶς, 132
εὔσημος, 195
εὔσπλαγχνος, 100
εὐσχημόνως, 187
εὐσχημοσύνη, 15
εὐσχήμων, 15, 79, 125
εὐτόνως, 58
εὐτραπελία, 152, 177
εὐφημία, 120
εὔφημος, 120
εὐφορέω, 137
εὐφραίνω, 61, 75
εὐφροσύνη, 75
εὐχαριστέω, 72, 188
εὐχαριστία, 72, 188
εὐχάριστος, 72, 188
εὐχή, 111, 120
εὔχομαι, 45, 120
εὔχρηστος, 172
εὐψυχέω, 54
εὐωδία, 150
εὐώνυμος, 47
ἐφ' ἱκανόν, 166
ἐφάλλομαι, 87
ἐφάπαξ, 109, 161
ἐφευρετής, 117
ἐφήμερος, 163
ἐφικνέομαι, 32
ἐφίστημι, 13, 15, 74, 134, 154, 162
ἐφοράω, 160
εφφαθα, 111
ἐχθές, 161
ἐχθὲς καὶ σήμερον καὶ εἰς τοὺς αἰῶνας, 166
ἔχθρα, 79
ἐχθρός, 79
ἔχιδνα, 135
ἔχω, 31, 125, 157
ἔχω κοινός, 70

Greek Index

ἔχω μέρος ἐν, 56
ἕως, 98, 162, 171
ἕως ὅτου, 162
ἕως οὗ, 162

ζάω, 16, 17, 95
ζεστός, 79
ζεῦγος, 110
ζευκτηρία, 60
ζέω τῷ πνεύματι, 52
ζηλεύω, 52
ζῆλος, 44, 58, 99, 152, 178
ζηλόω, 44, 52, 99, 152, 178, 182
ζηλωτής, 52
ζημία, 99, 119, 128
ζημιόω, 99, 118, 128
ζητέω, 11, 62, 120
ζήτημα, 49
ζήτησις, 49, 143
ζιζάνιον, 117
ζόφος, 42
ζυγός, 60, 104
ζύμη, 63, 176
ζυμόω, 63
ζωγρέω, 24, 37
ζωή, 95, 153
ζώνη, 30
ζώννυμι, 31
ζωογονέω, 95, 135
ζῷον, 7
ζωοποιέω, 95, 135

ἤ, 33, 36, 82, 112
ἡ ἄρτι ὥρα, 161
ἡ κοιλία βαστάζει, 17
ἡγεμονεύω, 138
ἡγεμονία, 138
ἡγεμών, 138
ἡγέομαι, 9, 72, 91, 138, 160
ἡδέως, 75
ἤδη, 161
ἥδιστα, 75
ἡδονή, 44, 55, 181
ἡδύνω, 157
ἡδύοσμον, 117, 152, 157
ἥδυσμα, 157

ἡδύσματα, 157
ἡδυσμός, 157
ἦθος, 41
ἥκω, 17, 32, 74
ηλι, 71
ἡλικία, 57, 103, 164
ἡλίκος, 57, 92
ἧλος, 60
ἡμέρα, 96, 161
ἡμέρα ἐξ ἡμέρας, 166
ἡμέρα σφαγῆς, 94
ἡμέτερος, 124
ἡμιθανής, 47
ἥμισυς, 109
ἡμιώριον, 164
ἡνίκα ἄν / ἐάν, 163
ἤπερ, 33
ἤπιος, 183
ἤρεμος, 115, 187
ἡσσάομαι, 95
ἥσσων, 14, 95, 175
ἡσυχάζω, 115, 136, 148
ἡσυχία, 61, 115, 136, 149
ἡσύχιος, 115, 136, 187
ἤτοι, 112
ἤτοι...ἤ, 112
ἡττάομαι, 35, 59, 95, 175
ἥττημα, 35, 59
ἠχέω, 151, 158
ἦχος, 9, 151

θάλασσα, 191
θάλπω, 24
θαμβέομαι, 155
θάμβος, 156
θανάσιμον, 46
θανατηφόρος, 46
θάνατος, 46
θανατόω, 27, 88
θάπτω, 47, 67
θαρρέω, 39, 183
θάρσει, 39
θαῦμα, 156
θαυμάζω, 62, 120, 187
θαυμάζω πρόσωπον, 62
θαυμάσιος, 156
θαυμαστός, 156
θαυμαστόω, 120

θεάομαι, 144, 189
θεατρίζω, 146
θέατρον, 21, 144
θεῖον, 22
θεῖος, 71
θειότης, 71
θειώδης, 32
θέλημα, 45, 116
θέλησις, 45
θέλω, 45, 116
θεμέλιον, 21, 26
θεμελιόω, 21, 56, 62
θέμις, 180
θεοδίδακτος, 158
θεομάχος, 154
θεόπνευστος, 121
θεός, 71
θεοσέβεια, 132
θεοσεβής, 132
θεοστυγής, 179
θεότης, 71
θεραπεία, 75, 80, 120
θεραπεύω, 75, 120, 145
θεράπων, 145
θερίζω, 60
θερισμός, 60
θεριστής, 60
θερμαίνομαι, 79
θέρμη, 22, 79
θέρος, 164
θεωρέω, 56, 144, 189, 194
θεωρία, 144
θήκη, 35
θηλάζω, 53
θῆλυς, 102, 196
θήρα, 24, 80
θηρεύω, 80, 159
θηριομαχέω, 154
θηρίον, 7
θησαυρίζω, 173
θησαυρός, 21, 36, 173
θιγγάνω, 88, 166
θλίβω, 123, 167
θλῖψις, 167
θνήσκω, 46
θνητός, 47
θορυβάζω, 9, 40
θορυβέω, 9, 129, 175

238

θόρυβος, 129, 151
θραύω, 168
θρέμμα, 7
θρηνέω, 40, 67, 106
θρῆνος, 106
θρησκεία, 120, 132
θρησκός, 132
θριαμβεύω, 35
θρίξ, 19, 74
θροέομαι, 61
θρόμβος, 19
θρόνος, 67, 138
θυγάτηρ, 28, 89
θυγάτριον, 89
θύελλα, 192, 194
θύϊνος, 196
θυμίαμα, 116, 140
θυμιάω, 140
θυμομαχέω, 10, 173, 179
θυμός, 44, 173, 182
θυμόω, 173
θύρα, 21
θυρεός, 192
θυρίς, 21
θυρωρός, 80
θυσία, 140
θυσίαν ἱλάσκεσθαι τὸν θεόν, 140
θυσιαστήριον, 67
θύω, 88, 140
θωή, 185
θώραξ, 19, 192

ἴαμα, 75, 104
ἰάομαι, 27, 75, 135
ἴασις, 75
ἴασπις, 121
ἰατρός, 75
ἴδε, 35
ἴδιοι, 44
ἴδιος, 124, 125, 170
ἰδιώτης, 82
ἰδού, 35
ἰδρώς, 18
ἱερατεία, 133
ἱεράτευμα, 133
ἱερατεύω, 133
ἱερεύς, 133

ἱερόθυτος, 140
ἱερόν, 21
ἱεροπρεπής, 133
ἱερός, 133
ἱεροσυλέω, 140, 182
ἱερόσυλος, 140, 182
ἱερουργέω, 133
ἱερωσύνη, 133
ἱκανός, 197
ἱκανός, 5, 34, 55, 57, 102
ἱκανότης, 5
ἱκανόω, 5
ἱκετηρία, 11, 120
ἰκμάς, 191
ἱλαρός, 75
ἱλαρότης, 75
ἱλάσκομαι, 65, 186
ἱλασμός, 65
ἱλαστήριον, 65
ἵλεως, 65, 186
ἱμάς, 60, 78
ἱματίζω, 31
ἱμάτιον, 30, 31
ἱματισμός, 30
ἵνα, 35, 136
ἱνατί, 26
ἰός, 18, 137
ἰουδαΐζω, 16
Ἰουδαϊσμός, 16
ἱππεύς, 191
ἱππικόν, 191
ἵππος, 8
ἱσάγγελος, 7
ἴσος, 141
ἰσότης, 141
ἰσότιμος, 141
ἰσόψυχος, 126
ἵστημι, 55, 119, 128, 134, 153
ἱστορέω, 48, 93, 189
ἰσχυρός, 58, 83, 119, 154
ἰσχύς, 154
ἰσχύω, 75, 154
ἴσως, 119
ἰχθύδιον, 62
ἰχθύς, 62
ἴχνος, 143
ἰῶτα, 198

καθά, 33
καθαίρεσις, 45, 170
καθαιρέω, 43, 45
καθαίρω, 29, 60
καθάπερ, 33
καθάπτω, 60, 157
καθαρίζω, 29, 48, 75, 185
καθαρισμός, 29
καθάρματα, 48
καθαρός, 29
καθαρότης, 29
καθέδρα, 67
καθέζομαι, 149
καθεξῆς, 145
καθεύδω, 46, 150
καθηγητής, 158
καθήκω, 125
κάθημαι, 3, 134, 149
καθημερινός, 163
καθίζω, 12, 134, 149
καθίημι, 43
καθίστημι, 12, 25
καθό, 33, 171
καθόλου, 55
καθοπλίζω, 191
καθοράω, 143
καθότι, 26, 171
καθώς, 26, 33, 80, 171
καθώσπερ, 33
καί, 7, 34
καί...καί, τέ...τέ, 7
καινός, 108, 161, 165
καινότης, 108, 165
καίπερ, 7
καιρός, 161
καίτοι, 7
καίτοιγε, 7
καίω, 22
κἀκεῖθεν, 98, 162
κακία, 14, 167, 179
κακοήθεια, 14
κακολογέω, 177
κακοπάθεια, 113
κακοπαθέω, 113
κακοποιέω, 14, 197
κακοποιός, 14
κακός, 14, 183, 197
κακοῦργος, 14

κακουχέομαι, 175
κακόω, 175
κακῶς, 14, 197
κακῶς ἔχω, 147
κάκωσις, 197
καλάμη, 117
κάλαμος, 103, 117, 198
καλέω, 24, 86, 107
καλλιέλαιος, 167
καλοδιδάσκαλος, 158
καλοποιέω, 184
καλός, 5, 14, 125, 168, 184
κάλυμμα, 30
καλύπτω, 39, 77
καλῶς, 58, 75, 168, 184
καλῶς ἔχω, 75
κάμηλος, 8
κάμινος, 22
καμμύω, 82, 111
καμμύω τοὺς ὀφθαλμούς, 82
κάμνω, 48
κάμπτω τὸ γόνυ, 120
κἄν, 7
κανών, 93, 103, 131
καπηλεύω, 68
καπνός, 22, 76
καραδοκία, 79
καρδία, 19, 126, 153
καρδιογνώστης, 90
καρπὸν ἀποδίδωμι, 137
καρπὸν φέρω, 137
καρπός, 60, 66, 89
καρπὸς τῆς κοιλίας, 89
καρπὸς τῆς ὀσφύος, 89
καρποφορέω, 137
καρποφόρος, 137
καρτερέω, 114
κάρφος, 196
κατ' ἀλήθειαν, 69
κατ' ἰδίαν, 77
κατά, 5, 99, 122, 163
κατὰ βάθους, 58
κατὰ κεφαλῆς ἔχω, 31
κατὰ λόγον ἀνέχομαι, 94
κατὰ μόνας, 7, 171
κατὰ πρόσωπον, 97

κατὰ συγκυρία, 74
καταβαίνω, 43
καταβάλλω, 78
καταβαρέω, 167
κατάβασις, 43
καταβιβάζω, 43
καταβολή, 15, 101
καταβολὴ σπέρματος, 17
καταβραβεύω, 87
καταγγελεύς, 8
καταγγέλλω, 8
καταγελάω, 75, 105, 177
καταγινώσκω, 87
κατάγνυμι, 19
καταγράφω, 198
κατάγω, 20, 142
καταγωνίζομαι, 35
καταδέω, 60, 84
κατάδηλος, 195
καταδικάζω, 94
καταδίκη, 94
καταδιώκω, 80, 143
καταδουλόω, 37
καταδυναστεύω, 168
κατάθεμα, 41
καταθεματίζω, 41
καταισχύνω, 146
κατακαίω, 22
κατακαλύπτω, 31
κατακαυχάομαι, 155, 174, 179
κατάκειμαι, 53, 95, 130
κατακλάω, 19
κατακλείω, 72
κατακληρονομέω, 130
κατακλίνω, 130
κατακλύζω, 62
κατακλυσμός, 62
κατακολουθέω, 63
κατακόπτω, 41
κατακρημνίζω, 161
κατάκριμα, 94
κατακρίνω, 94
κατάκρισις, 94
κατακύπτω, 17
κατακυριεύω, 35, 138
καταλαλέω, 176
καταλαλιά, 176

κατάλαλος, 176
καταλαμβάνω, 4, 13, 37, 93, 144, 159, 195
καταλέγω, 198
καταλείπω, 2, 43, 71, 131
καταλιθάζω, 88
καταλλαγή, 64, 105
καταλλάσσω, 64, 105
κατάλοιπος, 113
κατάλυμα, 21
καταλύω, 45, 85
καταμανθάνω, 160
καταμαρτυρέω, 195
καταμένω, 133
καταναλίσκω, 45
καταναρκάω, 42
κατανεύω, 148
κατανοέω, 144, 159, 194
καταντάω, 32, 74
κατάνυξις, 150, 160
κατανύσσομαι τὴν καρδίαν, 140
καταξιόω, 197
καταπατέω, 123, 179
κατάπαυσις, 136
καταπαύω, 26, 136
καταπέτασμα, 30
καταπίνω, 45, 53
καταπίπτω, 59
καταπλέω, 142
καταπονέω, 9, 175
καταποντίζομαι, 43
καταπράσσω, 66
κατάρα, 41
καταράομαι, 41
καταργέω, 27, 45, 54, 86, 132, 180
καταρτίζω, 5, 34, 101, 121
κατάρτισις, 5
καταρτισμός, 5
κατασείω, 148
κατασκάπτω, 45
κατασκευάζω, 20, 121
κατασκευάζω τὴν ὁδόν, 121
κατασκηνόω, 3, 95
κατασκήνωσις, 22
κατασκιάζω, 42

κατασκοπέω, 144
κατάσκοπος, 93
κατασοφίζομαι, 179
καταστέλλω, 37
κατάστημα, 15
καταστολή, 31
καταστρέφω, 137
καταστρηνιάω, 44, 182
καταστροφή, 45, 197
καταστρώννυμι, 88
κατασύρω, 20
κατασφάζω, 88
κατασφραγίζω, 198
κατάσχεσις, 4, 125
κατατίθημι, 69
κατατομή, 41
κατατρέχω, 139
καταφέρω, 75
καταφέρω ψῆφον, 28
καταφεύγω, 70, 141
καταφθείρω, 181
καταφιλέω, 90
καταφρονέω, 179
καταφρονητής, 179
καταχέω, 96
καταχθόνιος, 76
καταψύχω, 80
κατείδωλος, 83
κατέναντι, 97
κατενώπιον, 97
κατεξουσιάζω, 138
κατεργάζομαι, 25, 122, 196
κατέρχομαι, 43, 142
κατεσθίω, 45, 53, 152, 179, 182
κατευθύνω, 72
κατευθύνω τοὺς πόδας, 16
κατευλογέω, 18
κατεφίσταμαι, 13
κατέχω, 4, 24, 37, 123, 125
κατέχω εἰς, 143
κατηγορέω, 176
κατηγορία, 176
κατήγορος, 176
κατήφεια, 48
κατηχέω, 9, 158

κατιόομαι, 137
κατισχύω, 35, 155
κατοικέω, 2
κατοίκησις, 2
κατοικητήριον, 2
κατοικία, 2
κατοικίζω, 2
κατοπτρίζομαι, 96, 144
κάτω, 98
κατώτερος, 98
κατωτέρω, 150
καῦμα, 22
καυματίζω, 22
καῦσις, 22
καυσόομαι, 22
καύσων, 22, 192
καυχάομαι, 174
καύχημα, 174
καύχησις, 174
κεῖμαι, 95
κειρία, 30
κείρω, 41, 74
κέλευσμα, 32
κελεύω, 32
κενοδοξία, 174
κενόδοξος, 174
κενός, 54, 64, 118, 136
κενοφωνία, 177
κενόω, 54, 84, 86
κεντέω, 60
κέντρον, 8, 19, 60, 118
κεντυρίων, 191
κεραία, 118, 198
κεραμεύς, 35
κεραμικός, 53
κεράμιον, 35
κέραμος, 21
κεράννυμι, 96, 105
κέρας, 19, 118, 119
κεράτιον, 66
κερδαίνω, 68
κέρδος, 68
κέρμα, 106
κερματιστής, 68
κεφάλαιον, 35, 38, 49
κεφαλή, 19, 84
κεφαλὴ γωνίας, 21
κεφαλιόω, 78

κεφαλίς, 198
κημόω, 8
κῆνσος, 158
κῆπος, 59, 62, 117
κηπουρός, 59
κηρήθρα, 63
κηριον, 63
κήρυγμα, 120
κῆρυξ, 120
κηρύσσω, 9, 120
κῆτος, 62
κιβωτός, 36, 142
κιθάρα, 106
κιθαρίζω, 106
κιθαρῳδός, 106
κινδυνεύω, 42
κίνδυνος, 42
κινέω, 6, 106, 129
κιννάμωμον, 152
κίχρημι, 105
κλάδος, 117
κλαίω, 40
κλάσις, 19
κλάσμα, 20
κλαυθμός, 40
κλάω, 19
κλείς, 4, 67
κλείω, 111
κλέμμα, 182
κλέος, 78
κλέπτης, 182
κλέπτω, 182
κλῆμα, 117
κληρονομέω, 130
κλῆρος, 12, 28, 70, 113, 130
κληρόω, 28
κλῆσις, 24, 83
κλητός, 86
κλίβανος, 22
κλίμα, 131
κλινάριον, 67
κλίνη, 67
κλινίδιον, 67
κλίνω, 27, 95, 163
κλίνω τὸ πρόσωπον εἰς τὴν γῆν, 126
κλισία, 40

Greek Index

κλοπή, 182
κλύδων, 191
κλυδωνίζομαι, 6, 143
κναφεύς, 31
κνίσσα, 157
κοδράντης, 106
κοιλία, 19, 44, 127, 182
κοιμάομαι, 46, 150
κοίμησις, 150
κοινός, 146, 183, 195
κοινόω, 183
κοινωνέω, 70, 196
κοινωνία, 12, 70
κοινωνικός, 70
κοινωνός, 12
κοίτη, 18, 67, 182
κοίτην ἔχω, 17
κοιτών, 21
κόκκινος, 30, 31
κόκκος, 66
κολάζω, 127
κολακεία, 62
κόλασις, 127
κολαφίζω, 78, 197
κόλλα, 60
κολλάομαι, 60
κολλάω, 87
κολλούριον, 104
κολλυβιστής, 68
κολοβόω, 95
κόλπος, 19, 30, 191
κολυμβάω, 156
κολυμβήθρα, 191
κολωνία, 29, 39
κομάω, 74
κόμη, 19
κομίζω, 3, 25, 39, 67, 68, 130
κομμός, 67
κομψός, 75
κομψότερον, 75
κονιάω, 21, 30, 176
κονιορτός, 52
κοπάζω, 27
κοπετός, 67
κοπή, 88
κοπιάω, 48, 166
κόπος, 166, 167

κοπρία, 18
κόπτω, 41, 67, 78
κόραξ, 17
κοράσιον, 196
κορβᾶν, 140
κορβανᾶς, 21
κορέννυμι, 36, 192
κόρος, 104
κοσμέω, 14
κοσμικός, 16, 52
κόσμιος, 125, 187
κοσμοκράτωρ, 46, 138
κόσμος, 3, 15, 16, 115
κουστωδία, 191
κουφίζω, 193
κόφινος, 36
κράβαττος, 67
κράζω, 147
κραιπάλη, 178
κρανίον, 19
κράσπεδον, 4, 30
κραταιός, 37, 119, 155
κρατέω, 37, 145, 157
κράτιστος, 84
κράτος, 13, 119, 138, 155
κραυγάζω, 147
κραυγή, 40, 147
κρέας, 63
κρείσσων, 184
κρείττων, 83, 184
κρεμάζω, 60
κρεμάννυμι, 26, 60
κρεμάννυμι ἐπὶ ξύλου, 88
κρημνός, 106
κριθή, 66
κρίθινος, 66
κρίμα, 87, 93
κρίνον, 117
κρίνω, 28, 46, 87, 94
κρίσις, 87, 93, 127
κριτήριον, 93
κριτής, 94
κριτικός, 94
κρούω, 78
κρύπτη, 77
κρυπτός, 77
κρύπτω, 77, 126, 141
κρυσταλλίζω, 121

κρύσταλλος, 40, 121, 191
κρυφαῖος, 77
κρυφῇ, 77
κτάομαι, 4
κτῆμα, 125
κτῆνος, 8
κτῆσις, 125
κτήτωρ, 125
κτίζω, 15, 55, 101
κτίσις, 13, 101
κτίσμα, 101
κτίστης, 101
κυβεία, 176
κυβέρνησις, 72
κυβερνήτης, 143
κυκλεύω, 24
κυκλόθεν, 97
κύκλος, 138
κυκλόω, 138
κύκλῳ, 98
κυλισμός, 137
κύλιω, 137
κυλλός, 148
κῦμα, 191
κύμβαλον, 106
κύμινον, 117, 152
κυνάριον, 8
κυνέω, 120, 126
κύπτω, 17
κυρία, 84
κυριακός, 71
κυριεύω, 138
κύριος, 71, 84, 125, 138
κυριότης, 71, 138
κυρόω, 69, 119
κύων, 8
κῶλον, 18
κωλύω, 123
κώμη, 29
κωμόπολις, 29
κῶμος, 62, 178
κώνωψ, 85
κωφός, 76, 148

λαγχάνω, 28, 130
λάθρα, 77
λαῖλαψ, 194
λακάω, 153

Greek Index

λακτίζω, 78
λαλέω, 151
λαλιά, 151
λαμά, λεμά, 26
λαμβάνω, 3, 4, 130, 157
λαμβάνω θάρσος, 39
λαμβάνω πρόσωπον, 178
λαμπάς, 92, 96
λαμπρός, 15, 96
λαμπρότης, 96
λαμπρῶς, 180
λάμπω, 96
λανθάνω, 64, 77, 82
λαξευτός, 41
λαός, 39, 40, 115
λάρυγξ, 19
λατομέω, 41
λατρεία, 133
λατρεύω, 133
λάχανον, 117
λεγεών, 190
λεγιών, 190
λέγω, 107, 151
λεῖμμα, 114
λεῖος, 138
λείπω, 2, 118, 134
λειτουργέω, 120, 133, 145
λειτουργία, 120, 133, 146
λειτουργικός, 120, 146
λειτουργός, 120, 133, 146
λείχω, 106
λέντιον, 30
λεπίς, 19
λέπρα, 147
λεπρός, 147
λεπτόν, 106
λευκαίνω, 31
λευκός, 31, 96
λέων, 8
λήθη, 64
λῆμψις, 130
ληνός, 22
λῆρος, 177
λῃστής, 118, 129, 182
λίαν, 57
λίβανος, 116
λιβανωτός, 35
Λιβερτῖνος, 66

λιθάζω, 88
λίθινος, 53
λιθοβολέω, 88
λίθος, 53
λίθος τίμιος, 121
λιθόστρωτος, 22
λικμάω, 60, 123
λιμήν, 191
λίμνη, 191
λίμνη τοῦ πυρὸς καὶ θείου, 76
λιμός, 53
λίνον, 30
λιπαρός, 15
λίτρα, 193
λίψ, 47
λογεία, 5
λόγια, 151
λογίζομαι, 4, 104, 159
λογικός, 69, 168
λόγιος, 93, 152
λογισμός, 159
λογομαχέω, 10, 179
λογομαχία, 10
λόγος, 4, 26, 94, 121, 151, 160, 196, 198
λόγχη, 192
λοιδορέω, 177
λοιδορία, 177
λοίδορος, 177
λοιμός, 147, 167
λοιπός, 7, 35, 113, 134, 163
λουτρόν, 14, 29
λούω, 29, 96
λύκος, 8, 176
λύκος ἐν ἐνδύμασιν προβάτων, 176
λυμαίνομαι, 45, 175, 197
λυπέω, 140
λύπη, 140
λύσις, 50
λυσιτελέω, 5, 184
λύτρον, 132
λυτρόω, 132
λύτρωσις, 132
λυτρωτής, 132
λυχνία, 92

λύχνος, 92
λύω, 45, 132, 177
λωίων, 184

μαγεία, 101
μαγεύω, 101
μάγος, 101, 195
μαθητεύω, 63, 93
μαθητής, 63, 93
μαθήτρια, 63
μαίνομαι, 85
μακαρίζω, 75
μακάριος, 75
μακαρισμός, 75
μάκελλον, 68
μακράν, 98
μακρόθεν, 97
μακροθυμέω, 114, 150
μακροθυμία, 114
μακροθύμως, 114
μακρός, 103
μακροχρόνιος, 166
μάλα, 102
μαλακία, 147
μαλακός, 151, 182
μάλιστα, 57
μᾶλλον, 36, 102
μᾶλλον...ἤ, 36
μάμμη, 89
μαμωνᾶς, 192
μανθάνω, 93, 189, 194
μανία, 85
μάννα, 63
μαντεύομαι, 121
μαραίνω, 15, 51, 166
μαργαρίτης, 121
μάρμαρος, 121
μαρτυρέω, 195
μαρτυρία, 95, 195
μαρτύριον, 195
μαρτύρομαι, 34, 85
μάρτυς, 88, 195
μασάομαι, 53, 106
μαστιγόω, 78, 128
μαστίζω, 78
μάστιξ, 78, 147
μαστός, 19
ματαιολογία, 177

Greek Index

ματαιολόγος, 177
μάταιος, 172
ματαιότης, 172
ματάω, 164, 172
μάτην, 137
μάχαιρα, 88, 154, 190, 192
μάχη, 154
μάχομαι, 154
μεγαλεῖος, 119
μεγαλειότης, 83, 119
μεγαλοπρεπής, 15
μεγαλοπρεπὴς δόξα, 71
μεγαλύνω, 79, 92, 120
μεγάλως, 57
μεγαλωσύνη, 71, 83
μέγας, 57, 83, 92
μέγεθος, 57
μεγιστάν, 83
μέγιστος, 83
μεθερμηνεύω, 57
μέθη, 178
μεθίστημι, 27, 106, 134
μεθοδεία, 176
μεθύσκομαι, 178
μέθυσος, 178
μεθύω, 53, 178
μείζων, 83, 102, 166
μέλας, 31, 198
μέλει, 9, 160
μελετάω, 116, 134, 160
μέλι, 63
μέλισσα, 85
μελίσσιος, 85
μέλλω, 107, 162
μέλος, 19, 113
μέλω, 38
μεμβράνα, 198
μέμφομαι, 149, 176
μεμψίμοιρος, 176
μέν, 34, 36
μέν...δέ, 7
μενοῦν, 35, 36, 136
μενοῦνγε, 36
μέντοι, 36
μέντοι...δέ, 36
μένω, 133
μερίζω, 12, 70, 114, 146
μέριμνα, 9

μεριμνάω, 9
μερίς, 39, 113
μερισμός, 70, 114
μεριστής, 114
μέρος, 113, 130, 131
μεσημβρία, 47, 163
μεσιτεύω, 6, 85
μεσίτης, 6, 65, 85
μεσονύκτιος, 163
μέσος, 98
μεσότοιχον, 50, 190
μεσουράνημα, 76
μεσόω, 163
Μεσσίας, 133
μεστός, 36, 55, 67
μεστόω, 67
μετά, 99, 122, 163
μεταβαίνω, 70, 134
μεταβάλλομαι, 38
μετάγω, 20
μεταδίδωμι, 69
μετάθεσις, 27, 71
μεταίρω, 71, 134
μετακαλέομαι, 24
μεταλαμβάνω, 56, 130
μετάλημψις, 130
μεταλλάσσω, 28, 56, 136
μεταμέλομαι, 38, 140
μεταμορφόω, 27, 65, 135
μετανοέω, 38
μετάνοια, 38
μεταξύ, 98, 162, 195
μεταπέμπομαι, 145
μεταστρέφω, 27
μετασχηματίζω, 27, 66, 135
μετατίθεμαι ἀπό, 2
μετατίθημι, 27, 71, 135
μετατρέπω, 27, 135
μετέπειτα, 162
μετέχω, 53, 146
μετεωρίζομαι, 9
μετοικεσία, 151
μετοικίζω, 134, 151
μετοχή, 12
μέτοχος, 13
μετρέω, 70, 103
μετρητής, 104

μετριοπαθέω, 184
μετρίως, 150
μέτρον, 103
μέτωπον, 19
μέχρι(ς), 98, 161, 171
μέχρις οὗ, 161
μή, 108
μή πως, 136
μηδαμῶς, 108
μηδέ, 108
μηδείς, 108
μηδέποτε, 108
μηδέπω, 108
μηκέτι, 108
μῆκος, 103
μηκύνομαι, 72
μηλωτή, 30
μήν, 161
μηνύω, 9
μήποτε, 27, 108, 136
μήπω, 108
μήπως, 136
μηρός, 19
μήτε, 108
μήτηρ, 89
μήτι, 108
μήτιγε, 35
μήτρα, 19
μητρολῴας, 89
μιαίνω, 48, 183
μίασμα, 48, 183
μιασμός, 48
μίγμα, 104, 105
μίγνυμι, 105
μικρός, 84, 103, 150, 165
μιμέομαι, 83
μιμητής, 83
μιμνήσκομαι, 104
μισέω, 179
μισθαποδοσία, 141
μισθαποδότης, 141
μισθός, 38, 77, 141
μισθόω, 77
μίσθωμα, 77
μνᾶ, 106
μνεία, 104
μνῆμα, 67
μνημεῖον, 22, 67, 104

244

Greek Index

μνήμη, 104
μνημονεύω, 104
μνημόσυνον, 104
μνηστεύω, 103
μογιλάλος, 148
μόδιος, 36
μοιχαλίς, 181
μοιχάω, 181
μοιχεία, 181
μοιχός, 181
μόλις, 10, 168
μολύνω, 48, 183
μολυσμός, 183
μομφή, 33
μόνας, 7, 171
μονή, 3
μονογενής, 171
μονόομαι, 2, 7
μονόφθαλμος, 18
μορφή, 65
μορφόω, 65
μόρφωσις, 65
μοσχοποιέω, 83
μόσχος, 7
μουσικός, 106, 151
μόχθος, 166
μυελός, 19
μυέω, 93
μυθέομαι, 54
μῦθος, 48
μυκάομαι, 151
μυκτηρίζω, 105, 177
μυλικός, 22
μύλινος, 22
μύλος, 22
μυριάς, 109
μυρίζω, 115
μύριοι, 85, 109
μύρον, 115
μυστήριον, 77
μυωπάζω, 64
μώλωψ, 197
μωμάομαι, 39, 176
μῶμος, 48, 183
μωραίνω, 63, 157
μωρία, 63
μωρολογία, 177
μωρός, 63

ναί, 108
ναός, 21
νάρδος, 116
ναυαγέω, 142
ναύκληρος, 142
ναῦς, 142
ναύτης, 142
νεανίας, 102
νεανίσκος, 102
νεκρός, 46, 170, 172
νεκρόω, 27
νέκρωσις, 46
νεομηνία, 61
νέος, 108, 165
νεότης, 164
νεύω, 148
νέφος, 40
νεφρός, 127
νεωκόρος, 133
νεωτερικός, 164
νή, 26
νήθω, 30
νηπιάζω, 28
νήπιος, 28
νησίον, 92
νῆσος, 92
νηστεία, 53, 60, 61
νηστεύω, 60
νῆστις, 53, 60
νηφάλιος, 61, 188
νήφω, 160, 188
νίζω, 29, 96
νικάω, 35
νίκη, 35
νῖκος, 35
νιπτήρ, 29, 35
νίπτω, 29, 96, 185
νοέω, 159, 188, 194
νόημα, 127, 159
νόθος, 89
νομή, 8, 62
νομίζω, 41, 155
νομικός, 92, 95
νομίμως, 168
νόμισμα, 106
νομοδιδάσκαλος, 158
νομοθεσία, 92
νομοθετέομαι, 92

νομοθέτης, 92
νόμος, 32, 92, 198
νοσέω, 45, 147
νόσημα, 147
νόσος, 147
νοσσιά, 17
νοσσίον, 17
νοσσός, 17
νοσφίζομαι, 182
νότος, 47, 194
νουθεσία, 130, 158
νουθετέω, 130, 158
νουμηνία, 61
νουνεχῶς, 194
νοῦς, 127, 159
νύμφη, 89
νυμφίος, 89
νυμφών, 21
νῦν, 161
νυνί, 34
νυνὶ δέ, 34
νύξ, 42, 163
νύσσω, 116
νυστάζω, 150
νυχθήμερον, 163
νωθρός, 64, 180
νῶτος, 19

ξαίνω, 30
ξενία, 21, 193
ξενίζω, 64, 156, 193
ξενισμός, 156
ξενοδοχέω, 193
ξένος, 64, 193
ξέστης, 35
ξηραίνω, 51, 137, 147
ξηρός, 51, 92, 148, 191
ξύλινος, 196
ξύλον, 60, 88, 167, 192, 196
ξυράομαι, 41, 74

ὁ, 124
ὁ ἔσω ἄνθρωπος, 127
ὀγδοήκοντα, 109
ὄγδοος, 109
ὄγκος, 123
ὅδε, 124

Greek Index

ὁδεύω, 167
ὁδηγέω, 20, 93
ὁδηγός, 20, 72
ὁδοιπορέω, 167
ὁδοιπορία, 167
ὁδός, 16, 154, 167
ὀδούς, 19
ὀδυνάομαι, 9, 113, 175
ὀδύνη, 9
ὀδυρμός, 67
ὄζω, 150
ὅθεν, 26, 98
ὀθόνη, 30
ὀθόνιον, 30
οἶδα, 90, 104, 188, 194
οἰκεῖος, 44
οἰκέτης, 80
οἰκέω, 2
οἴκημα, 21
οἰκητήριον, 2
οἰκία, 22, 44, 126
οἰκιακός, 44
οἰκοδεσποτέω, 80
οἰκοδεσπότης, 125
οἰκοδομέω, 20, 101, 155
οἰκοδομή, 20, 101
οἰκοδόμος, 20, 80, 101
οἰκονομέω, 80
οἰκονομία, 80, 117, 197
οἰκονόμος, 13, 80
οἰκονόμος τῆς πόλεως, 4
οἶκος, 22, 44, 89, 126
οἰκουμένη, 39, 52, 171
οἰκουργός, 80
οἰκτιρμός, 100, 186
οἰκτίρμων, 100, 186
οἰκτίρω, 100, 186
οἴμαι, 155
οἰνοπότης, 178
οἶνος, 104, 118
οἰνοφλυγία, 178
οἷος, 29, 32
ὀκνέω, 150, 181
ὀκνηρός, 180
ὀκταήμερος, 163
ὀκτώ, 109
ὄλεθρος, 45
ὀλιγόπιστος, 50

ὀλίγος, 150
ὀλιγόψυχος, 48
ὀλιγωρέω, 179
ὀλίγως, 10
ὀλοθρευτής, 45
ὀλοθρεύω, 45
ὁλοκαύτωμα, 140
ὁλοκληρία, 75, 115
ὁλόκληρος, 6
ὀλολύζω, 40
ὅλος, 6, 34, 55, 105
ὁλοτελής, 34, 55
ὄλυνθος, 66
ὅλως, 69
ὄμβρος, 129, 164, 192
ὁμείρομαι, 100
ὁμιλέω, 37
ὁμιλία, 152
ὅμιλος, 40
ὄμμα, 19
ὀμνύω, 111
ὁμοθυμαδόν, 6
ὁμοιοπαθής, 44
ὅμοιος, 32
ὁμοιότης, 32
ὁμοιόω, 32
ὁμοίωμα, 32
ὁμοίως, 32
ὁμοίωσις, 32
ὁμολογέω, 34, 119, 124
ὁμολογία, 34
ὁμολογουμένως, 34
ὁμότεχνος, 101
ὁμοῦ, 195
ὁμόφρων, 160
ὁμῶς, 32, 142
ὅμως, 7, 32, 142
ὅμως μέντοι, 7
ὄναρ, 51
ὀνάριον, 8
ὀνειδίζω, 130, 176
ὀνειδισμός, 176
ὄνειδος, 84, 146
ὀνίνημι, 5, 55
ὄνομα, 29, 107, 120
ὀνομάζω, 90, 107
ὀνομάζω τὸ ὄνομα κυρίου, 120

ὄνος, 8
ὄντως, 69
ὄξος, 118
ὀξύς, 118, 165, 174
ὀπή, 78
ὄπισθεν, 97
ὀπίσω, 63, 97
ὁπλίζω, 122
ὅπλον, 55, 122, 192
ὁποῖος, 29, 142
ὅποτε, 163
ὅπου, 26, 97, 108, 125
ὀπτάνομαι, 144
ὀπτασία, 51
ὀπτός, 38
ὀπώρα, 66, 164
ὅπως, 80, 125, 136
ὅραμα, 51, 143
ὅρασις, 51, 143
ὁρατός, 143
ὁράω, 56, 93, 143, 160, 189, 194
ὀργή, 128, 173
ὀργίζω, 173
ὀργίλος, 173
ὀργυιά, 103
ὀρέγω, 44, 179, 181
ὀρεινή, 106
ὀρθότης, 168, 188
ὀρθοποδέω, 16
ὀρθός, 40
ὀρθοτομέω, 158
ὀρθρίζω, 163
ὀρθρινός, 163
ὄρθρος, 163
ὀρθῶς, 168
ὁρίζω, 12, 46
ὅριον, 131
ὁρκίζω, 56, 111
ὅρκος, 111, 124
ὁρκωμοσία, 111
ὁρμάω, 139
ὁρμή, 189
ὅρμημα, 189
ὁρμίζω, 143
ὄρνεον, 17
ὄρνις, 17
ὁροθεσία, 131

Greek Index

ὅρος, 106
ὅρος, 108, 131
ὀρύσσω, 47, 59
ὀρφανός, 2, 89
ὀρχέομαι, 106
ὅς, ἥ, ὅ, 124
ὁσάκις ἐάν, 163
ὅσιος, 43, 185
ὁσιότης, 43, 185
ὁσίως, 185
ὀσμή, 150
ὅσος, 102, 124, 162, 171
ὀστέον, 19
ὅστις, ἥτις, ὅτι, οἵτινες, αἵτινες, ἅτινα, 124
ὀστράκινος, 53
ὄσφρησις, 150
ὀσφῦς, 19
ὅταν, 162
ὅτε, 162
ὅτι, 26, 35, 124
οὔ, 108
οὗ, 97, 108, 125
οὐαί, 167
οὐδαμοῦ, 108
οὐδαμῶς, 108
οὐδέ, 108
οὐδείς, 108
οὐδέποτε, 108
οὐδέπω, 108
οὐκ, 108
οὐκέτι, 108
οὐκοῦν, 108
οὔκουν, 108
οὖν, 35, 136
οὔπω, 108
οὐρά, 19
οὐρανός, 76
οὖς, 19, 76
οὐσία, 126
οὔτε, 108
οὗτος, 124
οὕτως, 33, 57, 124, 145
οὐχ ὁ τυχών, 171
οὐχί, 108
ὀφειλέτης, 42, 107, 149
ὀφειλή, 42, 107
ὀφείλημα, 42, 107, 149

ὀφείλω, 42, 107, 149
ὄφελον, 107
ὄφελος, 5, 68, 184
ὀφθαλμοδουλία, 146
ὀφθαλμοὶ βεβαρημένοι, 150
ὀφθαλμοὶ καταβαρυνόμενοι, 150
ὀφθαλμός, 19, 144
ὄφις, 135
ὀφρῦς, 106
ὀχλέομαι, 167
ὀχλοποιέω, 40
ὄχλος, 40
ὀχύρωμα, 22
ὀψάριον, 62, 63
ὀψία, 163
ὄψιμος, 129, 164, 193
ὄψις, 19
ὀψώνιον, 38, 141

παγιδεύω, 80, 159
παγίς, 24, 42, 80
πάθημα, 44, 113
παθητός, 113
πάθος, 44, 182
παιδαγωγός, 73
παιδάριον, 28
παιδεία, 127, 158, 188
παιδευτής, 127, 158
παιδεύω, 127, 158, 188
παιδιόθεν, 164
παιδίον, 28, 89
παιδίσκη, 84
παίζω, 36
παῖς, 28, 84, 89
παίω, 78, 116
πάλαι, 161
παλαιός, 111, 161, 165
παλαιὸς ἄνθρωπος, 16
παλαιότης, 111, 165
παλαιόω, 165
πάλη, 154
παλιγγενεσία, 28, 38, 108, 135
πάλιν, 7, 36, 162
παμπληθεί, 6

πανδοχεῖον, 22
πανδοχεύς, 22
πανήγυρις, 61
πανοικεί, 44
πανοπλία, 192
πανουργία, 181
πανοῦργος, 181
πανταχῇ, 97
πανταχοῦ, 97
παντελής, 34, 166
πάντῃ, 97
πάντοθεν, 98
παντοκράτωρ, 71
πάντοτε, 166
πάντως, 27, 35
παρ αὐτοῦ, 44
παρά, 23, 66, 99, 102, 122
παραβαίνω, 177
παραβάλλω, 142
παράβασις, 177, 180
παραβάτης, 177
παραβιάζομαι, 172
παραβιάζομαι, 33
παραβολεύομαι, 42
παραβολή, 49, 114
παραγγελία, 32
παραγγέλλω, 32
παραγίνομαι, 32
παράγω, 40, 70
παραδειγματίζω, 146
παράδεισος, 76
παραδέχομαι, 3, 193
παραδίδωμι, 17, 69, 158
παραδίδωμι τὸ πνεῦμα, 47
παράδοξος, 171
παράδοσις, 158
παραζηλόω, 178
παραθαλάσσιος, 92
παραθεωρέω, 43
παραθήκη, 25
παραινέω, 5
παραιτέομαι, 11, 131
παρακαθέζομαι, 150
παρακαθήκη, 105
παρακαλέω, 24, 54, 86, 172
παρακαλύπτομαι, 77
παράκειμαι, 122

Greek Index

παράκλησις, 54
παράκλητος, 71, 77, 153
παρακοή, 177
παρακοινάομαι, 152
παρακολουθέω, 63, 74, 93
παρακούω, 82, 177
παρακύπτω, 17, 93, 144
παραλαμβάνω, 20, 93, 158, 193
παραλέγομαι, 142
παράλιος, 92
παραλλαγή, 28, 47
παραλογίζομαι, 176
παραλύομαι, 147
παραλυτικός, 147
παραμένω, 133
παραμυθέομαι, 54
παραμυθία, 54
παραμύθιον, 54
παρανομέω, 177, 180
παρανομία, 180
παραπικραίνω, 129
παραπικρασμός, 129
παραπίπτω, 2
παραπλέω, 142
παραπλήσιος, 33
παραπλησίως, 33
παραπορεύομαι, 40
παράπτωμα, 149, 178
παραρρέω, 50
παράσημος, 142, 148
παρασκευάζω, 80, 122
παρασκευή, 164
παρατεινω, 134, 150
παρατηρέω, 41, 144
παρατήρησις, 144
παρατίθημι, 25, 57, 69, 168
παρατυγχάνω, 189
παραυτίκα, 165
παραφέρω, 50, 134
παραφρονέω, 85
παραφρονία, 85
παραχειμάζω, 164
παραχειμασία, 164
παραχρῆμα, 165
πάρδαλις, 8
παρεδρεύω, 146

πάρειμι, 32
παρεισάγω, 74
παρείσακτος, 151
παρεισδύω, 151
παρεισέρχομαι, 151
παρεισφέρω, 169
παρεκτός, 47
παρεμβάλλω, 128, 191
παρεμβολή, 22, 29
παρενοχλέω, 167
παρεπίδημος, 64
παρέρχομαι, 32, 40, 71, 165, 177
πάρεσις, 43
παρέχω, 56, 74
παρηγορία, 54, 77
παρθενία, 18
παρθένος, 102, 103, 196
παρίημι, 148
παρίστημι, 69, 126, 153, 168
πάροδος, 40
παροικέω, 2, 151
παροικία, 151
πάροικος, 44, 64
παροιμία, 48
πάροινος, 178
παροίχομαι, 165
παρομοιάζω, 33
παρόμοιος, 33
παροξύνω, 173
παροξυσμός, 174
παροργίζω, 173
παροργισμός, 173
παροτρύνω, 79
παρουσία, 32
παροψίς, 35
παρρησία, 39
παρρησιάζομαι, 39, 152, 183
πᾶς, 6, 29, 55, 105
πάσχα, 8, 61
πάσχω, 57, 113
πατάσσω, 78, 88
πατέω, 35, 123, 190, 197
πατήρ, 71, 83, 89, 114
πατριά, 39, 89
πατριάρχης, 89

πατρικός, 89
πατρίς, 131
πατρολῴας, 89
πατροπαράδοτος, 158
πατρῷος, 89
παύω, 26
παχύνομαι, 64
πέδη, 60
πεδινός, 138
πεζεύω, 190
πεζῇ, 19
πειθαρχέω, 186
πειθός, 171
πείθω, 63, 171, 183, 186
πείθω τὴν καρδίαν, 39
πεινάω, 44, 53, 182
πειράζω, 159, 168
πειράζων, 46
πειρασμός, 159
πειραω, 168
πεισμονή, 171
πέλαγος, 191
πελεκίζω, 88
πέμπτος, 109
πέμπω, 25, 145
πένης, 118
πενθερά, 89
πενθερός, 89
πενθέω, 40
πένθος, 40
πενιχρός, 118
πεντάκις, 109
πεντακισχίλιοι, 109
πεντακόσιοι, 109
πέντε, 109
πεντεκαιδέκατος, 109
πεντήκοντα, 109
πεντηκοστή, 61
περαίνω, 34, 145
περαιτέρω, 7
πέραν, 98
πέρας, 34, 145
περί, 64, 99, 123, 138, 163
περιάγω, 20, 167
περιαιρέω, 143
περιαστράπτω, 96
περιβάλλω, 31
περιβλέπομαι, 144

περιβόλαιον, 30
περιδέω, 60
περίεργος, 181
περιέρχομαι, 40, 167
περιέχω, 24, 56, 145
περιζώννυμαι τὴν ὀσφύν, 121
περιζώννυμι, 31
περίθεσις, 31
περιΐστημι, 13, 153
περικάθαρμα, 48
περικαλύπτω, 39
περίκειμαι, 31, 138
περικεφαλαία, 192
περικρατής, 37
περικρύβω, 77
περικυκλόω, 24
περιλάμπω, 96
περιλείπομαι, 2
περίλυπος, 140
περιμένω, 133
πέριξ, 98
περιοικέω, 2, 108
περίοικος, 108
περιουσία, 171, 192
περιούσιος, 125, 171
περιοχή, 49
περιπατέω, 15, 190
περιπατέω τοῖς ἴχνεσιν, 83
περιπείρω, 116
περιπίπτω, 24, 37, 56
περιποιέομαι, 4, 141
περιποίησις, 4
περιραντίζω, 97
περιρήγνυμι, 153
περισπάομαι, 9
περισσεία, 102, 192
περίσσευμα, 192
περισσεύω, 102, 192
περισσος, 102
περισσός, 108, 170, 192
περισσότερος, 102
περισσοτέρως, 102
περιστερά, 17
περιτέμνω, 43
περιτίθημι, 128
περιτομή, 43
περιτομῆς, 170

περιτρέπω, 27
περιτρέχω, 139
περιφέρω, 25
περιφρονέω, 86, 179
περίχωρος, 131
περίψημα, 48
περπερεύομαι, 174
πέρυσι(ν), 161
πετεινόν, 17
πέτομαι, 17
πέτρα, 53
πετρῶδες, 53
πήγανον, 104, 117, 152
πηγή, 191
πηγὴ αἵματος, 148
πήγνυμι, 20, 60, 88
πηδάλιον, 142
πηδάω, 87
πηλίκος, 83, 92
πηλός, 52
πήρα, 36
πῆχυς, 103
πιάζω, 10
πιέζω, 123
πιθανολογία, 152
πικραίνω, 157, 179
πικρός, 157, 175, 178
πικρῶς, 140
πίμπλημι, 54, 55, 66, 67
πίμπραμαι, 147
πινακίδιον, 198
πίναξ, 35
πίνω, 53, 96
πιότης, 117, 173
πιπράσκω, 23
πίπτω, 27, 45, 46, 56, 59, 74, 84
πιστεύω, 25, 183
πιστικός, 30, 173
πίστις, 124, 183
πιστός, 27, 28, 183
πλανάω, 50, 99, 175
πλάνη, 99, 175, 181
πλανήτης, 167
πλάνος, 99, 175
πλάξ, 198
πλάσμα, 66, 83
πλάσσω, 66, 101

πλαστός, 59
πλατεῖα, 154
πλάτος, 103
πλατύνω, 111
πλατύς, 103
πλέγμα, 30, 74
πλείων, 102
πλέκω, 74
πλεονάζω, 84, 102, 192
πλεονέκτης, 44, 179
πλεονεξία, 44, 179
πλευρά, 19
πλέω, 142
πλέων, 143
πληγή, 78, 147, 167, 197
πλῆθος, 40, 102
πληθύνω, 84
πλήκτης, 175
πλήμμυρα, 62
πλήν, 36
πλήρης, 6, 66, 102
πληροφορέω, 34, 66
πληρόω, 7, 34, 36, 54, 55, 66, 67, 126
πλήρωμα, 7, 54, 67
πλησίον, 98, 108
πλησμονή, 36, 192
πλήσσω, 175
πλοιάριον, 142
πλοῖον, 142
πλόος, 142
πλούσιος, 192
πλουσίως, 58, 192
πλουτέω, 70, 192
πλουτίζω, 192
πλοῦτος, 192
πλύνω, 29, 97
πνεῦμα, 46, 47, 69, 71, 126, 152, 194
πνεῦμα ἀκάθαρτον, 46
πνεῦμα πονηρόν, 46
πνευματικός, 16, 127, 152
πνευματικῶς, 49, 127, 152
πνέω, 152, 194
πνίγω, 28, 47, 123
πνικτός, 28, 123
πνοή, 194
ποδήρης, 30

Greek Index

πόθεν, 26, 80, 98
ποιέω, 12, 25, 68, 101, 196
ποιέω τὸ ἱκανόν, 3
ποίημα, 101
ποίησις, 49, 196
ποιητής, 196
ποικίλος, 47
ποιμαίνω, 8, 72, 138
ποιμή, 8, 133
ποίμνη, 8
ποιός, 29
ποῖος, 29, 125
ποῖος, α, ον, 125
πολεμέω, 154, 190
πόλεμος, 154, 190
πόλις, 29
πολιτάρχης, 138
πολιτεία, 29, 39
πολίτευμα, 39
πολιτεύομαι, 16
πολίτης, 29
πολλάκις, 109, 111
πολλαπλασίων, 102
πολυλογία, 151
πολυμερής, 113
πολυμερῶς, 80
πολυποίκιλος, 47
πολύς, 57, 102, 111
πολύσπλαγχνος, 100
πολυτελής, 173
πολύτιμος, 173
πολυτρόπως, 29, 80
πόμα, 63
πονηρία, 14, 183
πονηρός, 46
πονηρός, 14, 147, 149, 178
πόνος, 113, 166
πορεία, 68, 167
πορεύομαι, 15, 70, 167
πορθέω, 45
πορισμός, 68
πορνεία, 181
πορνεύω, 181
πόρνη, 181
πόρνος, 181
πόρρω, 98
πόρρωθεν, 98, 161

πορρώτερον, 98
πορφύρα, 30
πορφυρόπωλις, 68
πορφυροῦς, 30, 31
ποσάκις, 111
πόσις, 53, 63
ποσός, 102
πόσος, 57, 102
ποταμός, 191
ποταμοφόρητος, 25, 62
ποταπός, 29
ποτέ, 56
πότε, 163
πότερον…ἤ, 82
ποτήριον, 35
ποτίζω, 53, 59
πότος, 178
πού, 10
ποῦ, 10, 97, 108, 125
ποῦ φανεῖται, 74
πούς, 19
πρᾶγμα, 94, 196
πραγματεία, 16, 196
πραγματεύομαι, 68
πραιτώριον, 22, 191
πράκτωρ, 139
πρᾶξις, 196
πρασιά, 40
πράσσω, 5, 16, 23, 196
πραϋπάθεια, 183
πραΰς, 183
πραΰτης, 183
πρέπω, 125, 188
πρεσβεία, 139
πρεσβεύω, 139
πρεσβυτέριον, 39
πρεσβύτερος, 102, 133, 166
πρεσβύτης, 102
πρεσβῦτις, 195
πρηνής, 126
πρίζω, 41, 174
πρίν, 161
πρό, 83, 99, 123, 161, 163
πρὸ θυρῶν, 162
πρὸ παντὸς τοῦ αἰῶνος, 166
πρὸ χρόνων αἰωνίων, 166

προάγω, 20, 74, 121
προαιρέομαι, 46
προαιτιάομαι, 176
προακούω, 76
προαμαρτάνω, 149
προαύλιον, 21
προβαίνω, 121
προβαίνω ἐν ἡμέραις, 165
προβάλλω, 72
προβατικός, 8
πρόβατον, 8, 29
προβιβάζω, 172
προβλέπομαι, 126
προβλέπω, 28
προγίνομαι, 74
προγινώσκω, 28, 90
πρόγνωσις, 90
πρόγονος, 89
προγράφω, 9, 198
πρόδηλος, 91
προδίδωμι, 69
προδότης, 17
πρόδρομος, 73
προελπίζω, 79, 183
προενάρχομαι, 15
προεπαγγέλλομαι, 124
προέρχομαι, 20, 121
προετοιμάζω, 121
προευαγγελίζομαι, 9
προέχω, 5
προηγέομαι, 102, 169
πρόθεσις, 116
προθεσμία, 164
προθυμία, 52, 153
πρόθυμος, 52, 153
προθύμως, 52
πρόϊμος, 129, 164, 193
προΐστημι, 72, 77
προκαλέω, 173
προκαταγγέλλω, 121
προκαταρτίζω, 121
προκηρύσσω, 120
προκοπή, 27
προκόπτω, 27, 84, 165, 196
πρόκριμα, 46, 179
προκυρόω, 119
προλαμβάνω, 159

προλέγω, 121, 130, 151
προμαρτύρομαι, 121
προμελετάω, 116
προμεριμνάω, 9
προνοέω, 25, 117, 126, 159
πρόνοια, 159
προοράω, 90, 143
προορίζω, 46
προπάσχω, 113
προπάτωρ, 89
προπέμπω, 4, 145
προπετής, 180
προπορεύομαι, 20, 121
πρός, 5, 33, 99, 123, 163, 171
πρὸς καιρὸν (ὥρας), 165
πρὸς κέντρα λακτίζω, 135
πρὸς ὀλίγον, 165
προσάββατον, 164
προσαγορεύω, 107
προσάγω, 10, 20
προσαιτέω, 11
προσαίτης, 11
προσαναβαίνω, 11
προσαναλίσκω, 152
προσαναπληρόω, 126
προσανατίθεμαι, 11
προσαπειλέομαι, 160
προσδαπανάω, 152
προσδέομαι, 118
προσδέχομαι, 3, 193
προσδοκάω, 9, 79
προσδοκία, 79
προσεάω, 7
προσεγγίζω, 10
προσεργάζομαι, 68
προσέρχομαι, 10
προσευχή, 120
προσεύχομαι, 120
προσέχω, 134, 160, 191
προσηλόω, 60
προσήλυτος, 29
πρόσκαιρος, 165
προσκαλέομαι, 24
προσκαρτερέω, 12, 134, 146, 169, 183
προσκαρτέρησις, 169

προσκεφάλαιον, 67
προσκληρόομαι, 87
προσκλίνω, 87
πρόσκλισις, 178
προσκολλάω, 87
πρόσκομμα, 111, 149
προσκοπή, 111, 149, 167
προσκόπτω, 78, 111
προσκυλίω, 137
προσκυνέω, 120, 126
προσκυνητής, 120
προσλαλέω, 151
προσλαμβάνομαι, 12, 20, 157
προσμένω, 133
προσορμίζομαι, 143
προσοφείλω, 42
προσοχθίζω, 174
πρόσπεινος, 53
προσπήγνυμι, 88
προσπίπτω, 78, 120, 126
προσποιέω, 83
προσπορεύομαι, 10
προσρήγνυμι, 78
προστάσσω, 32
προστάτης, 77
προστάτις, 77, 126
προστίθημι, 5, 67, 69, 134
προστρέχω, 139
προσφάγιον, 62, 63
πρόσφατος, 108
προσφάτως, 161
προσφέρω, 20, 25, 70
προσφιλής, 3
προσφορά, 140
προσφωνέω, 24, 147, 152
πρόσχυσις, 97
προσψαύω, 166
προσωπολημπτέω, 178
προσωπολήμπτης, 178
προσωπολημψία, 178
πρόσωπον, 19, 97, 115, 144
προτείνω, 153
πρότερος, 15, 109, 145, 161
προτίθεμαι, 25, 116
προτρέπομαι, 172

προτρέχω, 121, 139
προϋπάρχω, 17
πρόφασις, 43, 176
προφητεία, 126
προφητεύω, 126
προφήτης, 126, 133
προφητικός, 126
προφθάνω, 161
προχειρίζομαι, 28
προχειροτονέω, 28
πρύμνα, 142
πρωΐ, 163
πρωΐα, 163
πρωϊνός, 163
πρῷρα, 142
πρωτεύω, 83
πρωτοκαθεδρία, 79, 83
πρωτοκλισία, 79
πρῶτος, 83, 109, 161, 184
πρωτοστάτης, 84
πρωτοτόκια, 89
πρωτότοκος, 83, 89
πταίω, 149, 178
πτέρνα, 19
πτερύγιον, 21
πτέρυξ, 19
πτηνόν, 17
πτόησις, 61
πτύον, 60
πτύρομαι, 61
πτύσμα, 18
πτύσσω, 198
πτύω, 106
πτῶμα, 18, 149
πτῶσις, 45, 84
πτωχεία, 118
πτωχεύω, 118
πτωχός, 118, 172
πτωχὸς τῷ πνεύματι, 185
πυγμή, 19
πυκνός, 111
πυκνῶς, 111
πυκτεύω, 36
πύλη, 21
πυλών, 21
πυνθάνομαι, 11, 93
πῦρ, 22
πυρά, 22

Greek Index

πύργος, 22
πυρέσσω, 147
πυρετός, 147
πύρινος, 32
πυρόομαι, 22, 44, 80, 181
πυρράζω, 32
πυρρός, 32
πύρωσις, 22, 113
πωλέω, 23
πῶλος, 8
πώποτε, 56
πωρόω, 82
πώρωσις, 82, 155, 178
πῶς, 125

ῥαββί, 158
ῥάββι, 138
ῥαββουνι, 158
ῥαβδίζω, 78
ῥάβδος, 8, 60
ῥαβδοῦχος, 87, 139
ῥᾴδιος, 149
ῥᾳδιούργημα, 149
ῥᾳδιουργία, 149
ῥαίνω, 97
ῥακά, 64
ῥάκος, 30
ῥαντίζομαι τὴν καρδίαν, 185
ῥαντίζω, 30, 97, 185
ῥαντισμός, 97
ῥαπίζω, 78
ῥάπισμα, 78
ῥαφανίς, 63
ῥαφή, 31
ῥαφίς, 31
ῥεδή, 173
ῥέω, 62, 97
ῥῆγμα, 45
ῥήγνυμι, 78
ῥήγνυμι, 147, 153
ῥῆμα, 152, 196
ῥήτωρ, 94
ῥητῶς, 152
ῥίζα, 26, 117
ῥιζόομαι, 62, 155
ῥιπή, 96
ῥιπίζομαι, 6

ῥίπτω, 48, 128, 143, 161
ῥοιζηδόν, 151
ῥομφαία, 190, 192
ῥύμη, 154
ῥύομαι, 141
ῥυπαίνομαι, 48, 183
ῥυπαίνω, 48
ῥυπαρία, 48
ῥυπαρός, 48
ῥύπος, 48
ῥύσις, 62, 97
ῥύσις αἵματος, 148
ῥυτίς, 19
ῥώννυμαι, 49, 75

σαβαχθανι, 2
σαββατισμός, 164
σάββατον, 164
σαββάτου ὁδός, 103
σαγήνη, 142
σαίνομαι, 50, 62
σαλεύω, 6, 10, 129
σάλος, 191
σάλπιγξ, 106
σαλπίζω, 106
σαλπιστής, 106
σανδάλιον, 30
σανίς, 21
σαπρός, 14, 197
σάπφιρος, 121
σαργάνη, 36
σάρδιον, 121
σαρκικός, 16, 116, 127
σάρκινος, 16, 115, 116
σαρκὸς θέλημα, 44, 182
σάρξ, 18, 19, 66, 95, 115, 127
σὰρξ καὶ αἷμα, 115
σαρόω, 38
σατανᾶς, 46
σάτον, 103
σβέννυμι, 22, 27
σεαυτοῦ, σεαυτῷ, σεαυτόν, 124
σεβάζομαι, 120
σέβασμα, 120
σεβαστός, 138
σέβομαι, 120

σειρά, 60
σεισμός, 6, 192
σείω, 6, 9, 175, 182
σεληνιάζομαι, 147
σεμίδαλις, 63
σεμνός, 187
σεμνότης, 187
σημαίνω, 57
σημεῖον, 148
σημειόομαι, 104
σήμερον, 161
σήπω, 137
σής, 85
σθενόω, 155
σιαγών, 19
σιγάω, 148, 187
σιγή, 148
σίδηρος, 104
σιδηροῦς, 104
σικάριος, 89
σίκερα, 118
σιμικίνθιον, 30
σίναπι, 117, 152
σινδών, 30
σινιάζω, 38
σινίον, 38
σιρικός, 30
σιτευτός, 8, 173
σιτίον, 38, 63, 66
σιτιστός, 8
σιτομέτριον, 63
σῖτος, 66, 117
σιωπάω, 24, 148
σκανδαλίζω, 50, 111, 149, 178
σκάνδαλον, 81, 111, 149
σκάπτω, 45, 47, 59
σκάφη, 142
σκέλος, 19
σκέπας, 30
σκέπασμα, 30
σκευάζω, 121
σκευή, 55
σκεῦος, 18, 35, 38, 55, 89, 126, 192
σκεῦος κτάομαι, 18
σκηνή, 22
σκηνοπηγία, 61

σκηνοποιός, 22
σκῆνος, 18
σκηνόω, 3
σκήνωμα, 3, 18, 22
σκιά, 42, 114
σκιρτάω, 75, 87
σκληροκαρδία, 155
σκληρός, 62, 119, 175, 189
σκληρότης, 155, 178
σκληροτράχηλος, 155
σκληρύνω, 155
σκολιός, 40, 181
σκόλοψ, 118
σκόλοψ τῇ σαρκί, 167
σκοπέω, 24, 117, 144, 191
σκοπός, 34
σκορπίζω, 49, 70, 152
σκορπίος, 85
σκοτεινός, 42
σκοτία, 14, 42
σκοτίζομαι, 42, 64
σκοτόομαι, 42, 64
σκότος, 14, 42
σκύβαλον, 48
σκυθρωπός, 140
σκύλλω, 167
σκῦλον, 118, 140, 182
σκύμνος, 8
σκωληκόβρωτος, 147
σκώληξ, 85
σμαράγδινος, 121
σμάραγδος, 121
σμύρνα, 116
σορός, 67
σός, 124
σουδάριον, 30
σοφία, 90, 194
σοφίζω, 90, 189, 194
σοφός, 90, 194
σπάομαι, 127
σπαράσσω, 147, 153
σπαργανόω, 31
σπαταλάω, 180
σπάω, 43
σπεῖρα, 190
σπείρω, 59, 153
σπεκουλάτωρ, 9, 72, 88

σπένδω, 65, 140, 187
σπέρμα, 66, 89
σπερμολόγος, 82, 177
σπεύδω, 52, 165
σπήλαιον, 78, 182
σπιλάς, 42, 48
σπίλος, 48, 183
σπιλόω, 48
σπλαγχνίζομαι, 19, 100, 127, 186
σπογγίζω, 30, 96
σπόγγος, 96
σποδός, 22
σπορά, 89
σπόριμος, 59
σπόρος, 66
σπουδάζω, 52, 169
σπουδαῖος, 52
σπουδαίως, 52, 169
σπουδή, 52, 169
σπουδὴν εἰσφέρειν, 169
σπυρίς, 36
στάγμος, 35
στάδιον, 22, 103
στασιάζω, 129
στασιαστής, 129
στάσις, 10, 129, 179
στατήρ, 106
σταυρός, 88
σταυρόω, 88
στάχυς, 66
στέγη, 21, 114
στέγω, 114
στεῖρα, 18
στέλλομαι, 13
στέλλομαι ἀπό, 131
στέλλω, 122, 131
στέμμα, 4
στεναγμός, 40
στενάζω, 33, 40
στενός, 33, 40, 103, 167
στενοχωρέομαι, 37, 167
στενοχωρία, 167
στέργω, 99
στερεός, 141, 155
στερεόω, 155
στερέωμα, 155
στέφανος, 4, 141

στεφανόω, 79, 141
στῆθος, 19
στήκω, 153
στηριγμός, 141, 155
στηρίζω, 56, 60, 62, 128, 141, 155
στηρίζω τὸ πρόσωπον, 46
στιβάς, 117
στίγμα, 148
στιγμή, 165
στίλβω, 96
στοά, 21
στοιχεῖα, 54, 115
στοιχέω, 15
στοιχέω τοῖς ἴχνεσιν, 83
στολή, 30
στόμα, 19
στόμα πρὸς στόμα, 97
στόμαχος, 19
στρατεία, 190
στράτευμα, 190
στρατεύομαι, 190
στρατεύω, 190
στρατηγός, 139
στρατιὰ οὐράνιος, 7
στρατιώτης, 139, 190
στρατολογέω, 190
στρατόπεδον, 190
στρεβλόω, 57
στρέφω, 2, 27, 38, 137
στρηνιάω, 180, 182
στρῆνος, 180
στρουθίον, 17
στρώννυμι, 80, 153
στυγητός, 179
στυγνάζω, 42, 140
στῦλος, 21, 73
σύ, 124
συγγένεια, 44
συγγενής, 29, 44
συγγενίς, 44
συγγνώμη, 6, 7
συγκάθημαι, 149
συγκαθίζω, 150
συγκακοπαθέω, 113
συγκακουχέομαι, 113
συγκαλέω, 24
συγκαλύπτω, 77

253

Greek Index

συγκάμπτω τὸν νῶτον, 113
συγκαταβαίνω, 4
συγκατάθεσις, 6
συγκατατίθεμαι, 6
συγκαταψηφίζομαι, 109
συγκεράννυμι, 11, 105
συγκινέω, 79
συγκλείω, 142
συγκληρονόμος, 130
συγκοινωνέω, 12
συγκοινωνός, 12, 146
συγκομίζω, 67
συγκρίνω, 33, 57
συγκύπτω, 17
συγκυρία, 74
συγχαίρω, 75
συγχέω, 156
συγχράομαι, 12
σύγχυσις, 129
συζάω, 95, 135
συζεύγνυμι, 103
συζητέω, 37, 49
συζήτησις, 49
συζητητής, 49
σύζυγος, 13, 103
συζωοποιέω, 95, 135
συκάμινος, 167
συκῆ, 167
συκομορέα, 167
σῦκον, 66
συκοφαντέω, 176
συλαγωγέω, 24, 37, 118
συλάω, 182
συλλαλέω, 37
συλλαμβάνω, 17, 24, 144
συλλέγω, 157
συλλογίζομαι, 37
συλλυπέομαι, 140
συμβαίνω, 74
συμβάλλω, 10, 38, 49, 77, 160
συμβασιλεύω, 138
συμβιβάζω, 5, 46, 91, 104, 168
συμβουλεύω, 5, 117
συμβούλιον, 39, 117
σύμβουλος, 5

συμμαθητής, 63
συμμαρτυρέω, 195
συμμερίζω, 146
συμμέτοχος, 146
συμμιμητής, 83
συμμορφίζομαι, 65, 142
συμμορφόομαι, 65, 142
σύμμορφος, 65, 142
συμπαθέω, 100, 113
συμπαθής, 100
συμπαραγίνομαι, 12
συμπαρακαλέομαι, 54
συμπαραλαμβάνω, 20
συμπάρειμι, 3, 17
συμπάσχω, 113
συμπέμπω, 145
συμπεριλαμβάνω, 90
συμπίνω, 53
συμπίπτω, 43
συμπληρόω, 54, 142
συμπνίγω, 28, 47, 123, 168
συμπολίτης, 29
συμπορεύομαι, 4, 12
συμπόσιον, 40
συμπρεσβύτερος, 133
συμφέρω, 5, 12
σύμφημι, 6
σύμφορος, 5, 184
συμφυλέτης, 29
συμφύομαι, 72
σύμφυτος, 195
συμφωνέω, 6, 33
συμφώνησις, 6
συμφωνία, 6, 106, 151
συμψηφίζω, 109
σύμψυχος, 126
σύν, 123, 195
συνάγω, 12
συναγωγή, 12, 22, 29
συναγωνίζομαι, 13
συναθλέω, 166
συναθροίζω, 12
συναίρω, 4
συναιχμάλωτος, 84
συνακολουθέω, 63
συναλίζω, 13
συναλλάσσω, 65

συναναβαίνω, 4
συνανάκειμαι, 13
συναναμίγνυμι, 12, 105
συναναπαύομαι, 18, 136
συναντάω, 74
συναντιλαμβάνομαι, 77
συναπάγομαι, 12, 16, 50
συναποθνήσκω, 46
συναπόλλυμαι, 45
συναποστέλλω, 145
συνάπτω, 60
συναρμολογέομαι, 11
συναρπάζω, 145, 157
συναυλίζω, 13
συναυξάνομαι, 72
συνδέομαι, 11
σύνδεσμος, 60, 105
συνδοξάζομαι, 78
σύνδουλος, 85
συνδρομή, 12
συνεγείρω, 95, 135
συνείδησις, 90, 127
σύνειμι, 12
συνεισέρχομαι, 4
συνέκδημος, 4
συνεκλεκτός, 28
συνεπιμαρτυρέω, 195
συνεπιτίθημι, 13
συνέπομαι, 63
συνεργέω, 196
συνεργός, 101
συνέρχομαι, 4, 12, 18
συνεσθίω, 53
σύνεσις, 194
συνετός, 194
συνευδοκέω, 6
συνευωχέομαι, 53
συνεφίστημι, 13
συνέχης, 134
συνέχω, 10, 24, 37, 56, 72, 123, 134
συνήδομαι, 75
συνήθεια, 41
συνηλικιώτης, 164
συνῆλιξ, 164
συνθάπτομαι, 67
συνθλάομαι, 20
συνθλάω, 123

Greek Index

συνθλίβω, 123
συνίημι, 189, 194
συνίστημι, 105, 130, 153
συνοδεύω, 4
συνοδία, 4
σύνοιδα, 90
συνοικέω, 15
συνοικοδομέω, 20
συνομιλέω, 37
συνομορέω, 108
συνοράω, 93, 194
συνοχή, 9
συντάσσω, 32
συντέλεια, 54
συντελέω, 33, 54
συντέμνω, 54
συντηρέω, 104, 126
συντίθεμαι, 6
σύντομος, 165
συντόμως, 165
συντρέχω, 12, 15
συντρίβω, 20, 35, 123
σύντριμμα, 45
σύντροφος, 13, 89
συντυγχάνω, 10
συνυποκρίνομαι, 176
συνυπουργέω, 77
συνωδίνω, 113
συνωμοσία, 117
σύρω, 20, 127
συσπαράσσω, 147, 153
σύσσημον, 148
σύσσωμοι, 40
συστατικός, 130
συσταυρόομαι, 88
συστέλλω, 165, 197
συστενάζω, 40
συστοιχέω, 115
συστρατιώτης, 13
συστρέφω, 12
συστροφή, 117, 129
συσχηματίζω, 16
σφαγή, 88, 140
σφάγιον, 140
σφάζω, 88
σφόδρα, 58
σφοδρῶς, 58
σφραγίζω, 148, 198

σφραγίς, 69, 148, 198
σφυδρόν, 19
σχεδόν, 10
σχῆμα, 65, 116
σχίζω, 114, 153
σχίσμα, 49, 153
σχοινίον, 60
σχολάζω, 54, 164, 181
σχολή, 22
σῴζω, 75, 141
σῶμα, 18, 115
σωματικός, 18
σωματικῶς, 18, 69
σωρεύω, 169
σωτήρ, 141
σωτηρία, 141
σωτήριον, 141
σωφρονέω, 160, 194
σωφρονίζω, 158
σωφρονισμός, 188, 194
σωφρόνως, 188
σωφροσύνη, 61, 188, 194
σώφρων, 188

τὰ ἀγαθά, 192
τὰ ἔθνη, 170
τὰ παρόντα, 125
ταβέρνη, 22
τάγμα, 10
τακτός, 46
ταλαιπωρέω, 40
ταλαιπωρία, 167
ταλαίπωρος, 167
ταλαντιαῖος, 193
τάλαντον, 106, 193
ταλιθα, 28
ταμεῖον, 21
τάξις, 11, 29, 145
ταπεινός, 48, 146, 185
ταπεινοφροσύνη, 185
ταπεινόφρων, 185
ταπεινόω, 84, 103, 138, 146, 185
ταπείνωσις, 146, 185
ταράσσω, 6, 10, 129, 175
ταραχή, 6, 129
τάραχος, 10, 79
ταρταρόω, 76

τάσσω, 12, 26, 32, 55
ταῦρος, 7
ταφή, 67
τάφος, 67
ταχέως, 162, 165
ταχινός, 165
ταχύς, 165
τέ, 7
τέ...τέ, 7
τεῖχος, 190
τεκμήριον, 91
τέκνα φωτός, 28
τεκνογονέω, 17, 95
τεκνογονία, 17
τέκνον, 28, 89
τεκνοτροφέω, 25
τέκτων, 21, 102
τέλειος, 33, 115
τελειότης, 115
τελειόω, 26, 33, 54, 74, 115
τελείως, 55
τελείωσις, 66, 115
τελειωτής, 33
τελεσφορέω, 137
τελευτάω, 33, 46
τελευτή, 46
τελέω, 34, 54, 66, 74, 157, 187
τέλος, 34, 54, 136, 145, 158
τελώνης, 158
τελώνιον, 158
τέμνω, 41
τέρας, 148
τεσσαράκοντα, 109
τεσσαρακονταετής, 164
τέσσαρες, 109
τεσσαρεσκαιδέκατος, 109
τεταρταῖος, 163
τέταρτος, 109
τετράγωνος, 21
τετράδιον, 191
τετράκις, 109
τετρακισχίλιοι, 109
τετρακόσιοι, 109
τετράμηνος, 164
τετραπλόος, 110

Greek Index

τετραπλοῦς, 110
τετράπουν, 7
τετραρχέω, 138
τετράρχης, 138
τεφρόω, 23
τέχνη, 101
τεχνίτης, 101
τήκω, 96
τηλαυγῶς, 144
τηλίκος, 103
τηλικοῦτος, 92, 103
τὴν κεφαλὴν κλίνω, 136
τηρέω, 72, 126, 187
τήρησις, 22, 72, 187
τίθημι, 12, 25, 105, 128
τίθημι παρά, 69
τίθημι τὰ γόνατα, 90
τίκτω, 17, 72
τίλλω, 157
τιμάω, 38, 78
τιμή, 38, 78, 173, 187
τίμιος, 78, 173
τιμιότης, 192
τιμωρέω, 127
τιμωρία, 127
τίνω, 38, 57
τις, τι, 124
τίς, τί, 124
τίτλος, 198
τὸ βδέλυγμα τῆς
    ἐρημώσεως, 183
τὸ παρόν, 161
τὸ σκότος τὸ ἐξώτερον, 76
τοιγαροῦν, 136
τοίνυν, 136
τοιόσδε, 171
τοιοῦτος, 32, 125
τοιοῦτος, αὕτη, οὗτον,
    125
τοῖχος, 21
τοῖχος κεκονιαμένος, 176
τοκίζω, 105
τόκος, 105
τολμάω, 39
τολμηρότερον, 39
τολμητής, 39
τομός, 41, 118
τόξον, 192

τοπάζιον, 121
τόπος, 39, 119, 131
τόπος διθάλασσος, 92
τοσοῦτος, 102, 171
τότε, 161
τοὐναντίον, 36
τράγος, 8
τράπεζα, 67, 105
τραπεζίτης, 105
τραῦμα, 197
τραυματίζω, 197
τραχηλίζομαι, 91
τράχηλον ὑποτίθημι, 42
τράχηλος, 19, 91
τραχύνω, 138
τραχύς, 138
τρεῖς, 109
τρέμω, 6, 61, 79, 187
τρέφω, 25, 53, 126
τρέχω, 139
τρῆμα, 31, 78
τριάκοντα, 109
τριακόσιοι, 109
τρίβολος, 117, 118
τρίβος, 154
τρίβω, 164
τριετία, 164
τρίζω τοὺς ὀδόντας, 106
τρίκλινος, 80
τρίμηνον, 164
τρίς, 109
τρίστεγον, 21
τρισχίλιοι, 109
τρίτον, 109
τρίτος, 109
τρίχινος, 19, 74
τρόμος, 6
τροπή, 137
τρόπος, 80
τρόπος, 15
τροποφορέω, 114
τροφή, 63
τροφός, 25
τρόφος, 63
τροχιὰς ὀρθὰς ποιέω τοῖς
    ποσίν, 16
τροχός, 138, 139, 145
τρύβλιον, 35

τρυγάω, 60
τρυγών, 17
τρυμαλιά, 31, 116
τρυπάω, 31, 116
τρυφάω, 180
τρυφή, 180
τρώγω, 53
τυγχάνω, 4, 56, 119, 171
τυμπανίζω, 89
τυπικῶς, 114
τύπος, 19, 29, 65, 82, 114
τύπτω, 78, 114, 197
τυρβάζω, 9, 175
τυφλός, 18, 64
τυφλόω, 64
τυφόομαι, 174
τυφόω, 23
τύφω, 23, 174
τυφωνικός, 193, 194

ὑακίνθινος, 32
ὑάκινθος, 121
ὑάλινος, 21
ὕαλος, 21, 40, 121
ὑβρίζω, 175, 177
ὕβρις, 175, 177, 197
ὑβριστής, 175, 177
ὑγιαίνω, 75, 168
ὑγιής, 75, 168
ὑγρός, 96
ὑδρία, 35
ὑδροποτέω, 53
ὑδρωπικός, 147
ὕδωρ, 191
ὑετός, 129, 191, 192
υἱοθεσία, 25
υἱοὶ τῆς βασιλείας, 28
υἱοὶ τοῦ αἰῶνος τούτου,
    170
υἱοὶ τῶν ἀνθρώπων, 115
υἱός, 28, 89, 115
ὕλη, 167, 196
ὑμέτερος, 124
ὑμνέω, 106
ὕμνος, 106
ὑπάγω, 70
ὑπακοή, 186
ὑπακούω, 186

ὕπανδρος, 103, 187
ὑπαντάω, 10, 191
ὑπάντησις, 10
ὕπαρξις, 125
ὑπάρχω, 17, 125
ὑπείκω, 186, 199
ὑπεναντίος, 79
ὑπέρ, 64, 83, 102, 123
ὑπεραίρω, 129, 174
ὑπέρακμος, 164
ὑπεράνω, 83, 98
ὑπεραυξάνω, 57
ὑπερβαίνω, 149
ὑπερβαλλόντως, 102
ὑπερβάλλω, 102
ὑπερβολή, 102
ὑπερέκεινα, 97
ὑπερεκπερισσοῦ, 102
ὑπερεκτείνω, 169
ὑπερεκχύννομαι, 63, 96
ὑπερεντυγχάνω, 85, 120
ὑπερέχω, 37, 173
ὑπερηφανία, 174
ὑπερήφανος, 174
ὑπερλίαν, 57
ὑπερνικάω, 35
ὑπέρογκος, 174
ὑπεροράω, 43
ὑπεροχή, 83
ὑπερπερισσεύω, 102, 192
ὑπερπερισσῶς, 102
ὑπερπλεονάζω, 192
ὑπερυψόω, 79
ὑπερφρονέω, 174
ὑπερῷον, 21
ὑπέχω, 56
ὑπήκοος, 186
ὑπηρετέω, 145
ὑπηρέτης, 145
ὕπνος, 150
ὑπό, 23, 37, 99, 123, 163
ὑπὸ τὸν οὐρανόν, 52
ὑποβάλλω, 77, 174
ὑπογραμμός, 114
ὑπόδειγμα, 114
ὑποδείκνυμι, 57, 91
ὑποδέχομαι, 193
ὑποδέω, 31

ὑπόδημα, 30
ὑπόδικος, 94
ὑποζύγιον, 8
ὑποζώννυμι, 143
ὑποθήκη, 105
ὑποκάτω, 37, 98
ὑποκρίνομαι, 176
ὑπόκρισις, 176
ὑποκριτής, 176
ὑπολαμβάνω, 11, 130, 135, 155
ὑπόλειμμα, 114
ὑπολείπω, 2
ὑπολήνιον, 22
ὑπομένω, 114, 134
ὑπομιμνῄσκω, 104
ὑπόμνησις, 104
ὑπομονή, 114
ὑπονοέω, 155
ὑπόνοια, 155
ὑποπλέω, 142
ὑποπνέω, 192, 194
ὑποπόδιον, 67
ὑπόστασις, 65
ὑποστέλλω, 13, 27
ὑποστολή, 27
ὑποστρέφω, 50, 137
ὑποστρωννύω, 153
ὑποταγή, 187
ὑποτάσσω, 37, 177, 187
ὑποτίθημι, 158
ὑποτρέχω, 142
ὑποτύπωσις, 114
ὑποφέρω, 114
ὑποχωρέω, 71
ὑπωπιάζω, 10, 188
ὗς, 8
ὕσσωπος, 117
ὑστερέω, 48, 84, 118, 162
ὑστέρημα, 118
ὑστέρησις, 118
ὕστερος, 145, 162
ὕστριξ, 8
ὑφαίνω, 30
ὑφαντός, 30
ὑφάπτω, 22
ὑψηλὰ φρονέω, 174
ὑψηλός, 98, 103, 173, 174

ὑψηλοφρονέω, 174
ὕψιστος, 71
ὕψος, 76, 83, 103
ὑψόω, 83, 103
ὕψωμα, 76, 174

φάγος, 53, 179
φαιλόνης, 30
φαίνω, 90, 96, 144
φανερός, 90, 144
φανερόω, 90, 144
φανερῶς, 90, 144
φανέρωσις, 90
φανός, 92
φαντάζομαι, 144
φαντασία, 84
φάντασμα, 69
φάραγξ, 78
φαρμακεία, 101, 182
φάρμακον, 101, 104
φαρμακός, 101
φάσις, 9
φάσκω, 34
φάτνη, 22, 35
φαῦλος, 14
φέγγος, 96
φείδομαι, 13, 141, 150
φειδομένως, 150
φελής, 185
φέρω, 20, 25, 56, 75, 114
φεύγω, 13, 70, 141
φήμη, 9
φημί, 151
φθάνω, 32, 74, 121, 161
φθαρτός, 47
φθέγγομαι, 151
φθείρω, 45, 137, 181, 183, 197
φθινοπωρινός, 164
φθινόπωρον, 164
φθόγγος, 151
φθονέω, 178
φθόνος, 178
φθορά, 45, 137, 181
φιάλη, 35
φιλάγαθος, 55
φιλαδελφία, 99
φιλάδελφος, 99

257

Greek Index

φίλανδρος, 99
φιλανθρωπία, 99, 186
φιλανθρώπως, 186
φιλαργυρία, 179
φιλάργυρος, 179
φίλαυτος, 99
φιλέω, 55, 90, 99
φιλήδονος, 55
φίλημα, 90
φιλία, 99
φιλόθεος, 99
φιλονεικία, 10, 179
φιλόνεικος, 10
φιλοξενία, 193
φιλόξενος, 193
φιλοπρωτεύω, 44
φίλος, 13
φιλοσοφία, 194
φιλόσοφος, 194
φιλόστοργος, 99
φιλότεκνος, 99
φιλοτιμέομαι, 52
φιλοφρόνως, 186
φιμόω, 8, 149
φλογίζω, 23
φλόξ, 23
φλυαρέω, 177
φλύαρος, 177
φοβέομαι, 61, 79, 120, 187
φοβερός, 61
φόβητρον, 61
φόβος, 61, 120
φοῖνιξ, 167
φονεύς, 88
φονεύω, 88
φόνος, 88
φορέω, 31
φορέω τὴν μάχαιραν, 127
φόρος, 158
φορτίζω, 25
φορτίον, 25
φραγέλλιον, 89
φραγελλόω, 78
φραγμός, 50, 59, 131, 154, 190
φράζω, 57, 152
φράσσω, 27, 149
φράσσω στόμα, 149

φρέαρ, 78, 191
φρεναπατάω, 176
φρεναπάτης, 176
φρήν, 127
φρίσσω, 61
φρονέω, 127, 160
φρόνημα, 127
φρόνησις, 127, 189, 194
φρόνιμος, 194
φρονίμως, 194
φροντίζω, 160
φρουρέω, 72
φρυάσσω, 174
φρύγανον, 196
φυγή, 70
φυλακή, 22, 72, 84, 163
φυλακίζω, 84
φυλακτήριον, 4
φύλαξ, 72
φυλάσσω, 72, 126, 141, 187
φυλή, 39, 44
φύλλον, 117
φύραμα, 38, 105
φυσικὴν χρῆσιν, 18
φυσικός, 66
φυσικῶς, 66
φυσιόω, 174
φύσις, 29, 65
φυσίωσις, 174
φυτεία, 117
φυτεύω, 59
φύω, 18, 72
φωλεός, 78
φονέω, 24, 86, 147, 151
φωνή, 92, 147, 151, 152
φῶς, 23, 92, 95
φωστήρ, 96
φωσφόρος, 76
φωτεινός, 96
φωτίζω, 90, 95
φωτισμός, 90, 168

χαίρω, 49, 75
χάλαζα, 191
χαλάω, 43
χαλεπός, 168, 189
χαλιναγωγέω, 188

χαλινός, 60, 188
χαλκεύς, 104
χαλκηδών, 121
χαλκίον, 35
χαλκολίβανον, 104
χαλκός, 104, 106
χαλκὸς ἠχῶν, 106
χαλκοῦς, 104
χαμαί, 52
χαρά, 75
χάραγμα, 82, 148
χαρακτήρ, 65, 82, 114
χάραξ, 190, 191
χαρίζομαι, 42, 65, 70, 72, 186
χάριν, 26, 136
χάρις, 3, 70, 72, 184, 185, 188
χάρισμα, 70, 72
χαριτόω, 72, 186
χάρτης, 198
χάσμα, 78
χεῖλος, 92
χειμάζομαι, 193
χείμαρρος, 78, 191
χειμών, 164, 193
χείρ, 19, 119
χειραγωγέω, 20
χειραγωγός, 20
χείριστος, 14
χειρόγραφον, 198
χειροποίητος, 101
χειροτονέω, 12, 28
χείρων, 14, 95
Χερούβ, 83
χήρα, 89
χθόνιος, 76
χιλίαρχος, 191
χιλιάς, 110
χίλιοι, 109
χιτών, 30
χιών, 191, 193
χλαμύς, 30
χλευάζω, 105, 177
χλιαρός, 80
χλωρός, 32, 117
χοϊκός, 52
χοῖνιξ, 103

Greek Index

χοῖρος, 8
χολάω, 174
χολή, 18
χορηγέω, 126
χορός, 106
χορτάζω, 36, 53
χόρτασμα, 63
χόρτος, 117
χοῦς, 52
χράομαι, 15, 197
χρεία, 118
χρεία ἔχω, 107
χρεοφειλέτης, 42
χρή, 107
χρῄζω, 118
χρῆμα, 105, 192
χρηματίζω, 91, 107
χρηματισμός, 91
χρήσιμος, 172, 184
χρηστεύομαι, 186
χρηστολογία, 152
χρηστός, 132, 172, 184, 186
χρηστότης, 184, 186
χρῖσμα, 153
Χριστιανός, 16, 28
Χριστός, 133
χρίω, 153
χρονίζω, 150, 165
χρόνοις αἰωνίοις, 166
χρόνος, 161
χρόνος ἱκανός, 166
χρονοτριβέω, 164, 181
χρυσίον, 3, 104
χρυσοδακτύλιος, 4
χρυσόλιθος, 121
χρυσόπρασος, 121

χρυσός, 31, 104, 106
χρυσοῦς, 104
χρυσόω, 31
χρώς, 19
χυμός, 157
χωλός, 148
χώρα, 39, 62, 92, 131, 193
χωρέω, 13, 106
χωρίζω, 50, 70, 114
χωρίον, 62, 131
χωρίς, 114, 195
χῶρος, 47

ψάλλω, 106
ψαλμός, 106
ψευδάδελφος, 170
ψευδαπόστολος, 133
ψευδής, 175
ψευδοδιδάσκαλος, 158
ψευδολόγος, 175
ψεύδομαι, 175
ψευδομαρτυρέω, 195
ψευδομαρτυρία, 195
ψευδόμαρτυς, 195
ψευδοπροφήτης, 133
ψεῦδος, 175
ψευδόχριστος, 133
ψευδώνυμος, 107
ψεῦσμα, 175
ψεύστης, 175
ψηλαφάω, 143, 166
ψηφίζω, 108, 195
ψῆφος, 53
ψιθυρισμός, 181
ψιθυριστής, 181
ψίξ, 63
ψυχή, 95, 115, 126, 153

ψυχὴ ζωῆς, 7
ψυχικός, 16, 116
ψῦχος, 80, 164
ψυχρός, 80
ψύχω, 80
ψωμίζω, 53, 70
ψωμίον, 63, 70
ψώχω, 123

ὦ, 35
ὧδε, 97, 125
ᾠδή, 106
ὠδίν, 17, 113
ὠδίνω, 17, 113
ὦμος, 19
ὠνέομαι, 23
ᾠόν, 63
ὥρα, 161, 163
ὥρα πολλή, 163
ὡραῖος, 14, 164
ὠρύομαι, 151
ὡς, 10, 26, 33, 57, 80, 124, 136
ὡς ἄν, 163
ὡς ἐάν, 163
ὡς τάχιστα, 162
ὡσαννά, 120
ὡσαύτως, 33
ὡσεί, 10, 33
ὥσπερ, 33
ὡσπερεί, 33
ὥστε, 136
ὠτάριον, 19
ὠτίον, 19
ὠφέλεια, 5, 68
ὠφελέω, 77
ὠφέλιμος, 5

www.ingramcontent.com/pod-product-compliance
Lightning Source LLC
Chambersburg PA
CBHW050345230426
43663CB00010B/2000